SHIFTING
LANDMARKS

A Volume in the Series

Conjunctions of Religion & Power in the Medieval Past
Edited by Barbara H. Rosenwein

A full list of titles in the series appears at the end of the book.

PROPERTY,
PROOF, AND
DISPUTE IN
CATALONIA
AROUND THE
YEAR 1000

SHIFTING LANDMARKS

JEFFREY A. BOWMAN

Cornell University Press
Ithaca and London

This book is published with the aid of a grant from the Program for Cultural Cooperation between Spain's Ministry of Education, Culture and Sports and United States Universities.

Publication is also aided by a grant from the Book Subvention Program of The Medieval Academy of America.

First published 2004 by Cornell University Press

Printed in the United States of America

Library of Congress Cataloging-in-Publication Data
Bowman, Jeffrey A. (Jeffrey Alan), 1966–
    Shifting landmarks : property, proof, and dispute in Catalonia around the year 1000 / Jeffrey A. Bowman.
        p. cm. — (Conjunctions of religion & power in the medieval past)
Includes bibliographical references and index.
    ISBN 0-8014-3990-6 (cloth : alk. paper)
    1. Law, Medieval—Methodology. 2. Property—Spain—Catalonia—History—To 1500. I. Title. II. Series.
    KJ147.B69 2003
    340.5′5—dc21   2003013426

Cloth printing   10 9 8 7 6 5 4 3 2 1

CONTENTS

Preface   vii

Abbreviations   xiii

Introduction   1

PART I. COURTS AND CODES

1. *Sicut lex edocet:* Remembering and Forgetting the Written Law   33
2. Do Neo-Romans Curse? Land, Law, and Ritual   56
3. *Diligite iustitiam qui iudicatis terram:* Judges in Court and Society   81
4. Courts and the Administration of Justice   100

PART II: PROOFS AND STRATEGIES

5. Cold Cauldrons and the Smoldering Hand: The Judicial Ordeal   119
6. Fighting with Written Records   141
7. Community, Memory, and Proof: The Place of Witness Testimony   165

PART III. ENDINGS AND CONTEXTS

8. Winning, Losing, and Resisting: How Disputes Ended   185
9. Justice and Violence in Medieval Europe   211

Works Cited   249

Index   275

PREFACE

Maledictus qui transfert terminos proximi sui.
Cursed be he that removeth his neighbour's landmark.
      DEUTERONOMY 27:17

Quotienscumque de terminis fuerit orta contentio, signa, que antiquitus
constituta sunt, oportet inquiri . . .
Whenever a dispute arises about the boundaries of property, it is fitting to
investigate ancient landmarks . . .
      The Visigothic Code X.3.3

When we fight over property, we can rely upon an elaborate system of social, legal, moral, and intellectual traditions. We know, first of all, what property is, something of its relative value, what it would feel like to be deprived of it, and, with the help of experts, what constitutes a defensible legal claim to ownership. Disputes today tend to have a certain bounded framework of action, a certain rationality, and of course our whole social and political systems depend in part upon our faith that settlement of disputes can happen in relatively fair and predictable ways.

A thousand years ago, communities and individuals managed conflict differently. No single law code was accepted as authoritative. The competencies of different judicial assemblies were poorly defined. The judges and presidents of different courts were often intimately tied to the disputants who appeared before them. Courts lacked the institutionalized coercive power that modern courts rely upon to make their decisions stick. That this system worked differently, however, does not at all mean that it did not work well. In many parts of Latin Europe, the system through which property disputes were processed was, in its own way, highly refined and often effective; when it was not, it was at least a marvelous expression of norms and needs different from our own but no less reasonable and worthy of study.

This book examines how Europeans fought over property in the decades around the year 1000. It tells how people in one especially well-documented region on the edge of Latin Europe, the Province of Narbonne, came to disagree over who owned what; how they articulated their differences; how they sought to reconcile them; how they worked to thwart their opponents; and how the process of disputing defined property itself, not only in the immediate context of social and political life, but in the larger and longer process through which law developed during this period. These processes varied throughout Europe. Communities in the Province of Narbonne processed disputes in distinctive ways—relying heavily on formal courts, where professional judges evaluated proofs and issued decisions, and turning with unmatched frequency to written law. Although disputes in many parts of contemporary Europe sprang from similar causes, mechanisms to resolve conflict and the steps individual disputants took to protect their interests varied considerably. The Province of Narbonne thus cannot "stand" for all of Europe, but understanding these processes in a region where they are so well-documented can help us understand similar processes in other places where records are scarcer.

The richest source of information about the central Middle Ages is a body of records that describe people buying, selling, and giving away property. Most of these transactions were peaceful, but the records are punctuated by records of crisis in which litigants struggled for control of fields, mills, and vineyards. These cases present information of unusual interest—legal, cultural, even emotional—for here one finds traces of anger, confusion, violence, and the scramble to make disparate laws, traditions, and customs cohere in fair and practical resolutions. These conflicts teach us a great deal about law, society, and power around the year 1000, shedding light on the concerns of individual farmers, while at the same time helping us to trace broad social and political developments. Property disputes reflect tensions ranging from intimate conflicts between brothers and sisters to sweeping political struggles affecting the very shape of Latin Europe in a period of territorial, demographic, and economic growth.

Property disputes reveal to us the resources communities possessed— from the institutional to the conceptual—for resolving conflicts. In the Province of Narbonne the most important of these institutional resources were the judicial assemblies (often presided over by bishops and counts and staffed by professional judges) that adjudicated disputes. Conceptual resources, by contrast, included the legal and normative traditions that leaders and individual property-holders brought to bear upon the conflicts before them. These resources, in other words, were the diverse contents of the normative imagination—rich with terms, rules, and adages that could be cited, borrowed, combined, and reworked. Prominent among these was the written law of the *Visigothic Code*. These traditions afforded disputants, magnates, and legal professionals a vocabulary to describe conflicting claims. They constituted the conceptual tools for understanding tears in the social fabric.

The inhabitants of the Province of Narbonne often looked to the past for guidance, but their engagement with that past was not passive. The leaders and property-holders of the region reshaped the normative traditions they inherited from the late antique and Carolingian worlds. The "landmarks" of this book's title are thus both literal and figurative—both the physical markers that distinguished one vineyard from another and the time-honored authorities (like the *Visigothic Code*) to which property-holders appealed. Landmarks (in both senses) were at times movable. Property-holders shifted both material markers and the meaning of the law when it suited their interests and when they thought they could get away with it.

These disputes also reveal to us something more fundamentally epistemological: what these property-holders saw as *proof*. Some litigants presented written records to substantiate their claims; others presented witnesses; a small number appealed to judicial ordeals; and in a great many cases these different species of proof worked together. A full sense of the way people fought over property, and a full sense of the larger historical and cultural implications of disputes, depends upon close attention not only to what proofs were used, but how disputants shaped the various proofs into compelling, precedent-making, and sometimes misleading arguments. The disputes in question thus serve as a bridge between two levels of historical inquiry: inquiry into learned ideas about land, law, and justice, on the one hand, and, on the other hand, into the rough-and-tumble practice of daily life. The composite picture allows us to see the intimate connections between ink and parchment and sweat and earth.

From these disputes, we also gain a better understanding of the nature of conflict in this period. Europe in the year 1000 was politically fragmented, but such fragmentation does not necessarily mean life was chaotic. There were chronic tensions—but these tensions were fed more by incompatible and conflicting ways of understanding property than by the pervasive violence made to seem fundamental in many accounts of this period. In these conflicts, we see not the chaos of total oppositions, but rather the clash of legal ideas in tension: this was the deep conflict of this period and these disputes enable us to see this deeper cause in particular moments of action. Property disputes were serious matters for their participants, but they are less signs of a world convulsed in violence than signs of a world coursing with the vitality of normative traditions colliding in a period of rapid expansion.

The fraught diversity at work in this period extended even to the very meaning of property. Conflicts over the most basic human needs (water, salt, wine) were at the same time struggles over power, sanctity, and kinship. Throughout the Middle Ages, productive land was the most important form of wealth and the foundation of political power. At the same time, gifts of land to monasteries and churches were expressions of piety, and property-holders cultivated affective, personal relations with saints and their communities by giving and exchanging property. The distinction between public and private property at the heart of modern political thought did not obtain. At the heart of many disputes were fundamentally different conceptions of what it meant to own property, who could alienate it, and when.

In this distinctive landscape, the scattered cultural remains of earlier periods found new life. Scriptural passages encouraging generosity became legal aphorisms. Disputants and judges remade fragments of old law codes to fit their own needs. Understanding the changes and continuities of the tenth and eleventh centuries starts with the stories of individuals struggling with the pressing problems of how to distribute newly cleared land, how to divide valuable estates among heirs, and how to reconcile competing legal authorities. On the most mundane level, we can sketch the profiles of those who populated the vineyards and the courtrooms: the contemplative judge adapting ancient rules to new situations, the ambitious abbot striving to secure his hold on water rights, the industrious widow struggling to defend her land from aggressive neighbors (neighbors who might well include the ambitious abbot), and the dismayed niece who discovers that the ample inheritance she expected from her uncle was also claimed by the local cathedral chapter. Together, their achievements, their frustrations, their careful plans, and their desperate schemes lay bare the roots of conflict, trace the evolution of law, and map conceptions of proof. Together these stories yield a vivid picture of law and justice, property and power, change and continuity around the year 1000.

It is a great pleasure to thank the people and institutions who have been so generous to me while I wrote this book. My greatest debts are to my teachers. Phil Niles first made me think seriously about medieval history. Since my first day of graduate school, Tom Head has been a inspiring guide, wise counselor, and good friend. Paul Freedman has given generously his time and expertise. The late John Boswell has remained an inspiration.

In conversation and in correspondence, friends and colleagues encouraged, corrected, and inspired me. I especially want to thank Adam Kosto, Jason Glenn, Susan Reynolds, Dominique Barthélemy, Kathryn Miller, Nat Taylor, Michel Zimmerman, and Stephen White. Barbara Rosenwein and a second anonymous reader for Cornell University Press gave my manuscript as rigorous, informed, and sympathetic a reading as any scholar could want.

Their suggestions, queries, and criticisms have greatly improved the book. I alone am responsible for any remaining errors and infelicities.

A Solmsen Fellowship from the Institute for Research in the Humanities at the University of Wisconsin gave me the opportunity to revise the manuscript. I thank Paul Boyer and the other fellows at the institute for making my stay in Madison such a productive one. Kenyon College has supported my research and writing in numerous ways. I thank Kenyon's administration for giving me leave from my teaching responsibilities during the 2000–2001 academic year. At Kenyon, I have also enjoyed the support of my colleagues in the history department and throughout the college. In Kenyon's library, Cindy Wallace, Barb Chambliss, and Joan Pomajevich have been instrumental in helping me gain access to books and articles.

Research was generously supported by the French government with a Bourse Chateaubriand; by the Program for Cultural Cooperation between Spain's Ministry of Culture and United States Universities; by a Bernadotte E. Schmitt Research Grant from the American Historical Association; and by Kenyon College. Jaume Riera at the Arxiu de la Corona d'Aragó was especially welcoming and helpful, but I have benefited also from the warmth and wisdom of librarians and archivists in Paris, Perpignan, Barcelona, Vic, La Seu d'Urgell, and Madrid. I offer them my warm thanks.

A version of chapter 2 was originally published in *Viator* 28 (1997). I thank *Viator's* publishers for permission to reprint it here.

Finally, I thank those who have offered unstinting moral support and have even displayed occasional flashes of interest in Visigothic law: my parents and Jesse Matz.

ABBREVIATIONS

ACA	Arxiu de la Corona d'Aragó (Barcelona)
ACB	Arxiu de la Catedral de Barcelona (Barcelona)
ACU	Arxiu Capitular d'Urgell (La Seu d'Urgell)
ACV	Arxiu Capitular de Vic (Vic)
AESC	*Annales: Economies, sociétés, civilisations*
Agde	*Cartulaire du chapitre d'Agde.* Ed. Odile Terrin. Nîmes, 1969.*
AHDE	Anuario de historia del derecho español
AMidi	*Annales du Midi*
APO	Archives Départementales des Pyrenées-Orientales (Perpignan)
Archivo Condal	Federico Udina Martorell. *El archivo Condal de Barcelona en los siglos ix–x: Estudio crítico de sus fondos.* Barcelona, 1951.
Banyoles	*Diplomatari de Banyoles.* Ed. Lluís G. Constans i Serrats, vol. 1. Banyoles, 1985.
Barcelona	*Diplomatari de la Catedral de Barcelona: Documents dels anys 844–1260.* Ed. Àngel Fàbrega i Grau, vol. 1. Barcelona, 1995.
BEC	*Bibliothèque de l'École des Chartes*

*References in footnotes to sources marked with asterisks are to document numbers, rather than to page, folio, or column numbers. *Cuixà* 54, for example, refers to document 54 in the appendix to Abadal's article in *Analecta Montserratensia* 8 (1954). *Viage* 9, 13, refers to document 13 in volume 9 of *Viage literario a las Iglesias de España.*

Béziers	*Cartulaire de Béziers (Livre Noir).* Ed. J. B. Roquette. Paris and Montpellier, 1918–1922.*
BNF	Bibliothèque Nationale de France (Paris)
Cart. Rous.	*Cartulaire roussillonais.* Ed. B. Alart. Perpignan, 1880.*
Cat. Car.	*Catalunya Carolingia II: El Diplomes Carolingia à Catalunya,* part III, vol. 2, *Els comtats de Pallars i Ribagorça.* Ed. Ramon d'Abadal i de Vinyals. Barcelona, 1955.
CCM	*Cahiers de Civilisation médiévale*
Consagracions	Cebrià Baraut, *Les actes de consagracions d'esglésies de l'antic bisbat d'Urgell, segles X–XII.* La Seu d'Urgell, 1986.
Constitucions	*Les constitucions de Pau i Treva de Catalunya, segles XI–XIII.* Ed. Gener Gonsalvo i Bou. Barcelona, 1994.
CSMC	*Les Cahiers de Saint-Michel-de-Cuxa*
Cuixà	Ramon Abadal i de Vinyals. "Com neix i com creix un gran monestir pirinenc abans de l'any mil: Eixalada-Cuixà." In *Analecta Montserratensia* 8 (1954–55): 139–338.*
Gerri	*El monestir de Santa Maria de Gerri, colleció diplomàtica.* Ed. Ignasi M. Puig i Ferreté, 2 vols. Barcelona, 1991.*
Girona	*El Cartoral dit de Carlemany, del bisbe de Girona.* Ed. Josep María Marquès i Planagumà. Barcelona, 1993.*
Guissona	Domènec Sangés. "Recull de documents del segle XI referents a Guissona i la seva Plana." *Urgellia* 3 (1980): 195–305.*
HGL	Claude Devic and J. J. Vaissete. *Histoire générale de Languedoc avec des notes et les pièces justificatives,* 2d. ed. Toulouse, 1872–1904 (unless otherwise noted, references are to volume 5).*
IRMA	Ius Romanum Medii Aevi (Milan)
Lavaix	*El Cartoral de Santa Maria de Lavaix: El Monestir durant els segles XI–XIII.* Ed. Ignasi Puig i Ferreté. La Seu d'Urgell, 1984.*
Leges Visigothorum	*Leges Visigothorum.* Ed. Karl Zeumer, Monumenta Germaniae Historica, Leges I. Hanover, 1902; Reprint, 1973.
Lézat	*Cartulaire de l'abbaye de Lézat.* Ed. Paul Ourliac and Anne-Marie Magnou, 2 vols. Paris, 1984–87.*
LFM	*Liber Feudorum Maior: Cartulario real que se conserve en el Archivo de la Corona de Aragon.* Ed. Francisco Miguel Rosell, 2 vols. Barcelona, 1945–47.*
LFSB	*Liber Fidei Sanctae Bracarensis Ecclesiae.* Ed. Pe. Aveline de Jesus da Costa, 2 vols. Braga, 1965–78.*
Lib. Ant.	Libri antiquitatum I–IV, Arxiu de la Catedral de Barcelona (Barcelona).

Marca	Petrus de Marca and Etienne Baluze, *Marca Hispanica sive limes Hispanicus.* Paris, 1688.*
MCV	*Mélanges de la Casa de Velázquez.*
Nîmes	*Cartulaire du chapitre de l'église Notre-Dame de Nîmes, 876–1156.* Ed. E. Germer-Durand. Nîmes, 1872–1874.*
Notes hist.	Josep Mas. "Rúbrica dels Libri Antiquitatum de la Sèu de Barcelona." *Notes històriques del bisbat de Barcelona,* vol. 9 and 10. Barcelona, 1914–15.*
Oliba	*Diplomatari i escrits literaris de l'abat i bisbe Oliba.* Ed. Eduard Junyent i Subirà. Barcelona, 1992.*
Oviedo	*Colección de Documentos de la Catedral de Oviedo.* Ed. Santos Garcia Larragueta. Oviedo, 1962.*
Placiti	*I placiti del 'Regnum Italiae.'* Ed. C. Manaresi. Fonte per la storia d'Italia 92. Rome, 1955.*
RHDFE	*Revue historique de droit français et étranger*
RSJB	*Recueils de la société Jean Bodin pour l'histoire comparative des institutions*
Roses	*El Cartoral de Santa Maria de Roses, segles x–xiii.* Ed. Josep M. Marquès i Planagumà. Barcelona, 1986.*
Sant Cugat	*Cartulario de "Sant Cugat" del Vallés.* Ed. J. Rius Serra, 3 vols. Barcelona, 1946.*
Santa Anna	Jesús Alturo i Perucho. *L'arxiu antic de Santa Anna de Barcelona del 942 al 1200 (Aproximació històrico-lingüística)* 3 vols. Barcelona, 1985.*
Santa Cecília	F. X. Altés i Aguilo. "El diplomatari del monestir de Santa Cecília de Montserrat, I, anys 900–999." *Studia monastica* 36 (1994): 225–302; "El diplomatari del monestir de Santa Cecília de Montserrat, II, anys 1000–1077." *Studia monastica* 37 (1995): 301–94.*
Solsona	Antoni Llorens. "El documents dels segles x i xi de l'Arxiu Capitular de Solsona." *Urgellia* 11 (1992–93): 301–486.*
Urgellia	"Els documents del segles IX i X, conservats a l'Arxiu capitular de la Seu d'Urgell." Ed. Cebrià Baraut. *Urgellia* 2 (1979); 3 (1980); 4 (1981); 5 (1982); 6 (1983).
Viage	*Viage literario a las Iglesias de España.* Ed. Jaime and Joaquín Lorenzo Villanueva, 22 vols. Madrid-Valencia, 1803–1902.*
Vic	*Diplomatari de la Catedral de Vic, segles IX–X.* Ed. Eduard Junyent i Subirà. Vic, 1980.*

SHIFTING LANDMARKS

Aiguatèbia today (Author photo).

INTRODUCTION

During the first quarter of the eleventh century, Viscountess Guisla of Conflent controlled vast properties in the Eastern Pyrenees. At her death in 1025, she left generous bequests of land and moveable goods to a wide range of beneficiaries—monasteries, cathedral chapters, and members of her family.

Of special interest among the properties controlled by the viscountess was a *villa* near the valley of the River Tet. The *villa*, named Aiguatèbia, had for decades been among the core holdings of the vicecomital dynasty. In the years following the viscountess's death, Aiguatèbia's tithes became the subject of a bitter dispute—one in many ways typical of property disputes in this region. The disputants were two of Guisla's children: Bishop Ermengol of Urgell and his sister, Geriberga. Geriberga and her husband claimed that the late viscountess had sold them the tithes of Aiguatèbia prior to her death. Ermengol claimed that the tithes belonged rightly to him.

In September 1027, both parties appeared before a judicial assembly at the monastery of Sant Miquel de Cuixà, not far from Aiguatèbia. Geriberga's husband, Renard, brought a written record to substantiate his wife's claim and presented it to the assembly, composed of a judge named Guifré and a group of magnates. Bishop Ermengol bluntly rejected Renard's claims and dismissed the record as invalid. He called the purported sale strange, and doubted that his mother would have taken part in any such transaction. Judge Guifré doubted Renard too, expressing his own misgivings about accepting the record as proof.

In need of legal advice, Renard left the assembly and sought the guidance of a judge named Sendred. A few weeks later, the disputants, along with their supporters, met again, in a church further down the valley of the Tet. The disagreement continued. Ermengol continued to call the transaction unlikely, and he added another point of dispute: such a transaction would contravene rules in the *Visigothic Code* related to the alienation of property. Judge Sendred, acting on Renard's behalf, countered that the record was indisputably valid, and that even if the sale did not neatly conform to the demands of Visigothic law, the tithes had been transferred willingly. The viscountess had not been coerced, he argued, and the niceties of Visigothic law were less binding than a clearly recorded agreement executed with the consent of those involved.

Unable to resolve their differences, the parties postponed any final decision and scheduled a third hearing for late November at the monastery of Santa Maria de Ripoll. But when the appointed day arrived, Geriberga, Renard, and Sendred failed to appear. The bishop was left without opponents. Even so, Judge Guifré decided to press ahead, and ruled in the bishop's favor. This legal victory apparently did not fully relieve Ermengol of his anxiety about the disputed tithes or his ill-will: frustrated and angry with what he saw as Renard's erratic behavior, Ermengol damned the record that Renard and his wife had presented in court.

This case typifies, in many ways, the property disputes that are the subject of this book. Its occasion, the relations of its litigants, the involvement of various other parties, the contested relevance of written law, the variety of legal discourses in play, the tactics used to undermine opponents' proofs, and the place of the dispute in the long-term political history of the region—these elements characterize the processes of disputing more broadly in the province of Narbonne around the year 1000.

RECORDS, FAMILIES, AND PROPERTY

First of all, the dispute is typical for the way it appears to us, one thousand years later, in the form of a parchment drafted at the behest of one of the disputants, Bishop Ermengol. This region is rare for its wealth of surviving written records. Litigants up and down the social scale—from the episcopal scions of vicecomital dynasties like Ermengol to property-holders from much humbler social positions—were unusually attached to the creation and use of written records. One result of their attachment is that the body of evidence for this region is particularly rich.

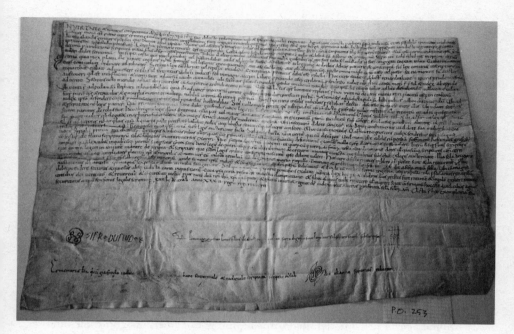

Arxiu Capitular d'Urgell, pergamin 253.

The record of this particular case survives as an original parchment in the Arxiu Capitular d'Urgell, but evidence about property disputes comes to us in various forms. The vast preponderance of source material consists of charters that record transactions relating to property rights, most of them created and stored by churches and monasteries. These include gifts, sales, exchanges, quitclaims, pleas, and testaments. Many of these records survive as tenth- and eleventh-century originals. The Arxiu de la Corona d'Aragó and the Arxiu Capitular d'Urgell, for example, contain many single-leaf original parchments related to Barcelona's comital family, the see of Urgell, and a range of monasteries and churches such as Sant Pere de Besalú, Sant Benet des Bages, and Sant Llorenç del Munt. Other records survive in cartularies compiled in the twelfth or thirteenth centuries. Scribes edited and arranged individual records to create selective catalogs of property rights such as the see of Urgell's *Liber Dotaliorum Ecclesiae Urgellensis* and the monastery of Sant Cugat's cartulary. Finally, some records survive only in the transcriptions of seventeenth-, eighteenth-, and nineteenth-century administrators and scholars. This rich body of evidence is not evenly distributed. The cathedral of Vic possesses hundreds of tenth- and eleventh-century records, although only a handful from Narbonne survive, none of them original. Béziers' cartulary contains just over a dozen records for the years between 1010 and 1060; for the same period, the see of Urgell can boast over four hundred. In general, records are concentrated in dioceses south of the Pyrenees in modern Spain: Barcelona, Urgell, Vic, and Girona.

The records of greatest interest for this study are the roughly 170 that mention disputes over property rights. Property disputes are recorded most often in two types of records: *placita* and quitclaims. Neither of these terms was used with precision. Both are difficult to translate. *Placitum* might mean a judicial hearing, the right to hold a hearing, a series of hearings related to a single case, an agreement reached by two opposed parties during litigation, or the document which recorded such an agreement. The meaning of the term thus moves between "a formal public court" and, as Stephen White proposes, a "discussion."[1] Quitclaims—*warpitoriae* or *werpitiones*—are less complicated. These were abandonments of property rights. One party renounced a claim to a particular piece of land, salt pan, or vineyard. Often this renunciation came when one party acknowledged that his or her claim to a disputed property was untenable.

Some *placita* provide detailed information about hearings and their outcomes, others provide only sketchy outlines. The eleventh century was a period of great creativity in diplomatic forms. Scribes often departed from traditional forms, adopting less formal, more anecdotal styles.[2] So it is not altogether surprising that these records are not consistent in the amount and type of information they supply. Some quitclaims record only that one party abandoned an unjust claim, while others furnish information about why the abandoning party had made a claim in the first place and how he or she had been brought to recognize that the claim was unjustified. Some documents record in detail the nature of conflicting property claims, the formation of a judicial assembly, and the processes by which disputants reached a settlement; others only note that there was an *altercatio* or a *contentio* between two parties.

The dispute between Ermengol and his sister resembles others in certain aspects of its initiation. Like other disputes, this one is best understood in the

---

1. Stephen D. White, "Inheritances and Legal Arguments in Western France," *Traditio* 43 (1987): 55–103.

2. For changes in diplomatic forms in this region see Michel Zimmerman, "Langue et lexicographie: l'apport des actes catalans," *Bibliothèque de l'École des Chartes* (hereafter *BEC*) 155 (1997): 185–205; and Adam J. Kosto, *Making Agreements in Medieval Catalonia: Power, Order, and the Written Word, 1000–1200* (Cambridge, 2001), 44–49.

context of the participants' long-term aspirations rather than as an isolated event. Ermengol had won earlier legal victories in the same way, by questioning the legitimacy of his opponent's records.[3] The bishop was a vigilant protector of the see of Urgell's property. He defended the see's rights often in court and he usually won. Bishop Ermengol's dispute with Geriberga and Renard was part of his sustained effort to consolidate the scattered pieces of his mother's estate. Prior to his dispute with Geriberga, the bishop already had pursued and won another case against his niece involving Aiguatèbia. A few years later, the bishop bought property at Aiguatèbia that another sister had inherited from their mother.[4] Like other key properties, Aiguatèbia was the subject of repeated litigation over the course of generations.[5] The dispute between Ermengol and Geriberga, in other words, must be seen in terms of Ermengol's defense of the see of Urgell's property rights and more specifically in his intense concern for property that had great personal significance to members of his family.

Once begun, the dispute between Ermengol and his sister was also typical in the way disputants appealed to and relied on a range of legal, ritual, and political discourses. Most notable among these was the ambiguously effective *Visigothic Code*, which Ermengol, like many other litigants, invoked to advance his case. Although the law was widely respected, this case clearly shows that even those well versed in the law of the *Code* were not always in agreement about how its rules should be applied. Then too, there were other authorities of a very different kind. Although Ermengol was handed an unequivocal legal victory by Judge Guifré, he was not satisfied until he had damned his opponents' record.

It may seem strange that Renard and Geriberga should have abandoned their case, but such disappearances were not unusual. The record of these hearings describes how Renard presented his wife's claim and how he sought professional counsel, but at a certain point Renard vanishes from the historical record. We can only guess why he and his advocate failed to attend the third hearing. The mercurial autumn weather in the Pyrenees may have prevented their arrival. The bishop himself apparently complained that the journey was an especially difficult one. Or Renard and Sendred may have stayed away because they anticipated an outcome in the bishop's favor; they may have wanted to avoid letting their presence lend legitimacy to a process they saw

3. Cebrià Baraut, ed., "Els documents del segles IX i X, conservats a l'Arxiu capitular de la Seu d'Urgell" (hereafter *Urgellia*), 390.
4. *Urgellia* 430.
5. *Urgellia* 203.

as flawed. Whatever the reason in this case, such abandonment of legal proceedings was not unusual. Frustrated disputants regularly left judicial assemblies in midstream or refused to accept court-ordered decisions. Such cases tell us two important things: (1) courts often lacked effective coercive power, and (2) disputants often perceived judicial processes in very different ways.

What we can expect to learn, then, from disputes like that between Ermengol and his sister is that litigants relied on a range of strategies to accomplish their goals; the process of disputing was inflected by several competing legal and ritual discourses; property rights were entangled with political and social relations; and, finally, property-holders displayed a rich variety of opinions about the justice and effectiveness of the mechanisms available to them.

One final feature of this case merits special attention: the prominent role played by judges. Judges like Guifré and Sendred—members of the special class of judges active in this region during the tenth and eleventh centuries—had extensive training. In this case, the two judges evaluated proofs and argued over the interpretation of written law. They also acted as advocates representing the interests of property-holders. Sendred in particular stood out for his experience. Ultimately Renard was not successful, but his belief that Sendred might help win his case was a reasonable one. Sendred enjoyed a stellar reputation by the time Renard sought him out. Moreover, he was especially well informed about the see of Urgell's property and about the legal strategies Bishop Ermengol and his supporters pursued. In 1025, Sendred had presided over the publication of Viscountess Guisla's will.[6] In the same year, he participated in another lawsuit related to the deceased viscountess's estate which also had pitted Ermengol against one of his relatives about property at Aiguatèbia. Sendred himself issued a decision in the bishop's favor.[7] In fact, Sendred almost certainly anticipated the outcome of the hearing at Ripoll that neither he nor his client attended. At Ripoll, Judge Guifré invoked a rule from the *Visigothic Code* that justified his decision to proceed despite the absence of one of the disputants. Two years earlier, Judge Sendred had invoked the very same rule to explain his own decision in favor of Bishop Ermengol. In short, Sendred not only had a well-established track record as a legal expert, he also had considerable experience dealing with the contested estate of Viscountess Guisla. He was learned, experienced, and deeply knowledgeable about the people and property involved in these cases.

6. *Urgellia* 401.
7. *Urgellia* 398.

Sendred's role here is important not only for the light its sheds on the region's legal system around the year 1000, but also for what it says in answer to a key historiographical question about this period: was this a period of radical, even revolutionary, change, in which traditional political structures shattered and longstanding social ties ruptured. Or was change in this period more gradual and marked by strong continuities. Was there, in other words, a feudal revolution?

Pierre Bonnassie, in his magisterial study of the social, economic, and political structures of tenth- and eleventh-century Catalonia, documents the region's rapid economic growth and traces the vicissitudes of some of the region's comital and vicecomital dynasties. In his account, and in those of other historians who share his view, an enduring Carolingian order frayed and crumbled during the late tenth century; widespread unrest and violence followed in the eleventh; and a "feudal revolution" precipitated a complex of abrupt social and political changes that included the proliferation of new types of servitude, the decay of public authority, the devolution of power from counts to viscounts to local castellans, a dramatic increase in the number of castles from which a new class of petty lords pillaged the countryside, and, finally, pervasive violence.[8]

Bonnassie's account of these transformations has won many adherents. Some accept his vision of the Feudal Revolution wholeheartedly, others propose modifications or amendments but in large part accept Bonnassie's account of sudden, catastrophic change. Thomas Bisson's approach, for example, focuses more narrowly on lordship and political culture, but he too argues that the early eleventh century was a time of upheaval. Bonnassie and Bisson both contend that an earlier public order was replaced by a newly private, newly exploitative order. Both scholars argue that the comital courts that were the hallmark of an earlier period suddenly lost their authority. Both agree that respected institutions foundered, and were replaced by ineffective alternatives or by personal violence. And finally, both suggest that the participation of professional judges in judicial assemblies and the citation of written law were signs of the continuing vigor of a Carolingian public order.

8. See references in chapter 9 below and Barbara Rosenwein and Lester Little, *Debating the Middle Ages: Issues and Readings*, part 2, "Feudalism and Its Alternatives" (Malden, Mass., 1998), 105–210.

Which brings us back to Judge Sendred. For Bonnassie, Sendred is the archetypal harbinger of a newly violent feudal world. Bonnassie cites the dispute over the tithes of Aiguatèbia as proof of change; the judges involved in the dispute, especially Sendred, were self-serving hucksters who contorted legal traditions to their own ends. Previously, such judges had worked to maintain a longstanding, equitable tradition of public order. But now Sendred and his ilk twisted the law, manipulated the courts, and cravenly sold their expertise to the highest bidder.[9] The picture Bonnassie paints of Renard's advocate is not a flattering one.

But the same Sendred makes a very different appearance elsewhere in the historiography of the Feudal Revolution. In an essay on the contours of the Feudal Revolution, Bisson makes a public hearing in 1022 an example of the coherent public order that the revolution destroyed. The dispute, in which Count Guifré of Cerdanya presided over a judicial assembly that issued a decision in favor of the monastery of Serrateix, is for Bisson a fine example of the sort of public administration of justice so favorably characteristic of the prerevolution order: "Here it is clear, and often explicit, that justice is determined by law, or by law-sanctioned writing. Was this order not public? The courts offered remedies to all on the basis of prescriptive authority expressive of God-ordained regalian power."[10] Key to this fine system of justice was the presiding judge's scrupulous respect for the written law. But the judge in question was Sendred. For Bisson, Sendred is no fomenter of feudal chaos but rather a stalwart defender of the traditional order. How could he play such a different role in Bisson's account? Why should Bisson and Bonnassie diverge so sharply in their opinions—the latter making Sendred part of degradation of public justice and an index to the cost of feudal chaos, the former making the same judge testament to the coherence of public order, the integrity of judicial institutions, and the enduring power of written law?

These questions are crucial to our understanding of the legal culture of this world, for the two faces of Sendred present us with an unresolved paradox that still confuses our knowledge of the nature and effects of conflict in this region and elsewhere. And the debate about European political and social order around the year 1000 hinges in part on how we answer key questions raised by property disputes. Did once-public courts slide irrevocably toward the indulgence of special interests, corruption, and anarchy? Were

9. Pierre Bonnassie, *La Catalogne du milieu du Xe à la fin du XIe siècle: Croissance et mutations d'une société*, 2 vols. (Toulouse, 1975–1976), 561.

10. Thomas N. Bisson, "The Feudal Revolution," *Past and Present* 142 (1994): 11–12.

late eleventh-century courts less effective than their tenth-century precursors? Did disputes become violent—or more violent—than they had been in the preceding centuries? To the extent that our dominant accounts say so—in the work of Bonnassie, Bisson, and other like-minded scholars—they overlook some key inferences we might make on the basis of close scrutiny of disputes like the one that pitted Geriberga against her brother, Bishop Ermengol. For such scrutiny finds as much continuity as change: disputes continued to spring from many of the same causes; disputants continued to appeal to many of the same authorities, to rely on the same varieties of proof, and to try to outmaneuver their opponents in the same ways, and judges continued to apply the same rules. To quantify the degrees of change and continuity at work here—to resolve the differences, in other words, between Bonnassie's Sendred and Bisson's, we need to let the records provoke more subtle responses. For what is true of Sendred, that he indicates both continuity and change, is true more generally of the many aspects of the process of fighting over property.

Accounts of violent transformation in this period depend upon emphatic distinctions between two orders: the earlier public order, characterized by stability and tradition, and the increasingly private, violent, and anarchic one that follows. But these distinctions are untenable in this period. To describe comital courts as public is to neglect the myriad social and ritual ties that bound those who participated in these assemblies. Certainly, a broad spectrum of society attended these assemblies, and this broad participation helped make them successful, but the litigants involved invariably had long-standing, private relations with the presiding authorities. In chapter 9, I show how the case involving Serrateix proves that public and private were, throughout this period, inextricable. Here I will simply note that the presiding count and his ancestors had been patrons of Serrateix for generations and that the putatively public obligation to administer justice was always entangled with the affective and spiritual affiliations between comital dynasties and religious foundations. The public proceedings were also always private; the relation between public and private was less one of ruinous and abrupt transformation than one of continuous interrelation.

When we pay this kind of attention to the full range of motives and involvements, more continuities emerge—including when it comes to the question of violence. Before we call references in records to *violentia* or actions committed *violenter* proof of genuine bloodshed or headcracking, we must remember that all scribal descriptions were themselves part of the disputing process. Bishop Ermengol's efforts to discredit the written record presented in court by his brother-in-law is a vivid reminder that not all written records enjoyed the universal assent or endorsement of the parties involved. The soundest conclusions we can draw from references to *violentia* are that the authors of these records wanted to discredit someone else's actions.[11] Violence may have occurred, and it may have occurred to greater degrees as one century gave way to the next, but any conclusions to this effect must be qualified by the recollection that complaints about violence were never neutral observations. Again, what may seem like change (toward greater violence) might just as easily be seen as continuity (of interested observation and description). We know a great deal about how Bishop Ermengol and Judge Guifré acted during the dispute over the tithes of Aiguatèbia and at other moments in their careers, but our relatively rich sense of their opinions and attitudes should not lead us to believe that these were universally shared. Renard and Geriberga certainly understood the dispute over the tithes of Aiguatèbia differently.

Approached from this angle, these disputes shed valuable light on the normative world of Latin Europe more generally. Sometimes what seems like violence or disorder might be better understood as a less institutional, bureaucratic, but no less effective means of resolving conflicts or as a means of negotiating relations with one's neighbors. Historians of premodern Europe in recent years have posed a range of questions about property disputes: Did small, face-to-face communities process conflict differently than do bureaucratized states? What role did ritual play in litigation? Were medieval courts especially inclined to issue compromise decisions? This research has fundamentally changed the way we understand law, order, and violence in medieval Europe. The "feud" is no longer seen as a senseless form of aggression, but as an institution with its own logic. Irrational proofs, like judicial ordeals, are seen to serve important social functions. Compromise is no longer seen as a sign of the degradation of justice but instead as a vital normative principle.[12]

11. For an example of *violenter*, see *Urgellia* 539. See also Stephen D. White, "Debate: The 'Feudal Revolution,'" *Past and Present* 152 (1996): 196–223; and Timothy Reuter, "Debate: The 'Feudal Revolution,'" *Past and Present* 155 (1997): 177–95.

12. Peter Brown, "Society and the Supernatural: A Medieval Change," in *Society and the Holy in Late Antiquity* (Berkeley, 1982), 302–32; Fredric L. Cheyette, "Suum cuique tribuere," *French Historical Studies* 6 (1970): 287–99; Wendy Davies and Paul Fouracre, *The Settlement of Disputes in Early Medieval Europe* (Cambridge, 1986); Thomas F. Head, Barbara Rosenwein, and Sharon Farmer, "Monks and Their Enemies: A Comparative Approach," *Speculum* 66 (1991): 764–96; Barbara Rosenwein, *Negotiating Space: Power, Restraint, and Privileges of Immunity in Early Medieval Europe* (Ithaca, N.Y., 1999), 6; Stephen D. White, "'*Pactum Legem Vincit et Amor Judicium*': The Settlement of Disputes by Compromise in Eleventh-Century Western France," *American Journal of Legal History* 22 (1978): 281–308; J. M. Wallace-Hadrill, "The Bloodfeud of the Franks," in *The Long-Haired Kings* (Toronto, 1982), 121–47; and Warren Brown, *Unjust Seizure: Conflict, Interest, and Authority in an Early Medieval Society* (Ithaca, N.Y., 2001).

Through a similarly revisionist point of view, the cases in question here emerge as evidence not of an order evolving from better to worse, but rather of an order with its own distinctive logic.

These are ways in which the records of disputes might reframe our account of this period's historical transformations. Such observations are the larger, ultimate goal of this book's investigations of property disputes. This is a book about the struggles of individual property-holders like Renard and Geriberga; it is at the same time a book about the complex tensions between change and continuity in a world characterized by uneven transformations. In these microhistorical dramas we see the peculiar ways in which venerable legal traditions changed. We witness the lofty figures of law transformed through earthy skirmishes over vineyards and mills. We see the impressive networks of professional judges fraying in the middle of eleventh century—as new institutions for managing conflict emerge. We see that comital courts may have dominated the administration of justice to a lesser degree as the eleventh century wore on, but that the assemblies that replaced them often interpreted the same varieties of proof in the same fashion. We observe competing landlords tugging legal traditions in different directions—not pulling them apart, but adjusting them to diverse interested purposes. We detect principled judges who insisted that the law should protect the poor, while at the same time wealthy and powerful litigants bent the law to their advantage. This is valuable not only because it enables us better to understand the challenges of making a living from the land in the eleventh century, but also for the way it allows us to trace the incremental, rather than catastrophic, transformations in the social, legal, and political spheres of the region—valuable for the evidence it gives of continuities in the process of disputing that bridge the entire period.

This approach allows us to focus our attention on individuals as well as institutions. If we allow for the fact that the administration of justice happened in different ways, we can ask the following questions: What tools did communities possess to process conflict? How did property-holders understand their rights? How did they try to substantiate their claims to disputed properties? In what ways, and with what effects, did they themselves remake written laws, compose narratives theorizing property claims, and try in other pragmatic ways to defeat their opponents? How was litigation over property related to broader political, social, and economic trends?

By attending not only to the institutional frameworks of justice but also to the experiences of individual disputants, I hope to discover some of the personal and social drama that pervaded disputes over property. And in the process I hope to emphasize certain key problems in the evaluation of the historical evidence. In many cases, information about the tactics used by individuals is more reliable and more clearly available than information about outcomes. We can draw some conclusions about the way disputes ended, but with far less certainty than we can draw conclusions about the way disputants tried to win. The records of disputes indicate the shape of arguments made before judicial assemblies, but they often fail to inform us about whether litigants were satisfied by court-issued decisions.

For this reason, the idea of "settlement" is less prominent in my account than in some other examinations of property disputes. In many cases, as in the case of the tithes of Aiguatèbia, we are left with little sense of what real effect particular judicial decisions had on the ways in which people exploited property. We must, in other words, look not only at what courts and judges did, but also at what litigants did—even when those litigants refused to comply with the decisions issued by judges, abandoned judicial assemblies, dragged their feet, or proposed uncommon ways of resolving disputes.

The greatest difficulty in reconstructing a complete picture of the moral, legal, and social world of the property-holders who appear in this book is that the records tend to record the attitudes and actions of some participants more fully and more sympathetically than others. Scribes tended to give little attention to opinions contrary to those handed down by the courts; surviving records tend to take the winner's side. These tendencies present a distorted picture—obscuring the experience of property-holders who (directly or indirectly) resisted the authority of courts, professional judges, and presiding magnates. Disputants who resisted the authority of courts are invariably portrayed as unscrupulous or belligerent, pursuing their own claims despite the very palpable injustice of these claims. The records put the least charitable construction on the actions of those who questioned legal proceedings. But whereas some of those who resisted the authority of the courts were motivated by self-interest, others were motivated by the conviction that the courts served only the interests of the powerful and interpreted the law to favor institutional litigants.

It may be hard to discern the difference and recapture expressions of dissent, but it is crucial to acknowledge the interested nature of the records and to see the resistance of some property-holders as signs of valid, positive, alternative legal positions. Rather than dismissing litigants who, like Renard, failed to appear in court as violent cranks, it is important to trace the logic in their decisions. Renard and other discontents were not simply renegades who refused to participate in a fair, orderly, stable legal system; they often represented coherent positions of resistance, evidence of much more thoughtful dissent and ordered disagreement than we have tended to see in tenth- or eleventh-century courts. When treated systematically, examples of noncompliance or resistance in the latter part of the eleventh century look less like signs of chaos and more like legal strategizing of the sort that had been taking place at least since the early tenth century.

With the field opened to include this greater diversity of legal activity, we can discover a similar kind of ordered irresolution in the judicial process at other levels. First of all, the judicial focus on proofs highlights the interplay of written and oral, and of law and ritual, around the year 1000. Litigants used various forms of proof—written records, judicial ordeals, witness testimony—that cannot be understood in isolation. In practice, different varieties of proof were almost always interdependent. For example, courts and litigants turned to judicial ordeals when written proofs were particularly problematic. Disputants relied on witness testimony to corroborate written records. In many cases, judges, disputants, and assemblies had to assess the interrelation of these different forms of proof.

And disputants appealed to a range of authorities. Some invoked custom. Others found in Scripture maxims to govern property relations and sanctions fitting for those who violated agreements. Most crucial was the role played by the written law of the *Visigothic Code*. Whereas accounts of this period tended to argue either that the code survived to dominate judicial proceedings or that it had fallen out of use, the cases in question here show that disputants and legal professionals used the *Visigothic Code* selectively. The citations reflect not rigid adherence but a flexible and pragmatic engagement with legal traditions. It was less a matter of whether the written law was applied than of how some disputants chose to invoke or activate that law.[13]

Property-holders and judges alike exploited this legal flexibility. When disputes flared up, competing claims tended to spring from the clash between fundamentally different ways of understanding property rights. It is common to see property disputes as epiphenomena of the violence that pervaded society; fighting over land was inevitably the consequence of living in a troubled time. But property disputes were rarely isolated acts of aggression between belligerent strangers. Rather, they were authentic efforts to negotiate evolving social, economic, and ritual relationships. Disputes were not the result of a fall into lawlessness. Most often they sprang from irreconcilable tensions between incompatible understandings of how property rights were enjoyed and transferred. A diverse set of normative authorities fostered incompatible systems of belief and interest and then led to misunderstanding and litigation. Disputants with conflicting interests understood rights differently, and the diversity of legal traditions allowed them to surround their conflicting claims with weighty historical authorities.

13. For a similar observation in another context, see Jill Harries, *Law and Empire in Late Antiquity* (Cambridge, 1999), 79–82.

We might begin to see how this is so by focusing on the most common cause of litigation: the challenged gift. Very often a church or monastery claimed property rights because someone (dead by the time the dispute unfolded) had left the property to the church as a bequest, while a second party (usually a lay person or group of lay people related to the putative donor) challenged the institution's claim. The challengers usually insisted that the property was rightfully theirs by inheritance. Some challengers claimed that they were unaware of the testament recording the alleged gift of their deceased relative; others insisted that their dead relative had never alienated the property at all. If the recipient institution presented proofs to support its claims, challengers might claim that these were defective, arguing that a testament was forged or that it had been superseded by other arrangements. In other cases, challengers accepted their opponents' claims that the deceased had made a donation, but argued that it was invalid. Family members might concede that a deceased relative had held a particular field or vineyard during his lifetime and had drafted a testament which included that field or vineyard, but sisters, sons, widows, and nieces argued that some properties were inalienable. Representatives of recipient institutions disagreed and presented the testament of the deceased as binding, citing rules which, in their eyes, supported an individual's right to alienate property at will. Tenth- and eleventh-century property disputes were often the temporary eruptions of cross-cutting tensions.[14]

We might see occasional disputes springing from lawlessness, aggression, or deceit. Sometimes disappointment might have motivated potential heirs to seek more than their fair share; sometimes monasteries eager to acquire a key mill or vineyard forced arguments about property rights, engineering new legal theories out of base material interest. But most disputes sprang both from differences of material interest *and* differences of legal interpretation. Different parties operated with incompatible but equally legitimate theories about the nature of property. Their contentions were based on tradition, and only if we allow for the coexistence of incommensurate but equally legitimate views can we accurately assess how disputes began and how they lingered.

Land was the most important form of wealth, but the significance of land was more than merely economic. Sales, donations, and disputes were meth-

14. See Patrick J. Geary, "Living with Conflicts in Stateless France: A Typology of Management Mechanisms, 1050–1200," in *Living with the Dead in the Middle Ages* (Ithaca, N.Y., and London, 1994), 139.

ods of participating in the society of monasteries and their patron saints.[15] Disputes over productive resources were at the same time struggles to reshape social, ritual, and political relations.[16] What land meant to churchmen and to lay people was sometimes at odds. Canons and monks encouraged potential donors to make gifts, while potential heirs saw their rights to the property of their kin as inalienable. Similar differences might obtain among the laity themselves: donors on the brink of death often had a heightened appreciation of the benefits of ritual intercession by monks and canons, while their kindred naturally remained more attentive to the material benefits of maintaining control over productive vineyards and lucrative mills. Noting that two parties each claimed a particular vineyard does not explain why each believed that the vineyard in question *rightly* belonged to it. Families were sometimes divided by deceit and greed, but most often they were riven by legitimate, though no less profound, disagreements about who owned a piece of land and when they were at liberty to alienate it. When disputes erupted in these cases, it was not because one party broke violently from some universally accepted understanding of property, but because different contexts determined the way property ought to be alienated. In the dispute between Ermengol and Geriberga, for example, several questions were in play: whether Viscountess Guisla had sold the tithes to her daughter, whether such a transaction was allowed by the *Visigothic Code*, and whether rules in the *Code* trumped other principles.

This recognition helps us see strife less as a sign of cataclysmic upheaval than a sign of the friction between different interpretations of belief and interest. To understand the disputants and their world, we should try to perceive the sense of justice at work in every claim. Examining this body of evidence with these interpretive principles in mind allows us to appreciate the multiple and at times contradictory normative claims that property-holders tried to reconcile. This approach gives us a better sense of the texture of daily life in the decades around the year 1000 and, finally, opens out into a more broadly comparative framework.

15. Stephen D. White, *Custom, Kinship, and Gifts to Saints: The* Laudatio Parentum *in Western France, 1050–1150* (Chapel Hill, N.C., 1988), 4; Chris Wickham, *The Mountains and the City: The Tuscan Appennines in the Early Middle Ages* (Oxford, 1988), 180; and Wendy Davies and Paul Fouracre, eds., *Property and Power in the Early Middle Ages* (Cambridge, 1995).

16. See Head, Rosenwein, and Farmer, "Monks and Their Enemies"; and Patrick J. Geary, "Land, Language, and Memory in Europe, 700–1100," *Transactions of the Royal Historical Society*, 6th series, 9 (1999), 171.

The Province of Narbonne is an especially promising arena to investigate the dynamics of conflict and the process of disputing. The abundance of sources, along with the region's cultural coherence and economic vitality, throw into high relief the changes and continuities that are the more general focus of this book. These changes and continuities are clarified further by a chronological focus on the years from 985 to 1060—years that saw transitions at all levels at the edge of the Latin Christian world.

Stretching along the Mediterranean from Béziers to the Llobregat River southwest of Barcelona, the province straddled the Pyrenees and reached inland to the mountain valleys of Pallars, Ribagorça, and Urgell. Tarragona to the south was in Muslim hands, and so dioceses north and south of the Pyrenees looked to Narbonne as their metropolitan. The bishops of Agde, Béziers, Maguelone, Lodève, Nîmes, Besalú, Carcassonne, Girona, Elne, Vic, Urgell, and Barcelona often met at synods and at the consecrations of churches. In 1043, for example, Archbishop Guifré of Narbonne presided over a council attended by the bishops of Girona, Carcassonne, Elne, Barcelona, Urgell, Coser, Vic, and Béziers.[17] Viscountess Guisla's testament signaled her connections to bishops scattered throughout the province by stipulating bequests of one mare each to the archbishop of Narbonne and the bishops of Béziers, Vic, Girona, Barcelona, Roda, Elne, and Carcassonne.[18] These are signs of an intense episcopal sociability that unified the province.

This regional coherence was reinforced by ties among elite families. The archbishop of Narbonne and the count of Barcelona were the two most important stars in a constellation of lay and ecclesiastical lordships that were distributed among the descendants of Count Guifré the Hairy of Barcelona. In the late ninth century, he encouraged resettlement of land that had been abandoned by its Christian inhabitants during the Muslim occupation. By the eleventh century, the counts of Barcelona, Urgell, Besalú, Cerdanya, Berga, and Empuriés were direct descendants of Guifré. The viscounts of Barcelona, Narbonne, and Béziers, the bishops of Besalú, Elne, Urgell, Girona, and Vic, and the archbishop of Narbonne were descendants of Guifré or married to his descendants. From Barcelona to Béziers, episcopal

17. Eduard Junyent i Subirà, ed., *Diplomatari i escrits literaris de l'abat i bisbe Oliba* (Barcelona, 1992) (hereafter *Oliba*), 149.
18. *Urgellia* 401.

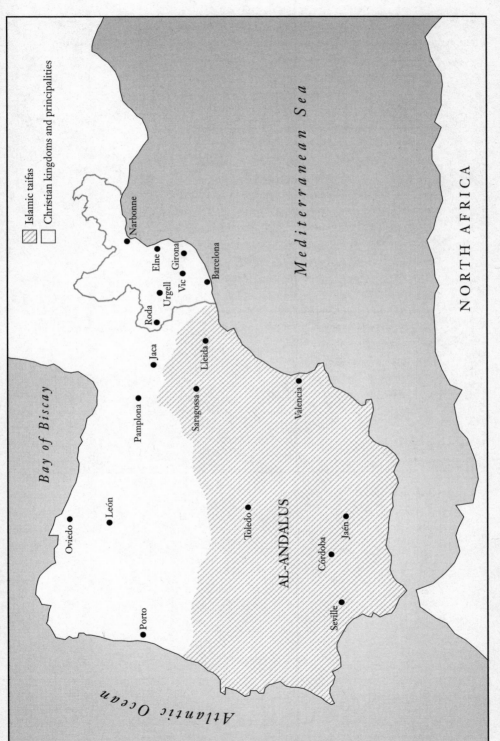

The Iberian Peninsula and Southern France

The Province of Narbonne, 985–1060

sees, major abbacies, and comital and vicecomital offices were monopolized by cousins, uncles, nephews, brothers, and sisters.

Ties among the region's elites were further strengthened by a vague but persistent sense of ethnic identity. The region's inhabitants identified themselves as Goths. This question of ethnic identity arises most frequently when people identify the law of the *Visigothic Code* as *lex noster*.

The outlook of both magnates and humbler property-holders was informed by the region's position on the edge of Latin Europe. Although the counts and bishops showed some lingering attachment to the Frankish political world, the economy and culture of the province were oriented toward the south and the Mediterranean. A long southwestern border facing Muslim al-Andalus was regarded by some as especially dangerous. Relations between Córdoba and Catalonia cycled between amity and animosity. During the latter half of the tenth century, Barcelona maintained diplomatic relations with Muslim Spain. At the same time, Muslim and Christian leaders regularly led raiding parties into each other's territory. The presence of Islam on the region's doorstep had important consequences both for leaders and for property-holders. Here too, Viscountess Guisla's testament reflects some of these conditions. The viscountess stipulated that several of her slaves were to be sold for the redemption of Christian captives in al-Andalus.

Administrative networks, shared dynastic histories, a sense of Gothic identity, and an unstable border with al-Andalus shaped the political and cultural world of the Province of Narbonne. These were key elements in creating a distinct legal environment. This consistency makes an informative foil to the continuities and the transitions that defined the years from 985 to 1060.

This period (985–1060) witnessed a transition at the edge of the Latin Christian world. Frankish kings lost power in the region after 985, and before 1060 the Gregorian Reform had yet to exercise any real influence. The counts of the Spanish March enjoyed a considerable degree of practical autonomy, even though they had also dutifully recognized Frankish kings as their overlords. When Andalusi armies threatened, the magnates of Catalonia expected aid and protection from Frankish kings in return for their loyalty. In 985, al-Mansur, the military leader of al-Andalus, led a devastating raid on Barcelona. The raiding army destroyed a great deal of property and took many of Barcelona's inhabitants prisoner as slaves or hostages. Count Borrell II of Barcelona appealed to King Lothair for help in repelling al-Mansur's raids. Lothair may have intended to respond to Borrell's call, but he died before organizing any military support. Borrell renewed his call for help to the newly elected Hugh Capet. Like his predecessor, Hugh failed to help the distressed inhabitants of Catalonia. Several factors may explain why

Frankish rulers responded so sluggishly to Borrell's urgent requests. The crisis on the Spanish March coincided with a period of instability for Frankish rulers, including a contested change of dynasties. Frankish kings had not engaged in military activity so far to the south for over a century, and the benefits of such an undertaking must have appeared uncertain. The count of Barcelona's troubles must have seemed remote to Lothair, Hugh, and their advisors. Whatever the reasons, their failure to act had political and cultural consequences. Attitudes toward the Frankish kings grew increasingly chilly after the sack of Barcelona. Historians, medieval and modern, have transformed the disaster into a source of national pride by celebrating 985 as the birth of an independent Catalonia.[19] The years around 985 provide a useful starting point, marking as they do watersheds in the political history of Francia and in the history of the region. The years around 1060, which saw another important set of political changes, mark a suitable end.[20] In 1059, political stability returned to the county of Barcelona as Count Ramon Berenguer I of Barcelona finally managed to contain an insurrection, led by a magnate named Mir Geribert. More generally, the count was developing innovative ways to exercise authority over the region's petty lords.[21] At roughly the same time, an acrimonious conflict between Archbishop Guifré of Narbonne and the city's viscount signaled shifting ideas about relations between lay and clerical power. First at a council of bishops and later to the pope himself, the viscount accused the archbishop of a litany of misdeeds: simony, bearing arms, building castles, dissipating the cathedral's wealth and relics, and, in general, behaving "like a devil" (*quasi diabolus*).[22] The viscount's campaign eventually resulted in the archbishop's excommunication. Archbishop Guifré was in part the victim of his own arrogance, in part the victim of local grudges, and in part the victim of growing discomfort throughout Europe with bishops who were indistinguishable from lay magnates. The conflict was a sign of shifting ideas about episcopal power. The struggle between viscount and archbishop was one manifestation of the inevitable collision of long-standing practices of the regional church with the imported

19. See Manuel Rovira i Solà, "Notes documentals sobre alguns efectes de la presa de Barcelona per al-Mansur," *Acta historica et archaeologica medievalia* 1 (1980): 31–53; Michel Zimmerman, "La prise de Barcelone par al-Mansur et la naissance de l'historiographie catalane," *Annales de Bretagne et des Pays de l'Ouest* 87 (1980): 191–218.

20. Thomas N. Bisson, *The Medieval Crown of Aragon: A Short History* (Oxford, 1986), 25.

21. Kosto, *Making Agreements*, especially chapter 4.

22. Claude Devic and J. J. Vaissete, *Histoire générale de Languedoc avec des notes et les pièces justificatives*, 2d ed. (Toulouse, 1872–1904) (hereafter *HGL*), 251.

ideas of Gregorian Reform.[23] The papacy took this occasion and others like it to assume an unprecedented level of involvement in local affairs. After 1060, the papacy, Cluny, and monasteries like Saint-Victoire de Marseille increasingly came to dominate monasteries and cathedral chapters that had until a generation earlier had been the exclusive preserve of the region's comital and vicecomital families.[24] The ties that had given the province some unity for two centuries were forever altered. Between 985 and 1060, then, a distinct legal environment in terms of the region's internal political structure and its relations with authorities beyond the ambit of local politics prevailed.

Longstanding traditions placed responsibility for adjudicating disputes on the shoulders of lay and ecclesiastical elites (counts, countesses, bishops, and viscounts). These same figures could also be found leading military raids, orchestrating Peace councils, and cultivating ties with monasteries and cathedral chapters. But although these magnates rightly occupy a large place in any account of the region's legal culture, disputes over fields, mills, and vineyards involved a broad cross-section of society, from the count and countess of Barcelona to humble widows eking out livings on undesirable lands. The region's social structure was a gradual continuum of social and economic gradations. Successful cultivators and speculators moved into the echelon of urban elites.[25]

The region's economy grew dramatically during this period. Recovering from the raid of 985 and subsequent smaller raids, magnates led their own raids into al-Andalus. These raids yielded booty and tribute payments. Gold began to trickle and then to flood into Latin Europe through Catalonia and other principalities in northern Spain. The Muslim-Christian frontier in Catalonia pushed to the south and to the west. Magnates and individual property-holders strove to bring land into cultivation in the newly won territories. Competition for newly available or newly desirable land intensified the impulses that fed litigation over property. The process of securing the fron-

23. Elisabeth Magnou-Nortier, *La société laïque et l'église dans la province ecclésiastique de Narbonne* (Toulouse, 1974), especially chapter 5.

24. Paul Freedman, *The Diocese of Vic: Tradition and Regeneration in Medieval Catalonia* (New Brunswick, N.J., 1983), 30–31; Anscari M. Mundó, "Monastic Movements in the East Pyrenees," in *Cluniac Monasticism in the Central Middle Ages*, ed. Noreen Hunt (London, 1979), 98–122.

25. José Enrique Ruiz Doménec, "The Urban Origins of Barcelona: Agricultural Revolution or Urban Development?" *Speculum* 52 (1977): 265–86; Pierre Bonnassie, "Une famille de la campagne barcelonaise et ses activités économiques aux alentours de l'an Mil," *Annales du Midi* (hereafter *Amidi*) 76 (1964): 261–303; Victor Farías Zurita, "Compraventa de tierras: Circulación monetaria y sociedad campesina en los siglos X y XI: El ejemplo de Goltred de Reixac," *Anuario de Estudios Medievales* 29 (1999): 269–99.

tier involved the construction of castles and towers which changed the political and social geography of the region.

These developments brought new wealth to a region whose inhabitants were already fairly prosperous. In much of the region, soil was fertile and easily worked. Wheat, barley, rye, pigs, sheep, cows, goats, figs, straw, cabbage, onions, flax, cheese, breads, and wine appear regularly in tenth- and eleventh-century records.[26] There was considerable variety in topography, soil, and climate. The fertile plain of Vic, for example, had a climate unlike Barcelona on the coast. Narbonne was sunny, dry, and mild. Urgell, on the other hand, had a cloudier, alpine climate. In the mountain valleys, trapping, hunting, and fishing played key roles. In the lower plains, game-filled forests gave way to carefully tended orchards. Many property-holders grew rich through the construction of terraces, cultivation of vineyards on those terraces, and wine production. Many others developed properties by constructing mills and irrigation canals. Some of the economic growth in this period was due to the influx of Andalusi gold, but much of it was due to human labor poured into developing fields, mills, and vineyards. Salt from coastal salt pans near Narbonne was renowned for its use in preserving fish. Salt formed the basis of local markets in Cardona and Gerri as well. Movable luxury goods also appear in records: silver, silk, weapons, books, furniture, linen, and Andalusi textiles.[27]

Some areas were more heavily settled than others. The narrow river valleys of the Pyrenees were densely populated from the eighth century. During the late ninth and early tenth centuries, many of the pent-up inhabitants of these valleys moved to the south to resettle the fertile plains near Bages and Vic. The climate of these newly repopulated zones was milder than that of the valleys of the high Pyrenees, but the terrain was still high and rugged. In coastal Languedoc, settlements like Narbonne or Elne crouched close to the sea, supplementing the produce of fields with fish and salt. South of the Pyrenees, the soil near the coast was less inviting. The inhabitants of Catalonia were, with notable exceptions like Barcelona, concentrated inland, away from the sea.[28] The *costa brava* did not appeal to medieval farmers in the way that it does to modern tourists.

Much of the rural population was dispersed in scattered farmsteads. In general, this was not a region of great latifundia, but one of individual manses on which families cultivated for self-sufficiency and carved out modest, com-

26. Paul Freedman, *The Origins of Peasant Servitude in Medieval Catalonia* (Cambridge, 1991), 43.

27. Bonnassie, *Catalogne*, 368, 419.

28. Freedman, *Origins of Peasant Servitude*, 24.

fortable livings.[29] Most varieties of land tenure were not especially onerous. Most agricultural property was allodial: farms, vineyards, mills, orchards, houses, churches, and towers were considered the outright property of their owners. The tolls and oppressive seigneurial exactions that characterized later centuries had not yet fallen upon the region's farmers.[30] Property-holders were accustomed to autonomy and opportunity.

In other ways, prosperity and peace were mixed with insecurities. Some of the region's inhabitants, for example, lived in small settlements that grew up alongside churches or near fortifications (*castra*). Churches were surrounded by envelopes of sacred space extending for thirty paces in every direction. Anyone within this area of sanctuary (*sacraria* or, in Catalan, *sagrera*) enjoyed special protections. Acts of violence and plunder were strictly forbidden and punished with heavy penalties. Initially, *sacrarias* housed clerics and served as warehouses for farmers. At times they became the nuclei of small, rural settlements, concentrating formally dispersed habitats.[31] The *sacrarias*, packed with wine, grain, and cured pork, reflect some of the prosperity of rural farmers while at the same time signaling some of the insecurity that accompanied daily life.

The province had a handful of important cities. Barcelona, which probably had a population of around 2,000 in the late tenth century, was the most important of these. It was already home to a modest textile industry, the importance of which would swell in later centuries. Smaller cities also had markets and served as administrative centers, but these were always tied to the rural hinterland. In general, urban development was closely linked and dependent upon agricultural growth. Many city-dwellers possessed farms beyond the city which required regular attention. Property disputes that erupted in the countryside often found their way to judicial hearings in the comital and episcopal palaces in the cities.

Cultivation tended to be managed by married couples and their children, rather than by more diffuse clan-like structures.[32] Inheritances were usually divided equally (or close to equally) among legitimate, surviving children, male and female. The conjugal unit was often important in property transactions, and married couples often executed property transactions together. At the same time, men and women, married and single, often bought and sold land independently. Women appear frequently as property-holders and as lit-

29. Bonnassie, *Catalogne*, 219–24.

30. Freedman, *Origins of Peasant Servitude*, 50, 70–71; Thomas N. Bisson, *Tormented Voices: Power, Crisis, and Humanity in Rural Catalonia, 1140–1200* (Cambridge, Mass., 1998).

31. See M. Fixot and E. Zadora-Rio, eds., *L'environnement des églises et la topographie religieuse des campagnes médiévales*, Documents d'archéologie française 46 (Paris, 1994).

32. Bonnassie, *Catalogne*, 266–70; Freedman, *Origins of Peasant Servitude*, 45–46.

igants in court. They continued to control their own property in marriage, often buying and selling land without the involvement of husbands or children.

Overall, records testify to a diverse and dynamic land market. What properties and resources particularly tended to become subject to dispute? Disputes arose over every type of productive resource. Often these were fields and vineyards. Sometimes churches or their tithes were disputed. Some disputes centered on very particular rights of exploitation. In one case, for example, a farmer named Odo accused his neighbor Sunifred of diverting a stream that traversed their adjoining properties in order to provide energy for a newly constructed mill. Sunifred's diversion had the unfortunate side effect of disabling an existing mill on Odo's property.[33] The terms scribes used most often to describe disputed properties were *alod, villa, terras, castrum, turris,* and *ecclesia.* These terms were flexible and lacked precise meanings.[34] On the most general level, terms like *villa, turris,* or *castrum* referred to complexes of property rights that might have included houses, fortifications, fields, uncultivated land, orchards, mills, vineyards, water courses, salt pans, and fish ponds. Disputes over churches or ecclesiastical property similarly involved buildings, income, pastures, fields, fishing rights, forests, and tithes.

The dynamism of the regional economy, the active land market, and intermittent territorial expansion explain in part why property rights were often disputed, but it is important to remember that the property rights over which people fought stood at the intersection of economics, politics, society, and religion. Most disputes sprang from structural tensions between potential heirs—tensions which might remain dormant for long periods of time until a catalyst (such as the death of a property-holder) brought them to the

33. J. Rius Serra, ed., *Cartulario de "Sant Cugat" del Vallés,* 3 vols. (Barcelona, 1946) (hereafter *Sant Cugat*), 317.

34. On patterns of landholding, see A. R. Lewis, *The Development of Southern French and Catalan Society, 718–1050* (Austin, Tex., 1965), 263–65, 382; Lluís To Figueras, "El marc de les comunitates pageses: *Villa* i parròquia en les diòcesis de Girona i Elna (final del segle IX—principi de l'XI)," in *Catalunya i França meridional, a l'entorn de l'any mil— La Catalogne et la France méridionale autour de l'an mil,* ed. Xavier Barral i Altet et al. (Barcelona, 1991), 212–39; Magnou-Nortier, *Société laïque,* chapter 1; Monique Bourin-Derruau, "Le Bas-Languedoc," in *Les sociétés méridionales aux alentours de l'an mil,* ed. Michel Zimmerman (Paris, 1991); Bonnassie, *Catalogne,* 215–16; Josep Maria Salrach, "Formació, organització i defense del domini de Sant Cugat en els segles X–XII," *Acta historica et archaeologica mediaevalia* 13 (1992), 138; Aline Durand, *Les paysages médiévaux de Languedoc* (Toulouse, 1998), 35–36, 81–85; Coral Cuadrada, *El Maresme medieval: Les jurisdiccions baronals de Mataró i Vilassar* (Barcelona, 1988).

surface. But larger political events also affected how people held and fought over property.

The turbulent relations between the caliphate of Córdoba and the magnates of Catalonia teach an important lesson in how politics and warfare affected law and property. The 985 sacking of Barcelona was the last time a Muslim army penetrated so far north in Latin Christendom. In 1010, 1013, and 1017, the count of Barcelona led counterraids on Córdoba. These raids may have enjoyed less success had they not coincided with political and social turmoil throughout Muslim al-Andalus, including a large-scale urban revolt in Córdoba in 1009 which drained the city of intellectual and military leaders. A series of coups and conspiracies culminated in the assassination of the caliph in 1024, ushering in a period of upheaval and collapse.[35] After two and a half centuries of remarkable stability, the Umayyad caliphate disintegrated into a host of smaller kingdoms.

Initially, the political fragmentation of al-Andalus may seem to have little to do with the mills and vineyards of Catalonia, but the two are intimately related. Records from the monastery of Sant Cugat provide compelling examples of how these broader political shifts ignited property disputes. The above-mentioned raids led by Count Ramon Borrell altered the shape of Catalonia's southern frontier. The success of these raids, however modest, prompted the region's inhabitants to reassess the value of property to the south and west of Barcelona. Vast areas of land previously considered perilous waste threatened by Andalusi raids now enjoyed some security; land along and beyond the Llobregat became newly desirable. For the monks of Sant Cugat near Barcelona, the situation afforded irresistible opportunities. Resting in Sant Cugat's archive were titles to much of this land, most in the form of privileges granted to the monastery by Charlemagne and his immediate successors. The monks had long ignored their claims to these properties. Because of their precarious position on the Muslim frontier, the rich vineyards and streams flowing into the Llobregat (easily adaptable to milling) had not claimed the monks' attention for more than thirty years. The raids on Córdoba not only seemed to make this land safer, but also suggested that the magnates of Catalonia were shifting their attention to the south. Such considerations sent the monks of Sant Cugat scurrying to dust off their Carolingian privileges so they could press claims to these lands.

The frontier was not, however, a barren wasteland. Other settlers had also seen opportunity there, had braved the rigors of the frontier, and had cultivated abandoned land. Scribes occasionally referred to the desolation of the

---

35. Peter C. Scales, *The Fall of the Caliphate of Córdoba: Berbers and Andalusis in Conflict* (Leiden, 1994), 213.

region, but these lands contained settlements, churches, and bridges.[36] The presence of these settlers was a great annoyance to the monks of Sant Cugat. Under the unswerving direction of Abbot Guitard, the monastery began to assert long-dormant rights, much to the consternation of the region's inhabitants, who had spent two generations building livelihoods on land that had not captured the interest of anyone else. In 1013, Guitard claimed in a comital court property held by a widow named Adelaide. He supported his claim to the property with a number of Carolingian documents. Adelaide made an impassioned plea to the court. She argued that her husband had cleared and cultivated the land, and in doing so had acquired the right to keep it.[37] Four years later, the same abbot, the same widow, and the same land were again the concern of a comital court. The abbot again appealed to royal and papal privileges; Adelaide again insisted on her right to hold the land because of long-term, unchallenged possession.[38] On both occasions, courts lavishly supplied with judges, counts, and bishops admitted that they were puzzled about how to proceed. Despite their contradictory claims and their different strategies of legitimation, both claimants appealed to two hundred year old authorities. Adelaide insisted on the right to her husband's property for her son. Sant Cugat insisted that royal privileges resolved all questions in the monastery's favor.

Property law on frontiers is always a challenge, and the decisions reached by these courts reflect their uncertainty. They eventually pursued a policy that favored Sant Cugat's claims in most cases, but which gave some (usually trifling) recognition of the rights of occupants like Adelaide. The Córdoba raid had consequences which the count of Barcelona had not anticipated: it provoked a rash of litigation. Sant Cugat's interest in the land worked by Adelaide and her neighbors was one sign of the monastery's programmatic effort to control land on the frontier. Virtually every one of the suits Sant Cugat initiated between 1010 and 1035 related to properties on the edge of Latin Christendom. These lawsuits were local symptoms of Latin Europe's economic and demographic expansion.[39]

The implications of political and military events extended into the prac-

---

36. Bonnassie, *Catalogne*, 128. See also Freedman, *Diocese of Vic*, 15, 21.
37. *Sant Cugat* 452.
38. *Sant Cugat* 464.
39. See Albert Benet i Clará, "Immigració ultrapirenenca a Catalunya en l'Edat Mitjana (ss. IX–XII)," *Actas del Congreso Internacional 'Historia de los Pireneos' Cervera 1988* (Madrid, 1991), 2:121–42; Stephen Bensch, *Barcelona and Its Rulers, 1096–1291* (Cambridge, 1995), 89–90; Robert Bartlett, *The Making of Europe: Conquest, Colonization, and Cultural Change, 950–1350* (Princeton, N.J., 1993); The instability of frontiers provoked litigation elsewhere as well. See, for example, Brown, *Unjust Seizure*, 204; and John Hudson, *Land, Law, and Lordship in Anglo-Norman England* (Oxford, 1994), 107–10.

tical and forensic details of how people tried to substantiate their property claims. Vast numbers of records were destroyed in the 985 sack of Barcelona. Some of Barcelona's inhabitants captured in the raid returned home to find that their property had been misappropriated and went to court to recover it. The destruction of so many records altered the nature of property litigation in Catalonia for generations. For decades to come, some disputants would substantiate their claims to disputed property by referring to records that had been lost or destroyed.

Tremors, large and small, in the social and political world brought conflicting claims to the surface. Once triggered, property disputes reflected competing understandings of how people acquired and kept property. Disputants voiced normative claims about how people held, transferred, and fought over property. The conflict between two coherent but incompatible understandings of how property rights were configured was at the core of many disputes. Monasteries and churches emphasized the importance of written titles and argued that individuals were free in almost every instance to alienate property as they saw fit. Lay challengers appealed to a different set of norms which emphasized collective interest in heritable propertyrights (sometimes referred to as a *hereditas*) and the importance of long-term possession. These conflicting conceptions of property reflect tensions in the social and economic world of the tenth and eleventh centuries, but they do not indicate chaos. Recurring patterns of claims and counterclaims suggest not a lawless free-for-all, but a world in which two coherent systems of property tenure and transmission coexisted with frequent discomfort. Disputes often occurred on the shifting frontier between the Latin world of the Province of Narbonne and Muslim *Hispania*, but they also occurred on the frontier between two conflicting views of how people held property. Disputes were always antagonistic and occasionally violent, but they were rarely senseless. With notable exceptions, disputants did not go to court merely because they were greedy, mean-spirited, or depraved. They went to court because they believed they had legitimate claims to property *and* they usually had good reasons for believing so.

In order to treat the complex interrelations that place property disputes between politics and proof, between innovation and tradition, and between justice and tactics, I have divided this book into three parts. Part one, "Courts and Codes," examines the institutional and intellectual resources communities possessed to process disputes. Part two, "Proofs and Strategies," explores the ways in which property-holders sought to substantiate their claims. Part three, "Endings and Contexts," places disputes from the Province of Narbonne in broader geographic and historiographic contexts.

Part one consists of four chapters. Chapter one, "*Sicut lex edocet*: Remembering and Forgetting the Written Law," describes the ways disputants and judges modified the law of the *Visigothic Code* in practice. Chapter two, "Do Neo-Romans Curse?" shows that ritual sanctions such as liturgical curses and sentences of excommunication occupied an important place in this legal system. Chapter three focuses on judges who, like Sendred and Guifré, took part in a dynamic, close-knit network of professional judges, fostered the regional attachment to written law and sought to forge lasting settlements. Finally, chapter four examines the protean organization of courts. Together, these four chapters describe the institutions and traditions that provided a vocabulary and a structure, however flexible, to the process of disputing.

Part two turns to the ways in which disputants tried to win disputes; the focus shifts from institutions and norms to the practice of disputing. Three chapters deal with the three main types of proof disputants used: judicial ordeals, written proofs, and witness testimony. Throughout these three chapters, I pay particular attention to how courts wrestled with unreliable and ambiguous proofs. Judges had to determine whether written proofs were legitimate and whether witnesses were well-informed and reliable. Each form of proof had particular strengths and weaknesses but in practice they were often interdependent.

In part three, "Endings and Contexts," I situate these property disputes in historical and historiographic contexts. Chapter eight, "Winning, Losing, and Resisting: How Disputes Ended," shows that most courts in the Province of Narbonne issued unequivocal decisions in favor of one disputant, but compromise was important in some cases. In addition to tracing the sorts of decisions that courts and communities made, I reconstruct the experience of disputants who were disappointed and who rejected court decisions. Chapter nine, "Justice and Violence in Medieval Europe," relates the courts and disputants of the Province of Narbonne to those throughout medieval Europe. First, the chapter places property disputes in the context of debates over the Feudal Revolution, arguing that the process of disputing displays important long-term continuities in the tenth and eleventh centuries. Finally, it turns to the question of how disputes in this region resembled those elsewhere. Many of the features of courts in the Province of Narbonne were distinctive, but there were parallels. For example, courts in Galicia and León at times relied on the *Visigothic Code* and the challenged bequests that provoked disputes in this region were common throughout Latin Europe.

In disputes like the one that pitted Ermengol against Geriberga and Renard, we see how individuals fought for property—wisely and foolishly, honestly and treacherously—and how people responded to conflicts which threatened the fabric of their communities. We see the regular challenges that property-holders confronted and the ways in which communities articulated and re-shaped notions of right and wrong, just and unjust. When read together, as a portrait of the region's legal culture, we see not only individual and community struggles but the larger contexts in which such struggles unfolded. They reveal not only individual challenges but fault lines in social structure—between lay and clerical property-holders, between institutions and families, between brothers and sisters. We can see the transmission of intellectual traditions—such as the law of the *Visigothic Code*—during a moment of transition in European history, and the ways in which premodern societies functioned with notions of law and justice which only dimly resemble those of modern states. This book aims to explore and to anatomize the stranger practices symptomatic of a period of gradual transition. In these disputes, one sees that what is most remarkable about this age is not its violence but rather its energy and resourcefulness.

PART I

COURTS AND CODES

CHAPTER ONE
SICUT LEX EDOCET: REMEMBERING AND FORGETTING THE WRITTEN LAW

J udges and disputants in Europe rarely referred to norms or rules during the tenth and eleventh centuries. When they did so, they usually invoked unwritten custom (*mos* or *consuetudo*) rather than written rules (*leges*). Few regions had a universally recognized written law (*lex*) and disputants or judges only infrequently appealed to *leges*. Litigation over property rights rarely involved the application of generalized rules drawn from law codes.

The Province of Narbonne was exceptional in this regard. People often relied on written rules to resolve difficult legal questions. Litigants invoked rules to support their claims to disputed mills, fields, and churches. Judges cited written law to legitimate their decisions. Scribes and judges drafted more documents, consulted more legal codices, and cited more rules than their contemporaries elsewhere in Europe. Understanding the significance of written law in the tenth and eleventh centuries is an essential first step toward understanding how people fought over property.

The inhabitants of the province had a special reverence for written law, especially for rules from the *Visigothic Code*. But although they exhibited a remarkable attachment to written law, they were not in its thrall. Judges and disputants constantly reshaped the traditions which they so greatly respected. I am primarily interested here in the ways people reinvented legal rules. Rules and codes were important features of the legal imagination of the region, but they did not determine the outcomes of disputes. As elsewhere, rules functioned in complex ways. People cited passages from the *Visigothic Code* as fundamental instructions for governing property relations, but their relation to the written law was more complicated than one of simple obedience. This warm embrace of a particular law code should not be mistaken for the systematic and impartial application of that code.

The people of the Province of Narbonne used written law selectively. Legal professionals drew many ideas from earlier legislation, but of all the rules available to them, they ignored many more than they adopted. Scribes, judges, and disputants adapted legal traditions to contemporary exigencies, pruning away inconvenient passages and splicing together fragments of unrelated legislation. Rather than the passive reception of a body of rules, these practices reflect a dynamic engagement with a constantly refashioned past. Citations of the *Visigothic Code* reveal the *Code's* enduring prestige, but they do not indicate that the *Code* survived as a system of law. The written law was not so much a set of commands determining the outcome of litigation, but rather a resource upon which disputants and judges drew, some more shrewdly than others. During the tenth and eleventh centuries, it served as a repository of ideas and gestures that legal professionals and disputants mined with discrimination and creativity.

Legal experts referred to the *Visigothic Code* more often than to any other legal authority, but the *Code* was not the only source of rules related to property.[1] Rules from the *Visigothic Code* were used alongside rules from other law codes, the canons of church councils, and scripture. Judges invoked passages from the prophet Jeremiah to support certain legal decisions, while narratives from the Book of Numbers were used to describe sanctions for violators of agreements. Resourceful disputants exploited the diffuseness of legal authority, citing any text that supported their claim. This legal flexibility is apparent not only in the range of authorities invoked, but also in the ways in which judges and disputants cited those authorities. Scribes, for example, lumped together the canons of Toledan councils and rules from the *Visigothic Code*. Legal authority was also cumulative. Invoking several rules from diverse sources did not mean that the foundation of a legal argument was in-

---

1. Several historians have noted the use of Visigothic law in Catalonia and Languedoc. See, for example, Bonnassie, *Catalogne*, 194–95; José Ríus Serra, "El derecho visigodo en Cataluña," *Gessamelte Aufsätzen zur Kulturgeschichte Spaniens* 8 (1940): 65–80; Walther Kienast, "Das Fortleben des gotischen Rechts in Südfrankreich und Katalonien," *Studien über die französichen Völksstamme des Frühmittelalters* (Stuttgart, 1968), 151–70; Michel Zimmerman, "L'usage du droit wisigothique en Catalogne du IXe au XIIe siècle: Approches d'une signification culturelle," *Mélanges de la Casa de Velázquez* (hereafter *MCV*) 9 (1973): 233–81; Aquilino Iglesia Ferreirós, "La creación del derecho en Cataluña," *Anuario de historia del derecho español* (hereafter *AHDE*) 47 (1977): 99–423; Roger Collins, "Visigothic Law and Regional Custom in Disputes in Early Medieval Spain," in *The Settlement of Disputes in Early Medieval Europe*, ed. Wendy Davies and Paul Fouracre (Cambridge, 1986), 85–104.

coherent, but rather that the position being argued was supported by a broad and authoritative consensus.

The cumulative effect of this selective use of written law was the promotion of certain understandings of how property rights were configured. Clerical disputants used written law to foster particular ideas about how people held property and when they could give it away. In particular, they invoked rules to promote the rights of individual property-holders to alienate property. They insisted that donations and sales were always irrevocable, but those made to churches and monasteries were especially so. While legal professionals emphasized rules which consolidated the rights of ecclesiastic property-holders, they passed over in silence rules in the same codes that protected the property rights of kindred or that limited an individual's right to alienate property. This transformation of written rules sheds valuable light on the ways in which disputants tried to win their cases. In particular, by looking at how these legal traditions were reshaped, we see that conflicting understandings of property and alienability were at the root of many disputes.

LEGES GOTORUM: THE LAWS OF THE GOTHS

When judges referred to *lex* or *leges*, they were usually thinking of the seventh-century *Visigothic Code*, also known as the *Forum Iudicum* or the *Liber Iudiciorum*.[2] The greatest achievement of Visigothic legislators, the *Code* went through several recensions during the seventh century, each of which added to the number of rules in the *Code's* twelve books. In his *Historia Gothorum*, Isidore of Seville described the original impulse behind the creation of the *Code* as King Leovgild's desire to amend earlier codes.[3] No copies of Leovgild's version survive, but it almost certainly formed the foundation of subsequent codes. King Recceswinth issued the version known as the *Liber Iudiciorum* in 654. King Ervig promulgated a revision in 681, and the final

2. The term *lex* had a broad semantic range in medieval Europe. At times, it referred with clarity and precision to particular rules drawn from particular codes. At other times, *lex* assumed a broader significance which did not correspond to any particular text but asserted that a transaction accorded with all that was just and authoritative. See Paul Fouracre, "'Placita' and Disputes in Later Merovingian Francia," in Davies and Fouracre, *Settlement of Disputes*, 33; and Rosamond McKitterick, *The Carolingians and the Written Word* (Cambridge, 1989), 38.

3. Isidore of Seville, *History of the Kings of the Goths, Vandals, and Suevi*, tr. Guido Donini and Gordon B. Ford, Jr. (Leiden, 1966), 24.

version was commissioned by Egica in 693. The *Visigothic Code* was thus the product of more than a century of tinkering by lawmakers.

Visigothic lawmakers were avid students of Roman law and they derived many rules directly from Roman sources. The *Visigothic Code* was the most Romanized and most comprehensive of the Germanic law codes created in early medieval Europe. It included detailed procedural rules for the organization of courts and the assessment of proofs—rules which tenth- and eleventh-century judges studied with keen interest. The *Code* not only provided a corpus of rules relating to property, injury, and inheritance, it also reflected on the role of law in society, concluding in grand echo of the *Theodosian Code* that "law is the instructress of life" (*lex est magistra vitae*).[4]

Tenth- and eleventh-century judges who turned to the *Code* for guidance found some of the *Code's* 527 rules more useful than others. Between 832 and 1300, only eighty-nine of those rules appeared in any form in records from Catalonia.[5] During the same period, only a dozen rules from the *Code* were used with any frequency. Quantitative assessments of this sort are an admittedly crude index of the way in which people understood legal authority, but the figures do show that tenth- and eleventh-century enthusiasm for the *Code* was very selective. The limited number of rules that scribes, disputants, and judges actually deployed poses a striking challenge to any unqualified notion of the "survival" of Visigothic law. Even the most expansive understanding of what might constitute the survival of a rule, applied to three centuries of records, yields a survival rate of less than 17 percent. The tenacity of certain elements of Visigothic jurisprudence is, indeed, impressive. But just as impressive as the survival of this legal tradition is the selectivity with which scribes and judges employed the rules of the *Visigothic Code*.

Disputants and judges were consistent in the types of rules they borrowed from the *Code*. Most citations of Visigothic law were related to one of three legal ideas: the irrevocability of gifts (especially gifts to churches), the freedom of property-holders to alienate their property without hindrance, and the notion that property transactions carried out through force or intimidation were not valid. Each of these ideas, supported by more or less scrupulous citations of rules from the *Code*, recurred frequently in charters. Relying on the legal authority of the *Code*, disputants and judges promoted particular conceptions of property rights, gifts, and alienability, ignoring a vast range of rules dealing with arson, theft, murder, adultery, Jews, personal injury, kingship, and a host of other issues.

4. *Leges Visigothorum*, Monumenta Germaniae Historica, ed. Karl Zeumer (Hanover, 1902; reprint, 1973), I.2.2.

5. Iglesia Ferreirós, "Creación del derecho," appendix 1, 401–6.

By looking at frequently invoked rules in Visigothic legislation, one sees that the practical significance of particular rules shifted over time. The use of a rule from Book V of the *Code*, *de transactionibus*, provides an example of change and continuity in legal ideas. The *Code's* Book V contained a title, "Concerning Exchanges and Sales," which included a rule stipulating that exchanges were as valid and as planent as sales, provided they were not undertaken under conditions of force or intimidation.[6] In the Province of Narbonne, variants of this rule appeared in thirteen records of donation or exchange between 950 and 1100.[7]

Roman legislators carefully distinguished sales from exchanges. Germanic law codes, even those indebted to Roman models, often collapsed distinctions that Roman jurists valued. The legal categories that were important to Roman jurists were clouded by seventh-century Visigothic legislators and further blurred by eleventh-century judges. In citations of these rules, the distinguishing features of the two types of transaction vanished before the rule's insistence on their shared validity. The rule does not define a type of prohibited behavior. Nor does it enumerate the sanctions related to a particular infraction. The rule does not explain the nature of sales or exchanges, but only asserts that both transactions enjoyed similar validity. The *Visigothic Code* distinguished several types of transaction by which property might be transferred (*donatio*, *commutatio*, and *emptio*), but litigants and judges ignored distinctions among the three. The claim that exchanges should share in the nimbus of unequivocal permanence that surrounded sales appealed to scribes, litigants, and judges in the tenth and eleventh centuries. The notion that sales and exchanges enjoyed equal validity became a sort of legal aphorism. Citations of the rule functioned mainly as assertions of the permanent nature of all alienations of property, whether sales, gifts, or exchanges. This legal notion was attributed not only to the *Visigothic Code*, but to a very broad understanding of legal authority—and was applied to a wide range of situations.

The rule in the *Visigothic Code* asserting the similar permanence of sales and exchanges also provided guidance about what made such transactions legitimate. The *Code*, borrowing from Roman law, prohibited transactions undertaken through force or intimidation (*per vim et metum*).[8] The many ref-

6. *Leges Visigothorum*, v.4.1.

7. See, for example, *Urgellia* 214; *HGL* 154; Bibliothèque Nationale de France (Paris) (hereafter BNF) Coll. Doat 55, f. 87; BNF Coll. Doat 58, f. 250; Arxiu de la Corona d'Aragó (Barcelona) (hereafter ACA) Ramon Berenguer I, 75; *El Cartoral de Santa Maria de Roses, segles x–xiii*, ed. Josep M. Marquès i Planagumà (Barcelona, 1986) (hereafter *Roses*), no. 7; Archives departementales de l'Aude H102.

8. Euric's code included two clauses invalidating any transactions which took place *per*

erences to this restriction in later records reflect the enthusiasm of tenth- and eleventh-century legal experts for some elements of Visigothic law. At the same time, the citations show that scribes and judges were at times unaware of or confused about the origins of the rules they cited.

The final version of the *Visigothic Code* included four different rules which invalidated coerced transactions.[9] Each dealt with a different type of transaction: *definitio*, *donatio*, *commutatio*, and *venditio*. While the distinctions between contracts, gifts, exchanges, and sales were serious matters for Visigothic legislators, they were less important when the rules were used in the tenth and eleventh centuries. Later scribes and judges seized on the idea that transactions undertaken through force or fear should be prohibited, but they paid little attention to the carefully drawn distinctions among different types of transactions. The phrase *per vim et metum extorta* ("exacted through force and intimidation") became a fragment of popular law and was frequently invoked by judges.[10]

Tenth- and eleventh-century judges knew that transactions *per vim et metum extorta* were not valid, but not all scribes and judges had a clear understanding of the origin of this prescription. The most immediate source was the *Visigothic Code*. Both Roman and Visigothic law were, to be sure, respected legal authorities, but eleventh-century scribes at times advanced even more elevated notions about the foundation of this prescription. Some claimed divine law was behind the prohibition: "Divine law and the commands of the Holy Fathers specifically teach that an exchange, sale, or donation which is not made through force or intimidation should have full validity."[11] Scribes and judges were usually eager to indicate the Visigothic origins of rules, but fanciful attributions like this one were not altogether uncommon. This scribe was in some sense citing the *Visigothic Code*, but he was also taking considerable liberties. His citation collapsed three of the four above-mentioned rules. The *Code* saw donations, sales, and exchanges as distinct legal activities, each of which was compromised by the presence of force or fear; the citation fused the three varieties of transaction together. Rather than citing a particular rule extracted from the *Code*, the scribe alluded to a legal fragment that was common to four discrete rules; he was synthesizing Visigothic law as much as applying it.

---

vim et metum. Codex Euriciani Leges ex Lege Baiuvariorum Restituae, ed. Karl Zeumer (Hannover, 1902), chapters 277 and 309.

9. *Leges Visigothorum*, II.5.8; V.2.1; V.4.1; V.4.3.

10. Compare Dominique Barthélemy's discussion of *droit demi-savant*. *La société dans le comté de Vendôme: de l'an mil au XIVe siècle* (Paris, 1993), 59–60.

11. Iglesia Ferreirós, "Creación del derecho," 304.

The fear and force prohibition proved particularly prone to adoption and modification by later scribes. Sometimes they indicated with meticulous care that the prohibition sprang from a particular rule governing a particular transaction in a particular body of law. At other times, they presented the prohibition as a piece of general legal wisdom with no particular source in legislation and applicable to any type of property transfer. Tenth- and eleventh-century judges grafted the force and fear prohibition onto unrelated legislation, embedding the *per vim et metum* clause in the middle of other rules.[12] In some citations, the four original transactions mentioned in the *Visigothic Code* remained distinct and scribes expressed awareness of the human roots of the legislation.[13] More often, the idea appeared without any reference to its legal status or its connection to particular rules. Even a document infused with a rhetoric of legality and citing specific rules from the *Visigothic Code* might refer to this prohibition with no hint that it was drawn from the *Code*.[14] Instead, the restriction became a formula that seeped into the language of property so pervasively that it no longer required any special reference to the origin of the rule.

INHERITANCE AND ALIENABILITY

The transformation of Visigothic rules governing inheritance shows how legal professionals adopted rules selectively and modified them. The *Visigothic Code* established clear guidelines for inheritance. The second title of Book IV, *de origine naturali*, consists of twenty detailed rules which determined inheritance portions due to children, aunts, uncles, nephews, nieces, grandparents, and posthumous children. If a parent died intestate, sons and daughters shared equally in the inheritance.[15] If a property-holder died intestate and there were no heirs in a direct line, collateral heirs were to divide the estate.[16] Finally, parents were constrained to alienate no more than one fifth of their property to beneficiaries other than children and grandchildren.[17] The *Code*, in other words, extended considerable protections to expectant heirs.

12. Petrus de Marca and Etienne Baluze, *Marca Hispanica sive limes Hispanicus* (Paris, 1688) (hereafter *Marca*), 217.

13. *HGL* 113.

14. See, for example, *Urgellia* 557, ACA Ramon Berenguer I, 25.

15. *Leges Visigothorum*, IV.2.2.

16. *Leges Visigothorum*, IV.2.3.

17. *Leges Visigothorum*, IV.2.18.

Of all these guidelines and restrictions governing inheritance, only one rule was invoked in later records: the last one in this section enjoyed a burst of popularity in the tenth and eleventh centuries. It dealt only with cases of inheritance for property-holders who had neither direct descendants nor the collateral heirs mentioned in the preceding nineteen rules. The rule stated that property-holders without children, grandchildren, or great-grandchildren were free of the constraints that bound other property-holders:

> Every freeborn man and woman, whether belonging to the nobility or of inferior rank, who has no children, grandchildren, or great-grandchildren, has the unquestionable right to dispose of his or her estate at will; nor can his or her command be set aside by any relatives belonging to the direct or to the collateral line. For those belonging to degrees of relationship other than that above, in the direct line, cannot, in the order of nature, receive the inheritance. Such relatives can, however, inherit from the intestate in accordance with the law which defines their rights.[18]

A dispute involving the monastery of Sant Cugat illustrates the type of situation that prompted judges and litigants to invoke this rule. In 1011, the abbot of Sant Cugat claimed that one Geribert was unjustly holding a tower. According to the abbot, the tower had been given to the monastery by Geribert's deceased brother, Adalbert. The gift, in the abbot's account, had been made with scrupulous attention to the law. Geribert did not contest the abbot's claim that his brother had made the gift, but he insisted that the gift was beyond his brother's rights and argued that he and his siblings had rights to the disputed tower which made Adalbert's gift invalid.[19] In a decision upholding the legitimacy of Adalbert's gift, the presiding judge cited five different Visigothic rules. Within this daunting thicket of citations was the rule governing inheritance and the freedom of property-holders to dispose of property as they wished:

> [Adalbert] then bequeathed [the tower] to the monastery and there was nothing about this that was contrary to the decree of the law . . . for it is clear that this castle (*castrum*) was Adalbert's according to the law . . . and he could do with it as he wished, for the law says: Every freeborn man and woman, whether noble or of lesser rank, who has no children, grandchildren, or great-grandchildren can do with his or her things as he or she pleases.[20]

18. *Leges Visigothorum*, IV.2.20, I have slightly modified the translation in Samuel P. Scott, *The Visigothic Code* (Boston, 1910), 130.

19. *Sant Cugat* 437. For a discussion of this case, see Marie Kelleher, "Boundaries of Law: Code and Custom in Legal Practice in Early Medieval Catalonia," *Comitatus* 30 (1999): 1–11.

20. *Sant Cugat* 437.

Viewed as a whole, the twenty rules in this section of the *Code* gave family members carefully defined legal interests in the property of their kin. But when the monks of Sant Cugat and other later disputants cited this rule, they usually omitted mention of the requirement that a property-holder have no descendants or heirs. References to this rule in tenth- and eleventh- century transactions never hinted at the goal of the original legislation: namely, to govern inheritance in those exceptional cases not covered by the preceding nineteen rules describing the rights of kin.

The metamorphosis of this rule is a striking example of how scribes, judges, and disputants reinvented Visigothic law. The omission of the first clause, which explained the conditions under which the rule could be applied, and the silent abandonment of the nineteen other rules governing inheritance transformed the rule's practical significance. Seventh-century Visigothic legislators would have found curious if not shocking the idea of unfettered alienability which scribes attributed to the *Code*. Visigothic law diligently protected the interests of potential heirs at the expense of the right of property-holders to alienate.[21] Thus, a provision originally intended for those exceptional property-holders who had no other claims on their estate became, in the tenth and eleventh centuries, an expression of the freedom of any property-holder, with or without kindred, to give without constraint. What appears at first blush to be continuity between the eleventh century and the Visigothic past is, in fact, a rupture with earlier ideas about property.

By the middle of the tenth century, scribes represented the right to alienate property (particularly to churches and monasteries) as fundamental to a host of legal traditions. While the monks of Sant Cugat and others pointed to the *Visigothic Code*, some scribes suggested that this right was guaranteed by a broad array of authorities: "A great part of authority states, as do Roman, Gothic, and Salic law, that any person shall have the freedom to donate or alienate his own things in the name of God."[22] Another scribe echoed this ample notion of legal authority: "Authority decrees, as do Roman, Salic, Gothic, and any other law, that a person shall have the right to do as he pleases—to give or donate his own things."[23] One scribe claimed that alien-

---

21. See Fernando de Arvizu, "Las causas de desheredación en el derecho altomedieval de Aragón y Navarra," *Mélanges offerts à Jean Dauvillier* (Toulouse, 1979), 1–14; and Katherine Fischer Drew, "The Family in Visigothic Law," in *Law and Society in Early Medieval Europe* (London, 1988), 10–11.

22. *HGL* 78; and *Catalunya Carolingia II: El Diplomes Carolingia à Catalunya*, part 3, vol. 2, *Els comtats de Pallars i Ribagorça*, ed. Ramon d'Abadal i de Vinyals (Barcelona, 1955) (hereafter *Cat. Car.*), 166.

23. "Multa declarat autoritas, et lex Romana sive Salica sive Gotha, sive qualiscumque lex, ut unusquisque homo de rebus suis propriis donare, aut cedere vel condonare voluerit,

ability was sanctioned by "all the rules of secular law."[24] Others insisted that the freedom to give away property was sanctioned by both written law and custom (*consuetudo* or *mos anticus*).[25] Scribes and judges presented the freedom to alienate property as an essential feature of a diffuse group of codes and customs and they suggested that this right was unmitigated by the presence of heirs or the choice of beneficiary. The *Visigothic Code's* endorsement of such a notion is qualified at best. The other imputed origins of this principle are even less convincing. Judges, scribes, and monastic or ecclesiastic disputants presented the gnarled fragment of a Visigothic rule as axiomatic to both *lex* and *mos*.

It is difficult to say whether this shrill insistence on the right to alienate and the fanciful attribution of this right to a host of more or less plausible authorities successfully eroded the property interests of heirs and kindred. Despite the heavy-handed rhetoric of alienability in citations, some disputants argued that the approval of kindred was required for the transfer of some property. Geribert, for example, maintained such an idea forcefully, if somewhat inarticulately, during his dispute with Sant Cugat.[26] The survival and modification of this rule from the *Code* may represent not general acceptance of the freedom to alienate so much as a prolonged struggle against deepseated traditions that emphasized the property rights of relatives. The constant affirmation that anyone could alienate any property rights at any time suggests not only that some disputants aggressively promoted this idea, but also that these disputants were trying to refute tenacious alternative understandings of how one held and transferred property—understandings which afforded more voice to the daughters, sons, brothers, sisters, nephews, and nieces of property-holders.

The conflicting claims of ecclesiastic or monastic beneficiaries of bequests and of kin groups were at the root of most disputes. It is perhaps not surprising that much of the legal reasoning, legal citation, and legal positioning in judicial assemblies centered on questions concerning the alienability of

---

habeat ad faciendum," in *Cartulaire du chapitre d'Agde*, ed. Odile Terrin (Nîmes, 1969) (hereafter *Agde*), 327. See also *HGL* 211.

24. "Omnes sanctiones secularium legum decernunt, ut si aliquis homo de rebus vel possessionibus suis alteri homini dare vel aliquo modo voluerit cedere, habeat ad faciendum," *HGL* 203.

25. *Cartulaire du chapitre de l'église Notre-Dame de Nîmes, 876–1156*, ed. E. Germer-Durand (Nîmes, 1872–1874) (hereafter *Nîmes*), 154; and *HGL* 120.

26. See *El monestir de Santa Maria de Gerri, col·lecció diplomàtica*, 2 vols., ed. Ignasi M. Puig i Ferreté (Barcelona, 1991) (hereafter *Gerri*), 1. On such approval generally, see Stephen White, *Custom, Kinship, and Gifts to Saints*.

property. Frequent tensions between the ecclesiastic beneficiaries of donations and other potential heirs sent judges and disputants searching for rules
to govern who could give what to whom. Legal experts tied to powerful
churches and monasteries shaped the rules of *Visigothic Code* into a tradition
supporting individual property-holders' freedom to sell or give away their
property. This "tradition" was hotly contested by other groups who, while
they often had less in the way of legal expertise, still had much to lose.

Most of the rules in the *Visigothic Code* were intended for general application. Visigothic legislators saw themselves as providing guidelines (and punishments) for society as a whole: "The law rules every order of the state, and
every condition of man; it governs wives and husbands; youth and age; the
learned and the ignorant; the polished and the rude. It aims to provide the
highest degree of safety for both prince and people, and, in renown and ex-
cellence, it is conspicuous as the noon-day sun."[27] Rules governing testamentary procedure, for example, were not written solely (or even primarily)
to govern transfers of property from laymen to churches. Similarly, the *Code's*
rules governing inheritance paid considerable attention to obligations to kindred.

Although scribes and judges tailored rules from the *Visigothic Code* in ways
that favored ecclesiastic and monastic litigants, some rules required less adjustment than others. One rule from the *Code's* Book V was originally intended to govern gifts to churches. Because of its specificity, it required less
tenth-century tinkering to make it especially appealing to ecclesiastic litigants:

> Concerning Donations to Churches. If we are compelled to do justice to the
> merits of those who serve us, how much greater reason is there that we should
> care for the property set apart for the redemption of our souls and the worship
> of God, and preserve it intact by the authority of the law. Wherefore, we decree
> that all property which has been given, either by kings, or by any other believ-
> ers whomsoever, to houses devoted to Divine worship shall eternally and irrev-
> ocably belong to said churches.[28]

Legal professionals could happily adopt this rule with few modifications and,
indeed, some scribes cited this rule very carefully. In a 980 will from Vic,
Isarn prefaced the appointment of his executors with a thorough citation of
the rule: "I order a document to be made to Sant Benet according to the rules

27. *Leges Visigothorum*, I.2.3; and Scott, *Visigothic Code*, 5.
28. *Leges Visigothorum*, V.1.1. I have slightly modified Scott's translation, *Visigothic
Code*, 143.

of the *Liber Iudicum*, where it says regarding donations to churches: If we are compelled to do justice . . ."[29] Most citations, however, were less precise than this one and tended to eliminate nuances in the original legislation. Much like the fear and force prohibitions, the rule governing gifts to churches was subject to modification. The rule's first sentence explains by analogy the importance of making pious donations to churches, likening such gifts to a donor's domestic obligations. Eleventh-century judges saw this prefatory material insisting on one's duties to one's *famulus* as an unnecessary and possibly confusing complication. The passage caused concern because it acknowledged, however vaguely, some collective interest in a property-holder's wealth—a feature of Visigothic law which made eleventh-century scribes and judges especially anxious. Citations of this rule thus often omitted the rule's prologue.[30]

In general, Visigothic lawmakers did not display the same concision shown by the framers of other Germanic law codes. They prefaced some rules with florid reflections on morals and society. These passages shed light on the social world of Visigothic legislators and on the excesses of seventh-century rhetoric. But tenth- and eleventh-century judges were primarily interested in these rules for practical reasons. Judges and scribes thought that such passages might very well obscure the most important parts. Deleting the clause about duties to the *famulus* made this rule less ambiguous by expunging reference to other potential claims on a property-holder, just as citations of inheritance rules often deleted passages related to the property rights of kindred. Churchmen cited this rule often in certain situations, but in other contexts they disregarded it altogether. It served as a way of suggesting to donors that their charitable impulses enjoyed an impressive legal sanction. The rule did not, however, deter clerics and monks from selling or exchanging ecclesiastic properties which, according to the rule, were supposed to remain eternally and irrevocably part of a church's patrimony.

The rules that judges and disputants ignored reveal as much as those they cited. In this case, the original context of a rule about gifts to churches is informative. Other rules from the same titleof the *Code* also aimed to protect the property of churches, but from different threats. One rule, for example,

29. Antoni Udina i Abelló, *La successió testada a la Catalunya altomedieval* (Barcelona, 1984), doc. 19. See also *Viage literario a las Iglesias de España*, 22 vols, ed. Jaime and Joaquín Lorenzo Villanueva (Madrid-Valencia, 1803–1902) (hereafter *Viage*), 15, 26.

30. *HGL* 161; ACA, Ramon Borrell, 64; *Viage*, 9, 20; *Urgellia*, 390; *Marca*, 206; *Liber Feudorum Maior: Cartulario real que se conserve en el Archivo de la Corona de Aragon*, ed. Francisco Miguel Rosell, 2 vols. (Barcelona, 1945–47) (hereafter *LFM*), 440; Domènec Sangés. "Recull de documents del segle XI referents a Guissona i la seva Plana." *Urgellia* 3 (1980) (hereafter *Guissona*), 62; *Oliba*, 131; and *Viage*, 15, 25.

noted that many churches were in disrepair because of the greed of priests. The rule specified that bishops were to set aside a portion of their revenue for the renovation of dilapidated churches.[31] Another rule from the same title attacked the arbitrary conduct of bishops at such length that it amounts to an essay on episcopal corruption. Among other complaints, the rule lamented that bishops manipulated legal reasoning to assume control of church property.[32] Visigothic lawmakers cautioned that greedy bishops legitimated their claims by taking advantage of legal loopholes. Seventh-century legislators were acutely aware that ecclesiastical property was particularly vulnerable to exploitation by the very people entrusted with its stewardship. Lawmakers attacked the subtle manipulation by which churchmen acquired for themselves land, houses, and vineyards that rightly belonged to their churches.

Visigothic legislators were clearly concerned about clerical manipulation of the law and exploitation of church property. The anxieties of these seventh-century legislators, however, left no trace in tenth- and eleventh-century legal practice. None of the rules deploring clerical avarice and corruption appeared in later records. Many of the region's bishops during this period were conscientious administrators and watchful shepherds, but there is little reason to think that the bishops of the year 1000 were significantly less worldly than their seventh-century predecessors. Scribes and judges never cited the rules in this section because, rather than encouraging lay donors to give and insisting that their gifts were irrevocable, these rules attacked clerical corruption and constrained clerical behavior. They suggested not that it was a pious duty to give to churches, but rather that such gifts were likely to be exploited for personal gain. Clerics were understandably skittish about invoking rules that railed against clerical manipulation of the law.

A rule from Book V of the *Code* further illustrates the modification of law in practice. The rule describes a number of ways by which a transaction might become valid and irrevocable and outlines measures for responding to challenged transactions. The rule is long but worth quoting at length if only to show the number of provisions it contains and to note the extent to which these were excluded from later citations:

Concerning Property Donated Verbally, or Conveyed by Instruments in Writing. Any property given away in the presence of witnesses can under no circumstances be reclaimed by the donor. And even if it should happen that what is given is situated elsewhere, the donation cannot, for that reason, be revoked, provided it is made in writing; because it is evident that the gift is absolute, when

31. *Leges Visigothorum*, V.1.5.
32. *Leges Visigothorum*, V.1.6; Scott, *Visigothic Code*, 148; and P. D. King, *Law and Society in the Visigothic Kingdom* (Cambridge, 1972), 154.

the instrument conveying it is in the name of, and for the benefit of him who receives it. It, however, must be noted, that if the donor should say that he neither delivered such an instrument nor directed it to be delivered, but that it was taken from him; then the party to whom the property was given may prove by witnesses that it was transferred to him, or directed to be so transferred by the donor, or placed under his control by the will of the testator; and when he shall have produced such testimony, the gift shall be deemed valid. Where he neglects to introduce competent testimony, he who executed the instrument shall make oath that he neither delivered it, nor directed it to be delivered, nor that he voluntarily executed it; and the instrument shall then be returned to him by whom it was claimed, and shall remain invalid, if the latter so desires. But it is proper to add, that if anyone should execute an instrument disposing of any property for the benefit of anyonewhomsoever, and, in his lifetime, should not deliver it to him for whose benefit it was made, and it should be found after the death of the former; he for whose benefit the donor has made disposition of said property, shall have the right to claim it, along with all the property therein described. . . .[33]

The quoted passage constitutes roughly half the rule, which goes on to add further conditions and qualifications. In tenth- and eleventh-century citations, this rule suffered more brutal editing than most. Although the rule presents a complex set of procedures and contingencies, even the most detailed citations of it in tenth- and eleventh-century records contained only its first sentence.[34] The fragment of this rule was often combined with other rules. The 977 record of the foundation of the monastery of Serrateix cites two passages from the *Code*: a rule concerning royal donations and a short section of the rule concerning the irrevocability of gifts.[35]

Like many other rules from the *Code*, this one dealing with the irrevocability of certain transactions was adapted to serve better monastic and ecclesiastic interests. The original legislation stipulated nothing about the identities of the parties involved. For the framers of the *Code*, the rule was applicable to anyone conveying property rights. When scribes cited the first sentence of the rule, they narrowed the rule's focus and claimed that it referred particularly to pious donations, as in this example from Urgell, where the rule was particularly popular: "Concerning gifts to the church of God or conveyed in writing, for any property given away in the presence of witnesses can in no way be reclaimed by the donor."[36] The scribe conflated two rules,

33. *Leges Visigothorum*, V.2.6; and Scott, *Visigothic Code*, 154–55.
34. See, for example, Udina i Abelló, *La successió testada*, doc. 7.
35. *Marca*, 122, citing *Leges Visigothorum*, V.2.2. and V.2.6. See also *El monestir de Santa Maria de Gerri, colleció diplomàtica*, ed. Ignasi M. Puig i Ferreté, 2 vols. (Barcelona, 1991) (hereafter *Gerri*), 7, citing *Leges Visigothorum*, V.2.6. and V.4.1.
36. *Urgellia* 689, citing *Leges Visigothorum*, V.2.6 and V.1.1.

one dealing with the permanence of transactions and the other dealing with donations to churches.

Tenth- and eleventh-century judges and disputants made focused use of the *Visigothic Code*. The alienability of property and the irrevocability of gifts were the two dominant themes that scribes and judges borrowed from Visigothic law. To the question of when a property-holder was free to alienate his or her property, scribes and judges replied that a person could alienate any property at any time. They stressed alienability by citing selected fragments of Visigothic legislation—fragments which, removed from their original context, minimized the property rights of kindred. Gifts were always irrevocable, but they were especially irrevocable when made to churches.

COUNTERARGUMENTS: LONG-TERM POSSESSION

Rules culled from the *Visigothic Code* and shorn of embarrassing contingencies became impressive components in the legal arsenals of property-holding institutions. The arguments about property made by churchmen were impressive, but they were not the only arguments available to disputants. Most of the interpretations and applications of written law described above served particular interests, namely, monastic and ecclesiastic recipients of gifts of property. Most appeals to written law thus favored ecclesiastic and monastic litigants. There is one notable exception to this general rule: lay property-holders appealed to Carolingian rules regarding a particular form of property tenure (*aprisio*) which supported claims of long-term occupants of land.

When churches and monasteries claimed disputed properties, they based their arguments on several related ideas: the freedom of property-holders to alienate property, the irrevocability of gifts to churches, the binding nature of written agreements, and the obligation to make pious donations. But the constant repetition of a smattering of rules from the *Visigothic Code* coupled with the fact that such property was, in fact, often disputed, suggests that not everyone accepted the oft-rehearsed clerical position. Monastic and ecclesiastic claims about the special nature of ecclesiastical property were, to some degree, wishful thinking on the part of churchmen rather than an indication of the way that most people understood fields, vineyards, and mills. Monks and clergy tried to erect a protective legal fence around gifts to churches, but they were not entirely successful.

Lay challengers rarely rejected these claims outright, but they appealed to a different set of principles to support their own claims. Lay challengers usually explained the foundation of their claims less fully than did the representatives of institutional litigants, but the normative principles to which they appealed nevertheless emerged with clarity and consistency. Challengers rarely invoked written rules or law codes, but they did appeal to a coherent set of ideas about property. Three related ideas constituted the core of most challenged gifts and sales. The first idea was that property that formed part of a family's *hereditas* could not be alienated. Members of a kin group instead insisted on their right to question or nullify alienations made unilaterally by other members of the kindred. The second distinct, but related, idea consisted of the notion that inheritance was, in some sense, automatic; testaments, executors, formal publications, and other elements of formal testamentary procedure were not necessarily wrong, but were unnecessary.[37] Challengers maintained that even documents created with scrupulous attention to legal propriety did not vitiate the rights of kindred. Finally, those who challenged bequests often claimed that having developed, cultivated, and occupied property generated rights to the continued undisturbed possession of that property. These ideas about property were clearly not compatible with those promoted by churches and monasteries, and conflict between these two incompatible sets of ideas was at the core of most disputes.

A few examples can provide a sense of how this clash of incompatible ideas manifested itself. The cathedral chapter of Béziers claimed a church held by Odo and his brothers. The chapter presented the testament of Odo's uncle, which recorded the uncle's gift of the property to the chapter. When asked by the judge to present proofs to refute the chapter's claim, Odo and his brothers responded: "We do not have any document, but both our grandfather and our father held this church as an alod."[38] Odo's laconic appeal to the rights of his ancestors failed to persuade the court, but his appeal was a legal argument rather than an admission of failure. Brief though it may have been, Odo presented a coherent claim to the disputed church. The case is typical in that the two disputing parties talked past each other. While Odo dismissed the judge's query about written proofs with some impatience, the canons, on the other hand, not only presented a charter but also described their proof

37. See Stephen White's discussion of inheritance practice in Western France, "Inheritances and Legal Arguments," 95, and his discussion of "implicit normative frameworks," "The 'Feudal Revolution,'" *Past and Present* 152 (1996): 214.

38. *Cartulaire de Béziers (Livre Noir)*, ed. J. B. Roquette (Paris and Montpellier, 1918–1922) (hereafter *Béziers*), 66; See also BNF coll. Doat 55, ff. 102–4; and *El Cartoral dit de Carlemany, del bisbe de Girona*, ed. Josep María Marquès, vol. 1 (Barcelona, 1993) (hereafter *Girona*), 100.

in a way that celebrated its written-ness.[39] Odo and his brothers only saw part of their *hereditas* which should rightly come to them, regardless of the documents so enthusiastically brandished by their opponents. A similar conflict between inheritance and written proofs was at play in 995, when judges questioned a group of lay people who were locked in a dispute with a local monastery:

> The judges asked them: "By what right do you retain this [property]?" They responded, "Our parents held it, and after their deaths, they appointed it to us . . ." Abbot Atto in his response said: "We have documents which are earlier and better, from the time of Emperor Louis, and from the time of Count Ramon, and the time of Count Isarn, and the time of Count Lupo. And [the property] should more rightly belong to the church of Saint Genesius through these documents than to those people through their ancestors.[40]

At the root of many disputes was a contest between written proofs and pious donations, on the one hand, and the interest of a group of lay people in property rights they understood as part of a collective inheritance, on the other.

Lay challengers often based their claims on the idea that unchallenged possession and cultivation of property generated rights. During the 990s in Barcelona, several lay people defended their right to a *villa* by saying that they had possessed it for more than thirty years without interruption or challenge.[41] Implicit in their response was the conviction that undisturbed possession for thirty years gave a property-holder the right to continued possession. A judge in another case dismissed one disputant's claims by remarking that he could support them neither by any legal proof nor by showing thirty years possession.[42] Some disputants claimed even longer possession. In Girona, three men defended their land from what they saw as the bishop's encroachment, claiming that, "between them and their kin they had held these [churches] by hereditary right (*iure hereditario*) for a hundred years and more without the assent of any bishop of the see of Girona."[43] Claims based on long-term possession appealed to a more formal foundation that did references to one's mother or grandfather, but the ideas were sympathetic.

Some disputants who based their claims on long-term possession were

---

39. They described the drafting of their charter as "tenuit cornua cum tincta." See *Béziers* 66.

40. *Cat. Car.*, 297; and *Urgellia* 560.

41. ACA Borrell II, 14.

42. ACA Berenguer Ramon I, 13. For another case involving a claim of thirty-year's possession, see Archives Départementales des Pyrénées-Orientales (Perpignan) (hereafter APO) Fonds Fossa, 12J24, no. 11; and *Urgellia* 252.

43. *Viage* 13, 23.

able to add a learned legal foundation to these claims by referring to Carolingian legislation regarding *aprisiones*. Charlemagne and his immediate successors had contrived *aprisio* grants as a way to integrate refugees from Muslim al-Andalus into the region's economy and, at the same time, to curb the power of local counts. Refugees, or *hispani*, were granted parcels of undeveloped land which they were expected to cultivate. Land brought into cultivation became the alodial property of the cultivators after thirty years. Carolingian rulers made such grants from the late eighth through the middle of the tenth century, with the greatest activity between 875 and 925.[44]

The popular embrace of the ideas behind *aprisio* grants proved more durable than the practice of Frankish kings issuing such grants. The Carolingian interest in attracting settlers and bringing land into cultivation waned as the Spanish March became more stable, immigration from al-Andalus slowed, and the activity of Frankish kings in the region diminished. Although the number of *aprisio* grants declined rapidly after 925, property-holders did not forget the nature of these grants. In the early eleventh century, when faced with churches holding impressive charters and privileges, lay tenants insisted that their long-term occupation and cultivation of properties gave them rights that could not be diminished by such documents, and they supported their claims by referring to Carolingian legislation. When lay challengers insisted that they had rights to property because they had cleared and occupied it, they were basing their claim on a rock solid (if somewhat anachronistic) legal foundation.[45]

When lay disputants appealed to the idea of *aprisio*, they presented their opponents and judges with an especially tricky problem. By claiming rights to property in this manner, lay disputants relied on a foundation in royal legislation for claims which were very much in keeping with the popular notion that a *hereditas* could not be alienated. They could claim that long-term possession established incontrovertible rights *and* could bolster their claims with reference to Carolingian legislation. Although *aprisiones* had their origin in royal policy, the ideas behind *aprisiones* were compatible with the arguments of less sophisticated lay disputants, like Odo, who, when called upon to sup-

44. Cullen Chandler, "Between court and counts: Carolingian Catalonia and the *aprisio* grant, 778–897," *Early Medieval Europe* 11 (2002): 19–44; and André Dupont, "L'Aprision et la régime aprisionaire," *Le Moyen Age* 71 (1965): 179–213, 375–99. See also Josep M. Salrach, *El procés de feudalització, segles III–XIII* (Barcelona, 1987), 206–7; Roger Collins, "Charles the Bald and Wifred the Hairy," in *Charles the Bald, Court and Kingdom*, ed. J. Nelson and M. T. Gibson (Oxford, 1981), 185–88.

45. Aymat Catafau, "Une famille Roussillonnaise du Xeme siècle," *Etudes Roussillonnaises* 12 (1993): 97. See also Susan Reynolds, *Fiefs and Vassals: The Medieval Evidence Reinterpreted* (Oxford, 1994), 107.

port his claim, could only mutter that the disputed property had belonged to his grandfather. To be sure, Odo's claim had a certain dignity to it, but courts found such arguments harder to dismiss when supported by the idea of an *aprisio*. With *aprisiones*, lay challengers had access to venerable royal privileges that were sympathetic to popular ideas about property and how it might be held, given, or alienated. What started as a program of grants designed to integrate immigrants and to bring new land into cultivation became a strategy for protecting property rights.

Bequests and donations became the objects of controversy less because of confused titles, ambiguous testaments, or endemic violence than because there were two conflicting conceptions of how property could and should be transferred. Although sons and daughters saw the *hereditas* as inalienable, churches claimed that transfers of property could be legitimated by properly executed testaments. Nieces and nephews saw kin as having unquestionable (although not always clearly defined) property rights; churches, on the other hand, claimed that individual property-holders had the right to alienate property as they saw fit. A judge in Urgell formulated with great economy the dominant clerical position that kinship ties did not establish legal property rights: "For it is true that not every woman is a man's wife, nor is every son a father's heir."[46] For this judge and others steeped in Visigothic jurisprudence (or, at least, the eleventh-century's particular version of Visigothic jurisprudence), one's legal identity as a property-holder was distinct from one's identity as a spouse, son, or nephew. Although his fellow-judges would have understood this argument, this concise formulation would have seemed strange or even outrageous to lay property-holders who offered as their entire legal argument a definition of their relation to a deceased putative donor.[47]

46. "Verum est enim, quia non omnis mulier uxor est viri nec omnis filius heres est patris," *Urgellia* 438.

47. Although alienability and irrevocability were the two themes that dominated the tenth- and eleventh-century use of the Visigothic legal heritage, there were other areas in which judges and property-holders relied on the *Code*. Visigothic law affected understandings of proof (see chapter 6, below), the role of judges (see chapter 3, below), testamentary procedure, and dowries. For testaments, see *Sant Cugat* 267; *Urgellia* 435, 490, 500 bis; *Diplomatari de Banyoles*, ed. LluísG. Constans i Serrats, vol. 1 (Banyoles, 1985) (hereafter *Banyoles*), 50; ACA Berenguer Ramon I, 88; ACA Ramon Berenguer I, 39; ACA Monacals Sant Llorenç del Munt 97; ACA Monacals Santa Cecília de Montserrat 58; Jean Bastier, "Le testament en Catalogne du IXe au XIIe siècle: une survivance wisigothique," *Revue historique de droit français et étranger* (hereafter *RHDFE)* 51 (1973): 380–81; Antoni Udina i Abelló, *La successió testada a Catalunya altomedieval: Textos i documentos* (Barcelona, 1984); and Nathaniel Lane Taylor, "The Will and Society in Medieval Catalonia and Languedoc, 800–1200." Ph.D. diss., Harvard University, Cambridge, Mass., 1995. For dowry rules, see ACA Ramon Berenguer I, 217; ACA Ramon Berenguer I, 34.

I have traced several of the ways in which Visigothic rules contributed to the legal vocabulary of tenth- and eleventh-century disputants. These examples show how large a role the *Visigothic Code* played in conditioning the ways people thought about and fought over property. But despite its apparent prestige, the *Visigothic Code* did not enjoy unique authority. One of the region's foremost legal thinkers, Judge Bonhom of Barcelona, acknowledged the primacy of Visigothic law but suggested that judges should also be familiar with Roman and Salic law as well.[48] In other words, the *Visigothic Code* was the most important source of legal ideas, but it was not the only source.

The idea that property-holders were always at liberty to alienate their property was supported in other bodies of law in addition to Visigothic legislation. One scribe cited a rule from the *Theodosian Code* which affirmed the similar validity of all gifts and sales made without fraud or violence.[49] During a 1024 dispute in Urgell, legal professionals referred both to Visigothic law and to a Frankish capitulary.[50] In 1042, Count Ramon of Pallars admitted that he had damaged the monastery of Lavaix. Eager to make amends, the count abandoned his claims to the monastery and renounced the right to administer justice in the monastery's territory, whether according to Frankish or Visigothic law.[51] References like these testify to the flexibility of legal authority.

Passages asserting the right to alienate property without hindrance or limitation invited this sort of multiple invocation.[52] The principle of freedom to alienate was presented as just and authoritative because of the general approval of several bodies of law. Scribes and judges sometimes stressed the special authority of the Visigothic law, but in other cases they appealed more

48. EscorialZ.ii.2, f. 35r. On Bonhom's career, see chapter 3.

49. *HGL* 189.

50. *Urgellia* 390.

51. *El Cartoral de Santa Maria de Lavaix: El Monestir durant els segles XI–XIII*, ed. Ignasi Puig i Ferreté (La Seu d'Urgell, 1984) (hereafter *Lavaix*), 24. For references to Salic law see *HGL* 138; and *Agde* 327.

52. "Multum declarat sive docet lex Romana vel Salica, ut unusquisque homo de res suas proprias habeat ad faciendum quod voluerit," *HGL* 173, citing *Leges Visigothorum*, IV.2.20; "Multum declarat auctoritas & lex Romanorum, & Gotorum, sive Salicorum, ut unusquisque homo de propriis rebus suis dare aut cedere aud condonare voluerit, licenciam habeat ad faciendum," *HGL* 211; and "Multum declarat auctoritas vel lex romana vel salica ut uniusquisque homo de res suas proprias ad faciendum quecumque voluerit . . ." in *Cartulaire de l'abbaye de Lézat*, ed. Paul Ourliac and Anne-Marie Magnou, 2 vols. (Paris, 1984–87) (hereafter *Lézat*), 335.

generally to the consensus of all written law. Since judges usually asserted that various legal codes were in agreement (at least with regard to the important questions), they felt little need to assess the relative merits of different *leges*. Litigants, judges, and scribes drew on Roman, Salic, and Visigothic law and often combined these if they had sufficiently mastered the repertory of legal fragments supporting the alienability of property.

The *Visigothic Code's* legislation regarding the alienation of property was, as I have already shown, considerably more complicated than tenth- and eleventh-century scribes suggested. The appearance of Salic law in this list of supporting authorities is even more surprising. Salic law contained no rules that remotely endorsed the idea advanced by such citations. In fact, the *Law of the Salian Franks* contains only two passages dealing with the transfer of property.[53] Although far less detailed than Visigothic legislation, Salic law is more restrictive in terms of the right to alienate property and never suggests that property-holders enjoyed the absolute liberty to sell, give, or exchange property rights without consideration for possible heirs. When disputants argued that Visigothic law supported the freedom to alienate, they were interpreting the law tendentiously; when they argued that Salic law supported the freedom to alienate, they moved past creative interpretation into the realm of pure fabrication.

Scribes, disputants, and judges also drew on canon law, most often the canons of Toledan Councils.[54] Many judges did not distinguish neatly between secular and canon law, conflating Toledan canons and rules from the *Code*. When judges cited more than one rule, they did so in order to show that a number of authorities concurred. In a 1054 transaction, judges cited six different rules from the *Code* and invoked the Toledan canons. Despite this heap of legal erudition, the transaction did not closely conform to *any* of the rules mentioned.[55] The execution of a will the same year in Urgell reveals similar attitudes toward written legal authorities. The procedure carefully followed Visigothic rules for the appointment of executors, but the record itself did not indicate that any particular rules were being applied. In a sanction clause, rather than invoking the *Visigothic Code*, which had at least indirectly provided the framework for this transaction, the scribe referred unconvincingly to the Council of Nicaea.[56] Visigothic rules, whether drawn

53. *The Laws of the Salian Franks*, tr. Katherine Fischer Drew (Philadelphia, 1991), numbers 46 and 59. See Paul Fouracre's discussion of earlier references to Salic law, "Carolingian Justice: The Rhetoric of Improvement and the Contexts of Abuse," in *La giustizia nell'alto medioevo (secoli V-VIII)* (Spoleto, 1995), 795.

54. See, for example, *Viage* 12, 8.

55. *Marca* 240. See also ACA Ramon Berenguer I, 71.

56. *Urgellia* 665.

from the *Code* or the canons of Toledan councils, enjoyed particular prestige, but they were far from the only source of legitimate legal authority. Legal professionals assumed that other authorities—Salic law, Frankish formularies, the *Theodosian Code*, the canons of church councils, and the Bible would not contradict each other in all important matters. One scribe expressed this search for consensus by asserting the conformity of Christian religious and Roman legal traditions: "Christian religion teaches and Roman authority affirms . . ."[57]

The inhabitants of the Province of Narbonne turned frequently to written law to govern their property relations. They relied on *lex* for guidance regarding testamentary procedure, inheritance, judging, proof, and property rights. Although disputants and judges embraced a range of written authorities, they did not do so indiscriminately. They used what they found useful in law codes and ignored the rest.

Professional judges were often judicious and thoughtful but, as the *Visigothic Code* cautioned, some legal professionals used the written law chiefly for their own benefit.[58] In certain cases, judges consulted the *Visigothic Code* because they needed guidance in resolving thorny legal questions. Just as often, however, citations of written law were less the result of considered reflection and careful study than of simple repetition. Certain rules drawn from canon law, the *Visigothic Code*, or scripture provided formulaic endorsements of certain ideas about property—ideas that some disputants were eager to promote. There were notable exceptions, but in general, the selective adoption and citation of written law favored a certain class of disputants: monastic and ecclesiastic institutions. In many cases, the Visigothic lawmakers of seventh-century Toledo would not have recognized their own work in the hands of the legal professionals of the year 1000. None of the dynamic reshaping of legal traditions occurred in the name of innovation. Judges and property-holders emphasized their deep respect for ancient legal traditions and tried to heed the prophet Jeremiah's injunction to "walk in the old paths." Judges and disputants may have altered the law in practice, but they did not set out to do so.

The many citations of written law are not the footprints of a coherent and enduring system of jurisprudence, but rather traces of a creative engagement with the legal past. Citations of *leges* do not suggest the survival of a legal system. Instead, one can trace the varied paths of particular ideas, precepts,

---

57. "Christiana religio edocet et auctoritas romana adfirmat ut quisque homo de res suas proprias ad ecclesiam Dei pro peccatis et neglegenciis que contrariis sibi videtur haberi in helemosina pro remedium anime sue domino Deo debet dari . . . ," *Lézat* 116.
58. *Leges Visigothorum*, I.1.9.

rules, and rule fragments.[59] Sometimes, citations of written law were merely signs of one disputant's attempt to secure property rights, to win a dispute, or to legitimate a claim. Invoking a rule is, after all, not quite the same thing as adhering to it. Gestures to written law were inspired both by respect for traditional legal authorities and by the self-interested desire to win disputes.

Citing a rule was one discrete move in the process of disputing, and that process had many features which fall outside any narrow understanding of law. Judges and disputants had complex understandings of legal authority which embraced not only rules about property drawn from the *Visigothic Code* but also the ritual sanctions and curses that are the subject of the next chapter.

59. Manuel C. Díaz y Díaz, "La Lex Visigothorum y sus manuscritos: Un ensayo de reinterpretación," *AHDE* 46 (1976): 163–224.

CHAPTER TWO
DO NEO-ROMANS CURSE?
LAND, LAW, AND RITUAL

In the hands of many property-holders, rules selected from the *Visigothic Code* proved useful instruments. The *Code* was widely accepted as the preeminent source of written law, but this venerable legal tradition was malleable. Judges and scribes tailored the law to their own needs. The written law—*lex*—was extraordinarily important in shaping the ways people fought over property in the Province of Narbonne, but it was not the only source of authority to which disputants appealed. Ritual was another important feature of the legal landscape. Like written law, ritual played a central role in structuring claims and counterclaims about mills, vineyards, and fields. When they bought, gave, and fought over property, property-holders often made solemn, liturgical appeals to the supernatural and the divine. The process of fighting over a field often involved the interplay of law and ritual, as religious communities used ritual sanctions (such as curses and excommunication) alongside recycled fragments of Roman and Visigothic legislation.

The role of ritual in property relations in this region has been underestimated. Francia of the year 1000 was not a coherent whole but rather a heterogeneous agglomeration of regions, each with a distinct identity. The Christian principalities of northern Spain were similarly diverse. Historians have outlined a number of characteristics that distinguished regions surrounding the Mediterranean (including the Province of Narbonne) from regions north of the Loire. There were important differences between Provence and Gascony, or between Catalonia and the Auvergne, but some scholars have described qualities that were shared by different parts of the south: the endurance of public authority (Carolingian notions of public authority disintegrated more slowly in the south than in the north), the predominance of alodial landholding (often linked to the vitality of a free peasantry), and a tenacious attachment to written law.[1]

Scholars often attribute the distinctive features of societies on the shores of the western Mediterranean to the longevity of Roman cultural ideals. The public courts, legal professionals, and the citations of written law all attest to the survival of a Roman cultural foundation which outlasted the decline of Roman political power and which continued to shape social relations well into the Middle Ages. Jean-Pierre Poly, for example, sees many elements of the social structure of Provence as indices of the region's *romanité*. This quality manifests itself most vividly in public courts where learned judges consulted Roman law.[2] Elisabeth Magnou-Nortier similarly points to the Roman origins of a wide range of phenomena in the Province of Narbonne. Judicial assemblies and references to Euric's Code are proofs of the vitality of Roman traditions. For Magnou-Nortier, even the Peace of God councils were indebted to a traditional legal vocabulary.[3] Christian Lauranson-Rosaz describes the importance of Roman ideas in the Auvergne. Citing the use of the *Theodosian Code* in a 1022 testament, he notes the survival of Roman law between the fifth and twelfth centuries.[4] Elsewhere, he describes the *romanité* of southern France consisting of values, practices, and attitudes inherited

1. Pierre Bonnassie identifies the vitality of urban societies, the strength of peasant liberties, the permanence of written law, and an enduring system of public justice as the most important distinguishing features of the south. See his "From the Rhône to Galicia: Origins and Modalities of the Feudal Order," in *From Slavery to Serfdom in Southwestern Europe* (Cambridge, 1991), 104–31.

2. Jean-Pierre Poly, *La Provence et la société féodale, 879–1166. Contribution à l'étude des structures dites féodales dans le Midi* (Paris, 1976), 45, 360. Jean-Pierre Poly, Martin Aurell, and Dominique Iogna-Prat emphasize the continuity of Roman ideas in Provence. See their "La Provence," in *Les sociétés méridionales*, ed. Zimmerman, 331; The survival of a public order is key to Bonnassie's argument. In the introduction to the current work and in chapter 9 below, I argue that the distinction between public and private is not a viable one in this period.

3. Magnou-Nortier, *Société laïque*, 111, 145, 203, 270; idem., "The Enemies of the Peace: Reflections on a Vocabulary, 500–1100," in *The Peace of God: Social Violence and Religious Response around the Year 1000*, ed. Thomas Head and Richard Landes (Ithaca, N.Y., 1992), 58–79; idem. "Recherches sur la fiscalité foncière durant le Haut Moyen Age: Premiers résultats," in *Historia económica y de las instituciones financieras en Europa: Trabajos en homenaje de Ferran Valls i Taberner*, ed. Manuel J. Peláez (Barcelona, 1989); and idem "La terre, la rente et le pouvoir dans les pays de Languedoc pendant le Haut Moyen Age," *Francia* 9 (1981): 79–115, 10 (1982), 21–66.

4. Christian Lauranson-Rosaz, "L'Auvergne," in *Les sociétés méridionales*, ed. Zimmerman, 24.

from antiquity. The endurance of these Roman values manifests itself most clearly, if not exclusively, in law.[5]

Arguments about the *romanité* of the south thus follow certain patterns.[6] They insist on the endurance of a Roman cultural foundation during the central Middle Ages and claim that this foundation is apparent in fragmentary citations of Roman vulgar law. What distinguishes north from south is the endurance of Roman legal categories: written law, proofs, testimony, the maintenance of clear divisions between public and private law. Basing their claims on sources from different parts of the south, historians have returned to the problem of the relationship between antiquity and the Middle Ages. Together, their work reflects a consensus that some type of Roman cultural presence was an important feature of meridional cultures during the tenth and eleventh centuries.

This insistence on the importance of *romanité* has generated some corollary beliefs which merit greater scrutiny. Among these is the more or less explicit dismissal of the role of ritual in the social, legal, and political worlds of lands skirting the Mediterranean. The legacy of *romanité* and written law is seen as antithetical to the influence of ritual. Attachment to written law and Roman traditions are seen as making the Mediterranean world impervious to the vulgar reliance on ritual that characterized northern Francia and other parts of Europe. If mentioned at all, ritual is seen merely as symptomatic of minor glitches in the otherwise well-oiled machinery of the very late Roman empire. Pierre Bonnassie, for example, laments the use of ritual sanctions, such as excommunication, as sorry substitutes for real and effective government. When such sanctions were deployed, they were perhaps the means to manipulate public opinion, but, Bonnassie claims, such measures were known to be ineffective.[7] The Romano-Visigothic tradition that was the foundation of public order in Catalonia left no room for curses. Elisabeth Magnou-Nortier dismisses the importance of ritual even more unequivocally. She insists that sanctions like excommunication were merely symbolic and that the ritual sanctions imposed by Peace Councils could have had lit-

5. Christian Lauranson-Rosaz, "La Romanité du Midi de l'an mil. Le point sur les sociétés méridionales," in *La France de l'an Mil*, ed. Robert Delort (Paris, 1990), 49–50.

6. For other discussions of *romanité*, see Michel Rouche, "Les survivances antiques dans trois cartulaires du sud-ouest de la France aux Xe et XIe siècles," *Cahiers de Civilisation médiévale* (hereafter *CCM*) 23 (1980), 93, 103; Marie-Louise Carlin, *La pénétration du droit romain dans les actes de la pratique provençale, Xie–XIIIe siecle* (Paris, 1967); Paul Ourliac, "Notes sur les actes français et catalans du Xe siècle," in *Les pays de Garonne vers l'an mil: La société et le droit: recueil d'études* (Toulouse, 1993); Bernard Bachrach, *Fulk Nerra, the Neo-Roman Consul, 987–1040: A Political Biography of the Angevin Count* (Berkeley, 1987).

7. Bonnassie, *Catalogne*, 652–53.

tle effect on public order. Magnou-Nortier grudgingly admits that relic cults may have had some claim on the impressionable *mentalité populaire*, but the romanized class of bishops, judges, and counts certainly would have been immune to their appeal.[8]

Magnou-Nortier's assessment of the antipathy of public authority and ritual is an extreme version of an idea that appears in many arguments about the *romanité* of the south. The appearance of ritual as a means of protecting property, coercing opponents, finding right, or assuring the longevity of an agreement is understood only as an index of how far courts had fallen from their pristine Roman clarity. Most scholars concur: in the choice between law and ritual, the south came down firmly on the side of law. This opposition of law and ritual is, however, a particularly deceptive anachronism. The legal practices of the south were indeed different from those of the north, and much of that difference lay in the frequent appeals to written law discussed above. The appearance of courts with sophisticated procedural norms, populated by legal professionals citing rules from the *Visigothic Code*, is striking. However, none of this enduring *romanité* precluded the use of rituals, which played a vital role in regulating social interaction even in the midst of romanizing legal procedures. Reliance on ritual does not necessarily indicate the collapse of authority, the absence of law, or the failure of government.[9] By the same token, Roman traditions, with their written rules and admirable clarity, did not drive out curses and sentences of excommunication but existed alongside them comfortably.

These relations between ritual and law and between ritual and *romanité* are particularly compelling problems, given recent scholarship emphasizing the fundamental role that ritual played in shaping ties within medieval communities. Barbara Rosenwein describes Cluniac liturgy as a form of ritualized aggression through which Cluniac monks protected their property. Patrick Geary has shown how monasteries coerced uncooperative neighbors through relic humiliations. Stephen White has pointed out the ritual impli-

8. Magnou-Nortier, *Société laïque*, 309. Others have argued persuasively that relic cults were integral features of the peace movements. The studies in Thomas F. Head and Richard Landes, eds., *The Peace of God* offer the best examination of these questions. See also Dominique Barthélemy, *L'an mil et la paix de Dieu: La France chrétienne et féodale, 980–1060* (Paris, 1999).

9. Michel Zimmerman has shown that in Catalonia the use of curses was most common between 950 and 1030. See his "Le vocabulaire latin de malédiction du IXe au XIIe siècle: Construction d'un discours eschatologique," *Atalaya, Revue Française d'Etudes Médiévales Hispaniques* 5 (1994): 40. The widespread proliferation of these clauses thus predates by as much as eighty years the period that Bonnassie identifies (1030–1060) as the violent collapse of public authority. Bonnassie, "The Formation of Catalan Feudalism and Its Early Expansion (to c. 1150)," in *From Slavery to Serfdom*, 156, and *Catalogne*, 539–646.

cations of gifts to churches and monasteries. Lester Little had drawn attention to the centrality of liturgical cursing as a strategy for defending monastic and ecclesiastic property.[10] Just as the regional studies mentioned above leave little doubt that Rome remained, in some way, important in the south, these scholars leave little doubt that one of the ways in which the people of tenth- and eleventh-century Europe negotiated their relations was through rituals.

These studies describing the importance of ritual rely primarily on liturgical sources, but the concerns of liturgy are not always far removed from the concerns of the cartulary. Lester Little suggests that the *si quis* clauses of charters were similar to liturgical clamors in which religious communities sought God's intervention:

> Many of the curses clamors abound with also appear in the sanction clauses of contemporary charters. This is no casual coincidence, for sanction clauses and clamors were integral parts of a single system for maintaining social order. . . . No alleged malefactor who became the object of ecclesiastical curses should have been surprised; there was ample warning. Virtually every ecclesiastical, especially monastic, possession and privilege was attested by a written instrument—a charter—and virtually every charter contained a sanction clause warning of dire consequences for anyone who contravened its terms.[11]

In what follows, I explore the role of ritual in the Province of Narbonne and the south more generally by examining types of ritual activity: curse clauses and excommunications. The survey of scholarship above provides a vantage point from which to examine whether the *romanité* of the south, and its concomitant devotion to written law, diminished the role of ritual in political, social, and economic relations. In other words, were curse clauses, relic elevations, and excommunications mere anomalies, or were they a vital part of the normative world of the Province of Narbonne in the tenth and eleventh centuries?

---

10. Barbara Rosenwein, "Feudal War and Monastic Peace: Cluniac Liturgy as Ritual Aggression," *Viator* 2 (1971): 129–57; Patrick Geary, "Humiliation of Saints," in *Saints and Their Cults: Studies in Religious Sociology, Folklore, and History*, ed. Stephen Wilson (Cambridge, 1983), 123–40; and Lester Little, *Benedictine Maledictions: Liturgical Cursing in Romanesque France* (Ithaca, N.Y., 1993). See also Jacques LeGoff, "The Symbolic Ritual of Vassalage," in *Time, Work and Culture in the Middle Ages*, trans. Arthur Goldhammer (Chicago, 1980), 237–87; Geoffrey Koziol, *Begging Pardon and Favor: Ritual and Political Order in Early Medieval France* (Ithaca, N.Y., 1991); and White, *Custom, Kinship, and Gifts to Saints.*

11. Little, *Benedictine Maledictions*, 52.

Records of sales, gifts, and judicial assemblies are more or less formulaic, and students of diplomatic long ago anatomized their constituent elements. Near the end of most charters, there is a clause (usually beginning with the words *si quis*) that establishes the penalties incumbent on anyone who contravenes the terms of the recorded agreement.[12] *Si quis* clauses were intended to ensure the permanence of gifts and to deter would-be violators of monastic and ecclesiastic property.[13]

Si quis clauses varied in content, but a few examples can provide a sense of their usual form. On 31 October 945, the bishop of Elne made a donation to his own church, Saint Eulalia:

> I am a donor of my alod to the church of Saint Eulalia in the see of Elne, mother of all the churches in Roussillon and in the Conflent. . . . If any worldly power, whether lay or clergy, of either sex, should try to take away any part of this [alod] from the church, first he shall incur the wrath of the almighty God, and he shall be apart from the consort of all Christians and beyond the limits of the Holy Church of God, and he should be separated from the kingdom of God. He shall feel himself receiving the judgment of Dathan and Abiron, and he shall be burned up in eternal flames with the traitor Judas. As the law of the Goths determines, he shall have to make double compensation of all of the above.[14]

The bishop's curse on violators of his gift includes a number of elements that were common in *si quis* clauses: the wrath of God; ritual affiliation of the violator with Judas, Dathan, and Abiron; rejection from Christian society and ritual, and the promise of suffering. After explaining the otherworldly torments that would befall a violator, the penal clause notes that violators would also be subject to the penalty specified in the *Visigothic Code* for unlawful appropriation of property—precisely the sort of citation used by historians as evidence of the Midi's enduring *romanité*.

A few years later, the count and countess of Carcassonne and their sons prefaced a gift by invoking rules from several law codes:

> We are firmly instructed by the writings of men, that anyone who wants . . . to sell or give away his/her own property shall have the complete freedom to do

12. See "L'examen de l'acte," in *Diplomatique médiévale*, L'atelier du médiéviste, no. 2, ed. Olivier Guyotjeannin, Jacques Pycke, and Benoît-Michel Tock (Turnhout, 1993); and A. Giry, *Manuel de diplomatique* (1894), 562–67, 855–58.

13. Barbara Rosenwein describes *si quis* clauses as "the monks' first line of defense." Head, Rosenwein, and Farmer, "Monks and Their Enemies," 772.

14. *HGL* 83.

so. This remains forever inviolable, as the first chapter of the third book of the law of the Romans wisely states: With a sale or purchase or a gift, so much is needed: if the party that arranged, gave, or sold did not act because of deception or violence, and if he should want to reclaim that which he sold or gave, it shall in no way be permitted. Similarly, as the rule of Salic Law makes known: A sale, purchase, or gift which has not been extracted through force or intimidation shall be valid in every way.[15]

The count and countess invoked rules from the *Theodosian Code*, Salic Law, and the *Visigothic Code*. Having insisted on the gift's conformity with the demands of Roman, Visigothic, and Salic law, the donors specified the boundaries of the property. Finally, the scribe spelled out the penalties that violators of the gift could anticipate:

> And if it should come about, which we do not believe to be true, that we donors, or any of our children, or heirs, or successors, or any sent or appointed person should come against this alod to trouble or disrupt it, or should want to [do so], first he shall incur the wrath of God, and shall be beyond the limits of the Holy Church of God, and the plagues which battered Egypt shall come upon them. As the ground swallowed up Dathan and Abiron, so shall it swallow them up in unquenchable flames and dazzling light, and as Ananias and Sapphira were battered in their bodies because of their greed, so they shall feel in their bodies. Let the sword devastate them on the outside, while fear terrorizes them on the inside.[16]

When these donors (the count and countess) and recipients (the monks of Montolieu) wanted to ensure the permanence of the gift, they did not rely solely on scrupulous citations of Roman property law, nor did they rely exclusively on the daunting litany of ritual, social, and somatic censures that would batter anyone foolhardy enough to trouble the monastery's new property. Citations of written law and vivid invocations of torment both frame the donation. The patterns of acquiring, alienating, and fighting over property were conditioned both by rules and by curses.

The canons of the cathedral at Nîmes relied on curses to protect the chapter's property, suggesting that overly acquisitive neighbors would be afflicted with leprosy.[17] A 959 donation to Sant Cugat threatened would-be violators with exclusion from the church and emphasized that they would, "not be worthy to accept the body and blood of our Lord Jesus Christ." Scribes at Sant Cugat, like those in Elne and Carcassonne, combined financial penalties from Visigothic law with a rich constellation of scriptural villains to whom violators were solemnly linked:

15. *HGL* 89.
16. *HGL* 89.
17. *Nîmes* 66.

And it shall be like the keepers of these idols, Zaroen and Arfaxat, who were turned into coals in the passion of apostles Simon and Jude. God shall submerge him, just as he submerged Sodom and Gomorrah, and as he submerged Simon Magus because of the Speech of Peter and Paul. He shall be cursed and consumed, as Galerius was with his idols, and afterward at the time of judgment he shall pay double however much this [agreement] mentions.[18]

Sant Cugat's records are particularly rich sources for many reasons, not the least of which is the monastery's close ties to Barcelona's comital family. Sant Cugat was not the isolated backwater, removed from the traditions of written law and comital authority that characterized Catalonia in the tenth and eleventh centuries.[19] The monastery was not forced to rely on curses because it had no other means of defending itself. On the contrary, it was one of the principal guardians of the Romano-Visigothic ideals and written law. Professional judges, comital courts, and citations of written law appear frequently in the monastery's records. Nevertheless, for the legal minds at Sant Cugat, curses were a central element in ensuring the longevity of agreements.

The same willingness to combine curses and written law was apparent in the comital courts of nearby Barcelona. The counts and countesses of Barcelona regularly presided over courts that relied both on the legal reasoning of professional judges and on curses: "Let him be excommunicated and be punished in the underworld with the traitor Judas, and associated with Dathan and Abiron, whom the earth swallowed alive, and joined with Herod, who lives in fire with worms feeding on his flesh and soul, and he shall be anathema, that is, guilty in the judgment of the Lord, and be crucified cruelly in eternity."[20] The *si quis* clause of a 1002 donation made by Count Ramon Borrell threatened violators with the penalty prescribed by Visigothic law and also with the wrath of God, judgment alongside Judas, and long-term suffering in brutal flames.[21]

The bishop and chapter of Urgell relied on a similar blend of legal and ritual sanctions to protect their property. Would-be violators were threatened with liturgical penalties and fines.[22] Like the canons at Nîmes who cursed their enemies with leprosy or the canons of Urgell who threatened to deprive their dying enemies of intercessory psalms, monks in nearby Gascony displayed a fiery creativity in formulating spiritual penalties:

18. *Sant Cugat* 61.
19. J. M. Salrach, "Formació, organització i defense del domini de Sant Cugat."
20. *Marca* 227.
21. ACA Ramon Borrell 64.
22. *Urgellia* 362.

Truly, if any of my progeny or any contrary person should rise up against this donation, he shall be anathematized from the part of God and excommunicated and he shall incur the wrath of God. [God's] mercy and the intercession of all the saints shall profit him nothing. He shall have his part with Judas Iscariot, who betrayed the Lord, and Dathan and Abiron, whom the earth absorbed. His soul [shall be] submerged in an infernal cesspool, and he shall be expunged from the book of life, unless he repents, and pays the fine . . . as it is stipulated in the decrees of the book of the judges.[23]

The book of the judges to which the charter refers is the *Liber Iudiciorum*, or *Visigothic Code*. Here again the threat of the infernal sewer and the authority of the legal codex worked together. At the monastery of Lézat, curses were an important aspect of even relatively minor transactions:

If anyone should rise up to disturb this charter of foundation, first he shall be subject to the indignation and excommunication of the Lord, and shall mix in misery with the traitor Judas and shall be shut off from all association of the Holy Church of God of the faithful. They shall have their part with Cain the fratricide and the most unhappy Herod the parricide. Just as the earth swallowed Dathan and Abiron, so shall hell swallow them. They shall remain excommunicated and cursed, and they shall never hear the voice of the Lord. And they shall be cursed from the top of their heads to the soles of their feet, and their children shall be orphans and their wives widows. And they shall never be in the memory of God and they shall be cursed walking, standing and sitting, eating and drinking, sleeping and waking, the leprosy of Naaman the Syrian shall be upon them and they shall consort with Nebuchadnezzar, Caiaphas, Pilate, Doec, and Holofernes and all the enemies of God whom, from the beginning, God has cursed and whom he has banished from himself forever. They shall sink into the sewer of Gehenna, to endure the pains of misery forever.[24]

Professional judges played a smaller role in disputes involving Lézat than they did in Urgell, Cerdanya, or Barcelona, but the monks of Lézat clearly had a vivid sense of how judicial courts were supposed to operate. One scribe included curses as well as a brief description of the functioning of comital courts:

If any enemy of God, which let not be true, should want to disturb this charter, first he shall incur the wrath of God and shall have part with Dathan and Abiron and Judas Iscariot in hell, and as the flames burned the stalk, so shall his body and soul be consumed in fire. All the curses which are contained in the Old and New Testaments shall descend upon him. Afterward the clerics or leaders of this church shall go to the count and the bishop of Toulouse and make a com-

23. B. Cursente, "La Gascogne," in *Les Sociétés meridionales*, ed. Zimmerman, 284–85.
24. *Lézat* 268.

plaint, and the count and bishop for the love of God and Saint Martin and for the health of their souls shall make justice and shall have the property held by Saint Martin and by the clerics belonging to this place.[25]

The monks of Lézat saw no tension between dramatic curses and a system of courts administered by counts and bishops; curses and courts were complementary aspects of managing property.

Curse clauses varied, but the possible elements of a *si quis* curse might be divided into four rough, overlapping categories: specific liturgical sanctions (e.g., excommunication), deprivation of intercession, earthly sufferings, and affiliation with the enemies of God. Most clauses drew elements from each of these categories.

Excommunication was usually the first sanction mentioned in curse clauses. Excommunicated parties were cut off from the Church and its ritual; they were deprived of the Eucharist and removed from the community of believers. Although this two-pronged exclusion constituted the core of excommunication, it remained a flexible sanction which admitted degrees of severity. According to Hincmar of Rheims, writing in the ninth century, a bishop could unilaterally excommunicate an offender, but the more serious sentence of anathema required the consent of fellow bishops and superiors. This distinction between excommunication and anathema remained operative in the eleventh century. The canons of the 1027 Council of Toulouges specified that violators were subject to excommunication, and if they remained unrepentant for three months, the sanction of anathema would be added.[26] Some scribes specified that their excommunication was the most serious penalty or emphasized the implications of being separated from the body of Christ.[27] A sentence of excommunication could be intensified with threats of anathema, marantha, or being stricken from the book of life. Curse clauses usually insisted that guilty parties be deprived of intercession and sometimes specified that a violator's removal from this world to the next would be unaccompanied by the singing of psalms.[28] Violators were deprived of saintly intercession and incurred the saints' wrath.[29] A sentence of excommunication thus could be more or less severe, but there is little evidence

---

25. *Lézat* 1163; Lézat's *si quis* clauses provide other rich examples of the combination of legal and ritual discourses. Paul Ourliac notes that features of tenth- and eleventh-century *si quis* clauses at Lézat reflect the long-term continuity of Roman contractual practices. See Ourliac, "Notes sur les actes," 247.

26. Little, *Benedictine Maledictions*, 32.

27. *Oliba* 105; Bourin-Derruau, "Le Bas-Languedoc," 76.

28. *Urgell* 263.

29. *Nîmes* 49; *Lézat* 803.

that in practice these different shades of excommunication conformed to any regular set of guidelines.[30]

After threatening excommunication, curse clauses emphasized that violators' eternal suffering would be both physical and spiritual: "He shall incur the wrath of the almighty God and both body and soul shall be filled with curses, and with the cursed [who shall be] on the left at the end, they shall hear: 'Go, cursed one, into the eternal fire that is prepared for the devil and his angels,' and they shall burn in the fire of Gehenna with Dathan and Abiron and their helpers now and forever."[31] Most of the prescribed suffering would occur during violators' eternal sentence in the fires of Gehenna, but the bodily suffering of some violators would begin in this world:

> They shall be cursed in the city and cursed in the fields. Their properties and their cellars shall be cursed. Their food and their relics shall be cursed. They shall be cursed on the inside of their bellies, and in the fruit of their lands, and in their herds and flocks. They shall be cursed coming and going. The Lord shall send upon them hunger and pestilence, and fruitlessness in all of the works they do, for he shall oppose them and they shall lose quickly because of their awful subtleties in which they abandon the Lord. The Lord shall bring upon them pestilence, so they sorrow over all the land they possess. He shall bring need, fever, cold, heat, summer, foul air, and blight, and he shall persecute them so that they perish. The Lord shall hand them over into the courts of their enemies. Their corpses shall be food for birds and beasts of the earth, and no one shall drive them away. They shall be struck with blindness, stupidity, insanity; they shall tremble at midday, just as the blind man is used to trembling in the shadows. And their flocks shall not be guided. Their heads shall be cursed through each of the seven portals: the nostrils, and ears, and eyes, and mouth. Their brain, their hair, shoulders, arms, hands, fingers, forehead, eyelids, tongue, teeth, throat, chest, back, heart, stomach, navel, inside, outside, and backside—vitals, groins, hips, knees, fibia, ankles, feet, soles, joints [articuli], veins, joints [juncturae], viscera, bones, and marrow shall be cursed.[32]

This curse, remarkable for its comprehensiveness, added that anyone who knowingly spoke, ate, or slept with the violators would be subject to the same dizzying array of punishments. Other curses specified that violators' days

30. Elisabeth Vodola outlines the evolution of excommunication in canon law in *Excommunication in the Middle Ages* (Berkeley, 1986). Richard Helmholz describes the gradual "judicialization" of excommunication in the twelfth century in "Excommunication in Twelfth-century England," *Journal of Law and Religion* 11 (1994–1995): 235–53. See also Geneviève Edwards, "Ritual Excommunication in medieval France and England, 900–1200," Ph.D. diss., Stanford University, 1997.

31. *Lézat* 235, quoting Matthew 25:41.

32. BNF, coll. Baluze 117, ff. 317–318.

would be short, their children would be orphans, and they would suffer from leprosy. When cataloging such earthly sufferings, scribes sometimes resorted to categorical curses, condemning violators to suffer all the plagues of Egypt or all the curses of the Old and New Testaments.[33]

The fourth and final aspect of curses in *si quis* clauses allowed for considerable variety. Violators were solemnly associated with the enemies of God. Here, scribes had the opportunity to display their familiarity with lesser-known scriptural narratives. *Si quis* clauses promised that violators would share in the eternal fate of figures such as Dathan, Abiron, and Judas who were renowned for the depravity of their conduct and for the intensity of their sufferings. A Narbonne curse specified that violators would be submerged like Pharaoh and his army.[34] In other transactions, the cursed shared the infamy of Ananias and Sapphira, Beelzebub, Galerius, Herod, Nero, Pilate, Zaroen and Arfaxat, Simon Magus, the inhabitants of Sodom and Gomorrah, Chore, Caiaphas, Holofernes, and Nebuchadnezzar.

This part of a *si quis* clause, with its assortment of villains, relied on the idea of affiliation. A violator of monastic or church property was linked to figures who provided touchstones for evaluating the violator's spiritual health. Dathan, Abiron, and the rest of this miserable troop provided an anecdotal method of describing the liturgical, sacral, and ritual implications of violating ecclesiastical property. Scribes and property-holders thus encoded property rights (and challenges to them) with significance by drawing on scriptural narratives of redemption and perdition. Curse clauses used scriptural events to guarantee the permanence of gifts and to impress upon would-be violators the magnitude of the sin of challenging ecclesiastic property rights. Dathan and Abiron, for example, served as a shorthand warning to those who questioned the inviolability and sanctity of such transactions. As just punishment for having challenged the priestly authority of Moses, the rebellious Dathan and Abiron were swallowed whole by the earth.[35]

Challengers to the authority of an agreement could expect a similarly decisive fate. Scribes equated challenges to ecclesiastical property not only with the violation of legal rules but also with the disruption of ritual order. Figures drawn from Scripture were used to represent both healthy and unhealthy attitudes to property. A couple who gave an alod to a church or monastery was adhering to the injunctions of Jeremiah, Luke, and John, as well as to those of the *Visigothic Code*.[36] Those who challenged such dona-

---

33. *HGL* 89; *HGL* 189; *Lézat* 270; *Lézat* 87; *Béziers* 58; *Béziers* 63.
34. BNF, coll. Doat 55, f. 94.
35. The story of Dathan and Abiron appears in Numbers 16:12–15, 25–34.
36. See, for example, *Gerri* 1; *Lézat* 1295; *Urgellia* 602.

tions, on the other hand, not only contravened the written law; they were also the peers of Dathan, Abiron, and Judas.

For modern historians, curse clauses are not easy to interpret. Would donors have understood the references to the earthy fates of Dathan and Abiron or to the more obscure villains who populate curse clauses? Would recipient monks have explained to donors the significance of Dathan and Abiron's usurpation of priestly authority prior to accepting gifts? Did monks explain to donors the important Roman origins of the contractual procedures they culled from the scraps of the *Theodosian Code* or the codices of Visigothic law, or would this knowledge have been part of any meridional donor's innate *romanité*? When donors tried to reclaim gifts, did they think of themselves as breaking the law, challenging the local saint, or simply reclaiming what was rightly theirs?

The complex fusion of ritual and legal discourses in these documents provokes many questions about the rules and norms that governed property relations around the year 1000. Although I do not pretend to offer complete answers to each of these question, I can propose one axiom for the study of charters: whatever interpretive attitude is assumed toward a record should be applied consistently to each of its constituent parts. Certain clauses should not be privileged as particularly rich sources of social or legal history while other clauses are considered irrelevant. Scholars who note the endurance of Roman contracts or Visigothic testamentary procedure often share a curious willingness to reject curses as ineffectual or unworthy of notice. When explicitly formulated, this dismissive attitude toward curses is attributed to the scant evidence for their effectiveness. The same accounts which airily dismiss the importance of curse clauses because there is little evidence for their effectiveness happily enshrine the appearance of fragments of Roman law as evidence of the continuing vitality of a civilization.

There are admittedly few sources describing clerical understanding of how curses worked or how donors responded to ritual sanctions; there is similarly little evidence to suggest that donors to monasteries and cathedral chapters felt particularly bound by Roman legal formulae, or felt particularly Roman when performing such transactions, or that anyone actually ever paid one of the financial penalties so carefully specified by the *Visigothic Code*.[37] It is a reckless skepticism that selects one part of a record as reflective of an essential cultural foundation and dismisses other parts of the same record as irrelevant background noise. If one dismisses curses as trivial, formulaic, and

37. For a similar caution about seeing continuities in citations of Roman law, see François Bougard, *La justice dans le royaume d'Italie de la fin du VIIIe siècle au début du XIe siècle* (Rome, 1995), 222.

legally unimportant, one should similarly dismiss citations of Roman law as insignificant and mindless repetitions, rather than presenting them as proof of the vitality of Roman jurisprudence and the endurance of a Roman cultural foundation.

MAKING GOOD ON THREATS

Si quis clauses were conditional. They described what would happen if someone were to violate the terms of an agreement. Curses took effect when someone took (or tried to take) property that belonged to a monastery or church. The curses were usually suspended when the offending party satisfied the offended party by abandoning any claim to the contested property. Although curses doubtless had some value as deterrents, they were not idle threats. When things went awry, prelates, clerics, and monks imposed the sanctions they had threatened.

Numerous surviving records of excommunication show that people took the conditions in curse clauses seriously. Although the precise theological implications of excommunication exercised the minds of canonists, in practice excommunication was embedded within and often indistinguishable from a chain of curses.[38] In Nîmes in 1066, two bishops excommunicated and cursed anyone who troubled an agreement:

> We, Bishops Froterius and Elefantus, and all the canons and clergy of Saint Mary, excommunicate and curse those men and women, who shall be damned in this manner: all the curses of the Old and New Testaments shall come upon those who do so. They shall be with Judas the traitor in hell, and at the day of their death they shall not receive communion nor shall they be buried in a Christian cemetery, unless they or someone on their behalf should come to the canons of Saint Mary to make satisfaction for this misdeed.[39]

The bishops further stipulated that the offending parties were liable for double damages as specified by law, *secundum legem*. In 1090, the bishop of Béziers struggled to protect his cathedral church, which was suffering at the hands of some violators described as "false Christians, enemies of God, and sacrilegious destroyers of our Church" ("falsi Christiani, inimici Dei, et nos-

---

38. Michel Zimmerman notes the indiscriminate use of the four main terms of ritual sanctions: maledictus, damnatus, excommunicatus, anathemitizatus in "Le vocabulaire latin," 45.

39. *Nîmes* 150.

tre Ecclesie sacrilegi destructores").[40] The bishop formed a coalition of ecclesiastical magnates, including the archbishop of Narbonne and the bishops
of Maguelonne, Nîmes, Lodève, Agde, and Albi. These bishops excommunicated and cursed those accused by the bishop of Béziers:

> Having heard what is written about the complaint and the destruction of the
> church of Béziers, . . . by the authority of God and of the apostles Peter and Paul,
> and all of God's saints, and by our own authority, we curse and excommunicate,
> and anathematize the above-mentioned violators of sacred property, and any of
> their helpers in this affair, and anyone who approved of it, and any who now
> takes, or subsequently shall take from the *honor* of Torrilias (about which this
> dispute took place), and all the tithe collectors, and their ministers, and all those
> who shall give to them any of the tithes or benefits of *cens* from this *honor*. He
> shall be cursed and excommunicated and anathematized, and separated from
> every gathering of Christians. They shall be cursed waking, sleeping, standing,
> sitting, lying, eating, drinking, speaking, remaining silent, above, below, on the
> left, on the right, before, and behind. The earth shall absorb [them] as it ab-
> sorbed Dathan and Abiron. They shall be participants in hell with the traitor Ju-
> das Iscariot, and they shall be damned along with the others to whom the Lord
> God says, "Go away from us." Leprosy shall come upon them from one gener-
> ation to the next. Their children shall be orphans and their wives widows. They
> shall be taken out of their homes and they shall wander. The plagues, which God
> gave to Pharaoh and his people, shall come upon them, and they shall be anath-
> ema, marantha. They shall incur all of the curses of the Old and New Testa-
> ments, until they come to their senses and make satisfaction to the Lord God
> and the holy martyrs Nazarius and Celsus regarding this dispute, and to their
> own bishop and to his canons.[41]

The record from Béziers is particularly elaborate, but bishops regularly
formed such cursing coalitions. In 1043, Bishop Oliba of Vic told a council
of bishops at Narbonne how the monastery of Sant Miquel de Cuixà, despite
its daunting collection of royal and apostolic privileges, had been laid waste
by certain "depraved and perverse men."[42] Nineteen bishops were moved by
Oliba's complaint. They decided to help the monastery and to encourage
others to do likewise by issuing a collaborative excommunication. Excommunications like these, affirmed by several bishops at large councils, not only
troubled violators' souls by depriving them of Christian burial or ritual intercession, but also galvanized networks of churchmen in support of their
beleaguered colleagues. Those who ignored the bishops' sentence of excommunication and continued to associate with excommunicated parties found

40. *Béziers* 90.
41. Ibid.
42. *Oliba* 149. In 1022, Oliba convinced a council of bishops to excommunicate violators of the see of Vic's property. See *Oliba* 68.

themselves excommunicated as well. The collective action of the clergy thus forced the broader community to become involved in conflicts. The consequences of a struggle over a particular property were no longer restricted to the principal parties in a case. An excommunication could move a threatened church into a position of greater strength by polarizing both lay and clerical communities. With the broad public decree of such sanctions, people were forced to take sides.

Coalition building was one of Oliba's particular strengths, but he was not alone. In 991, Bishop Salla of Urgell excommunicated two entire dioceses which he felt had been unjustly removed from his authority by "perverse men" (*pravi et perservi homines*).[43] These dioceses would enjoy no priestly ministry or absolution until the disputed property was returned.[44] In justifying his action, Salla invoked the episcopal power of binding and loosing and mentioned restrictions on bishops bearing arms. In doing so, he compared the liturgical sanctions of the clergy to the material weapons of lay barons.[45] After promulgating this excommunication with the assistance of two other bishops, Salla notified other bishops in the region, described the difficulties that led to his decision, and encouraged them to cooperate with his sentence.[46]

Bishops might augment the severity of their sentence with terms like anathema and marantha. Neither term enjoyed precise canonical significance, and the nuances of such intensifiers may have been lost on the excommunicated parties, but the use of such terms reveals some attempts to calibrate the severity of ritual sanctions. Just as bishops could adjust the severity of excommunications, so too could they target them in different ways. When Oliba of Vic organized the excommunication of Cuixà's enemies, he exempted certain people from any possible danger: "We exempt from this chain of excommunication Count William and his son, and Count Ramon and his brothers and sons, because we find it unworthy to subdue those with excommunication who we know have long been defenders and patrons of the monastery."[47] Similarly, when Salla of Urgell excommunicated two dioceses, he exempted Countess Ermengard and her children from the sentence, specifying that they would continue to enjoy the normal benefits of liturgy and intercession.[48] At roughly the same time in northern France,

43. *Urgellia* 225.
44. *Urgellia* 224.
45. Salla's scruples about bearing arms do not seem to have been widely shared by his fellow-bishops. The bishops of Barcelona, Girona, and Vic all participated in and died during a military expedition to Córdoba in 1010.
46. *Urgellia* 225.
47. *Oliba* 149.
48. *Urgellia* 224.

Bishop Fulbert of Chartres displayed similar subtlety when considering the value of ritual sanctions. Writing to the bishop of Paris sometime before 1023, he explained his rationale for pursuing a particular policy regarding one of the enemies of the Church:

> With regard to the woman from Laon who is committing sacrilege by ravaging your church's possessions, we have put off excommunicating her for the following reasons: first, because there was no one who would dare to notify her that we had excommunicated her; second, since it would be of little or perhaps no profit to you if she were excommunicated in our church without knowing of it; third, because we believe that this could be done to better advantage in a provincial council of our fellow bishops.[49]

Fulbert's explanation makes clear that the publication of a sentence of excommunication was important and that networks of bishops provided much of the real muscle behind these threats. Excommunication was not merely a formulaic threat. Bishops fashioned sentences to meet particular goals. They tried to ensure the cooperation of neighboring clergy by informing them of the reasons behind particular sentences and tailored excommunications by excluding certain parties from sanctions and singling out others for particular reproof. In short, excommunication was not a crude or exotic tool but one which bishops used regularly and with considerable finesse.

When bishops excommunicated someone, their action was directed toward the restoration both of a compromised social order and of an eternal order. Excommunications and curses bound the temporal order of law and property to the eternal, sacred order.[50] An excommunication called for the immediate intervention of the supernatural in earthly affairs. Through excommunications, the clergy created a state of hostility between God, the saints, and the community of the faithful, on the one hand, and the violators of church property, on the other. Having created this tension between the temporal and the eternal, bishops carefully announced their sentences to the community. At the end of the excommunication liturgy, bishops threw burning candles representing offending parties to the floor of the church and crushed out their flames; having completed the liturgy, bishops were instructed to explain their sentence to the public.[51] A sentence of excommunication thus not only brought about the involvement of the supernatural in

49. *The Letters and Poems of Fulbert of Chartres*, ed. Frederick Behrends (Oxford, 1976), no. 79.

50. See Roy A. Rappaport, "The Obvious Aspects of Ritual," in *Ecology, Meaning, and Religion* (Richmond, Calif., 1979), 173–222.

51. See, for example, a liturgy in Etienne Baluze, *Capitularia regum Francorum* (Paris, 1677), 2, 666–67.

daily life—like the liturgical humiliation of a saint's relics, the processions of relics and reliquaries at peace councils, or the judicial ordeals which were occasionally used as proofs—but also communicated information to the violators of church property and to members of the surrounding community.

RESPONDING TO EXCOMMUNICATION: THREE CASES

The question of how excommunications worked (or failed to work) is a tricky one. Records reveal that clerics devoted time and energy to excommunicating people, but they rarely describe how the recipients of such sentences responded to their spiritual and social peril. Evaluating the efficacy of ritual sanctions is notoriously difficult. Occasional clerical complaints about the inefficacy of excommunication suggest that it failed to have the desired effects. These same complaints, however, are often delivered in surprised tones suggesting that when an excommunication was cavalierly disregarded it was an exceptional circumstance which caused particular consternation.[52]

Despite these difficulties, scattered evidence suggests that ritual sanctions were effective clerical and monastic strategies for protecting property and dealing with enemies. In 1018, Jofre Maier abandoned a castle to the monastery of Gerri. He explained that his action was prompted by the excommunication that had been enacted against him: "I, Jofre Maier, because of the excommunication that I heard of and for the fear of God and the blessed Mary, examined myself, and I came before Count Ramon and Countess Valentia at Castle Mur and abandoned any claim on this land [condamina] into the hand of Abbot Arnold such that neither I nor my progeny will claim it."[53] Relative to the excommunications at Urgell or Cuixà, the stakes in this affair were small. Nevertheless, the case shows that on a local level excommunication could be an effective means of responding to lay aggression *and* that such sanctions were compatible with other fora of dispute processing. Jofre performed his quitclaim in a comital court of the sort that often administered justice in the region, but according to his own words (or, at least, the scribe's account of Jofre's words), his renunciation was prompted

52. The abbot of Sant Pere de Roda complained to Pope Benedict VII in 1022 that violators of the monastery's property had ignored a sentence of excommunication. He noted that he and other bishops had tried to defend the monastery's property and asked that the pope reaffirm the sentence of excommunication. See *Oliba* 72.

53. *Gerri* 4. This record includes one of the earliest references to *convenientiae* in the region. See Kosto, *Making Agreements*, 38–39.

by a sentence of excommunication and the fear of God, not by his respect for comital authority or written law.

In Béziers, the cathedral chapter successfully used excommunication to soften a recalcitrant bishop. The canons of the cathedral church of Saint Nazaire claimed that property which rightly belonged to the chapter was being unjustly held by Bishop Arnold of neighboring Maguelonne. The canons showed Bishop Arnold a charter to substantiate their claim. Arnold replied only that he would look into the matter. Having examined the canons' charter, which presumably contained a *si quis* clause like other charters from Béziers, the bishop's attitude changed. He traveled to Béziers and, influenced by his fear of excommunication and by the supplication of the bishop of Béziers and his canons, Bishop Arnold changed his previously dismissive attitude: "His heart began to fear such a great excommunication, and he was silent because of the decree which the clerics had in their donation. The Lord Bishop Bernard [of Béziers] along with his clerics started to demand of Lord Bishop Arnold with a most humble voice that he give up and abandon to God and to the chapter of Saint Nazaire his claim to the gift which he had held unjustly for so long. And he did so."[54] Again in this case, the threat of excommunication prompted the chapter's opponent to reconsider his position.

In 1059, the viscount of Narbonne leveled a number of charges at Narbonne's archbishop, Guifré, before a council of bishops at Arles. His attack on Guifré's poor stewardship included a bewildering range of accusations against the viscount, including building castles, abusing the chapter's wealth, neglecting his liturgical responsibilities, and selling the cathedral's silver to Narbonne's Jews. In an impassioned plea to the assembled bishops, the viscount described how he could have borne all these offenses, but he had labored under an unfair excommunication which oppressed him greatly: "All of this mattered little. But he [Archbishop Guifré] cruelly and unjustly excommunicated me, my wife, and all our land—so cruelly that no one was baptized there, nor did anyone receive communion, nor was anyone properly buried."[55] After pleading for the intervention of Guifré's fellow bishops, the viscount expressed his doubts about the validity of an excommunication issued by anyone as clearly misguided as Archbishop Guifré. The viscount's suspicion about the force of the archbishop's sentence shows that while bishops adjusted the severity of their excommunication, laymen could harbor their own ideas about the gravity of the ritual sanctions imposed upon them. Although the viscount did not blindly accept the significance of the archbishop's sentence of excommunication, he was also made distinctly uneasy by

54. *Béziers* 70.
55. *HGL* 251.

the archbishop's cessation of his normal ritual duties. The viscount suspected that Guifré's excommunication might well be invalid or powerless, but he did not want to take any chances when the stakes were so high.

These three documents from Gerri, Béziers, and Narbonne record very different types of conflict. The charter from Gerri describes a comital court in which a layman abandoned his claim to a castle that the court ruled was owned by a monastery. The record from Béziers shows that the bishop and chapter of one see mobilized a number of persuasive strategies against the bishop of another. The third document is a viscount's complaint to a synod of bishops about his suffering under the sentence of excommunication issued by an unjust archbishop. All three records, however, concur that a wide range of people (and not just easily impressionable crowds) responded to excommunications: in one case a lay property-holder, in another a bishop, and in another a viscount. By one admittedly crude test, excommunications worked. The monks of Gerri and the canons of Béziers retrieved their property. Each of these struggles suggests that ritual played a pivotal role in conflict. Contests over property and authority, even those processed in arenas like comital courts, could be inflected, influenced, and determined by ritual.

These confluences of law and ritual were not precipitated only by extraordinary circumstances. They occurred even during the most mundane transactions. The professional judges that were such a remarkable feature of courts in the south were, after all, often priests. The technicians of the written law were also the celebrants of Christian ritual. A charter from Agde described a judge receiving the routine testimony of several witnesses regarding an oral testament. The witnesses testified about the deceased's deathbed bequests, and the concise description of the judge's role in the transactions shows him shifting from one idiom to another:

> When the judge had heard these witnesses giving good testimony, which did not vary but was like one testimony, he entered into the Church of Saint Stephen. They placed their hands over the most holy altar. And they said, swearing by God, the Father almighty, and his son Jesus Christ, and the Holy Spirit, that is the triune and one God, above whose altar we touch our hands, and hold each other swearing [an oath regarding] this affair, that we have testified truly, and rightly, and that we testify faithfully, and that we testify truly and not falsely. This [testament] was executed within the time limits, as the law of the Goths indicates [*sicut in lege Gothorum resonat*].[56]

The judge moved seamlessly from orchestrating sacramental oaths over an altar to consulting a law code in order to confirm that procedure had conformed to the demands of Visigothic law.

56. *Adge* 323.

Scribes did not neatly distinguish between legal sanctions (such as the fines stipulated by the *Visigothic Code*) and ritual sanctions (such as excommunication or solemn association with Dathan and Abiron). Property, law, and ritual were linked in an improvised collection of rules, symbols, and practices, cobbled together from a number of sources. Pierre Bourdieu's supple account of the complicated origins of norms and rules suggests that any thorough understanding of law must include an appreciation of the role of ritual and the symbolic:

> The absence of a genuine *law*—the product of the work of a body of specialists expressly mandated to produce a coherent corpus of juridical norms and ensure respect for its application, and furnished to this end with coercive power—must not lead us to forget that any socially recognized formulation contains within it an intrinsic power to reinforce dispositions symbolically.[57]

Bourdieu's work provides insight into how Dathan, Abiron, and Jeremiah might inhabit a legal world alongside the *Visigothic Code*. The proud claims of legality and conformity to rules made by judges and scribes should not seduce us into the belief that antique rules alone constituted the normative world of the central Middle Ages. Judges and scribes insisted that transactions adhered to the rule of Visigothic law. But such rules were only one part of the system through which people understood property rights, not the system itself. Law and liturgy, rules and rituals, codes and curses were intertwined.

The conflicting positions of the scholars who first studied the problem of law and *romanité* in the south has been neatly summarized by Christian Lauranson-Rosaz. One group of scholars argued that Roman legal ideas endured during the Middle Ages; another set claimed that citations of written law were relatively unimportant and that Roman legal traditions survived in such fragmentary and corrupt forms that it was hardly appropriate to call it survival at all.[58] The positions described by Lauranson-Rosaz have framed most subsequent treatments of the problem.

Although they reached different conclusions, both camps posed the question in more or less the same way: Did Roman law survive into the Middle Ages? As I suggested in the last chapter, the frequent resort to the idea of "survival" may be the real stumbling block in assessing the significance of ci-

---

57. Pierre Bourdieu, *Outline of a Theory of Practice* (Cambridge, 1977), 21.
58. Lauranson-Rosaz, "La romanité," 53–54.

tations of written law in charters. Law codes, after all, are not independent historical agents; they do not do things by themselves. The terms of the debate might fruitfully be changed if we thought less about whether a legal system were maturing, surviving, dying, or reviving, and instead devoted more attention to what use people made of the different elements of that legal system. If one poses the question in terms of "survival," any discussion naturally turns away from the strategic maneuvers of particular people to judgments about the health or frailty of the system. Legal systems and law codes do not "survive"; bits of them, however, are found useful by people who continue to deploy them in constantly evolving ways. Challenging the positivist model of law as a comprehensive system of rules which determines human interaction, and at the same time questioning the organic model which sees laws and legal systems as surviving or dying, enables us to see medieval judges and disputants as agents who reshaped property and social relations with rules (and curses) rather than as passive conduits of a legal tradition.

Historians might benefit from the work of legal scholars who provide alternate models for understanding law. One of the central projects of legal scholarship since the early 1980s has been to examine law as a semiotic system. In its crudest form, this debate examines the ways in which law resembles literature and language as a way of making meaning. One of the corollary questions that emerges is whether there are meaningful connections between judges and lawyers, on the one hand, and poets and literary critics, on the other. Other formulations ask more generally whether judging and reading can be linked through the idea of interpretation. James Boyd White represents one branch of these investigations. In *Heracles' Bow: Essays on the Rhetoric and Poetics of the Law*, White aims

> . . . to set forth as vividly as I can my sense of law as a social and cultural activity, as something we do with our minds, with language, and with each other. This is a way of looking at the law not as a set of rules or institutions or structures (as they are usually envisaged), nor as part of our bureaucracy or government (to be thought of in terms of political science or sociology or economics), but as a kind of rhetorical and literary activity. One feature of this kind of activity is that it must act through the materials it is given—an inherited language, an established culture, an existing community—which in using it transforms.[59]

White's poeticizing of law is, of course, only one exploration of these ties, and one that is far from universally accepted. Robert Cover, for example, argues that any equation of criticism and judgment is bound to obscure the vi-

59. James Boyd White, foreword to *Heracles' Bow: Essays on the Rhetoric and Poetics of Law* (Madison, Wisc., 1985), x–xi.

olence that is an essential part of judicial decisions.[60] Cover himself, however, insists that positive rules and the instruments of their enforcement are only one part of the normative worlds we inhabit. Communities construct normative worlds by drawing on a complex mixture of rules, narratives, myths, and visions of the future.[61] Legal scholars are far from agreeing on how to envision the connection between law, literature, narrative, and violence, but these debates themselves afford valuable alternatives to the rigid model which sees law as a transparent and coherent system of commands. Whether one embraces White's "cultural resources" and "inherited language" or Cover's *nomos*, law is less a determined and determining system than it is a repertory of texts, symbols, and practices which are creatively, and at times violently, used to reshape communities.

These expansive conceptions of law and its uses are valuable not only when examining the origin of civil rights and judicial violence (as Cover does) or the poetics of the lawyer's craft (as White does), but also when looking at property disputes. Taking, for example, White's idea of "cultural resources" in place of the more conventional model of "the survival of Roman law" allows us to account for the combination of two discrete discourses. The law codes which furnished the written rules had much in common with the Scripture that provided tropes for cursing. Both are normative, authoritative texts. Both describe (one with commands, the other through narrative) which categories of human behavior are to be encouraged and which are to be punished. Together, rules and rituals distinguished the legal from the illegal, the good from the bad, the blessed from the damned. Antitypes drawn from Scripture located potential violators of ecclesiastic and monastic property within the economy of Christian redemption and damnation. Rules from Visigothic law classified the same transactions according to whether or not they were lawful, whether or not they were contracts. Both Scripture and the *Theodosian Code* were parts of the "inherited language" of Provence, Languedoc, and Catalonia. The resonant qualities of the contract and the curse encoded property transactions. The host of figures with whom a violator was ritually associated provide a rich constellation of images which engaged donors and violators in a symbolic world of punishment, isolation, redemption, and suffering. The scribes who made charters drew on this inherited cultural language. Making a charter was an act of *bricolage* relying on an im-

60. Robert Cover, "Violence and the Word," *Yale Law Journal* 95 (1986): 1601–29. For an overview of Cover's work, see Carol J. Greenhouse, "Reading Violence," in *Law's Violence*, ed. Austin Sarat et al. (Ann Arbor, Mich., 1992), 105–39.

61. Robert Cover, "Nomos and Narrative," in *Narrative, Violence, and the Law: The Essays of Robert Cover*, ed. Martha Minow, Michael Ryan, and Austin Sarat (Ann Arbor, Mich., 1992), 101.

provised set of tools for describing, determining, and altering the social and economic landscape. Two sets of metaphors about property, one drawn ultimately from Roman and Visigothic law and the other from the narrative of Christian redemption, were thus fused.[62]

During the tenth and eleventh centuries, scribes from the south cursed with energy, violence, and persistence. Churches and monasteries protected their possession with a dual nimbus of legal and sacral authority. Gifts to monasteries and churches involved donors in networks of giving and receiving that tied donor, saint, and community.[63] Transfers of property not only involved parties in contractual agreements but also in affective and personal bonds with saints and religious communities—bonds with ritual implications. Given these ties, it is not at all surprising that breaking agreements affected both one's ritual and one's legal status, and that the threat of curses accompanied gifts and quitclaims. The astonishing feature of records from the Province of Narbonne and its neighbors is not the endurance of written law nor the ritualizing of property relations. Instead, it is the facility and elegance with which scribes combined these two discourses. Neo-Romans though they doubtless, in some sense, were, the inhabitants of the Midi cursed and juggled relics along with the least romanized of their northern counterparts.

In the landscape of tenth- and eleventh-century Europe, Roman architectural elements were recycled in monastic construction. The Roman monuments which dotted the countryside of Gaul and Iberia were ever-present echoes of the antique past; they were exploited as models and as inexpensive sources of building material. The fragments of Roman law that appeared in charters thus found physical reflections in the Pont de Gard, the Temple of Diana, the Maison Carrée at Nîmes, and in countless lesser monuments. Xavier Barral i Altet presents the tenth-century altar at the monastery of Sant Miquel de Cuixà as one particularly compelling example.[64] At Cuixà, a Ro-

62. This reliance on several normative discourses is, of course, not unique to the Midi or even to medieval Europe. For an early thirteenth-century example from the Orléanais, see Thomas Head, *Hagiography and the Cult of the Saints: The Diocese of Orléans, 800–1200* (Cambridge, 1990), 190; For a useful comparison in a modern context, see Sally Falk Moore, *Social Facts and Fabrications: "Customary" Law on Kilimanjaro, 1880–1980* (Cambridge, 1986), 44–45.

63. See Barbara Rosenwein, *To Be the Neighbor of St. Peter: The Social Meaning of Cluny's Property, 909–1049* (Ithaca, N.Y., 1989).

64. Xavier Barral i Altet, *Le paysage monumental de la France autour de l'an mil* (Paris, 1987), 21. See also Pierre Ponsich, "La table de l'autel," *Les Cahiers de Saint-Michel-de-Cuxa* (hereafter *CSMC*) 6 (1975): 41–65; and Josep Maria Salrach, "El comte-bisbe Miró Bonfill i l'acta de consagració de Cuixà de l'any 974," *Acta historica et archaeologica medievalia* 10 (1989): 107–24.

man capital of white marble from Narbonne was used in the construction of the monastery's main altar. Such examples of architectural recycling provide captivating images of the palpable presence of Rome in the Middle Ages. The altar which incorporated this vestige of Rome was consecrated in 974 at a ceremony attended by the bishops of Elne, Girona, Vic, Urgell, Toulouse, Coser, and Carcassonne. After describing the history of the monastery, the gathering, and the altar itself, a scribe recorded how the bishops completed their consecration:

> But if someone wants to dare to neglect our warning, and led astray by confusion replaces it, and unless he corrects himself and humbly comes to make satisfaction to this same church, he shall be prevented from approaching the limits of the Holy Church of God. Then the vengeance for sacrilege shall be conferred [upon him], and he shall be driven to compound according to both worldly and holy laws. He shall be handed over into savage and infernal flames along with the most unspeakable traitor Judas, to whom he shall be sent by God. He shall feel the judgment of the divine law condemning Dathan and Abiron. Unless he corrects himself, he shall descend living into hell to be crucified eternally just like these transgressors, where the worms do not die, and the fires never fade and where because of the extreme heat snow quickly changes to water, and where transgressors endure intolerable stenches and indescribable torments. And besides [there shall be] the pains which the Holy Church of God sings regularly against transgressors in the psalm. Like the fire that burned up the forest and like the flame that burned up the mountains, thus shall the almighty God persecute him in his fury, and in his anger he shall expel them. He shall fill their faces with shame, and they shall want the name of the almighty God. They shall be ashamed and troubled through all time, and they shall be confounded and they shall perish.[65]

The bishops stressed that the monastery would be protected by both the worldly and the holy law. As in those agreements which at the same time cited written law and cursed, so too in the use of antique architectural elements, the dominant mode was not slavish imitation of the Roman past. Instead, the inhabitants of the Province of Narbonne employed a vital archaeology, adapting fragments of the (textual and architectural) past to new uses. The fragment of white marble which made its way from the center of antique Narbonne to the Pyrenean Cuixà of the late tenth century is less proof of the endurance of *romanité* than it is a testament to the improvisation that was one of this culture's most compelling features. When the inhabitants of the medieval Midi used Roman fragments to build, they built altars.

65. Ramon Abadal I de Vinyals, "Com neix i com creix un gran monestir pirinenc abans de l'any mil: Eixalada-Cuixà," in *Analecta Montserratensia* 8 (1954–55) (hereafter Cuixà) 99.

CHAPTER THREE
DILIGITE IUSTITIAM QUI IUDICATIS TERRAM: JUDGES IN COURT AND SOCIETY

As the disputes over Viscountess Guisla's property at Aiguatèbia suggest, judges played an extremely important role in processing disputes. Indeed, judges' activities are more thoroughly described in surviving records than those of disputants themselves. The sheer number of references to judges is remarkable, but the accumulation of such references does little to indicate what judges did, how they understood their work, or how others saw them. The term *iudex* (judge) in medieval Europe had many meanings. References to *iudices* in most regions were rare, and those judges who do appear elsewhere in Europe little resemble those in this region. The term *iudex* did not always and everywhere suggest specialized legal training as it did in the Province of Narbonne. In Western France, *iudices* played informal roles in disputes and rarely referred to written rules as their contemporaries in Catalonia and Languedoc did.[1] Even when they did invoke rules, judges usually were not seen as having a special status; they were indistinguishable from the witnesses or oath-helpers who also participated in judicial hearings.[2] In Burgundy, *iudex* might refer to people who appeared in court largely because of their close connection to one of the disputants.[3] In ninth-century Brittany, men with reputations for being trustworthy served as judges, but there is little indication that they were considered experts in the "law." Knowledge of

1. Stephen White, *Custom, Kinship, and Gifts to Saints*, 72–73, 77–78; idem., *"Pactum Legem Vincit et Amor Judicium,"* 293.
2. Barthélemy, *La société dans le comté de Vendôme*, 655–58.
3. Georges Duby, "The Evolution of Judicial Institutions," *The Chivalrous Society*, trans. Cynthia Postan (Berkeley, 1977), 30–31.

local history was more important than training in a body of rules.[4] In England, references to *iudices* appear only in certain areas and seem to refer to a type of select witness rather than to legal experts.[5]

Even in other parts of Mediterranean Europe, *iudex* did not mean quite the same thing that it meant in the Province of Narbonne. In eleventh-century Provence, *iudices* might refer to groups of advisers who supported opposing parties in a dispute.[6] In the twelfth-century near Toulouse, judges were not those who applied rules to cases before them, but rather ". . . individuals or groups capable of pressuring the disputants to accept their judgment, come to an agreement, or recognize that their claims were unjust. They were able to do this because of their great status or because they were friends, perhaps relatives; in any case, frequent associates."[7] Judges from other regions played important roles in property disputes because they had special knowledge of the facts of a case or because their opinion was respected by the disputants, not because they possessed special legal skills or pursued a career as a judge. *Iudex* in many places meant something closer to the modern notion of arbiter, counselor, adviser, or community leader.[8]

To be a *iudex* in the Province of Narbonne meant something quite particular. Judges were distinguished by training, appointment, and social status. There is little evidence related to how judges were educated, but it is abundantly clear that they were expected to have specialized training. They were supposed to be well-versed in the *Visigothic Code*—or at least in certain parts of the *Code* dealing with property, proofs, and testamentary procedure. Some judges even emphasized their academic accomplishments in their signatures.[9] Most were in clerical orders, and when they signed documents, they identified themselves with both judicial and clerical titles: *sacer et iudex, presbiter et iudex*, or *levita et iudex*.[10] Judges also expressed a lofty sense of their

4. Davies, "People and Places in Dispute in Ninth-Century Brittany," in *Settlement of Disputes*, ed. Davies and Fouracre, 78–79, 82–83.

5. Patrick Wormald, "Disputes in Anglo-Saxon England," in *Settlement of Disputes*, ed. Davies and Fouracre, 163.

6. Some tenth-century judges in Provence did, however, display a keen interest in written law. See Geary, "Living with Conflicts in a Stateless France," 132.

7. Fredric L. Cheyette, "Suum cuique tribuere," *French Historical Studies* 6 (1970): 292.

8. Conclusion to *Settlement of Disputes*, ed. Davies and Fouracre, 216–17.

9. See the examples discussed in Yolanda García López, *Estudios Críticos de la 'Lex Wisigothorum'* Memorias del Seminario de Historia Antigua V (Alcalá, 1996), 83.

10. There were exceptions: one judge signed a document *iudex et miles*, and another *laicus, qui et iudex*. Antoni Llorens, "El documents dels segles x i xi de l'Arxiu Capitular de Solsona," *Urgellia* 11 (1992–93): 301–486 (hereafter *Solsona*) 112; and Josep Mas, "Rúbrica dels Libri Antiquitatum de la Sèu de Barcelona," in *Notes històriques del bisbat de Barcelona*, vol. 9 and 10 (Barcelona, 1914–15) (hereafter *Notes hist.*), 500.

own importance in their signatures and seals. Judge Salomon, for example, had a distinctive monogram which he applied to transactions he witnessed. The signature of Judge Guifré of Vic ("Guifredus, gratia Dei iudex") reflected the same confluence of ritual and legal discourses apparent in the simultaneous use of Visigothic law and curses.[11]

By his own account, Guifré was a judge "by the grace of God," but judges generally derived their earthly authority from the counts, countesses, and bishops who appointed them to perform a range of legal tasks.[12] Foremost among those tasks was that of forging lasting solutions to disputes. In this region, disputes very often ended up in courts presided over by bishops and counts. These courts were not the only path by which a distressed property-holder might try to resolve a dispute, but they were a particularly important one. Disputants might try to end a dispute through bilateral negotiation with little involvement from legal professionals, or they might turn to self-help to redress perceived wrongs. Indeed, tenth- and eleventh-century records provide numerous examples of such self-help, some of which I discuss below. Fleeting traces of such extra-judicial strategies allow us to reconstruct something about the ways in which disputants viewed their options. But although disputants doubtless tried to resolve their differences in a variety of ways, property-holders in the Province of Narbonne turned frequently and enthusiastically to formal courts with professional judges. Disputants saw bringing their disputes before judges as an especially appealing or inevitable choice. Despite gaps in the historical record, ample evidence shows that comital and episcopal courts staffed by professional judges were the dominant means of resolving property disputes in this region. In this chapter and the next, I concentrate on litigation in formal courts, because that is precisely the avenue most disputants took.

As I have already suggested, the most remarkable feature of these courts was the corps of professional judges who studied written law, heard disputes, evaluated evidence, and issued judgments.[13] The careers of professional judges provide the best opportunity to explore how courts functioned. This is true not only because of the prominence of judges in the sources and their responsibility for the interpretation and application of the written law, but

11. *Oliba* 99; and Arxiu Capitular de Vic (hereafter ACV) Calaix 6, 1207.

12. The *Visigothic Code* suggested that in some cases judges were to be chosen by mutual agreement of litigants. *Leges Visigothorum*, II.1.27. In a few cases, this idea is echoed in later records. See, for example, F. X. Altés i Aguilo, "El diplomatari del monestir de Santa Cecília de Montserrat, I, anys 900–999," *Studia monastica* 36 (1994): 225–302 (hereafter *Santa Cecília*), nos. 181, 191.

13. Of the 176 disputes considered here, 93 were heard by at least one professional judge.

also because the presence of such a corps of professional judges is unparalleled in tenth- and eleventh-century Europe.

By calling these judges professional, I mean to draw attention to several important features of the judiciary. First, they executed a range of legal tasks over extended periods of time. They were not *ad hoc* adjudicators, stepping in temporarily to resolve thorny problems. Judges often knew the disputants who appeared before them, but the role they played in disputes was not one based primarily on their relations to disputants or on knowledge of particular cases. Second, they were expected to possess specialized knowledge of rules related to procedure and property—knowledge which they brought to bear on the cases before them. Finally, they enjoyed a professional identity in the broader social world. Many judges thought about what it meant to exercise their professional responsibilities and worked closely with their fellow-judges. Many occupied positions of social and economic prominence.

A LEGAL TEXTBOOK FOR THE ELEVENTH CENTURY

A single manuscript provides a vivid glimpse of the world of these judges. In 1010 and 1011, Judge Bonhom of Barcelona compiled two similar collections of legal texts. One of these manuscripts was lost when fire destroyed Ripoll's library in the nineteenth century. The second manuscript, known as the *Liber Iudicum Popularis*, survives.[14] In this compilation, Bonhom included a text of his own authorship on judges and judging, a handful of passages from Isidore's *Sentences* and *Etymologies*, a treatise on geometry, a list of Visigothic kings, a list of Frankish kings, a calendar indicating the feast dates of saints important in and around Barcelona, and an extensive glossary. All of these texts combined occupy only a small portion of the manuscript; the centerpiece of Bonhom's compendium was a copy of the *Visigothic Code*.

The centrality of the *Code* in Bonhom's manuscript confirms what is apparent from diplomatic evidence, namely that Visigothic law played a large role in the legal imagination of the region's inhabitants. But beyond echoing the importance of Visigothic law, the manuscript affords a picture of one eleventh-century judge thinking about his profession. Bonhom's prefatory

14. Escorial z.II.2. See F. Valls i Taberner, "El 'Liber Iudicium Popularis' de Homobonus de Barcelona," *AHDE* 2 (1925), 200–212; Anscari M. Mundó, "El jutge Bonsom de Barcelona, cal·lígraf i copista del 979 al 1024," in *Scribi e Colofoni: Le sottoscrizioni di copisti dalle origini all'avvento dell stampa*, ed. Emma Condello and Giuseppe de Gregorio (Spoleto, 1995), 269–88; and García López, *Estudios Críticos*, 84–95.

essay, the glosses which peppered the *Code*, and the glossary-appendix reveal something of how judges understood their profession, how they interpreted the law, and how they adjudicated disputes. In this manuscript, we witness Bonhom's effort to compose a useful compendium for the practicing judge, while at the same time reflecting upon the social obligations of judges.

Bonhom's preface is a sort of mirror for judges meant to serve as a sobering introduction to the texts that follow. He begins by tracing the divine origins of the law. Here he establishes a theme that recurs throughout the manuscript: the intimate relation of divine justice and earthly justice.

> The Law (*lex*) was first given to the just man Moses; grace and truth, however, were made through Jesus Christ. Therefore to use it well and to judge rightly are the highest blessing; to use it badly and to judge worse is the highest condemnation and a terrible curse. By this curse the just judge is saved, and the unjust is eternally condemned. Oh, you who wish to be a judge and to know the law, first listen and learn about the path on which you will embark.[15]

Bonhom draws on Scripture to develop further this point. He refers to Isaiah 30:21, and the *Book of Wisdom*, I, 1: "Love justice you who judge the earth." (*Diligite iustitiam qui iudicatis terram*). He cautions that judges should fear doing to others anything that they would not want done to themselves, a precept which he notes is the command of both law (*lex*) and prophecy (*propheta*). When describing the judge's social obligations, Bonhom emphasizes that earthly judges are themselves subject to divine judgment. Those who judge wrongly are eternally separated from God and his saints for their iniquity. But if the costs of being a bad judge are momentous, the rewards for good judging are commensurately impressive. A just judge earns a share in an eternal life where none are hungry, none sick, and all are clothed in perpetual light. The first part of Bonhom's preface thus argues that being a good judge is not merely knowing a set of rules, or being able to evaluate proofs. To be a good judge—to apply the law wisely—is to be an instrument of divine justice.

Bonhom's vision thus bridges theology and judicial practice. The link between divine judgement and earthly judgement has concrete implications. A conception of judgement based on Scripture and divine justice should ramify in the daily life of judges. In particular, judges must be especially sensitive to the poor, the weak, and those without protection. They should not oppress widows and orphans with their power. The links Bonhom established among divine justice, earthly law, and a concern for the welfare of the humble is most clearly articulated in his preface, but Bonhom does not abandon

15. Escorial z.II.2, f.iv.

this theme elsewhere in the manuscript.[16] Judging justly requires not only *lex*, but also grace and truth (*gracia* and *veritas*).

Having described the social and spiritual foundation of judges' responsibilities, Bonhom turns to the threats to justice against which judges must guard. Chief among these is greed. Bonhom warns judges against allowing their judgment to be corrupted by money. Those who judge rightly but expect a reward for doing so commit a "fraud in Christ."[17] Bad judges evaluate cases not on their merits but according to gifts to be gained; they do not resolve a case until the purse of the accused is exhausted.[18] Judges seduced by gold, silver, clothing, or money are consigned to eternal suffering: "For short pleasure, eternal suffering; for moderate happiness, enduring sadness." Drawing again on the *Book of Wisdom*, Bonhom describes such judges as "like wolves at sundown," thinking only of this life and not of the next.[19]

Greed is the most dangerous threat to justice, but Bonhom describes others as well, such as consideration for the status of a person.[20] Bonhom criticizes verbose judges who want only to hear their own pronouncements and who fail to listen to the people who appear before them. Judgments made in anger also violate justice. In his most economical formulation, Bonhom divides the threats to justice into four categories: "Human judgment is perverted in four ways: fear, greed, hate, and love." Whenever decisions are informed by these emotions, equity is violated and the innocent suffer. After voicing his concerns about the failures of those who wield authority, namely princes and judges, Bonhom offers a concise catalog of threats to the spiritual health of a community: "Wisdom without good works, age without religion, youth without obedience, a woman without chastity, a lord without strength, a proud pauper, an unfair king, a neglectful bishop, a priest without learning, an undisciplined mob, a contentious Christian, and a people without law. Thus does justice suffocate."[21]

Bonhom's ideas were not without forerunners. A ninth-century copy of the *Visigothic Code* from this region also included a preface on the duties of

16. This argument is not uncommon in early medieval discussions of justice. King Cnut's laws, for example, mandated that the weak should be judged with special leniency. *The Laws of the Kings of England from Edmund to Henry I*, ed. and trans. A. J. Robertson (Cambridge, 1925), 207. For another English example, see Michael Treschow, "The Prologue to Alfred's Law Code: Instruction in the Spirit of Mercy," *Florilegium* 13 (1994): 79–110.

17. "Qui recte iudicat et premium exinde hic remunerationis expectat fraudem in Xpo perpetrat." Escorial z.II.2, f.3r.

18. Escorial z.II.2, f.2v.

19. "principes eius in medio eius quasi leones regient; iudices eius lupi vespere non reliquebant in mane." *Book of Wisdom* 3, 3.

20. Escorial z.II.2, ff.2v–3r.

21. Escorial z.II.2, f.3r.

judges. The earlier preface advised judges to be cautious, vigilant, and learned, and encouraged them always to bear in mind their relation to the eternal judge.[22] Bonhom thus was not alone in his efforts both to respect the law of the *Visigothic Code* and to articulate the special responsibilities of judges. Bonhom's linking of divine and earthly judgment also mirrors understandings of justice that were prevalent in the Visigothic kingdom centuries earlier when various versions of the *Code* were first promulgated.[23] The *Code* cautions that justice might be corrupted through greed or incompetence, and stipulates that judges who unnecessarily delay cases and thereby cause litigants additional expense are to be punished.[24] Another passage, which notes that judges often accepted excessive payments, restricts the amount judges could receive.[25]

Bonhom's anxieties about judicial greed had Carolingian precedents as well, the most famous of which is a poem by Theodulf of Orléans. Born and educated in Spain, Theodulf spent time at Charlemagne's court before becoming bishop of Orléans. In 798, he was sent as a royal representative and itinerant judge to administer justice throughout the Midi. His extensive tour through Septimania included visits to Nîmes, Béziers, Agde, and Carcassonne. In Narbonne, the assembled crowd greeted him with special enthusiasm because they recognized him as a fellow Goth. Theodulf's poem is in part a memoir of his experiences in the courtrooms of the Midi and in part advice to judges on how to administer justice. Theodulf saw the task of adjudicating disputes as a difficult one, agreeing with Bonhom that the greatest threat to justice was greed: "Often I see that judges leave the laws to those who offer bribes and follow gold with greedy throat and mouth."[26] Theodulf's account of the harried judge struggling to make impartial decisions suggests that everyone tried to sway his opinion—not only litigants, but also the judge's servants and even his wife. "The people eagerly offered gifts, thinking that, if they gave, whatever they wanted would be done. . . . One of-

---

22. BNF MS Lat 4668, f.1r–v.

23. Carlos Petit, "*Iustitia y Iudicium* en el Reino de Toledo: Un Estudio de Teología Jurídica Visigoda," *La giustizia nell'alto medioevo (secoli V–VIII)*, 843–932.

24. *Leges Visigothorum*, II.1.18, II.1.20.

25. *Leges Visigothorum*, II.1.24; See King, *Law and Society*, 116–121; and *Leges Visigothorum*, II.1.30.

26. *Paraensis ad Iudices*, in MGH Poetae Latini I, no. 28, with title *Versus Teudulfi episcopi contra iudices*, 493–517; Nikolai Alexandrenko, "The Poetry of Theodulf of Orleans: A Translation and Critical Study," Ph.D. diss., Tulane University, 1970, 162. See also Gabriel Monod, "Les moeurs judiciaires au VIIIe siècle d'après la 'Paraenesis ad Judices' de Theodulf," *Revue Historique* 35 (1887) 1–20; and Ann Freeman, "Theodulf of Orleans: A Visigoth at Charlemagne's Court," in *L'Europe Héritière de l'Espagne Wisigothique*, ed. Jacques Fontaine and Christine Pellistrandi (Madrid, 1992), 185–94.

fered both crystal and gems from the East if I should contrive to get possession of another's fields. Another brought a large number of fine golden coins, which were struck with Arabic letters and characters, and coins of white silver imprinted with a Roman stamp, if only he might procure a farm, land, a house."[27] He catalogs the exotic treasures by which litigants tried to influence judges: livestock, multicolored rugs, silver cups, ancient decorated vases, skins from Córdoba, wax tablets, and purple and red garments. The practice of bribery, in Theodulf's accounts, was crude and pervasive: "There is no one who does not give, and no one who does not take bribes."[28] Although Theodulf, like Bonhom, saw greed and bribery as the most prominent threat to justice, he allowed that judges might accept modest gifts like wine, eggs, chickens, and fodder—as he had himself done—if these were given out of affection rather than from a desire to influence decisions.[29]

Theodulf was eloquent on the topic of the challenges of judging. Alcuin's *Liber de virtutibus et vitiis* devoted to judges provided another model. Calling on judges to maintain high moral standards, Theodulf and Alcuin represented one type of response to the problem of corrupt judges, but such concerns could take other courses. Some Carolingian legal reforms aimed to eliminate corruption among judges by prohibiting gifts to them.[30] These legislative measures had counterparts in liturgy; the Sacramentary of Gellone, for example, included a mass against bad judges.[31]

Bonhom shared several important ideas about judging with Theodulf and Alcuin. All three saw greed as the main threat to the judge's integrity. All encouraged judges to prefer rewards in the next life to riches in this one. All suggested that judges should be attentive to the demands of the written law and, at the same time, be merciful in the exercise of justice. Theodulf, like Bonhom two centuries later, claimed that it was among a judge's duties to see that the weak were not oppressed by the powerful. In Bonhom's preface, as in Theodulf's poem, the rewards for good judging are great and the punishments for bad judging are severe. In describing the two paths a judge might

27. *Versus Teudulfi,* lines 166–82, trans. Alexandrenko, "Poetry of Theodulf," 166.

28. *Versus Teudulfi,* line 258; Alexandrenko, "Poetry of Theodulf," 170.

29. *Versus Teudulfi,* lines 284–88.

30. Régine Le Jan, "Justice royale et pratiques sociales dans le royaume Franc au IXe siècle," *La giustizia nell'alto medioevo (secoli IX–XI)*, 52.

31. *Liber Sacramentorum Gellonensis,* ed. A. Dumas (Turnhout, 1982), no. 424, 427. See also Janet L. Nelson, "Kings with Justice, Kings without Justice: An Early Medieval Paradox," *La giustizia nell'alto medioevo (secoli IX–XI)*, 802. Late antique and Merovingian sources had complained about the crisis of justice in Gaul. See Marie-Bernadette Brugières, "Réflexions sur la crise de la justice en Occident à la fin de l'Antiquité: L'apport de la littérature," *La giustizia nell'alto medioevo (secoli V–VIII)*, 165–218.

take, Theodulf contrasted the surging waters of Acheron with the pleasant calm of Paradise.[32]

Bonhom's ideas about judging were neither especially sophisticated nor strikingly original. But in the broader context of early medieval writing about judges, his work is significant. A couple of Carolingian churchmen had reflected on the responsibilities of judges and the dangers of judicial corruption, but few earlier law codes devoted the degree of attention to judging that Bonhom did. The *Visigothic Code* provided a number of rules describing judicial responsibilities and prerogatives, rules which influenced Bonhom and his colleagues, but most codes gave only scanty treatment to the duties and responsibilities of judges. The *Laws of the Salian Franks* and the *Burgundian Code* instruct that corrupt judges were to be punished, but offer little insight into how judges were appointed or the range of their responsibilities. The *Lombard Laws* offer only slightly more guidance, tracing a range of duties that judges performed (adjudicating disputes, investigating runaway slaves, issuing passports) and stipulating penalties for those who judged contrary to the law.[33] On the Iberian Peninsula, some early *fueros* (municipal charters) refer to judges, but in general they say little about the appointment, responsibilities, or social position of judges.[34] The *Usatges of Barcelona* merely repeated a Carolingian capitulary stating the judges should judge fairly.[35] The Aragonese *Vidal Mayor* expresses concerns about bribery and prohibits judges from accepting payments, gifts, or jewels for rendering justice.[36]

A thorough treatment of how judges should be appointed and how they should hear cases would wait until the thirteenth-century *Siete Partidas*, which included an extensive section on the duties of judges and arbitrators. This Alfonsine code established serious punishments for overstepping judicial authority and required that judges recuse themselves from criminal cases involving members of their own family or cases involving their own property.[37] The numerous rules about judging in *Siete Partidas* placed less emphasis on the social responsibilities and empathy than had Bonhom. Judges

---

32. *Versus Teudulfi*, lines 9–14.

33. Katherine Fischer Drew, trans., *The Lombard Laws* (Philadelphia, 1973) 157, 164.

34. The late twelfth-century *Fuero de Cuenca* spells out the duties of *iudices* who acted as heads of municipal government. See *The Code of Cuenca: Municipal Law on the Twelfth-Century Castilian Frontier*, ed. James F. Powers (Philadelphia, 2000), 5–6, 109–14.

35. *The Usatges of Barcelona: The Fundamental Law of Catalonia*, trans. Donald Kagay (Philadelphia, 1994), 99.

36. Gunnar Tilander, ed. *Vidal Mayor: Traducción Aragonesa de la Obra* in excelsis dei thesauris *de Vidal de Canellas*, Leges Hispanicae Medii Aevi VI, 3 vols. (Lund, 1956), II, 2.

37. *Las Siete Partidas*, trans. Samuel Parsons Scott, ed. Robert I. Burns (Philadelphia, 2001), III, IV, ix; III, IV, x.

might at times take pity, but they should avoid becoming emotionally entangled with those who appeared before them. They should not, for example, be moved by weeping plaintiffs.[38]

In other words, although Bonhom's preface was rudimentary, it was still an impressive accomplishment. Few law codes described in any depth the role of the *iudex*, and even fewer practicing judges attempted to do so. Bonhom's compendium shows that eleventh-century judges thought carefully about the nature of judicial authority and the special responsibilities of those who administered justice. In the context of tenth- and eleventh-century courts, the chief importance of Bonhom's work is that it shows that judges articulated a sense of their professional identity—an identity that involved a spiritual component and a sense of special social responsibilities. Judges had, in other words, particular and weighty responsibilities derived both from Scripture and from written law. The portrait of the judge Bonhom paints is an idealized one. Many disputants did not see judges in such a positive light. It does, however, show that judges like Bonhom identified how judges *ought* to behave and strove to articulate a professional identity closely related both to the written law of the *Visigothic Code* and to Scripture.

BONHOM AND HIS COLLEAGUES

Bonhom's manuscript affords a window into the legal imagination of the early eleventh century. Alone, it would be enough to establish a place for Bonhom as an example of the activities of learned legal professionals during a period when judges of this sort were uncommon. Bonhom was not, however, a disengaged student of justice. His reflections are all the more compelling because, like Theodulf before him, Bonhom based his work on his experiences as a practicing judge. Bonhom left an ample record of his work in the tumult of the courtroom as well as in the quiet of the scriptorium. Between roughly 980 and 1024, Bonhom's name appears in 120 documents from several different locations, including the cathedral at Vic, the monastery of Sant Cugat, the comital palace in Barcelona, the cathedral in Barcelona, and the abbey of Sant Pere de les Puelles. He probably received his earliest training at Vic. After several years in Sant Cugat's scriptorium, he moved to Barcelona in 994 where he was intimately connected to both the comital and episcopal courts. During the course of his career, he prepared and witnessed donations, exchanges, sales, and testaments. He even expressed his reserva-

38. *Siete Partidas*, III, IV, xiii.

tions about the nominal sovereignty of Frankish kings in Catalonia.[39] And, of course, he adjudicated disputes.

Bonhom's career is impressive, but it was not unique. Many other judges enjoyed similar careers. Pons Bonfill Marc of Barcelona was born in the late tenth century, the son of a noted judge, Ervig Marc. From the 990s until 1010, the senior judge served the count and countess of Barcelona and the counts of Cerdanya. Given Ervig's success and his connections, it is hardly surprising that his son Pons would want to follow in his footsteps. Although it is usually impossible to gain thorough information about judges' families, the careers of Ervig Marc and Pons Bonfill Marc suggest that the profession of judging ran in families. In another family, two brothers became judges.[40] The younger Pons first appeared as *clericus* in a 1010 dispute involving the monastery of Sant Cugat.[41] He was trained in Barcelona, benefiting from the expertise of judges like Bonhom. Over the course of three decades, he appeared as a judge throughout Catalonia. Like his father, he enjoyed particularly close ties with Barcelona's cathedral chapter and the comital court, where he became a close advisor to Countess Ermessenda. Between 1010 and 1033, Pons heard at least twelve disputes. By 1024, Pons's expertise commanded a significant honorarium. Bishop Ermengol of Urgell awarded him 300 solidi (an amount far exceeding the 20 solidi allowed by the *Code*) for his part in "bringing [the case] to legitimate ends, with the help of God."[42] References to payments to judges were rare, but fees of this sort must have been an especially attractive feature of the profession. Such payments provoked the concern of judges like Bonhom who, in one of his several discussions of how greed distorted justice, cautioned judges against thinking too much about comfort in this life rather than salvation in the next.[43]

One of Pons's colleagues had a long career similar in many respects to his own. Guifré of Vic first appeared as a judge in the same dispute in which Pons made his judicial debut. Like Pons, Guifré adjudicated disputes (at least thir-

39. Anscari Mundó, "La datació de documents pel rei Robert (966–1031) a Catalunya," *Anuario de Estudios Medievales* 4 (1967): 13–34; and idem., "El jutge Bonsom de Barcelona," 281.

40. *Oliba* 130; and *Marca* 204. Jane Martindale identifies an example of two judges coming from the same family during the same period in western France in "'His Special Friend' Dispute Settlement and Political Power within the French Kingdom from the Tenth to the Twelfth Centuries," *Transactions of the Royal Historical Society*, 6th series, 5 (hereafter *TRHS*) (1995), 45.

41. *Sant Cugat* 437. See also José María Font Rius, "Entorn de la figura de Ponç Bofill Marc Jutge comtal de Barcelona, a les primeres del segle XI," *Boletim da Faculdade de Direito* 58 (1982): 377–95.

42. *Urgellia* 390.

43. Escorial z.II.2, f. 2v.

teen of them between 1010 and 1039) and witnessed documents in several different places. Although the two judges frequently worked together, Guifré's career centered in the areas surrounding Vic and Urgell, while Pons always maintained his close ties to Barcelona. When Guifré died in 1039 after more than three decades as a judge, he left a detailed testament, which was solemnly published in Vic's cathedral in the presence of two of his former colleagues (Adalbert and Gerald), the entire chapter, and Bishop Oliba. He left the bulk of his estate, which included houses, vineyards, alods, and tithes, to his sons. His widow and their daughters also received bequests. Some cows and a quantity of premium wine were to be sold to pay his funeral expenses. Guifré's testament also included an impressive list of movable goods, including overcoats, silverware, leather garments, a very fine cape, a cotton shirt, a fur coat, animal hides, a felt mattress, and a number of unidentified books. Given his frequent references to Visigothic law, it is not unlikely that at least one of these was a copy of the *Visigothic Code*.[44] Guifré left his best mule to Bishop Oliba, asking the bishop to ensure that his bequests to his children would be scrupulously honored. The solemnity of the proceedings, the splendor of the bequests, and the range of beneficiaries all reflect Guifré's wealth and his importance in the community.

Bonhom, Guifré, and Pons Bonfill Marc were surrounded by a host of other judges whose careers testify to the sophistication of courts in this region and to the importance of professional judges in adjudicating disputes. Between the late 1020s and the 1050s, Judge Adalbert appeared in more than a dozen transactions. In addition to approving sales, he heard a number of disputes and executed Guifré's testament.[45] Judge Arnau participated in the adjudication of three disputes and attended the dedication of a new basilica at Ripoll along with three other judges.[46] There were two judges named Bernat, one active in Rousillon in the first part of the eleventh century and the other around Girona in the 1070s and 1080s.[47] Renard's advocate during the dispute over the tithes of Aiguatèbia, Sendred of Cerdanya, had a similarly productive career. A Judge Guisad worked in Barcelona in the 1030s and 1040s, occasionally hearing disputes but apparently focusing his energies

44. *Oliba* 137. Tenth-century bequests occasionally included copies of the *Code*. See, for example, *Cartulaire roussillonais*, ed. B. Alart (Perpignan 1880), 12; For Guifré's role in the administration of episcopal castles, see Kosto, *Making Agreements*, 186.

45. *Oliba* 130; *Notes hist.* 545; *Oliba* 154; *Santa Cecília* 184; and *Notes hist.* 678.

46. *Oliba* 83; *Urgellia* 425; *Urgellia* 427; *Oliba* 104; *Urgellia* 530.

47. For the earlier Bernat, see *Oliba* 100; *HGL* 193; and *Oliba* 154. For the later Bernat, see *Girona* 143; Jesús Alturo i Perucho, *L'arxiu antic de Santa Anna de Barcelona del 942 al 1200 (Aproximació històrico-lingüística)*, 3 vols. (Barcelona, 1985) (hereafter *Santa Anna*), 114; BNF coll. Baluze 116, f. 169; and *Girona* 148.

on probate.[48] Judges Isarn, Marc, Miro, Oliba, Per, Ramon, Salomon, Seniofred, Vivas, and Guitard all appear in a half dozen or more transactions during the tenth and eleventh centuries. These were among the most productive, but their labor was shared by many others who also witnessed testaments, approved sales, and adjudicated disputes.

References to judges in records usually concentrate on the performance of professional activities. Records of sales or judicial assemblies usually afford little insight into the personal or social lives of the judges who participated. But occasionally documents offer stray details about other aspects of judges' lives. The bequests recorded in Judge Guifré's testament, for example, hint at his economic and social position. Other judges apparently enjoyed similar prosperity. Many were active in buying, selling, and trading land. Judge Borrell, for example, participated in the resolution of several disputes between 979 and 1013.[49] During the same years, he also engaged in wide-ranging economic activity, buying and selling different properties and exhibiting a keen interest in mills.[50] Judge Teudisclus constructed and held a tower, which eventually passed into the possession of the cathedral of Barcelona.[51] Judge Orús of Barcelona also bought and sold property. In 1008, he was involved in exchanges of property with both the bishop of Barcelona and the bishop of Girona, a pair of transactions which suggest both the judge's wealth and the lofty position of those with whom he did business.[52] In 1014, shortly after his death, Orús's widow and children were involved in a dispute over a property which the judge had cultivated and developed.[53] Judge Adalbert and his wife purchased property, made donations with their children, and, in one case, received a generous gift.[54] The gift was not apparently tied to any litigation be-

48. ACA Berenguer Ramon I, 97; *Notes hist.* 500; *Notes hist.* 504; ACA Ramon Berenguer 40; ACA Ramon Berenguer 54; Arxiu de la Catedral de Barcelona (hereafter ACB), Lib. Ant. IV, f. 155, d. 365.

49. *Diplomatari de la Catedral de Barcelona: Documents dels anys 844–1260*, ed. Àngel Fàbrega i Grau, vol. 1 (Barcelona 1995) (hereafter *Barcelona*), 201; *Sant Cugat* 317; and *Sant Cugat* 438.

50. *Diplomatari de la Catedral de Vic, segles IX–X*, ed. Eduard Junyent i Subirà (hereafter *Vic*), 455; and ACA Monacals Sant Llorenç del Munt 27, 41, 42, 54, 64. The boundary clause of another record noted Judge Borrell as a property-holder. See ACA Ramon Borrell 90.

51. ACB Lib. Ant. II, f. 106, doc. 324.

52. ACB Lib. Ant. I, f. 112, doc. 277; ACB Lib. Ant. II, f. 99, doc. 306; and *Notes hist.* 245, 266. In 1002, Judge Orús sold land and a vineyard near Barcelona. *Diplomatari de la cartoixa de Montalegre (segles X–XII)*, ed. Pérez i Xavier Gómez (Barcelona, 1998), 21.

53. Francesch Carreras i Candi, "Lo Monjuích de Barcelona," *Memorias de la Real Academia de Buenas Letras de Barcelona* 8 (1906): 197–450, 321, no. 252. Orús's widow, Maria, was mentioned the same year in another document, ACA Ramon Borrell 108.

54. ACA Ramon Berenguer I 90, 97, 123.

fore the judge, but one cannot help but remember Bonhom's concerns about the gifts that litigants showered upon judges.

There were, of course, significant differences between judges like Pons Bonfill Marc or Bonhom, who worked in Barcelona's comital court, and more obscure judges like Riculf, who made a single appearance in a record from Béziers, or Sesuldus whose career may have been limited to witnessing a single donation.[55] Some judges left ample records of distinguished careers and of their own financial dealings; other judges had more modest careers. Despite these differences, judges were, as a class, rich. They often bought, sold, and traded large pieces of property. They accumulated significant estates that included both land and movable goods. Many judges were also closely tied not only to comital and episcopal courts, but to counts and bishops themselves. Some spent much of their time in the entourage of counts or bishops. Judges not only advised lay and secular magnates on questions of law, they were also intimate advisors and business partners.

It is hard to know how Bonhom would have responded to the apparent financial comfort of his peers on the bench or whether that taste for comfort and the enterprising spirit of these judges ever slid into a dangerous greed. Their training, their wealth, and their positions made them very influential, but such achievements were always accompanied by the snares and temptations Bonhom mapped out for aspiring judges. Occupying these positions of power, they were subject to the manifold dangers so carefully described by Theodulf and Bonhom.

JUDGES IN COURT

Judges were distinguished by training in Visigothic law, by their wealth, and by their connections. The many references to judges afford a glimpse of their personal, economic, and social lives, but the richest descriptions of judges focus on what they did in court. Although records offer only tentative and fragmentary information about judges' families and friendships, they provide

55. *Béziers* 54; and *Solsona* 11. M. Carmen del Camino Martínez suggests that some judges in remote Pallars were not comfortable writing, unlike Bonhom and his urban associates. See "Notas sobra la escritura en Pallars en el siglo XI," *Actas del Congreso Internacional 'Historia de los Pireneos' Cervera, 1988*, vol. 2, Historia Medieval, Moderna, y Contemporanea (Madrid, 1991), 94. For a more positive account of the literacy of judges in this area, see Pierre Bonnassie and Jean-Pascal Illy, "Le clergé paroissal aux IXe–Xe siècles dans les Pyrénées orientales et centrales," in *Le Clergé rural dans l'Europe médiévale et moderne*, ed. Pierre Bonnassie (Toulouse, 1995), 153–66.

more complete descriptions of what judges did when people appeared before them to fight over property. Judges' activities in court are dealt with at greater length in subsequent chapters, but some preliminary observations are appropriate here.

Bonhom's preface on judging is the richest expression of how eleventh-century judges understood their work, but fragmentary descriptions of judicial activity in other records shed additional light. Diplomatic records generally favor the concrete over the abstract, devoting their attention to particular pieces of property in particular transactions rather than to explorations of how judges should perform their job, but occasionally scribes included descriptions of how judges understood their position and whence they enjoyed their authority. The decision in a 1002 dispute issued by three judges began: ". . . we find it written in the opinions of the early Fathers that a judge should compose a written judgment about any contested issue, and should seal it with his hand, lest in the future anyone should bring up this conflict again."[56] These judges expressed their sense of the role they played in resolving conflicts and their conviction that judges should consider the long-term prospects of the decisions they issued. In two different decisions, Judge Pons Bonfill Marc stressed the importance of trying to ensure that the settlements reached in court would remain unchallenged: "Since it is agreed that appointed judges are the source of solutions, it is considered just that the orders of judges be especially recorded, lest in the future some dispute arise from doubt about how the case of business should be brought to legitimate ends."[57] Another judge stressed that disputants had a duty to honor the authority of judges.[58]

Given the status of the *Visigothic Code*, it is not surprising that many judges defined their role with language drawn from the *Code*. The *Code* defined a *iudex* as someone, "sent to direct cases and to determine the outcome of suits according to the laws," and judges from Agde to Urgell to Sant Cugat incorporated this passage, or portions of it, into their signatures.[59] Short references like these do not, of course, articulate notions of justice and law in the same way that Bonhom's prologue does, but even these fragmentary claims give a sense of how judges formulated ideas about their professional duties. Judges saw themselves as playing a central role in resolving conflicts, making peace, and formulating stable agreements.

56. *Viage*, 13, 22.
57. *Sant Cugat* 529. See also ACB Lib. Ant. III, f. 6, doc. 15.
58. *Marca* 204.
59. *Leges Visigothorum*, II.2.5. See, for example, *HGL* 57; *Agde* 323; *Béziers* 14; *Sant Cugat* 139; *Viage* 13, 20; *Urgellia* 539.

In addition to intervening in moments of crisis, judges also performed routine legal transactions, such as approving donations, sales, and exchanges. They ensured that testaments conformed to Visigothic rules. They were consulted about the establishment and management of the growing number of castles in Catalonia. They witnessed the dedications and consecrations of churches and cathedrals. When a Barcelona woman was concerned because she had lost some documents related to her property, she sought professional advice from Judge Orús.[60]

Some judges specialized in certain types of transactions. Guifré, for example, was almost exclusively involved in settling property disputes. Pons Bonfill Marc, on the other hand, participated in more than seventy transactions from the 1010s to the 1030s which included disputes, sales, exchanges, testaments, and other types of transactions. More than once he served as a sort of appeal judge.[61] Orús of Barcelona, after returning from captivity in Córdoba, became an expert on legal aspects of relations between Christian Barcelona and Muslim Córdoba. He worked to secure the release of Christian captives still in al-Andalus. Around 1000, he composed a document for the Count of Barcelona supporting the count's right to sell the property of Jews of Barcelona who had died in captivity.[62]

Judges often worked in a number of different places. Bonhom's career, divided between Vic and Barcelona, is a good example. Judges were often closely tied to cathedrals, monasteries, or comital courts, but their professional duties often required them to travel. Adalbert worked both in Girona and near Barcelona.[63] Judge Borrell appeared in documents related to the see of Vic, the monastery of San Llorenç del Munt, the see of Barcelona, the monastery of Sant Pau del Camp, and the monastery of Sant Cugat.[64] Dacho worked in Vic and Urgell.[65] Judge Solomon worked near Vic and throughout Roussillon.[66] Renard's advocate, Judge Sendred, worked throughout Cerdanya. The frequent movement of judges to hear cases is noteworthy for several reasons. Even though judicial expertise was concentrated in certain densely populated areas—Barcelona and Vic, for example—the movement of judges made this expertise more widely available.

The itinerance of judges strengthened the professional ties throughout

60. *Barcelona* 72.
61. *Sant Cugat* 512; *Sant Cugat* 527.
62. ACA Ramon Borrell 45.
63. *Girona* 8; *Notes hist.* 678.
64. *Vic* 455; *Barcelona* 201; ACA Monacals Sant Llorenç del Munt 41, 45; *Lavaix* 3; BNF coll. Moreau 18, ff. 134–36; *Sant Cugat* 438.
65. *Vic* 465; Arxiu Capitular de Vic (hereafter ACV) Calaix, 6, 1303; *Urgellia* 278.
66. *Cart. Rous* 25, 26, 32; *Oliba* 76, 77, 78, 87, 130; *Solsona* 54; *Guissona* 1.

the region. Disputes were often adjudicated by panels of two or three judges. The length of some judicial careers, regular travel, and frequent collaboration allowed judges to build close working relationships with their colleagues. Guifré and Pons Bonfill Marc, for example, adjudicated disputes together on seven different occasions.[67] Such partnerships might be close and long-lasting, but they were not exclusive. In addition to working closely with Marc, Guifré also witnessed transactions or heard disputes with other judges, including Adalbert, Orús, Bonhom, Dacho, Borrell, Vivas, and Salomon. During more than two decades of judging, Adalbert worked with Pons Bonfill Marc, Vivas, Salomon, Guisad, Ramon, and Per. The abundance of legal expertise deployed in eleventh-century courts was not the result of individual judges working in isolation, but rather of the frequent interaction of a great number of judges working closely with one another.

Although many judges traveled, their distribution throughout the Province of Narbonne was uneven. Lézat's cartulary, from the northwest perimeter of the province, contains records of disputes which refer to written law and to formal processes of adjudication, but does not contain a single reference to a professional judge.[68] In stark contrast stands Sant Cugat's cartulary, in which fourteen out of twenty disputes between 985 and 1060 involved professional judges. Fifteen of the twenty-two cases recorded in the see of Urgell's cartulary involved professional judges. At Vic during the eleventh century, six of eleven cases were heard by judges.[69] Barcelona was, as Bonhom and others attest, particularly well endowed with professional judges, but judges flourished in Vic, Urgell, and Girona as well.

The nature of this corps of judges changed over time. The network of dynamic, learned judges represented by Bonhom flourished during the first three decades of the eleventh century. Of those judges whose careers can be traced through more than a half dozen transactions, all were active between 995 and 1035. During the second half of the eleventh century, fewer judges studied written law, fewer adjudicated disputes, and fewer worked collaboratively. Judges remained an important feature of the legal landscape during the latter part of the eleventh century, but they were less well trained and less closely connected to one another than they had been during the first decades of the century. Judges continued to adjudicate disputes, but after 1040 the impressive regional network deteriorated.[70]

67. *Notes hist.* 344, 345; *Oliba* 89, 104,
68. In one case, the abbot and the rectors of the monastery had a record that they felt entitled them to a certain property. They brought the document to some *iudices*, but from the context it seems clear that these were nonprofessional mediators. *Lézat* 1295.
69. Freedman, *Diocese of Vic,* 118.
70. I discuss these changes in chapter 9 below.

Judges cultivated a professional identity in society. Once earned, the title *iudex* remained with its bearer even when he was not sitting in court. Bonhom, Orús, Guifré, and Pons Bonfill Marc were referred to as *iudices* not only when they heard cases but also when they bought and sold property. In a handful of cases, judges were mentioned not in relation to their judicial position but in relation to other members of their families. Bonadona, for example, was identified in one transaction as the daughter of Judge Bonhom and his wife Widella.[71] When they assessed written proofs, judges were particularly impressed by earlier transactions that had been drafted or approved by other judges.[72]

The judges of this region differed in important ways from most of their European contemporaries. They frequently (if selectively) relied on written law for rules about property, inheritance, proof, and testamentary procedure. They even appealed to written law to justify their own judicial power. When they adjudicated disputes, they depended on their collective expertise. They sought the opinions of fellow judges and of prominent or knowledgeable members of the community. They strove to forge lasting agreements among disputing parties, and they were confident that enduring agreements were those formulated in conformity with written rules and scrupulously recorded. Judges valued compromise and mutual agreement, but these took second place to law and procedural rigor.

The vitality and coherence of the judiciary is doubtless one of the reasons that so many property disputes in the Province of Narbonne were processed by formal courts. Compromise decisions, informal mediators, and out-of-court settlements played smaller roles in negotiating conflict here than in many places. Several factors contributed to the stability of these courts. The region's comital and vicecomital dynasties presided over the courts that provided an institutional framework in which judges practiced their profession. The frequent cooperation of bishops and counts (discussed in the next chapter) further strengthened judicial assemblies. Connections among the region's judges and their ties to major property-holding chapters and monasteries allowed judges to rely on each other for advice and support. The widespread and enduring enthusiasm for Visigothic law afforded an authoritative ideological foundation for elements of judicial practice.

All of this is indeed impressive, but the presence of legal professionals applying a written law is no guarantee of stability or fairness. It is difficult to gauge the degree to which daily judicial practice corresponded to the lofty ideals expressed by Bonhom and his colleagues. At times, the image of judges

71. ACA Ramon Berenguer I 70.
72. ACA Ramon Borrell 114.

in records pursued a life apart from the actions of actual judges. The role of judges shifted during the eleventh century, but there was no corresponding adjustment in the impressive epithets drawn from the *Visigothic Code*. Despite their frequent invocations of the *Code*, judges' decisions often drew on several different legal and normative traditions. Finally, judges were particularly effective at serving the desires of the powerful rather than protecting widows, orphans, and the poor, as Bonhom and Theodulf argued judges should. The rules from the *Code* they cited most frequently were those that afforded important advantages to large property-holding institutions. Their interpretations of Visigothic law tended to favor monasteries and cathedral chapters over widows and orphans. Just as some property-holders viewed rules from the *Visigothic Code* as unjust or irrelevant, some property-holders were skeptical of the justice dispensed by professional judges.[73] Some distrusted professional judges and saw their expertise as sophistry. Bonhom's manuscript can show us something of how judges thought about and presented their profession, but it should not persuade us that judges were always especially kind to orphans or that Bonhom's colleagues were always fiercely resistant to the bribes which they were certainly offered.

Judges did not always meet the high moral standards to which they were urged by Bonhom, but, if we are to believe their own accounts, some judges tried tirelessly to do so. Occasionally, even the energetic Bonhom admitted fatigue. He added a notation apologizing for the sloppy appearance of his document and for the numerous characters that he had crossed out. Recalling the words of Psalm 131, Bonhom explained that his eyes had been oppressed with sleep.[74]

73. See chapter 8 for a discussion of disputants who rejected or resisted settlements.

74. *Sant Cugat* 267; Bonhom, recalling Psalm 131:4, apologizes that the document appears "cum litteras rasas et superpositas in diversis locis, quia occupati era oculi mei somno et palebre mee dormitacione."

CHAPTER FOUR
COURTS AND THE
ADMINISTRATION OF JUSTICE

COUNTS, COUNTESSES, AND BISHOPS

Property-holders in the Province of Narbonne usually sought to resolve their differences in judicial assemblies that involved dozens of people from great magnates to crowds of peasants. Judges' investigations and decisions dominate the accounts of disputes in surviving records, but other officials and members of the community played important roles. In this chapter, I turn to the courts in which disputants fought and judges judged, examining the roles played by magnates, low-level officials, and *boni homines*.

When judges listened to the petitions of disputants, they were usually acting under the authority of lay and ecclesiastic lords, often counts and bishops. Judges articulated a notion of their own competence based on their knowledge of written law, but they enjoyed the authority to judge because they were appointed to do so. In the dispute in 1011 between the monastery of Sant Cugat and Geribert (see chapter 1), the monastery's abbot brought his complaint before a judicial assembly:

> ... the abbot ... rose up with documents and the claims of the blessed Cugat, and took his complaint into the city of Barcelona, to the palace and the court of the prince [Count Ramon Borrell] and his wife, where there were many great men and bishops (Deusdé, bishop of Barcelona, Borrell, bishop of Vic, and Pere, bishop of Girona), in order to petition and accuse Geribert and his brothers. Several judges were also there: Guillem of Girona and Guifré of Vic, whom the count had ordered to examine the case.[1]

1. *Sant Cugat* 439.

The count and countess listened to petitioners in the comital palace surrounded by their followers and by the judges they appointed to adjudicate disputes. The by-now familiar Judge Guifré of Vic and his colleague, Judge Guillem, heard the complaint and evaluated competing claims at the behest of the count and countess. Counts, countesses, and bishops presided over judicial assemblies and were the ultimate sources of their authority. The counts and countesses of Barcelona most often presided over these assemblies in the comital palace in Barcelona.[2] The great gatherings of comital courts took place at least two or three times a year and lasted several days. These assemblies probably discharged a range of military, fiscal, and diplomatic functions, but surviving records describe only the lawsuits that were adjudicated.[3] Just as Abbot Guitard brought complaints to Barcelona's comital court, other disputants sought justice at the courts of the counts and countesses of Urgell, Cerdanya, and Carcassonne.[4] Disputants often sought justice at the count's residence or bishop's palace, but even well-established courts were quasi-itinerant. The counts and countesses of Barcelona presided over assemblies in Barcelona's cathedral, at the cathedral church of Saint Peter in Vic, and at Sant Cugat.[5] Occasionally, hearings took place at or near disputed properties. This proximity presumably made it easier to gather information about the properties and to identify knowledgeable witnesses.[6] Some assemblies took place when magnates had gathered for important occasions, such as for the dedication of a church or for a saint's feast.[7]

Aggrieved disputants sought help wherever counts, countesses, and bishops held court. They brought their *altercatio* (disagreement) to the court's attention and asked the count, countess, bishop, assembled magnates and judges to investigate their claims. Some disputes were resolved quickly, with judges and magnates issuing decisions in a single hearing. In other cases, investigations into conflicting claims required more time, and hearings could drag on for days or months, as in the dispute over the tithes of Aiguatèbia. Some petitioners requested the court's attention several times before their complaint received a hearing.[8] In some cases, a petitioner's initial complaint

2. *Barcelona* 201; *Barcelona* 345; *Sant Cugat* 437; *Sant Cugat* 464; ACB Lib. Ant. IV, f. 110, d. 279.

3. Bonnassie, *Catalogne*, 182.

4. *Solsona* 23; *Viage* 13, 23; *Urgellia* 390; *Viage* 13, 22; *HGL* 175; *Marca* 232.

5. For judicial assemblies elsewhere, see *Urgellia* 278; *Viage* 6, 20; ACB Lib. Ant. IV, f. 110, d. 279; ACA Berenguer Ramon 22; *Oliba* 64.

6. ACA Berenguer Ramon 13; *Sant Cugat* 479; *Urgellia* 372; *Oliba* 95.

7. *Barcelona* 224; *Urgellia* 416.

8. BNF Moreau 20, ff. 165–76; *Sant Cugat* 612.

led only to an agreement to hold a judicial assembly at a later date.[9] Some litigants requested delays in order to gather the proofs necessary to support their cases.

The idea that it was a count's duty to administer justice was a Carolingian legacy. The model of a public tribunal (*mallus publicus*) presided over by a count was one of the more enduring Carolingian administrative innovations and one whose afterlife is clearly apparent in this region. The role of the count as president of judicial assemblies is reflected in records of hearings and in other texts. The mortuary roll of Count Bernat Tallaferro, for example, praised the count for his fair judging.[10] A few year's earlier, Oliba of Vic wrote a poem honoring Count Ramon Borell in which he described the count as *iustus iudicio*.[11] Judge Bonhom was thinking of the count of Barcelona when, in his copy of the *Visigothic Code*, he described the prince's duty to appoint judges. Counts and justice were closely related in the legal imagination of the region.

Judges at times described how they were appointed. Judge Sendred, for example, noted that his authority to resolve a 1025 dispute was derived from both Visigothic law and from a comital commission: "I, Judge Sendred, accept these proofs, according to the order of the law and by the direction of my lord, Count Guifré."[12] Fifteen years later, the same judge articulated a similar understanding of his right to judge disputes: "I, Sendred, judge by order of the countess and by legal command contained in the *Liber Iudicum*."[13] On different occasions, the counts of Urgell and Barcelona both appointed Pons Bonfill Marc to hear cases, a testament not only to the comital responsibility for appointing judges but also to this particular judge's high reputation.[14] Many counts had resident judges in their retinues. Judge Arnau was a member of the court of Count Ermengol II of Urgell, and the Count of Besalú traveled with a judge to hear disputes.[15]

Although the comital responsibility for presiding over judicial assemblies was widely understood, in practice courts assumed many different forms. Most assemblies took place under the auspices of combined presidencies, in which two or more counts, countesses, viscounts, and bishops took part. Just as judges evaluated evidence in teams, so too were courts usually held in the

9. *Urgellia* 278; *Oliba* 130.

10. *Oliba,* "Textos Literaris," 9.

11. *Oliba,* "Textos Literaris," 1.

12. *Urgellia* 398.

13. *Urgellia* 539.

14. *Urgellia* 390; *Guissona* 2. "Qui iussus atque informatus a principe et a primatibus patrie est dirimere causas." *Sant Cugat* 529.

15. *Urgellia* 425; APO Fonds Fossa 12J24, no. 11.

presence of groups of lay and ecclesiastic magnates. The authority of counts and countesses was complemented by that of the other notables who attended. The bishop of Urgell sought justice in Barcelona's comital court in 1002, and his suit was heard by the count, countess, and the bishop of Barcelona.[16] In 1017, a woman brought a suit against Sant Cugat in an assembly presided over by the count and countess of Barcelona, the bishops of Vic and Barcelona, the viscount of Barcelona, two judges, and several magnates.[17] The countesses of Carcassonne, Barcelona, and Cerdanya presided over judicial assemblies with their sons and other *optimates*.[18] A case involving the monastery of Ripoll was heard by the count and countess of Barcelona, the count of Urgell, the archbishop of Narbonne, the bishop of Urgell, the bishop of Vic, the bishop of Barcelona, two viscounts, and a number of other notables.[19] In some cases, bishops, usually accompanied by canons and judges, presided over courts.[20] Counts, and to a lesser extent bishops, thus had a widely recognized responsibility for the administration of justice. Alone and in groups, lay and ecclesiastic magnates were expected to organize judicial assemblies, appoint judges, gather *boni homines*, and resolve the complaints of aggrieved property-holders. This responsibility was widely recognized, but the composition of assemblies was never rigidly defined.

Just as the composition of these courts was fluid, so too were their competencies. At first glance, the variety of comital, episcopal, and vicecomital courts seems like a hopelessly complicated tangle of overlapping competencies and jurisdictions. With such a profusion of different courts and the lack of any clear guidelines, it is not always obvious why a particular case was heard by one assembly rather than another.

Only rarely did the authority of a particular assembly or its president become the subject of controversy. In 899, the archbishop of Narbonne complained to Charles the Simple about a practice that he claimed was becoming common in his diocese. The archbishop deplored the fact that counts and their judges were hearing more cases involving clerics in comital courts.[21] In the final decades of the eleventh century, churchmen again strove to limit the jurisdiction of lay courts over the clergy. But between the time of the arch-

16. *Urgellia* 278.
17. *Sant Cugat* 464.
18. *HGL* 161; *Marca* 143; *Urgellia* 493. For other cases in which counts heard cases together with viscounts or bishops, see ACA Borrell II 14; *Viage* 15, 34; *Barcelona* 345; BNF coll. Moreau 18, f. 160; *Oliba* 56; *Sant Cugat* 437; *Sant Cugat* 452.
19. *Viage* 6, 20.
20. *Barcelona* 274; *HGL* 158; *Oliba* 22, 99, 105.
21. Magnou Nortier, *Société laïque*, 283.

bishop of Narbonne's complaint and discussions about jurisdiction informed by the impulses of the Gregorian Reform nearly two hundred years later, there were few attempts to distinguish neatly the competencies of different courts. During much of the tenth and eleventh centuries, bishops and abbots submitted without hesitation to the authority of comital courts.[22] Disputes between lay people were frequently adjudicated in episcopal courts.[23] Apparently, litigants and judges were not troubled by the many different configurations of magnates that presided over judicial hearings.

The boundaries between different courts were fluid and ill-defined, but they were not without occasional tensions. A 990 case in Barcelona involved a conflict between the count's right to judge and the bishop's right to judge. Sindared, the *custus monete*, or keeper of the mint, brought a complaint to Count Borrell's court. The count was surrounded by the bishop of Barcelona, the bishop of Girona, some of the count's nobles, and a group of *boni homines*. The presence of such a group was, the scribe noted, customary when the count administered justice. Sindared accused a cleric of having produced counterfeit coins:

> When he heard this case, the count, not hesitating, wanted to exercise justice immediately, as is customary, in order to snatch away the discovered evil and prevent any future [wrong] from being done. Hearing this, the lord bishop who was present, claiming the count's mercy so that [the count] should observe [the bishop's] *honor* [authority and privileges], to which the bishop had recently succeeded by royal appointment, as in the royal orders, that no one but the bishop of the church should constrain inhabitants of the church's land. The lord count, hearing his speech, freely said: "I have observed and will continue to observe the *honor* of your see. I want to have the power to constrain priests, as was done with your predecessors. This much I want so that justice might not suffer, but will be pursued in this manner.[24]

The bishop seems to have believed that the count was overstepping his legitimate authority because the alleged wrongdoer was a cleric. The bishop's concern is notable, but what is perhaps more striking is the effortlessness with which the count dismissed the bishop's protest. The newly appointed bishop had, it seems, yet to grasp the range of the count's powers. In 1023, a similar argument about the legal separateness of the clergy was more per-

22. *Urgellia* 390; *Viage* 15, 34; Josep M. Salrach, "Práticas judiciales, transformación social y acción política en Cataluña (siglos IX–XIII)," *Hispania* 57 (1997): 1012.

23. Federico Udina Martorell, *El archivo Condal de Barcelona en los siglos ix–x: Estudio crítico de sus fondos* (Barcelona, 1951) (hereafter *Archivo Condal*), 207; *Urgellia* 380. See also Bonnassie's discussion in *Catalogne*, 182–85.

24. *Barcelona* 201.

suasive, when a cleric accused of murder argued successfully that his case belonged in an ecclesiastic rather than in a comital court.[25]

In 1024, the canons of the see of Urgell claimed that a property dispute in which they were involved should not be heard by the count of Urgell's court, because it was a secular tribunal. They supported their claim to immunity from comital judgment by appealing to canons from the sixth-century Council of Orléans: "The clergy are to be judged in the audience of the bishop, not by secular judges, for it is contrary to divine law (*fas*) that the divine should be subject to the judgment of the secular. It is also stated in the Council of Orléans that churches should remain in the power of the bishop in whose territory they are."[26] Such careful citation of a rarely used source of written law reflects considerable research on the part of these litigants. The canons' assertion seems like a forerunner of the type of claims about the autonomy of ecclesiastic property that would become increasingly common in the latter part of the eleventh century. But if the canons seem at first blush like Gregorians *avant la lettre*, their subsequent behavior makes their motivations in the case more difficult to understand. Despite their unequivocal and carefully supported resistance to adjudication in the count's court, the same canons argued a different case the following year in the same comital court without protest.[27]

The claims made by the canons regarding the legal separateness of the clergy are interesting, but they are also exceptional. Their swift retreat from the position so carefully argued a year earlier suggests that their argument was more an attempt to influence the outcome of a particular case than an indication of the chapter's ongoing commitment to the legal autonomy of ecclesiastical property.

The few cases in which clerical disputants argued that they should not be subject to comital justice were exceptional. On those few occasions when churchmen made such claims, they seem to have rung a little hollow, even when supported by impressive citations of conciliar legislation.[28] When it suited their interests, the canons of Urgell retreated from their claim to exemption from comital justice and the canons of the Council of Orléans were quietly reshelved. In Barcelona, the count acknowledged the bishop's concern about his privileges, but set aside the bishop's objection with little hesitation. Arguments for the legal separateness of the clergy were opportunistic

25. ACB Diversorum B 134.
26. *Urgellia* 390.
27. *Urgellia* 398.
28. Magnou-Nortier argues that bishops in the Province of Narbonne maintained a clear sense of duty and competence relative to the monks and clergy in their dioceses until the middle of the eleventh century. *Société laïque*, 283–85.

and sporadic. Occasional attempts to articulate a particular competence were rare departures from the normal interpenetration of comital and episcopal justice. There is little evidence of the jealously guarded jurisdictions that would became increasingly common in the twelfth and thirteenth centuries.

The authority of judicial assemblies in the tenth and eleventh centuries was in some sense collective. Lay and secular lords were charged with the duty of resolving disputes and appointing judges, but they did so collaboratively. The interwoven quality of episcopal and comital power makes it difficult to define with precision how courts delimited their own authority, but the murkiness is not particularly surprising. The administration of justice was just one of many arenas in which bishops and counts cooperated closely. The same cooperation was also apparent in the region's Peace councils.[29] The occupants of episcopal sees most often sprang from comital and vicecomital dynasties. It is not at all surprising to see these bishops working in close cooperation with their brothers, uncles, aunts, and nephews. The complementarity of comital and episcopal power, rather than their competition, was one of the hallmarks of social, political, and legal organization in the Province of Narbonne.[30]

The activities of the counts, countesses, and bishops who presided over judicial assemblies are less fully described in records than the activities of the judges whom they appointed or the disputants who sought justice from them. Records usually describe the groups of magnates who presided over courts but say little about the role court presidents played in hearings. Judges questioned witnesses, consulted law books, assessed proofs, and, occasionally, coerced uncooperative disputants, but it is difficult to determine what presiding counts and countesses did while their appointees were thus occupied.

The fact that judges' activities are recorded in greater detail is in itself significant. On the most rudimentary level, the more ample representations of judges' activities further confirm their central role in processing disputes. Even when presiding magnates intervened more directly, they often left fi-

29. On the Peace of God in this region, see Jeffrey A. Bowman, "Councils, Memory, and Mills: The Early Development of the Peace of God in Catalonia," *Early Medieval Europe* 8 (1999): 99–130. Paul Freedman warns against seeing episcopal courts as indices of comital weakness. *Diocese of Vic*, 18; idem., "Le pouvoir épiscopal en Catalogne au Xe siècle," *Catalunya i França meridional, a l'entorn de l'any mil*, ed. Barral i Altet et al. (Barcelona, 1991), 174–80.

30. The close cooperation of counts and bishops in the administration of justice was not unique to the Province of Narbonne. In eleventh-century Burgundy, the *mallus publicus* was often jointly presided over by counts and bishops. See Duby, "The Evolution of Judicial Institutions," 25. For Italian examples, see Bougard, *Justice dans le royaume d'Italie*, 239.

nal decisions to judges. While presiding over a judicial hearing in Cerdanya, Countess Ermengard relied on the counsel of judges to resolve the case: "When [Countess] Ermengard heard the great complaint and petition of the abbot and his monks, she listened to him carefully, and asked for advice from the judges and the lords about how she could justly bring to an end such a large complaint and serious conflict."[31] Acting on the advice of her judges, the countess instructed that knowledgeable witnesses be sought and questioned. In this case, as in many others, the countess listened carefully to the case before her but relied on the opinion of judges in formulating a solution. The countess endorsed the judges' opinion, rather than formulating and issuing her own.

Occasionally, however, court presidents assumed more active roles. Counts and countesses at times led investigations or made decisions of the sort they usually left to judges. In one case, the abbot of Sant Cugat brought a complaint before the count and countess of Barcelona, the bishops of Urgell, Vic, Elne, and Barcelona, and a group of *optimates*. The count and countess made the decision with the approval of the judge and other magnates, rather than the other way around: "When both parties had argued furiously about this, the count and countess, with the gathering of bishops and powerful men, and the approval of the judges, gave and imposed the following decision between the two parties."[32] The same two litigants returned to the comital court four years later. Again the count presided, but the court's decision in the second hearing was based on the opinion of the judges.[33] Even over the course of a few years, in cases involving the same two disputants, the respective roles of judges and court presidents varied. In 1036, when Abbot Guitard asked Countess Ermessenda to adjudicate a dispute between the monastery and a layman named Dagobert, the countess evaluated his claims accompanied by her nobles but without the usual team of judges.[34] Ermessenda herself assessed the proofs, rejected the document offered by Dagobert as false, and awarded possession of the property to the monastery.

In cases involving Sant Cugat, the especially active participation of the count and countess was due in part to the comital family's close ties to the monastery. But some of the countess's activity in these hearings must also be attributed to her individual ideas, objectives, and strengths. The case involving Dagobert is but one example of Ermessenda's dynamic engagement (as president, judge, and litigant) with the law over several decades. In 1018, the

31. *Marca* 143.
32. *Sant Cugat* 452.
33. *Sant Cugat* 464.
34. *Sant Cugat* 542.

recently widowed countess was involved in a dispute with Count Hug of Empúries. Hug claimed an alod which the countess insisted belonged to her son. The countess proposed that both parties submit their disagreement to a judicial assembly. Hug suggested instead that they settle their differences through a trial by combat. In an assembly presided over by Bishop Oliba of Vic and his brother (Count Bernat of Besalú), the countess explained to Hug that resolving disagreements in the manner he proposed was contrary to Visigothic law. Ermessenda's appeal to written law did not impress Hug: "When [Hug] did not want to accept what [Ermessenda] said . . . without the authority of the Gothic law, [he] violently invaded all that Ermessenda and her son possessed."[35] Visigothic law was not only a tool for judges like Bonhom; it was also a tool for particularly sophisticated lay magnates, like Countess Ermessenda who, in this case, persuaded the assembled magnates that her son's claim to the property was superior to Hug's.[36]

The countess's enthusiasm as both judge and litigant for the use of the *Visigothic Code* was a part of a family tradition. Judicial assemblies in Barcelona often involved reference to the *Code*, but Ermessenda most likely learned how to administer justice and how to use the law from her mother, Countess Adelaide of Carcassonne. In 1002, the monks of the monastery of Saint-Hilaire brought to Ermessenda's mother their dispute with the city's viscount. In consultation with other members of the court, the countess ruled in favor of the monastery, citing a rule from the *Visigothic Code* to support her decision.[37] The counts, countesses, bishops, and viscounts who presided over judicial assemblies usually played a less-engaged, more ceremonial role when disputes were adjudicated in their presence, but occasionally magnates like Countess Ermessenda displayed some of the same legal skills they valued in the judges they appointed.

SAIONES, ADVOCATES, AND BONI HOMINES

Judicial assemblies took place in crowded rooms. Records of hearings emphasize that counts and judges were surrounded by their followers, notable members of the community, low-level officials, and spectators. Like the crowded, bustling hearings Theodulf of Orléans described two centuries earlier, tenth- and eleventh-century courts involved many people. After court presidents, judges, and the disputants themselves, the most important par-

35. *Oliba* 56. See also Kosto, *Making Agreements*, 51–52.
36. For a discussion of Hug's motivations and actions in this case, see chapter 8 below.
37. *HGL* 161.

ticipants in judicial assemblies were minor judicial officials (*saiones*) who enforced decisions, the advocates who represented some disputants, and the *boni homines* who witnessed the proceedings.

By the middle of the ninth century, the *saio* was a regular, but far from universal, feature of courts in the region. For the tenth and eleventh centuries, there are roughly twenty-five widely scattered references to *saiones* who, like judges, were comital appointees.[38] Unlike judges, *saiones* worked alone; there are no cases in which more than one *saio* attended a hearing or witnessed a transaction. The legal activities of *saiones* were more restricted than those of judges. They usually appeared as witnesses to judicial hearings and only rarely as witnesses to routine transactions like sales or donations.[39] *Saiones* discharged some of the same functions ascribed to them in the *Visigothic Code*. Counts made them responsible for executing the decisions of judicial assemblies, bringing people before tribunals, extracting oaths from witnesses, and assuring that disputants adhered to the terms of decisions.[40]

Most *saiones* are identified only in witness lists. Such references suggest that they were considered valued signatories to agreements but provide little sense of how they participated in deliberations. In a handful of cases, one catches a glimpse of *saiones* playing more active roles. During a 988 dispute involving the monastery of Sant Cugat, the monastery's opponent, Sentemir, was accused of having destroyed his brother's testament. Sentemir denied any knowledge of the document's existence and any part in its destruction. Sentemir's fraud was discovered in the midst of an abortive judicial ordeal, and the court had to decide both how to distribute the disputed property and whether to punish Sentemir for having first concealed and then destroyed the testament.[41] The members of the court explored several possible solutions. The *saio* proposed that Sentemir be reduced to servitude and handed over to the abbot of Sant Cugat, noting that such a penalty was in keeping with the law. The presiding bishop, the judge, and the abbot representing Sant Cugat opted for a more lenient settlement. They ordered Sentemir to compensate the monastery, the bishop, the judge, and the *saio*. But the court left him with his freedom and, incidentally, a new, more intimate relationship with the monastery.[42] At least occasionally, *saiones* offered their opinions

38. *Saiones* appear only in records of comital courts. The 1018 dispute between Count Hug and Countess Ermessenda further shows the link between the *saio*'s office and comital authority. Witnesses testified that the count of Barcelona exercised regalian rights over the disputed property, noting that the count had collected customary revenues and that he had maintained a judge and a *saio*. See *Oliba* 56.

39. For two exceptions, see *Oliba* 36 and *Agde* 330.

40. *Leges Visigothorum*, II.1.18, II.1.21, II.1.26.

41. I discuss Sentemir's case in chapter 5 below.

about how to resolve disputes and punish wrongdoers.

A tenth-century case from Vic provides additional clues about the tasks performed by *saiones*. In 953, a woman named Sabida sold a slave, Samuel, to Brunikard. Sabida explained that Samuel had come into her possession because he had been reduced to slavery for the murder of her son: "By this document I sell to you my slave, who was transferred to me in court by the hand of the *saio*, by order of the judges, because I had filed a suit against him because he had murdered my innocent son."[43] In a case from Carcassonne, judges similarly ordered a *saio* to execute their decision.[44] These few cases, combined with passages from the *Visigothic Code*, show that *saiones* were responsible for executing courts' decisions.

The cases also suggest that *saiones* were inclined to formulate severe, punitive solutions. The cases from Vic and Sant Cugat that offer the clearest descriptions of *saiones* in action both dealt with questions of servitude. At Vic, the *saio* had been responsible for handing over a homicide who had been reduced to slavery; at Sant Cugat, the *saio* argued unsuccessfully that a disputant should be reduced to slavery. Focusing on these same records, Pierre Bonnassie argues that "the judicial machine, throughout the early Middle Ages, functioned as a system for the enslavement of the free poor. This was so to a very late date. In Catalonia, for example, the public tribunals were still pronouncing condemnations to slavery as late as 933, 987, and 988."[45] Bonnassie is right to point to the fact that the *saio* wanted to render Sentemir unfree, but his conclusion about the function of the "judicial machine" invites qualification. The threat of servitude did indeed hang over Sentemir, but it did so only briefly. The *saio's* proposal was largely out-of-step with the opinions of the other members of the court, who disregarded the suggestion. The presiding bishop, judge, and even Sentemir's opponent rejected the *saio's* proposal and instead formulated a solution that "pleased both parties." The case from Sant Cugat is an interesting one, but Bonnassie puts more pressure on this single, idiosyncratic example than it can bear.

The judges and magnates who presided over courts were thus, at least occasionally, assisted by minor officials. Some disputants also sought assistance in court. Most property-holders represented themselves, organizing their own arguments and presenting their own proofs. Some disputants, like Renard in the dispute over the tithes of Aiguatèbia or Hug during his conflict with Countess Ermessenda, appointed advocates to represent their interests

42. *Sant Cugat* 218.
43. *Vic* 279.
44. *HGL* 43.
45. Bonnassie, "The Survival and Extinction of the Slave System in the Early Medieval West, Fourth to Eleventh Centuries," in *From Slavery to Feudalism*, 36.

during disputes. Appointing a legal representative, a *mandatarius* or *assertor*, was an option usually reserved for disputants of wealth and prestige, most often lay and clerical magnates.[46] The *mandatarius* appointed by a magnate might initiate a complaint on the magnate's behalf. In other cases, a *mandatarius* would respond to the complaints of other petitioners and answer questions posed by judges.[47] It is not always clear whether these representatives had special training or whether they were considered especially persuasive arguers, but in some cases professional judges, such as Sendred of Cerdanya, represented other disputants in court. At least one advocate seemed to think that representing his client required as much eloquence as it did legal expertise; the bishop of Barcelona's legal representative described himself as *poeta et levita*.[48]

Numerically, the most significant group of people who heard disputes was neither judges nor magnates, but *boni homines*. It is generally impossible to determine the precise number of *boni homines* who attended any given hearing, because records usually list a number of *boni homines* by name and note that many others were in attendance. Groups of *boni homines* or *boni viri* appeared at nearly every dispute, but records devote little attention to the activities of the prominent members of the community (*optimates, proceres*, and *nobiles*) who were present at judicial assemblies. The roles they played in adjudicating disputes, reconciling disputing parties, or enforcing courts' decisions remain obscure. Most often, they remained silent witnesses to the more visible and vocal deliberations and maneuvers of judges and disputants.[49]

The general silence about their activity should not be mistaken as a sign of their insignificance. The very presence of the *boni homines* is an important reflection of participation in the administration of justice by prominent members of communities. The participation of *boni homines* offered broad guarantees that court decisions would enjoy broad support.[50] Proofs were presented, decisions issued, and oaths taken in their presence. They constituted the collective memory of the agreements reached in courts. As subsequent chapters will show, this memory played a crucial—if not always

46. *HGL* 57; *Sant Cugat* 218; *Viage* 15, 34; *HGL* 168; *Oliba* 62; *Urgellia* 203; *Sant Cugat* 512; *Barcelona* 274; *Urgellia* 252; *Viage* 13, 23; *Cart. Rous.* 32; *HGL* 158. In another case involving Barcelona's chapter, legal representatives were referred to as *causidici*. ACB Diversorum B 134.

47. *Barcelona* 274.

48. ACB Lib. Ant. I, f. 175, doc. 461.

49. See Bonnassie, *Catalogne*, 187; and Paul Ourliac, "Juges et justiciables au XIe siècle: les *boni homines*," *Recueil de mémoires et travaux publié par la société d'histoire du droit et des institutions des anciens pays de droit écrit* 16 (1994): 17–33.

50. The role of *boni homines* was acknowledged in Visigothic law. *Leges Visigothorum*, II.1.30; IX.1.21; X.1.17. See King, *Law and Society*, 101.

successful—role in ensuring that resolved disputes did not erupt again.

In some cases, *boni homines* played active roles. In 998, the abbot of Montolieu accused two brothers of having unjustly taken an alod that rightly belonged to the monastery. The record of the abbot's complaint resembles many others, although there is no mention of a formal judicial assembly.[51] In this case, there were neither presiding magnates nor the investigations of professional judges. Instead, the brothers abandoned their claim to the disputed property, noting only that they did so in the presence of the *boni homines*, twenty of whom were named. In 1040, a disputant abandoned an alod to the archbishop of Narbonne and the cathedral chapter in an agreement reached through the intervention of *boni homines*: "When the archbishop and the canons petitioned [the disputed property] from me, I did not want to give it to them at all, but through the involvement of the *boni homines* to call us back to an agreement of peace I saw that I could in no way keep it by my right."[52] Groups of *boni homines* at times persuaded disputants to abandon their claims without citations of written law, evaluation of proofs, or the authority of magnates.[53]

A final example of the participation of *boni homines* in the adjudication of disputes dates from 1081. Elizarius brought a complaint to Count Hug of Empúries, successor to the count of the same name who had wrangled with the countess of Barcelona roughly sixty years earlier. Elizarius said that the abbot of the monastery of Roda was infringing on his rights to a mill, some tithes, and a fief. All of these, Elizarius claimed, were part of his rightful inheritance from his eponymous father. The monastery's abbot claimed that the disputed properties had reverted to the monastery in full on the death of the senior Elizarius. The abbot offered to prove his claim, but before he could do so, the *boni homines* hearing the case in a comital court intervened: "Meanwhile the *boni homines* (Dalmacius, Ramon, Renard, and his brother and several others along with the already-mentioned judges) advised the abbot to give his parts of the fief to Elizarius the petitioner which his father, also Elizarius, had held until the day of his death. The other third of the mill he will give totally as a donation into the power of the monastery."[54] The *boni homines* interrupted the investigation, suggesting that the validity of the abbot's proof was less important than forging a workable compromise.

Cases in which *boni homines* intervened so actively were exceptional. More often, professional judges dictated procedure and would have been eager to

51. BNF coll. Doat 69, ff. 82–83.
52. BNF coll. Doat 55, ff. 102–4.
53. See, for example, *Solsona* 54.
54. *Roses* 8.

consider the sort of proofs offered by the abbot of Roda. But while exceptional, such cases point to the role that *boni homines* might play in the absence of, alongside of, or even within more formal courts. They bolstered the authority of the presiding counts, viscounts, and bishops. They recalled earlier agreements. They encouraged disputants to compromise. As these cases show, informal and formal mechanisms for resolving disputes might coexist even within a single court. Seeing professional judges and *boni homines* working together should come as no great surprise. The less formal intervention of *boni homines* was not necessarily incompatible with the procedures of more formal courts.[55] As in Pierre Toubert's *Latium*, learned judges and *boni homines* worked together to resolve disputes.[56] Learned legal professionals working in concert with larger groups of community members may be less a sign of confusion or decadence than a distinguishing feature of tenth- and eleventh-century justice. If the collective intervention of the *boni homines* is often the most scantily described feature of these courts, it does not mean that their role in settling disputes and keeping them settled was insignificant. The few cases in which *boni homines* played active roles show that they were capable of doing so effectively. One can imagine judicial assemblies in which disputants had to respond to the interlocking pressures of, on the one hand, judicial questioning and, on the other, counseling from the *boni homines*. Although judges demanded written proofs, *boni homines* might remind disputants of the desirability of formulating workable compromises. In this way, *boni homines* doubtless influenced the course of many disputes, even if such subtle and informal interventions leave few traces.[57]

Property disputes were adjudicated in several different types of assembly. There were comital, episcopal, vicecomital, and abbatial courts. Neither judges, nor counts, nor disputants made systematic attempts to describe the limitations or competencies of each. In a handful of cases, disagreements arose about the authority of a judicial assembly, but in every one of these cases, disputants seem to have raised the question with the hope that their case might be moved to what they perceived as more sympathetic *fora*. In

55. The eleventh-century shift from adjudication by literate judges to informal mediation by *boni homines* is not nearly as abrupt or unequivocal as some have argued. Magnou-Nortier, *Société laïque*, 277–78. See chapter 9 below.

56. Pierre Toubert, *Les structures du Latium médiévale*, 2 vols. (Rome, 1973), 1229–54, 1292–1303.

57. See Geary, "Extra-Judicial Means of Conflict Resolution," in *La Giustizia nell'alto medioevo (secoli V–VIII)*, 2 vols, Settimane di studio del Centro italiano di studi sull'alto medioevo 42 (Spoleto, 1995), 601. For a broad discussion of the range and effectiveness of collective action of this sort, see Susan Reynolds, *Kingdoms and Communities in Western Europe, 900–1300* (Oxford, 1984).

other words, the only people who discussed the power of particular courts were disputants trying to extricate themselves from difficult situations. Claims about the limited competency of some assemblies, such as the appeal to the canons of the Council of Orléans made by Urgell's chapter, were instrumental attempts to accomplish something rather than being systematic examinations of how courts were organized.

This profusion of courts with ill-defined jurisdictions did not, in general, provoke conflicts over rights and privileges. Aside from the few cases mentioned above, there is little to suggest that courts struggled against each other. This relatively peaceful coexistence is due, in large part, to the widespread understanding of the count's responsibility for the administration of justice and to the intimate ties of lay and ecclesiastical magnates; the interaction of different courts was more characterized by cooperation than competition. Carolingian ideas about the cooperation of bishops and counts meshed nicely with local politics in this region, where the same families dominated episcopal and comital offices.

Counts shared with other magnates the responsibility for the administration of justice, the organization of courts, and the appointment of judges. They presided over courts with countesses, other counts, bishops, and viscounts. Even in areas characterized by stability and coherent leadership, the composition of courts was protean. The groups of magnates who presided over judicial assemblies often played only minor roles in assessing evidence, questioning witnesses, and issuing decisions about disputed property. They usually left the nitty-gritty of dispute processing to judges. There were, to be sure, notable exceptions. Counts sometimes assumed a very active role and issued decisions after having consulted judges and *boni homines*. Comital authority established the legitimacy of tribunals and made disappointed litigants more likely to adhere to courts' decisions, but counts did not necessarily decide which disputant's claim was superior.

This fluidity in the composition and organization of judicial assemblies should not be mistaken for confusion. Although considerable flexibility existed in the shape of courts, the overall impression is not one of chaos. Judges strove to issue decisions that conformed to the demands of a complex legal tradition that included the *Visigothic Code*, other sources of written law, and custom. The intimate cooperation of lay and ecclesiastic magnates shows that such courts were not only informed by law codes that were centuries old; they were also in-step with contemporary political and social realities.

The task of administering justice—of orchestrating assemblies, evaluating proofs, and issuing decisions that were widely accepted as legitimate and compelling—is not an easy one in any century. The fragmentation of political structures in the tenth and eleventh centuries posed additional challenges to courts in the Province of Narbonne. Despite these challenges, the courts proved to be impressive, enduring institutions that relied on several related strengths: the personal prestige of the lay and ecclesiastic magnates, the close and frequent cooperation of those magnates, the learned application of law by professional judges, and the broad participation of prominent members of the community. Professional judges, written law, comital authority, and the cooperation of lay and ecclesiastic magnates made these courts particularly sophisticated mechanisms for resolving property disputes. The flexibility apparent in the organization of those same courts was not so much a sign of instability as it was a source of strength.

PART II

PROOFS AND STRATEGIES

CHAPTER FIVE
COLD CAULDRONS AND THE
SMOLDERING HAND: THE
JUDICIAL ORDEAL

In part 1: *Courts and Codes,* I described the resources communities possessed to resolve disputes (written law, professional judges, ritual, and judicial assemblies). In part 2, I turn from those traditions and institutions to the question of how disputants tried to win disputes. I examine the kinds of evidence disputants used when called upon to substantiate their claims to vineyards and mills and the ways in which they used them. This discussion of how disputants argued their cases centers on the interlocking problems of proof and strategy. Proof means simply the different materials that disputants presented and judges evaluated to determine the outcomes of disputes. By strategy, I mean the array of appeals, moves, and gestures through which disputants tried to succeed both in and out of court.[1] Disputants tried to protect their property, bolster their social standing, and thwart their enemies in many ways—some shrewd, others clumsy, some honest, others less so.

Proof and strategy are closely related. Most disputants, after all, tried to achieve favorable outcomes in court by presenting documents or witnesses in order to substantiate their claims to disputed property. But although proof and strategy are closely related, they are not the same thing. Together, written rules and long-standing customary norms governed what proofs disputants might use to convince judges of the legitimacy of their claims, but

---

1. For strategy in medieval litigation, my argument is indebted to Stephen D. White, "Proposing the Ordeal and Avoiding It: Strategy and Power in Western French Litigation, 1050–1110," in *Cultures of Power: Lordship, Status, and Process in Twelfth-Century Europe,* ed. Thomas N. Bisson (Philadelphia, 1995), 89–123.

disputants' knowledge of and attitude toward those rules and norms varied. Disputants often had their own idiosyncratic ideas about what made particular documents relevant or what made particular witnesses desirable. Sophisticated disputants shaped relatively modest proofs into convincing cases; less skilled disputants lost in court even though they had marshaled impressive proofs. Unscrupulous disputants forged documents or tried to manipulate the outcome of judicial ordeals. Just as disputants exploited ambiguities in Visigothic inheritance rules, so too they exploited ambiguities in rules about proof. The courts and codes discussed above structured the possibilities available to disputants and judges alike, but these rules and norms did not *determine* the behavior of disputants in and out of court.

By framing this discussion in terms of proof and strategy, I hope both to describe the framework of norms governing proof *and* to suggest the ways in which individual disputants maneuvered within that framework. Litigants, whether medieval or modern, rarely go to court to display their approval of a system of courts or their enthusiasm for rules governing evidence. They go to court because they want to verify and publicize their rights and to defeat opponents who threaten their well-being; they go to court in order to win.

Disputants relied on three types of proof: written records, witness testimony, and judicial ordeals. Given the regional enthusiasm for written law, it comes as little surprise that written proofs often loomed large in disputes. Disputants frequently presented a wide range of documents in court, including records of sales, royal privileges, and testaments. Witness testimony was also common. Witnesses often testified about their knowledge of boundaries or of earlier transactions. Judicial ordeals were the least common variety of proof. Given a legal environment which combined a highly romanized Visigothic law with dense curse clauses, the use of the ordeal of boiling water alongside the evaluation of written evidence seems less incongruous than it otherwise might.

Disputants often used these different proofs in conjunction with one another. In practice, the different varieties of proof often became interdependent. One variety of proof might become indistinguishable from another. To mention one example, explored at greater length in chapter 6, disputants sometimes presented witnesses in court who testified about the contents of lost documents. Fastidious judges had to decide whether to evaluate such evidence as a written proof or as witness testimony. In practice, the boundaries between the three types of proof were porous, but there is, at least initially, some analytic value to looking at each separately. This chapter and the two that follow discuss the three varieties of proof, but although these types of proof are examined separately, treatment of each dramatizes how the value of each type must be understood in relation to the other two.

The term "ordeal," or *Iudicium Dei*, refers to several different methods of proof which relied on the intervention of the divine in human affairs. When human judges or mediators were unable to determine the outcome of a case, they asked God to do so. The proband was subjected to a test which revealed something important about the case. The outcome of an ordeal might determine the validity of a property claim or, in cases where the proband was accused of a crime, guilt or innocence. Judicial ordeals enjoyed their greatest popularity in Europe between 800 and 1200.[2] Although the use of ordeals was widespread, enthusiasm for them was never universal. Even while courts regularly relied on ordeals, critics (including Agobard of Lyons, Peter the Chanter, Atto of Vercelli, and Ivo of Chartres) questioned their use either because they suspected that ordeals did not provide reliable judgments or because they feared that to invoke divine assistance in mundane human affairs was to tempt God. Hostility to the ordeal among churchmen and intellectuals grew during the twelfth century, and in 1215, the Fourth Lateran Council prohibited them. Although the Council's decree did not put an end to the use of ordeals in Europe, it did reflect growing discomfort with the procedure and hastened its decline.[3]

The most common form was the ordeal of the boiling water, also known as the ordeal of the cauldron. The proband plunged his hand into a cauldron of boiling water and removed a ring or stone. If, after several days, the proband's hand was healing without infection, his or her claim would be considered legitimate. In other ordeals, probands were expected to walk across a row of white-hot ploughshares or, less frequently, to eat a consecrated piece of cheese. In order for any ordeal to work, certain conditions had to obtain. The medium—whether boiling cauldron or consecrated goat cheese—had to be properly blessed, the proband had to be properly prepared, and God's intervention had to be properly petitioned.

In the Province of Narbonne, the judicial ordeal was a very uncommon form of proof. Starting a discussion of proofs and strategies with the least common type of proof makes sense for several reasons. Of the three types of proof, the ordeal is the most alien to modern understanding. Written proofs

2. Robert Bartlett, *Trial by Fire and Water: The Medieval Judicial Ordeal* (Oxford, 1986), 13.

3. Jean Gaudemet, "Les ordalies au moyen Age: Doctrine, legislation, et pratique canoniques," *Recueils de la société Jean Bodin pour l'histoire comparative des institutions* (hereafter *RSJB*) 17 (1965): 99–135; John W. Baldwin, "The Intellectual Preparation for the Canon of 1215 against Ordeals," *Speculum* 36 (1961): 613–36; and Bartlett, *Trial by Fire and Water*.

and witness testimony still constitute evidence in modern courts; the ordeal is, on the other hand, in continental and Anglo-American legal traditions distinctly medieval. Because the ordeal is, to modern eyes, so odd, its origin, function, and evolution have attracted scholarly attention to a much greater extent than has, for example, witness testimony. There is another important reason to begin with the ordeal. In cases involving the ordeal, the status of different types of proof was often seen as problematic by the participants themselves. Those few cases involving ordeals seem to have vexed medieval judges as much as they puzzle modern historians. Such cases thus afford a compelling introduction to the logic of proof in tenth- and eleventh-century courts. They allow us to see judges wrestling with the question of how to interpret disparate forms of proof and disputants trying to exploit the judges' uncertainty. It is perhaps precisely because ordeals were relatively uncommon that they prompted scribes, judges, and disputants to reflect upon how proofs should be evaluated.

In this region, the ordeal was invoked in only a handful of cases, but these few cases reveal a great deal about how disputants tried to substantiate their claims and about how courts assessed proofs. Before drawing broader conclusions about the significance of the ordeal as proof and as strategy, it is worth reviewing the dossier of cases involving ordeals, devoting particular attention to the first recorded case.

In March 988, a representative of the monastery of Sant Cugat accused a man named Sentemir of concealing his brother's testament. According the monastery's witness, Sentemir had instructed his wife to burn the missing will, and she had complied. The monks of Sant Cugat were particularly concerned about this document because it had allegedly stipulated a generous bequest to the monastery. The dispute thus began as many others did, with a monastery or church quarreling with the kindred of a recently deceased property-holder over an estate.

Although the origin of the dispute was mundane, its resolution was odd. In order to recover the bequest recorded in the destroyed document, Sant Cugat's representative, Pons, went before a court presided over by Bishop Gondemar of Barcelona, Abbott Odo of Sant Cugat, and Judge Bonhom of Barcelona. Pons presented a witness, a priest named Ennego, who testified that he had seen the missing testament and was familiar with its contents. Sentemir denied any knowledge of the testament and any part in its destruction. Despite the priest's testimony and the judge's aggressive questioning, Sentemir refused to admit any wrongdoing. Finally, in order to clear himself, Sentemir offered to undergo the ordeal of the boiling water: "As he persisted thus in his iniquity, he sought the *iudicium Dei* by cauldron . . . claiming that he would maintain himself healthy in it by some curses and incantations which he knew." Sentemir's pluck in the face of authorities like the bishop of Barcelona and the abbot of Sant Cugat is impressive. He did not, however, have the chance to try out the incantations about which he had so confidently boasted. Before he could circumvent the ordeal's justice with his magic, Sentemir's hand burst into flames, revealing his guilt: "But his incantations availed him nothing, and his hand suddenly appeared burned up. Revealed thus in his malice and his falsehood, by the order of the judge he confirmed a confession of how he had lawlessly and unjustly ordered his wife to burn the will."[4] The defeated Sentemir, his smoldering hand a testament to his misdeeds, abandoned the disputed property to the monastery. The court's *saio* recommended that Sentemir be reduced to servitude and handed over to the monastery, but Sentemir asked for and received the bishop's mercy.

A few features of this case are worth highlighting. The first is that the use of the ordeal was proposed by Sentemir rather than by the judge or by the presiding bishop. Judge Bonhom, Bishop Gondemar, and Abbot Odo seemed content to restrict themselves to the proofs offered by Sant Cugat's representative—namely, witness testimony about the contents of a lost document. When Sentemir proposed the ordeal, the judges and his opponents, even though they were inclined to rely on the witness testimony they had already heard, accepted his proposal. The record depicts Sentemir as a charlatan, but his proposal that he clear himself through the ordeal apparently met with no resistance from other members of the court. The judge and the other members were suspicious of Sentemir, but no one suggested that the ordeal he proposed was unacceptable. The judge and Sentemir's opponents accepted the ordeal as a proof, even if they did so reluctantly.

Sentemir, if we can trust the scribe's account of his motivations, seems to have seen the ordeal in a purely instrumental sense. He viewed it not as a proof (a way to get to the bottom of a complicated situation), but as a strategy (a way to get out of an uncomfortable position). He suggested the ordeal precisely because he thought that he could manipulate its results more easily than he could manipulate other proofs. Sentemir's ideas about proof were, admittedly, out-of-step with those of the other members of the court, but they are especially worth noting because they reflect differences of opinion about what constituted compelling proof in property disputes.

Sentemir made two important miscalculations about proof which led, in turn, to two blunders. First, he seems to have thought that the destruction of his brother's testament would vitiate Sant Cugat's claim to his brother's estate. He was wrong. The court was happy to hear the evidence provided by the witness who had seen the testament before it met its fiery end at the hands of Sen-

4. *Sant Cugat* 218.

temir's wife. He probably should have known better; courts regularly heard witness testimony about lost documents, and Sant Cugat tended to keep a vigilant watch on its property. Sentemir's second miscalculation was in thinking that he could manipulate the results of the ordeal and thereby extricate himself from a tight spot. Here too, Sentemir was wrong. But his second miscalculation is more understandable. Although ordeals may have been used in this region prior to this case, they have left no records. Neither Sentemir nor anyone else present at the hearing had much, if any, experience conducting, undergoing, or assessing judicial ordeals. Sentemir was mistaken in thinking that he could use magic to avoid the ordeal's justice, but his belief that the ordeal was the type of proof most amenable to improvisation is understandable.

The ordeal put a dramatic end to Sentemir's case and, more generally, to his brief career as a thorn in Sant Cugat's side. But it did so in a way that no one probably would have expected. Even if the ordeal provided the court with important information about the relative legitimacy of the claims made by Sentemir and Sant Cugat, the ordeal did not unfold as ordeals were expected to—that is, with Sentemir snatching something from the cauldron and being examined several days later to see whether he was healing without infection. Instead, the document explains, "his hand suddenly appeared burned up." It is admittedly hard to know exactly what the scribe meant by this formulation, but it sounds more like an account of localized spontaneous combustion or a metaphoric attempt to portray Sentemir's palpable, red-handed guilt, than it does the systematic unfolding of a judicial ordeal. In this case and in many others, ordeals ended not in determinations emerging as planned by the court, but rather in felicitous short-circuits.

The next recorded ordeal occurred in the year 1000. Like the dispute between Sentemir and Sant Cugat, this case also involved a challenged bequest and a testament. The canons of Elne's chapter and the niece of the chapter's recently deceased schoolmaster (*caput scole*), Auriolus, quarreled over the division of Auriolus's estate. Elne's canons brought a written testament before a judge in an episcopal court. Auriolus's niece, Ermeld, and her husband, Elderic, brought a conflicting testament before the same court. The judge examined both documents, and after having read them over more than once, he became convinced that the document presented by Ermeld and Elderic was illegitimate. The judge described it as "most false" and "contrary to the law." He also noted that the couple's document lacked the necessary signatures and seals. Instead of these, he complained of "phony seals and signatures."[5]

Despite his rejection of the document submitted by Ermeld and her husband, the judge still did not issue a decision in the chapter's favor. He offered

5. *HGL* 158.

the married couple another chance to vindicate their claim: "The judge asked Elderic whether he dared to try the *iudicium Dei*, so that he would not remain in this knowing fraud and that this charter, which he presented in court, would not be known as a lie." Elderic agreed to undergo the ordeal to prove that his written proof was legitimate and the judge began to prepare him. But before the proposed ordeal could take place, a group of local notables intervened. Three men, with the support of other *boni homines*, went before the bishop and encouraged him to find another way to resolve the dispute. The bishop agreed and encouraged the disputants to formulate a compromise, which they did. Elderic and Ermeld eventually abandoned their claim.

The case involving Elne's chapter and the schoolmaster's niece resembles Sentemir's in some ways. In both cases, a testamentary bequest was challenged by a member of the deceased's family. In both cases, judges tried to establish the legitimacy of different claims by examining written evidence. In both cases, written proofs were somehow problematic. In both cases, courts, disputants, and judges appealed to the ordeal only after finding other proofs deficient. Finally, in neither case did the ordeal determine the outcome of the case. The ordeal was proposed and accepted as a proof, but before the ordeal was executed and assessed, something went wrong. In the first case, Sentemir's hand peremptorily appeared all burnt up; in the second, prominent members of the community encouraged the bishop to find an alternative solution to the disagreement. The two conclusions are, of course, quite different, but they might both be called felicitous short-circuits.

The next recorded ordeal took place in 1016. In a donation to the church of Sant Vicenç, Viscount Beremund outlined the turbulent history of property that he was giving to the church. In reviewing the property's history, he was presumably trying to establish his right to alienate it. He explained that his rights had been affirmed in an earlier judgment in which he had recovered property from one of his own agents, Sendred (not to be confused with Judge Sendred). According to the viscount, Sendred's thievery and misdeeds had been so various that it would have taxed his endurance to have recounted them all. In an assembly of lay and clerical magnates, Beremund had asked Sendred to return the things he had taken. Sendred refused to do so and appealed to the ordeal: "[Sendred] did not want to accept any decision, but confiding in his own magical incantations, he said that he would be judged by the boiling water of the *iudicium Dei*. But God, who knows all hidden things, wanted to reveal openly in this presence his most iniquitous deception. . . . Sendred put his hand in the cauldron, cruelly his heart and flesh were burned, and his savage theft was revealed to all who were there."[6]

6. BNF coll. Moreau 19, ff. 87–88; Partially published in *Viage* 8, 31. For a roughly

Sendred's was the first case in which the ordeal seems to have determined the outcome of a dispute. He plunged his hand into the cauldron of boiling water and his claims were subsequently considered illegitimate. The account of this ordeal, however, leaves many questions unanswered. For example, the donation does not record either party presenting witnesses or written proofs prior to the ordeal, although they may have done so. Although the account is sketchy, it does provide valuable information about the proband, Sendred, who, like Sentemir, proposed the ordeal not in the hope that it would reveal the truth, but in the belief that he could avoid a just settlement through "evil arts."

In 1037, the ordeal again played a role in Sant Cugat's litigation. Abbot Guitard brought a complaint before Countess Ermessenda, the bishop of Barcelona, and a group of magnates. The abbot claimed that one Bernat had unjustly seized part of a *castrum* that rightly belonged to the monastery. The abbot presented a royal privilege to support his claim. The relevant passage from this privilege was read aloud to the court. The presiding magnates declared that the case would be determined according to the rules of the *Visigothic Code*. Abbot Guitard accepted this decision and began to make the appropriate arrangements. Bernat flatly rejected the proposal and suggested his own alternative: "I will neither make nor receive any other law (*directum*) but this one: if you agree, we will send two youths to the judgment of the almighty God in cold water. From this it will appear to whom these rights belong."[7] Despite their clearly stated preference for Visigothic procedure, the countess, the bishop, and the magnates accepted Bernat's proposal. One boy would represent the monastery, another would represent Bernat. Whichever of the two the water accepted would win for his sponsor the disputed property. If the water accepted or rejected both boys, the property would be divided. Both parties agreed to these terms.

The ordeal began. According to Sant Cugat's cartulary, the youth representing Sant Cugat was initially accepted by the water, but the water did not retain him. The water did not receive Bernat's boy at all. It is, of course, difficult to imagine exactly what this process looked like to the gathered observers. The record does not, for example, explain who determined what constituted being accepted by the water or what constituted being rejected by it. Presumably, this decision was made by the countess, the bishop, and

---

contemporary ordeal in which the proband was also burned all the way to the heart, see *Cartulaire de Notre-Dame du Ronceray*, in *Archives d'Anjou*, t. III, ed. P. Marchegay (Angers, 1854), no. 313; and Dominique Barthélemy, "Diversité des ordalies médiévales," *Revue Historique* 280 (1988), 10.

7. *Sant Cugat* 545. For the use of *pueri* as representatives in ordeals see, Barthélemy, "Diversité des ordalies," 17–18.

the magnates, but one cannot be sure. Nor does the record explain how long the ordeal lasted. But although the account leaves much to the imagination, it does suggest that the results of such ordeals were not immediately apparent to those who witnessed them. There was evidently ample room for disagreement and interpretation. Despite its ambiguous beginning, the ordeal did yield a decision in the case, albeit an equivocal one. Neither Sant Cugat nor Bernat managed to prove their right to the property, so the judges divided it. The disputants promised to make no future claims on the portion allotted to their opponents and arranged for the erection of new markers indicating boundaries between their portions.

This is a strange case even within the narrow context of disputes involving ordeals. It is the only case involving a bilateral ordeal and youths serving as proxies. In this respect, it resembled a trial by combat in which disputants elected champions to fight on their behalf.[8] This ordeal did precipitate a resolution to the dispute, but the conclusion reached was a compromise. The difficulty of assessing the ordeal's results and the ordeal's equivocal decision both dramatize how volatile the ordeal could be as a means of determining whose claim to a disputed property was superior. Prior to the procedure, the disputants and judges discussed the possible outcomes of the bilateral ordeal, and specified how each of those outcomes would effect the redistribution of property rights. Despite their clear discussion of how to proceed, the situation that unfolded—two hapless youths sinking and bobbing ambiguously—conformed to none of the scenarios which the court had foreseen.

The case also reflects the flexibility of procedure, even in relatively formal courts. The judges, bishop, and countess blithely accepted their own inability to dictate the rules according to which a suit was to be adjudicated. The judges advocated the use of evidentiary procedure drawn from Visigothic law, but their preference became irrelevant when Bernat insisted that the only outcome he would accept would be one determined by ordeal. When one disputant did not accept the court's proposed method of adjudicating a dispute and proposed an unconventional alternative, even relatively strong courts sometimes had little choice but to accept the alternative.

This is the only recorded case in which a lay disputant used the ordeal and enjoyed some measure of success. It is hard to know what went through Bernat's head as he tried to retain control of the disputed *castrum*, but he almost certainly knew that when Sant Cugat litigated over property rights, Sant Cugat usually won. He also probably knew that the royal privilege the

8. The only case in which a disputant proposed a trial by combat was the 1018 dispute between Countess Ermessenda of Barcelona and Count Hug of Empúries. *Oliba* 56.

monastery presented in court would weigh heavily in the monastery's favor. Additionally, he may have suspected that the Visigothic procedure proposed by the judges often favored institutional disputants like Sant Cugat. Finally, Bernat may have recognized that unilateral ordeals usually did not help one's case. There is, in fact, no tenth- or eleventh-century case in which a unilateral ordeal actually benefited the person who undertook (or agreed to undertake) it. In other words, Bernat may well have known that his case looked weak, and he may well have sensed that unilateral ordeals did not help disputants with weak cases.

Bernat's unique proposal, that the disposition of the *castrum* be governed by a bilateral ordeal with proxies, was thus a particularly savvy one. After all, Bernat ended up with half the disputed *castrum*. With this partial victory, Bernat was considerably more successful than many other disputants who fought Sant Cugat with more conventional proofs. Moreover, he was more successful than disputants like Sentemir who proposed a unilateral ordeal, lost the property he claimed, and was nearly handed over into servitude. Bernat established his right to half the *castrum* against a powerful and shrewd disputant, and he managed to do so without even having to stick his own arm into a cauldron of boiling water.

The few remaining eleventh-century cases involving ordeals are less complicated. In 1044, the abbot of Sant Pere de Roda complained to a comital court about men who, the abbot claimed, had usurped some of the monastery's vineyards.[9] The laymen accused by Sant Pere's abbot were represented by a representative named Berenguer. The monastery's abbot presented a charter, made by the presiding count's predecessor, to substantiate his claims. Berenguer provided neither documents nor witnesses to support the claims of those whom the monastery accused. The accused vacillated as to whether they wanted to participate in the hearing at all. The presiding counts and the judge, frustrated with a dispute that had already dragged on through several sittings, ordered an ordeal of cold water to determine the rightful owner. The document does not describe any of the details surrounding the procedure, but reports that the ordeal yielded a decision in the monastery's favor. Although the court awarded the property to the monastery, it noted that this was a provisional arrangement. Less than a final determination, the ordeal and the decision in the monastery's favor appear to have been attempts to coax the lay disputants to submit to a comital judgment. The decision reached was subject to revision if the other disputants agreed to have their claims assessed by more conventional procedures.

The ordeal was also proposed in 1064 near Barcelona and in a 1080 case

9. BNF coll. Moreau 20, f. 165.

involving the monastery of Sant Pere de Roda.[10] In 1081, Urgell's bishop petitioned a woman named Bonadonna and her six children to go before Judge Albert. The bishop claimed that they were unlawfully violating the see's right to certain tithes.[11] Bonadonna and her children rejected the bishop's claim, and the judge ordered her to undergo the ordeal. The judge's command prompted a swift change of heart. Terrified by the judge's suggestion that she undergo the ordeal, Bonadonna admitted her sin, begged for mercy, and promised to respect the see's rights. In 1100 in Vic, Arbert Salamon agreed to submit to the ordeal of boiling water to prove that the lord of Taradell had no rights over his person or property. Just before he underwent the ordeal, the disputing parties reached a compromise agreement with the advice of a group of noteworthy men.[12]

There were, thus, nine disputes involving the ordeal in the Province of Narbonne between 950 and 1100.[13] The records of these nine cases are certainly the most informative sources regarding the use of the *judicium Dei*, but two other types of sources shed additional light on attitudes toward ordeals: the acts of Peace councils and manuscripts of the *Visigothic Code*.

THE ORDEAL IN LEGISLATION

At the Council of Vic in 1033, an assembly of lay and ecclesiastic magnates promulgated legislation intended to protect church property, to establish areas of asylum surrounding churches, to prohibit injury to clerics, and to forbid the destruction of the houses of clerics and peasants. The assembly also confirmed a Truce of God, during which there was a blanket prohibition on acts of violence weekly from Thursday evening to Monday morning, during liturgically important dates such as Easter, and on the feasts of local saints like Felix of Girona and Eulalia of Barcelona. Violators of the truce were subject to severe penalties. Excommunication was prominent among these sanctions, but, in certain cases, the ordeal of the cold water might be used to punish wrongdoers: "If anyone should do wrong to another person during this Truce, he will compensate him double and afterward will amend doubly to the see by the judgment of the cold water. If someone should intention-

10. ACA Ramon Berenguer I, 305; *Viage* 15, 17.

11. *Urgellia* 947.

12. ACV Calaix 6, 2213.

13. A laconic reference from Montserrat in a testament mentions *iudicium Dei*. See *Santa Cecília* 87.

ally kill another person during the Truce, he will be damned to exile for all the days of his life."[14] Peace councils in Narbonne in 1054, Vic in the 1060s, Barcelona in 1064, and Roussillon in 1065 included similar legislation mandating the use of the ordeal of the cold water to punish violators of the Truce.[15]

References to the ordeal in Peace legislation marked several noteworthy departures from those in diplomatic records. Canons of Peace councils were, unlike records of disputes, prescriptive. Rather than describing deliberations and hearings, Peace councils specified sanctions to be applied in the event of future infractions. There is much to suggest that Peace legislation was influential, but there is no evidence that sanctions like those promulgated at Vic in 1033 were applied systematically. In other words, the lay and ecclesiastic magnates who gathered at Vic knew about the ordeal and believed, in principle, that imposing it was an appropriate response to violations of the Truce, but there is no evidence that any violator of the Truce actually underwent the ordeal described in the canons.

Peace legislation described the function of the ordeal in a fundamentally different way than did records of litigation. The canons of Peace councils specified that the ordeal was to be used as a punishment rather than as a proof. Ordeals were not to be used to determine guilt or innocence, or to determine who should rightly possess a disputed alod. Instead, the ordeal was to be applied after guilt had been determined.

A final difference between the ordeal in Peace legislation and the ordeal in disputes lay in the sort of ordeal specified. Peace legislation specified the ordeal of cold water, rather than the ordeal of boiling water more commonly mentioned in records of property disputes. The appearance of the ordeal in the canons of Peace councils may have made ordeals more familiar to the judges, churchmen, and lay magnates who presided over courts as well as to a wider public, but it is striking how little the ordeals described in the canons of Peace councils resembled the ordeals occasionally proposed as proofs in court.

The canons of Peace councils were not the only source to which judges and disputants might turn for guidance about when and how to use ordeals. Judges could find some authoritative sanction for the ordeal's use in the *Visigothic Code*. A single rule in the *Code* allowed for the use of the ordeal of the boiling water. The rule mandated that in certain cases those accused of crimes might

14. *Les constitucions de Pau i Treva de Catalunya, segles XI–XIII*, ed. Gener Gonsalvo i Bou (Barcelona, 1994) (hereafter *Constitucions*), 3.

15. Giovanni Mansi, *Sacrorum Conciliorum Nova et Amplissima Collectio*, vol. 19 (Venice, 1774), col. 829; and *Constitucions* 4, 5, and 6.

prove their innocence through the ordeal and suggested that this was appropriate when witness testimony seemed untrustworthy.[16] It is difficult to say when this rule was added to the corpus of Visigothic legislation, but most of the earliest extant manuscripts, including an early ninth-century manuscript from Girona, include some version of the rule.[17] Tenth- and eleventh-century judges who consulted copies of the *Visigothic Code* would have found included therein a rule entitled, "How a judge investigates cases using the test of the cauldron."[18]

The treatment of the rule in one eleventh-century manuscript reflects some of the same judicial ambivalence that is apparent in records of disputes. In chapter 3 above, Bonhom of Barcelona served as a particularly well-documented example of the region's professional judges. As noted, Bonhom's most impressive achievement was the compilation of two legal manuscripts which included the *Visigothic Code*. The treatment of the ordeal in Bonhom's manuscript is another example of how this compilation reflects the scholarly and practical concerns of professional judges. Bonhom excluded the only rule sanctioning the use of the ordeal from his manuscript. There are several possible reasons he did so. He may have doubted, as some modern scholars do, that the rule belonged in any official recension of the *Code*. He may have thought that the ordeal was out of place in the context of the *Code*'s other rules. Or Bonhom's omission may have been based less on his historical jurisprudence than on his practical experience; a long career on the bench may have convinced him that the ordeal simply was not a good way of establishing facts. Or perhaps he based his own compilation at least in part on manuscripts, now lost, which did not include the rule. Finally, although one should not lightly accuse Bonhom of negligence, he may have omitted the rule through carelessness. Whatever the reason, his omission did not go unnoticed. A different, roughly contemporary, scribe noticed that the rule was missing and inserted it in the manuscript.[19] Bonhom's hesitation and the later interpolation show that professional judges were not entirely agreed on the ordeal's rightful place as a proof.

The curious history of this single rule in this single manuscript becomes even more interesting when one remembers that Judge Bonhom was a member of the court that heard the 988 case between Sant Cugat and Sentemir. In other words, Bonhom acted as judge in at least one case involving a pro-

16. *Leges Visiogthorum*, VI.2.2.

17. Javier Alvarado Planas, "Ordalías y derecho en la España Visigoda," *De la Antigüedad al Medievo, siglos IV–VIII: III Congreso de Estudios Medievales* (*Y*vila, 1993), 481.

18. See Yolanda García López, "La Tradición del Liber Iudiciorum: Una revisión," *De la Antigüedad al Medievo, siglos IV–VIII*, 386–9.

19. Escorial Z.II.2, f. 142r.

posed ordeal. If he knowingly excluded the rule from his manuscript because he thought it was not a legitimate form of proof, Sentemir's case must have informed his decision. Remembering the case two decades after the fact, he may have seen the ordeal as an unpredictable way of conducting an inquiry. He may not have considered the ordeal a good way of adjudicating disputes over property rights, but he omitted the ordeal not because he was not familiar with how it might be used (and possibly abused) by judges and disputants. Bonhom had seen the ordeal in action at least once.

The dialog about the ordeal apparent in this manuscript did not stop with the insertion of the rule. Long after Bonhom's death, a twelfth-century hand inserted a more elaborate set of guidelines (*ordines)* for performing ordeals. These instructions were not limited to the ordeal by cauldron mentioned in Visigothic law. The later contributor to Bonhom's manuscript also included the ordeal of the cold water and the ordeal of the bread and the cheese. These additions instructed judges to have mass celebrated prior to the examination and described how to prepare the media (water or cheese) and probands for the procedure. The water and cauldron were blessed, and God's intervention was solicited. Priests were to recite another prayer when the cauldron started to grow warm, noting as they did so famous examples of God's justice such as saving Susanna from her false accusers, protecting Shadrach, Meshach, and Abednego from Nebuchadnezzar's wrath, and keeping Daniel safe in the lions' den.

If the proband was, like these scriptural prototypes, innocent, whatever wound his or her hand incurred would show no signs of infection. Not all probands were, however, expected to be innocent: "But if he has lies and unjustness, his hand will appear burnt by the fire so that all people will know the strength of our Lord, Jesus Christ, who will come with the Holy Spirit to judge the living and the dead by fire."[20] The twelfth-century interpolator eagerly devoted much more attention to the use of ordeals than either Bonhom or the eleventh-century scribe who inserted the Visigothic rule. But some of the difficulties anticipated by the twelfth-century scribe were the same as those confronted by judges in the decades around the year 1000. The instructions recognized the problem of disputants who tried to avoid the ordeal's justice through duplicity or sorcery. It warned against disputants like Sentemir who, according the Sant Cugat's record, tried to contaminate the ordeal's justice by using "herbs or demonic incantations."

The scribe who so richly augmented the material related to ordeals in Bonhom's manuscript was not the lone voice making a place for the ordeal

20. G. Baist, "Ritual de pruebas judiciales tomado de un códice del Escorial," *Boletín Histórico* (1880): 139.

in twelfth-century legal practice. The Catalan jurists who framed the *Usatges of Barcelona* saw several different roles for the ordeal. For example, peasant women accused of adultery could clear themselves by undergoing the ordeal, while their social betters might achieve the same through oaths or judicial duels.[21] Ironically, these twelfth-century amplifications of the legal significance of judicial ordeals—the rules in the *Usatges* and the additions to Bonhom's manuscript—came in a period when ordeals were being subjected to the increasingly widespread criticism that would lead to their condemnation at the Fourth Lateran Council.

There was thus a learned legal discourse related to ordeals that was, at least in theory, available to disputants and judges in the eleventh century. Judges could, if they chose, appeal to *leges* which approved certain uses of the ordeal. But, seventh- and eighth-century Visigothic legal ideas were always transformed in practice. Just as judges and disputants adapted and transformed Visigothic rules about property-holding and alienability, so too they adapted rules about proofs in similar ways.

Although judges and disputants could have referred to Visigothic legislation to authorize their use of the judicial ordeal, the handful of cases involving ordeals conformed poorly to the *Code*'s prescriptions. The area of greatest congruity between theory and practice was probably that of problematic evidence. The *Code* specified that the ordeal might be appropriate in cases where other proofs were suspicious. In several of the disputes, other proofs were, indeed, problematic. In the 988 case at Sant Cugat, a document had been destroyed. In 1000 at Elne, opposing litigants presented contradictory testaments, one of which was considered a forgery. In 1044 at Sant Pere de Roda, one party refused to appear in court. In 1100 in Vic, neither party could provide evidence to support its claim.

Courts may have been attentive to the *Code*'s suggestion that the ordeal was appropriate when other proofs were suspect, but in every other area practice diverged from legislation. The *Code* specified that the ordeal be used by those who had been accused of crimes. In tenth- and eleventh-century cases, the ordeal's use had dilated beyond the criminal cases mentioned by the *Code*. Probands were no longer those accused of crimes but litigants in property disputes.

Although judges who accepted ordeals as proofs may have had Visigothic legislation in the back of their minds, they never actually cited the Visigothic rule when considering an ordeal. The record describing the 988 case involv-

---

21. Joan Bastardas, ed. *Usatges de Barcelona: El codi a mitjan segle XII* (Barcelona, 1984), trans. Donald J. Kagay as *Usatges of Barcelona: The Fundamental Law of Catalonia* (Philadelphia, 1994), canon 89; see also canon 50.

ing Sant Cugat echoed the language of the *Code* but never cited the single rule referring to ordeals. Judges generally did not hesitate to invoke the Visigothic origins of rules, so their reluctance to do so in this case is all the more remarkable. Elsewhere in the Iberian Peninsula, in a case in Galicia in 1025, the Visigothic rule was explicitly invoked when an ordeal was being considered.[22]

Relations between written legal traditions and judicial practice were complex. Charters, the canons of Peace councils, and copies of the *Visigothic Code* indicate that judges were familiar with the ordeal. But although judges occasionally allowed the use of ordeals in judicial assemblies and magnates gathered at Peace councils suggested that it be used to punish violators of the Truce of God, the small number of cases involving ordeals and the tepid response of most judges to proposals for ordeals suggest that most courts preferred to avoid them.

The ordeal's place in the legal history of medieval Europe has long inspired scholarly interest. Historians have devoted considerable attention to the ordeal, often at the expense of examining more common forms of proof. They have asked whether the procedure is rational or irrational, whether the ordeal's origins lie in the misty northern forests of common law or in the sunny public *fora* of the Roman Mediterranean, or whether judicial ordeals are common to all cultures.[23] Scholars have asked whether all types of ordeal have common origins, or whether the different ordeals, such as ordeal by combat and ordeal of the bread and the cheese, are so different that they should not be considered varieties of the same phenomenon.[24] Some have argued that the ordeal should be explained as a functional way of resolving inflammatory questions within small communities, while others have suggested that the ordeal should be seen as an instrument of mercy, sparing those who might otherwise suffer severe punishments.[25]

22. J. M. Fernandez del Pozo, ed., "Alfonso V rey de León," in *León y su Historia*, vol. 5 (León, 1984), 165–251, doc. 10; García López, "La Tradición del Liber Iudiciorum"

23. For an overview of the question of the ordeal's origins, see Aquilino Iglesias Ferreirós, "El proceso del Conde Bera y el problema de las ordalias," *AHDE* 51 (1981): 1–221; and Alvarado Planas, "Ordalías y derecho"; For the ordeal's Roman roots, see Wood, "Disputes in Fifth- and Sixth-Century Gaul," in *The Settlement of Disputes*, ed. Davies and Fouracre, 7–22. For a reassertion of the ordeal's essentially Germanic character, see R. C. van Caenegem, "Reflexions on Rational and Irrational Modes of Proof in Medieval Europe," *Tijdschrift voor Reschtsgeschiedenis* 58 (1990): 263–79. See also Jean Gaudemet, "Les Ordalies au Moyen Age"; and Colin Morris, "*Judicium Dei*: The Social and Political Significance of the Ordeal in the Eleventh Century," *Studies in Church History* 12 (1975): 95–111.

24. Barthélemy, "Diversité des ordalies."

25. Brown, "Society and the Supernatural"; Rebecca Colman, "Reason and Unreason in Early Medieval Law," *Journal of Interdisciplinary History* 4 (1974): 571–91; Ian C. Pilar-

To some of these questions about the origins or rationality of the ordeal, cases from this region contribute little in the way of answers. The question of whether the ordeal's origin was Germanic or Roman, for example, seems to have rarely vexed eleventh-century judges. Moreover, if professional judges did not concern themselves with the ordeal's origin, the question of origins almost certainly did not trouble Sentemir, Bernat, or Bonadonna—litigants who underwent (or nearly underwent) judicial ordeals.

This region's dossier of disputes involving the ordeal does, however, allow us to see how the ordeal functioned in particular contexts—how ordeals operated as proofs in property disputes. Because ordeals were one component of a much larger set of rules, customs, and techniques which constituted the legal world of the region, they are best understood in relation to other proofs and other strategies. Ordeals were not everywhere and always the same. In Catalonia, where professional judges presided over public courts, where written law played an important role in shaping legal ideals, and where, as the next chapter will show, disputants often relied on written proofs to establish their claims, the ordeal as a proof must have been understood and employed differently than in places where the same conditions did not obtain. Indeed, the form and function of judicial ordeals varied considerably not only from one region to the next but even from one dispute to the next.[26] Different types of proof cannot be understood in isolation; attitudes toward the ordeal are related to other ideas about law, proofs, and authority. Thus, although these few cases involving the ordeal may not contribute much to our understanding of the ordeal's origin or its rationality, there are compensating advantages to an approach which sees each instance of the ordeal as part of a particular dispute and each dispute as grounded in a distinctive set of conditions under which judges and disputants operated.

The first conclusion to draw about the ordeal should by now be obvious, but it is worth repeating: the ordeal was a very uncommon form of proof.[27] Between 900 and 1100, fewer than ten cases of the ordeal are recorded. All

---

czyk, "Between a Rock and a Hot Place: The Role of Subjectivity in the Medieval Ordeal by Hot Iron," *Anglo-American Law Review* 25 (1996): 87–112; Margaret E. Kerr, Richard K. Forsyth, and Michael J. Plyley, "Cold Water and Hot Iron: Trial by Ordeal in England," *Journal of Interdisciplinary History* 22 (1992): 573–96; Paul Hyams, "Trial by Ordeal: The Key to Proof in the Early Common Law," in *On the Laws and Customs of England: Essays in Honor of Samuel E. Thorne*, ed. Morris S. Arnold, Thomas A. Green, Sally A. Scully, and Stephen D. White (Chapel Hill, N.C., 1981), 90–126; C. M. Radding, "Superstition to Science: Nature, Fortune, and the Passing of the Medieval Ordeal," *American Historical Review* 84 (1979): 945–69.

26. See White, "Proposing the Ordeal," 91.

27. Robert Bartlett's otherwise admirable study exaggerates the prominence of the ordeal in eleventh-century Catalonia. See his *Trial by Fire and Water*, 27.

of the ordeals undertaken or proposed involved water, whether boiling or cold. There were no ordeals by iron, and none of the more exotic varieties of ordeals, such as the ordeal of the cross or the ordeal of the bread and cheese, occurred. With a single exception, ordeals were unilateral.[28] For every case which involved the ordeal, there were dozens which relied exclusively on written proofs or witness testimony.

Those cases in which the ordeal played a part were extraordinary. Since the most common proofs were documents and witness testimony, every proposal of the ordeal (whether by a judge or disputant) constituted an attempt to exploit an unusual type of proof.[29] Every proposal raises questions about why a disputant or judge chose to rely on this exotic alternative to conventional proofs. Perhaps because ordeals were so uncommon, they often unfolded in unpredictable ways and, as noted, tended to end in "felicitous short-circuits." Even when the ordeal was proposed as a method of proof, it rarely determined the outcome of a dispute in the manner anticipated by disputants, judges, and courts.[30] Judges and disputants might reasonably expect that they would have the opportunity to back out of an ordeal even after they had proposed it. In 1000, the judge's proposal that one of the disputant's undergo an ordeal seems to have prompted the disputants to reach a compromise. The bilateral ordeal at Sant Cugat in 1037 yielded an ambiguous decision. At Urgell, the mere mention of the ordeal terrified one disputant into abandoning her claim.[31] In only one case did an ordeal take place and yield an unequivocal decision in favor of one disputant.[32]

Ordeals tended to short-circuit in ways that had beneficial effects. There are no recorded complaints about the injustice of decisions involving the ordeal. Records of cases involving ordeals insist that these cases arrived at just ends. Even alleged scoundrels like Sentemir were inspired by the results of the ordeal, however quirky and unpredictable those results were, to abandon unjust claims. But the ordeal's role in bringing these cases to such satisfying ends was anything but straightforward. When ordeals were proposed, they rarely unfolded according to preconceived plans. The proband's hand burst into flames before the procedure or the benevolent intervention of *boni homines* rendered the ordeal unnecessary. Proposing the ordeal may have resulted in outcomes considered fair by most of the participants, but these out-

28. *Sant Cugat* 545
29. As Stephen White argues, "A decision to propose an ordeal must be sharply distinguished from a decision to hold one." White, "Proposing the Ordeal," 93.
30. White, "Proposing the Ordeal," 101.
31. *Urgellia* 947.
32. *Viage* 8, 31.

comes rarely emerged methodically. When ordeals did take place, they almost never provided clear proof of one disputant's right to a disputed property. Instead, they prompted disputants to compromise, or revealed their treachery, or inspired members of the local community to involve themselves more actively in a dispute.

The unpredictable character of ordeals may have contributed to their tarnished image. Judges and probably other members of the community were suspicious of ordeals and of the disputants who proposed them. Property disputes were always adversarial, but the quality of the adversaries in cases involving the ordeal was different. The ordeal was seen as susceptible to fraud. Disputants who proposed ordeals were seen as untrustworthy, heterodox, and deceitful. In cases that did not involve the ordeal, disputants with no legitimate right to a disputed property might be described as confused, misinformed, or even ill-tempered, but they were rarely described as malevolent. In cases involving the ordeal, on the other hand, scribes often portrayed disputants as conniving and malicious.

Although anachronistic, the modern distinction between civil and criminal law might shed light on decisions to use the ordeal. Most tenth- and eleventh-century litigation (however rancorous) resembled modern civil suits. Two or more parties understood the disposition of property rights in conflicting ways. Each strove to offer a compelling account of its own claim in order to attain a favorable outcome. Cases involving ordeals inched toward the criminal in that at least one of the disputants was trying to deceive rather than to persuade. Some disputants who proposed ordeals did so because they believed that they could circumvent God's judgment with charms or incantations. Ordeals were apparently seen as more subject to manipulation than other proofs. Disputants who proposed the ordeal were depicted as disreputable, duplicitous, dangerous, and engaging in unwholesome commerce with supernatural forces. The ordeal was recognized as one component of the forensic landscape—one way to prove a claim—but proposing the ordeal was also associated with treachery.

The canons of Peace councils and legislation in the *Visigothic Code* also reflected this link between ordeals and disreputable litigants. In Peace legislation, the ordeal was proposed as a method of punishing someone whose guilt had been established rather than as a method of determining guilt or innocence. In disputes over property rights, the ordeal was probatory; in Peace councils, it was punitive. The very purpose of the ordeal was thus as protean as its procedure. The *Visigothic Code*'s suggestion that the ordeal be used for suspicious witnesses doubtless strengthened the connection between this type of proof and a particular type of disputant.

Medieval legal procedure paid a great deal of attention to the reputation of litigants, witnesses, and those accused of crimes.[33] Reputations are, of course, ephemeral and difficult to reconstruct. The task of separating rumor from reality is one of the challenges of understanding records that present only one perspective. Just as we should take with a grain of salt the positive image of judges presented in Bonhom's copy of the *Visigothic Code*, so too we should not accept without reservation the negative portrayals of some defeated disputants. The portrait of Sentemir in Sant Cugat's cartulary, for example, is not flattering. But had he been given the opportunity, he doubtless would have offered a more sympathetic account of his own decisions and motivations regarding his brother's estate and his day in court. The only surviving account of Sentemir's dispute with Sant Cugat leaves many questions unanswered. Did his hand burst into flames or was the scribe trying to render the vivid, collective sense of Sentemir's wrongdoing that pervaded the court? Was Sentemir an unscrupulous crook who would stop at nothing to cheat Sant Cugat of its rightful property, or was he the innocent victim of the monastery's aggressive drive to accumulate property?

There are good reasons to be cautious in our judgment of particular litigants, but caution should not lead us to admit defeat in the face of partial and laconic records. Informal and semiformal social categories like reputation sometimes misfire egregiously and in doing so can damage the social, financial, and even physical well-being of innocent victims; but much of the time those same mechanisms worked fairly well, providing judges with useful information for forging lasting and equitable judgments. There are some natural (though admittedly vague) limits to the extent that a disputant's reputation might be unjustly besmirched. The widespread participation of members of the community in judicial assemblies presumably limited the extent to which disputants could simply fabricate lies about their opponents. The inhabitants of this region were, as the next two chapters will demonstrate, adept at assessing written documents and witness testimony. They did not hesitate to reject unconvincing records or testimony. Portrayals of defeated disputants in records did not have to be charitable, but they did have to be plausible if they were to provide a defense against subsequent legal challenges. In other words, there was probably a degree of consensus that hovered around the negative picture of Sentemir. Whether he merited the profound suspicion shown by all of those around him or not, in legal terms, rumor became reality.

These questions about whether Sentemir actually burned his brother's testament, whether he really lied, and whether he intended to circumvent the

---

33. With specific reference to the ordeal, see Hyams, "Trial by Ordeal," 106–8.

justice of the ordeal with magic are indeed interesting, but they are not the most important questions. No descendants of Sentemir are trying to clear his name or to reclaim property lost a millennium ago. If records cannot always satisfy our understandable curiosity about the personalities of tenth-century litigants, the use of magical charms and incantations, or the possibilities of spontaneous combustion, they can still give us a vivid picture of the world in which those litigants moved. We will never have access to Sentemir's anxieties and hopes as he (allegedly) instructed his wife to burn his brother's will or proposed to undergo a judicial ordeal, but we can understand something of how Sentemir's contemporaries understood his actions. We can reconstruct how judges and disputants interpreted Sentemir's statements and choices, how Sentemir and his contemporaries understood proof.

Judges accepted ordeals as a type of proof, but they did so with little enthusiasm. If some disputants saw the ordeal as an opportunity to fabricate a legitimate claim in the absence of documents and witnesses, the region's judges had a different attitude. When judges began hearings, they often provided disputants with some idea of the types of proof they would welcome. They usually invited claimants to submit written proofs or to present knowledgeable witnesses. Judges never initiated an investigation with the suggestion that the ordeal might be a legitimate proof. But although the ordeal was never a judge's first choice, judges always accepted ordeals when they were proposed by disputants. Judges, like Bonhom who omitted the Visigothic rule from his legal compilation, displayed a mixture of discomfort and acceptance. They recognized that the ordeal might be a legitimate proof, but they usually turned to it only once a disputant had rejected other proofs.

That is not to say that judges never proposed the ordeal themselves. They too might use alternative, unusual proofs strategically. Judges might, for example, propose an ordeal in order to intimidate intractable litigants and to dissuade them from pursuing groundless suits.[34] In 1081, Judge Albert proposed the ordeal as a proof, and thereby inspired a disputant to renounce her unjust claim with astonishing speed. The judge's use of the ordeal was, however, no sign that he was abandoning venerable Visigothic legal traditions or minimizing the importance of written records. On the same day he frightened Bonadonna from her litigious course, Judge Albert executed another document relating to property in the same *villa* in which he cited a Visigothic rule stressing the importance of written documents in legal transactions.[35] Disputants with tarnished reputations were thus not the only ones who used the ordeal strategically.

34. White, "Proposing the Ordeal," 113.
35. *Urgellia* 948.

The ordeal was rarely the only type of proof involved in a dispute. The ordeal's deployment was always related to the availability and status of other proofs. It was proposed because available written proofs were defective or problematic.[36] Different proofs were intimately related in courts throughout Europe, but the nature of these relations was often regionally distinctive. Even when the same body of written law informed legal practice, the boundaries between different proofs might vary considerably from one place to the next. In eleventh-century León and Galicia, for example, ordeals were commonly used to verify oaths and witness testimony even when there was no suggestion that the testimony in question was considered suspect.[37] Thus, in two corners of the Iberian Peninsula, both steeped in Visigothic law, the links between testimony and the ordeal or between written proofs and testimony varied.

The ordeal was an unusual, even quirky, practice. But it merits a prominent place in any exploration of how disputants tried to win cases. Judges encouraged disputants to provide particular types of proof. When such proofs were unavailable or inconclusive, and when disputants refused to accept standard forensic procedures, judges might turn to the ordeal of the boiling water. Certain disputants—particularly ones considered to be disreputable—saw the ordeal as a last-ditch effort to win cases when other proofs were against them. The ordeal thus occupied a small but important niche in the practice of disputing. Despite their relative infrequency, cases involving the ordeal help frame broader questions about how disputants gathered proofs and how judges assessed them. Keeping in mind the interdependence of different proofs so vividly demonstrated by cases involving the ordeal, the next two chapters examine two less exotic varieties of proof that appeared more frequently, tended to yield less equivocal results, and provoked less judicial discomfort: written records and witness testimony.

36. See Bartlett, *Trial by Fire*, 26; White, "Proposing the Ordeal," 99.
37. See, for example, a dispute heard by Alfonso V of León in March 1024. "Colección Diplomática de Alfonso V," doc. IX, pp. 244–45.

CHAPTER SIX
FIGHTING WITH WRITTEN RECORDS

Written records played a large role in litigation. The enormous body of surviving records from this region suggests that people there were more committed to the written word than many of their contemporaries. Judges often cited rules that emphasized the importance of creating written records of a range of transactions.[1] At the same time, they pointed to the practical advantages of written records, advising property-holders to keep records to avoid conflicts and to prevent agreements from passing into oblivion.[2] Judges and property-holders were concerned about

---

1. For example, a judge in Urgell wrote: "Et lex iudicialis hoc dicit et iustitia hoc affirmat ut scripture ex omnibus intercurrant causis" (*Urgellia* 557). Another judge echoed the same sentiment: "Est in antiquitus regularibus institutum et in gothorum legibus est decretum ut inter comutantes gesta scripturam intercurrant, quatinus uno animo firmetur et corroboretur" (*Sant Cugat* 536). For similar citations, see ACA Ramon Berenguer I, 8; *Sant Cugat* 528; ACA Berenguer Ramon I, 54; ACA Monacals Sant Llorenç del Munt 129. A widely copied tenth-century formulary from Ripoll included the Visigothic rule stressing the importance of written proofs. ACA Monacals MS Ripoll 74, f. 151v. Compare *Leges Visigothorum*, II.1.23, II.2.5. See also Michel Zimmerman, "Un formulaire du Xe siècle conservé à Ripoll," *Faventia* IV / 2 (1982): 25–86.

2. ACV Calaix 6, 1833; *Girona* 78; *Lézat* 1295; ACA Ramon Berenguer I, 8; *Sant Cugat* 528; *Sant Cugat* 536; ACA Berenguer Ramon I, 54; ACA Monacals Sant Llorenç del Munt 129; On the idea of writing as a substitute for memory, see Franz H. Bäuml, "Varieties and Consequences of Medieval Literacy and Illiteracy," *Speculum* 55 (1980): 237–65; Paul Hyams, "The Charter as a Source for the Early Common Law," *The Journal of Legal History* 12 (1991): 173; and James Fentress and Chris Wickham, *Social Memory* (Oxford, 1992).

the longevity of agreements, and they placed considerable faith in the power of the written word to ensure stability of these agreements. Monks and churchmen saw documents as fundamental tools for defending property rights.[3] In the Province of Narbonne more than most places in Europe, litigation turned on the evaluation of written proofs.

When judges investigated conflicting property claims, the availability of written records was one of their chief concerns. Procedure in court very loosely conformed to Visigothic law, which dictated that proofs were to be sought from both parties to a dispute and that witness testimony and documents were the preferred forms of proof.[4] Judges usually asked disputants to prove their claims with either written proofs (*cartas* or *scripturae*) or witness testimony.[5] Disputants relied most often on records of earlier sales and donations, but many presented testaments or records of earlier judicial hearings. Disputants often presented two or three records, and sometimes as many as a half dozen.[6] If they were able, they built cases by presenting in court dossiers of written proofs.

Some disputants supported claims with records of royal or papal privileges. The see of Urgell's legal representative compiled a dossier of proofs to support the see's right to the church of Curcitia. In court, he began by presenting the testaments of two former counts of Urgell. Both of these indicated that the disputed church belonged to the see. He then presented three Carolingian royal privileges issued by Louis the Pious and Charles the Bald. Finally, he offered two papal privileges. Relevant passages from these documents were read aloud in court.[7] The success of the see's representative depended on the number, authority, and diversity of written proofs he presented. Major monasteries protected their vineyards, mills, and fields with similar textual compendia.[8]

From the middle of the tenth century, monastic foundations determined

3. *Oliba* 63.

4. *Leges Visigothorum*, II.1.23, II.2.5.

5. In some cases, they simply asked disputants for any *indicium ueritatis* (index of truth). See *Urgellia* 252. See also ACA Ramon Borrell 13; Gustave Desjardins, ed. *Cartulaire de l'abbaye de Conques eu Rouerque* (Paris, 1879), no. 18; *Urgellia* 570; *Béziers* 66.

6. *Sant Cugat* 470.

7. *Urgellia* 390. The see also appealed to the document recording the cathedral's consecration in 839. See Cebrià Baraut, *Les actes de consagracions d'esglésies de l'antic bisbat d'Urgell, segles X–XII* (La Seu d'Urgell, 1986) (hereafter *Consagracions*), 2. For roughly contemporary cases relying on Carolingian privileges in northern Italy, see Antonio Padoa Schioppa, "Aspetti della giustizia milanese nell'età Carolingia," *Archivio Storico Lombardo* 114 (1988): 9–25; and Ross Balzaretti, "The Monastery of Sant' Ambrogio and Dispute Settlement in Early Medieval Milan," *Early Medieval Europe* 3 (1994): 1–18.

8. BNF coll. Doat 71, ff. 295–97.

that papal privileges were especially desirable proofs, and they aggressively pursued these proofs. They dispatched representatives to Rome to acquire these valuable affirmations of property rights. The monastery of Sant Miquel de Cuixà was precocious in developing its archival abilities and received the region's first papal privilege in 950. Other monasteries quickly followed Cuixà's example: Arles-sur-Tech (968), Sant Pere in Besalú (979), Gerri (966), Sant Pere de Roda (974), and Sant Joan de les Abadesses (1016).[9]

The privileges which the abbots of Sant Cugat and bishops of Urgell brandished with such enthusiasm enjoyed a certain prestige in court, but they suffered some limitations as proofs. They were broader in scope than the records of sale or donation most disputants presented, and their breadth could prove a liability. Privileges usually confirmed rights to dozens of scattered churches, mills, and fields without describing the history of these properties. A royal privilege might assert that a particular *villa* belonged to Sant Cugat, but it would not indicate how Sant Cugat had acquired that *villa*. In weighing the merits of different claims, judges strove to reconstruct the histories of disputed properties. They tried to trace how a *villa* or an alod had been transferred from one party to another. Royal and papal privileges were impressive, but they often failed to provide information that judges regarded as essential.

The need for detailed information about the histories of disputed properties explains in part why litigants like the see of Urgell and the monastery of Sant Cugat relied on such a range of written proofs. Each type of record supported property claims in a different way. A comital testament might explain how property came into the see's possession, while royal and papal privileges demonstrated that the comital bequests recorded in the testament enjoyed the continuous approval of political and spiritual authorities beyond the horizon of local politics. The most successful litigants were those who assembled and presented different forms of written proof and could weave those different proofs into coherent narratives about the history of disputed properties.

The use of royal and papal privileges in court was confined to a handful of cases. Only cathedral chapters and major monasteries were able to acquire and deploy such impressive authorities. The strategy of presenting numerous and varied written proofs thus favored ecclesiastic and monastic dis-

---

9. Thomas Deswartes, "Rome et la spécificité catalane. La papauté et ses relations avec la Catalogne et Narbonne (850–1030)," *Revue Historique* 294 (1995): 28. Usually the involvement of the papacy in disputes was limited to issuing privileges, but on at least one occasion, the bishop of Barcelona sought more direct intervention from Pope Sylvester II. Educated at Ripoll, he was familiar with the political world of Catalonia. *Papsturkunden (896–1046)*, ed. Harald Zimmerman, 2 vols. (Vienna, 1984–85), no. 395.

putants. Important monasteries and cathedral chapters could rely on types of proof that were not available to smaller institutions and individual property-holders. Few churches or monasteries had the archival, intellectual, and legal resources to present cases in the manner that Sant Cugat, the chapter of Vic, or the see of Urgell did; no lay disputants had such resources.

Assessments by courts of disputants' claims were determined both by the variety of proofs presented and by the ways in which disputants used those proofs to argue their case. Resourceful disputants used modest proofs in novel ways. Abbot Guitard of Sant Cugat, for example, used records of sale and donation with great ingenuity. In 1017, Guitard accused a woman named Gondesalva of occupying an alod the monastery had received as a gift. Gondesalva denied the abbot's claim, explaining that she and her husband had purchased the property from another couple, Esteve and Argotamia. Gondesalva presented three different documents to substantiate her version of the property's past. The first of these recorded the purchase of the alod that she and her husband made. The second recorded an earlier transaction by which Argotamia had received the property as a gift from her mother, Ennegon. The third document recorded Ennegon's purchase of the alod. With records of two sales and a gift, Gondesalva traced the disputed alod's path through four successive owners. She and her husband were evidently canny real estate speculators. Her presentation of proofs shows that early eleventh-century land markets were active and that individual lay disputants used written records with care.

No one questioned the authenticity of Gondesalva's chain of documents, but the indefatigable Abbot Guitard did not admit defeat. After Gondesalva completed her presentation, the judges asked Guitard whether the monastery had written proofs to support its claim. The abbot explained that the original record specifying Sant Cugat's rights, along with countless other documents, had been destroyed in the 985 sack of Barcelona. Because of this disaster, the abbot had no record of the monastery's right to the disputed alod. Despite these difficulties, Guitard claimed that he could prove the monastery's claim by using the boundary clauses in documents related to neighboring properties. According to the abbot, records related to properties adjoining the disputed property would establish Sant Cugat's unshakeable right in the matter.

Guitard presented six documents, dating from between 987 and 1007. He described the six transactions in detail, noting whether they were sales or donations and naming the parties to each. He then specified the location of the properties mentioned relative to the disputed alod, pointing out where they bordered each other. Finally, he quoted boundary clauses from each of these six records which described the disputed property as within Sant Cugat's domain.[10] Although both Gondesalva's and Guitard's arguments are recorded in some detail, the deliberations of the judges, unfortunately, are not. The judges were confronted by two particularly strong cases, each argued in a very different way. In the end, they decided that Gondesalva's sequence of written proofs was inconsistent, but they did not suggest that she was guilty of any deceit. One of her three records had misrepresented the boundaries of the alod in question and, in doing so, had unjustly removed it from Sant Cugat's dominion. After evaluating the nine records presented by the two disputants, the judges decided in the monastery's favor. Despite Gondesalva's ultimate failure, the case shows that lay disputants could make sophisticated legal arguments amply supported by written proofs. Widows may not have been able to procure privileges or to employ legal experts, but they did maintain dossiers of documents related to their property rights and they knew how to use them. Gondesalva's proofs were ultimately rejected as less persuasive than Guitard's boundary clauses, but she made a thorough, consistent, and well-documented case.

The case reveals a great deal about how disputants presented written proofs and how judges evaluated them. Guitard admitted that he had no original record which tied the disputed alod to his monastery, but he asserted that he could prove the monastery's claim with secondary proofs. Judges were enthusiastic about written proofs and they were flexible in the sorts of documents they would consider. Gondesalva's claim was finally rejected because the judges ruled that the description of the alod in one of her charters was not consistent with descriptions of the alod in the two other documents she presented or with the boundary clauses in the documents Abbot Guitard submitted. For the judges, the case turned on the comparison of various parts of the nine different records presented by the two disputants. The judges pored over the nine documents looking for flaws, contradictions, and inconsistencies.

There was evidently more than one way to prove a claim. Even though both disputants appealed to written proofs, they understood proof in very different ways. Gondesalva's argument was chronological, while Guitard's was topographic. Gondesalva reconstructed the history of the disputed property, tracing the series of transactions which transferred the alod from one property-holder to the next. Guitard ignored the history of the property altogether, making no attempt to trace how the alod had come into Sant Cugat's possession. Instead he based his argument on the premise that the disputed alod (whatever its history) had to fit into a coherent landscape of property relations. Gondesalva documented transactions, while Guitard documented boundaries. Gondesalva followed the alod through time; Guitard

10. *Sant Cugat* 497.

located the alod in space. In this case, the two types of argument stood in stark opposition to one another. More often, disputants relied on some combination of the two forensic strategies, appealing to both history and topography. The judges in this case decided in Guitard's favor, but courts in general did not show a preference for one type of argument over the other. An argument as carefully documented as Gondesalva's would, in most cases, have persuaded the judges that the litigant's claims were legitimate.

Courts accepted many types of written proof, but older documents were usually considered to have greater authority. According to Visigothic law, documents that had been unchallenged for a year and a day were to remain unchallenged.[11] Several cases in which both disputants relied on written proofs show that judges considered older documents more persuasive. In 1020, the abbot of Serrateix brought a complaint before a comital court. The abbot and his advocate claimed that two properties rightly belonging to the monastery were being held unjustly by a woman named Emo and her husband. The abbot presented "legitimate documents confirmed according to the law by the former count's own hand," which recorded the donation of the alod to the monastery. The judge examined the monastery's document and found it truthful (*invenit eam veridicam*). He then asked Emo why she held the land. Emo and her husband presented a document that recorded their purchase of the property from one Arnold, who happened to be present at the hearing. He corroborated Emo's story and explained how the property had come into his possession. After hearing the evidence presented by both sides and examining the documents, the judge ruled in the monastery's favor because the abbot's charter was older than Emo's.[12] In a 995 case, the abbot of Saint-Genis similarly stressed the antiquity of his monastery's claim, saying that his documents were better and older (*scripturas anteriores et meliores*) than his opponent's.[13] In addition to age, judges also paid attention to the origins of records, looking favorably upon those created by other professional judges. Judge Pons Bonfill Marc, for example, was impressed when a disputant in his court submitted a document drafted by Judge Guifré of Vic.[14]

Disputants often used a variety of types of written proofs. There was not an especially rigid judicial criteria for evaluating written proofs, but judges assessed with care and sophistication the relative merits of the records presented. They especially appreciated time-tested documents and those that provided detailed information about a disputed property's past. In complex

11. See, for example, *Marca* 109, citing *Leges Visigothorum*, II.5.1.
12. *Oliba* 62.
13. *Cat. Car.* 297. See also *Oliba* 83.
14. *Urgellia* 438.

cases, judges often had to evaluate several written proofs. When they did so, they examined the written proofs for inconsistencies in both form and content. The ability to identify such inconsistencies was at the heart of the judge's task, just as the ability to weave a coherent narrative around records was every disputant's goal.

PROBLEMS WITH WRITTEN PROOFS I: FORGED AND FLAWED DOCUMENTS

When one party had written proofs to support its claim and the other party had none, courts usually decided in favor of the litigant with written proofs. But when both disputants had written proofs, judges had to accept some documents as convincing and reject others as forged, flawed, or irrelevant. In their attempts to resolve the conflict between Sant Cugat and Gondesalva, for example, judges compared the boundary clauses of several documents, searching for discrepancies. As they assessed the relative merits of conflicting records, judges always confronted the possibility that some of the proofs disputants submitted were forged. Although courts were flexible about the types of written proof they honored, they did not accept written proofs without scrutinizing them carefully. When it came to evaluating proofs, judges were flexible but they were also discriminating.

Even legitimate documents from reputable sources might be ambiguous. In a 1007 case, judges claimed that the records proffered by one disputant did not clarify the situation: "They showed them some documents, which were old. They were not able by these to discover the entire truth of the matter."[15] A court in Urgell rejected a document both because it recorded testimony which had not been properly received by a professional judge and because the testimony did not relate to the disputed property.[16] In a case during which Sant Cugat relied on royal and papal privileges, the judges were unable to determine the merits of the monastery's claim despite (or perhaps because of) the abundance of documents Sant Cugat submitted: "[The judges] thoroughly read the privileges and grants and examined the petitioners verbally, but it was not discovered who first gave this land to the monastery, nor was it ascertained that the church should possess it, since it had remained uncultivated for many years."[17] The court's uncertainty about Sant Cugat's rights points to the problem of ambiguous documents and un-

15. APO Fonds Fossa, series 12J24 n. 11.
16. *Guissona* 2.
17. *Sant Cugat* 464.

derscores the possible weakness of privileges as proofs. Individual documents had to make sense in their own right, but they also had to fit into a coherent history of the disputed property.

The ambiguity of valid documents was not the only difficulty judges faced when evaluating written proofs. There were other compelling reasons to distrust documents. Documents could, of course, be forged.[18] Judges understood this possibility and rejected some records as outright fakes. A dispute at Elne, which eventually involved the proposal of a judicial ordeal, began with a judge assessing two conflicting testaments: "The judge heard [the testament] read and reread, and found it deceitful and most false, and contrived against the law . . ."[19] The judge's decision regarding the validity of the testament included several discrete criticisms. The document was not only deceitful; it was also technically flawed, lacking the necessary seals and signatures. In Barcelona, a man named Bonhom (not to be confused with Judge Bonhom) allegedly used a series of fraudulent records to appropriate his sister's property while she languished in captivity in Córdoba.[20] In 996, the abbot of Santa Cecília of Montserrat lost a case over a disputed alod when the judges hearing the case found that the record presented by the abbot was deceitful.[21] Some disputants admitted during the course of an investigation that they had presented forged records.[22] In other cases, disputants realized that they had themselves been duped during earlier transactions. When a disputant named Renard saw his opponent's impressive "truthful records" (*veridicae scribturae*), he recognized that the document by which he had hoped to prove his claim was a "*scribtura apofrica* [sic]."[23] In other cases, a forgery was revealed only through the judges' examination of records, the interrogation of witnesses, and comparison of the questionable document with other records.

Scheming disputants went to great lengths to fabricate illegitimate documents and to persuade others that these were genuine. In 1032, Bishop Oliba of Vic and Sendred of Gurb reached an agreement regarding the tithes of

---

18. On forgery in the Middle Ages, see Giles Constable, "Forgery and Plagiarism in the Middle Ages," *Archiv für Diplomatik* 29 (1983): 1–41; and Elizabeth A. R. Brown's rejoinder to Constable, "*Falsitas pia sive reprehensibilis*: Medieval Forgers and Their Intentions," *Fälschungen in Mittelalter*, MGH Schriften, no. 33, vol. 1 (Hannover, 1988), 101–20. Despite certain differences, Constable and Brown agree that forgery was especially common during the eleventh and twelfth centuries.

19. *HGL* 158.

20. ACB Diversorum B 138.

21. *Santa Cecília* 96.

22. *Sant Cugat* 510.

23. *Urgellia* 560. See also *Girona* 59; *Sant Cugat* 542; and ACA Ramon Borrell 104.

several churches which the see and the Gurb clan fought over intermittently for nearly two centuries. In settling the affair (at least temporarily), Oliba described the origins of the dispute, tracing a series of legal maneuvers which reflected poorly on his episcopal predecessors. Bishop Frujà (972–993) gave tithes within the *castrum* of Gurb to Bonfill, brother of Sendred, lord of Gurb. This gift was confirmed by Frujà's successor, Arnulf (993–1010). When Bonfill died, Arnulf transferred the tithes to Sendred's son, Berenguer. Relations between the Gurb clan and the chapter remained amicable; Berenguer was even a canon in Vic's chapter. When Borrell succeeded Arnulf on the episcopal throne in 1010, he confirmed Berenguer's right to the tithes. But when Berenguer himself was elevated to Elne's episcopal throne, a major dispute (*tanta discordia*) over the tithes erupted. Bishop Borrell seized the property and launched a war of shifty diplomacy.[24] He falsified documents in order to advance his own claims and to discredit Berenguer. In 1017, he brought his forgeries to a council of bishops in Narbonne. The forgeries, which Borrell claimed were made during the episcopate of the long-dead Frujà, indicated that the tithes of Gurb rightly belonged to Vic's cathedral chapter. Borrell asked the archbishop of Narbonne and the assembled bishops to confirm his documents and to excommunicate Berenguer and his allies. Persuaded by Borrell's forgeries, they complied.

Not long after orchestrating this ambitious program of deceit, Borrell died while returning from an expedition to al-Andalus. When Oliba became bishop of Vic, Berenguer asked him to reconsider their case. After much negotiation, Berenguer and his brother proved to Oliba's satisfaction that the records Borrell had presented at the council in Narbonne were fakes. Oliba restored the tithes to the Gurb clan, adding the condition that a member of the Gurb family remain a member of Vic's chapter. The dispute over the tithes of Gurb was complicated and protracted. Although Oliba restored the peace temporarily, an ultimate resolution to the conflicting claims had to wait another 180 years.[25] It was only through the tenacity of the Gurb clan and Bishop Oliba's apparent willingness to listen that the forged proofs were finally discredited. For Borrell, Oliba's document-forging predecessor, episcopal stewardship at times demanded campaigns of deception.

The written proofs Borrell presented in Narbonne were forged and passed off as genuine. In other cases, the question of the validity of written proofs was less straightforward. Judges devoted energy and care to assessing the merits of written proofs, but they were at times unable to say whether a document was acceptable or not. During the 1027 dispute between Bishop Er-

24. *Oliba* 105.
25. Freedman, *Diocese of Vic*, 129–30.

mengol and his sister Geriberga, Geriberga's husband, Renard, presented a written record that substantiated his wife's claim to the tithes of Aiguatèbia. Ermengol and Judge Guifré questioned the record's legitimacy, but Renard's advocate, Judge Sendred, firmly supported its value. The disagreement between the bishop and his sister became a contest between two professional judges who disagreed about how to assess a particular written proof and how to interpret Visigothic law. Aside from showing how professional judges assumed roles of advocacy, the case also demonstrates that documents might muddy a situation rather than clarify it.

Renard's charter, in fact, so frustrated the judges that they made the general observation that documents often inspired doubt and controversy. Despite regular repetition of the idea that written proofs prevented conflict, judges at times conceded that the availability of written proofs did not always make a case straightforward. Undeterred, Sendred still insisted that his client's charter had some validity. Sendred's tireless defense of Renard's flawed document did not persuade the court that Renard and his wife had a better claim to the property than the bishop—who seems to have presented no proofs and to have contented himself with the public expression of his belief that the transaction recorded in his opponent's document struck him as unlikely.

Invalid documents ranged from charters that were willfully and maliciously fabricated to documents whose signatures did not meet the demands of rigorous judges. A judge examining a testament from Urgell found that most of its prescriptions were valid, but part of the document was disqualified because it contained unspecified elements that were contrary to written law (*contra legem*).[26] Other documents were disregarded entirely because of technical flaws. During a dispute at Lézat, one party's record was deemed unacceptable because it lacked the proper dating formula and the scribe's name.[27] A struggle between the bishop of Urgell and the monastery of Santa Cecilia further illustrates how carefully courts examined the technical features of documents submitted as proofs. Durand, the abbot of Santa Cecilia, claimed that his monastery had held a particular church for over one hundred years. The presiding judge ordered that evidence be gathered. Both parties offered written proofs to substantiate their claims. The abbot referred to records of donations made to his monastery by Count Borrell of Barcelona and Count Ermengol I of Urgell. The see's case rested on a bundle of papal and royal privileges. The judges compared the signatures on some of the monastery's records and concluded that one record was invalid.[28] The judges rejected the abbot's proof

26. *Urgellia* 438.
27. *Lézat* 409.
28. *Urgellia* 390.

on diplomatic grounds and ruled in favor of the see of Urgell. Judges thus assessed written proofs in terms both of form and of content.

Having a document declared invalid was, of course, damaging to one's case, but it was not always as damaging as might be expected. In this case, despite the fact that his document was found to be importantly flawed, Abbot Durand succeeded in persuading the court that the transactions recorded in it should not be considered altogether invalid. The abbot argued for the partial validity of his document much in the same way that Judge Sendred had argued that Renard's claims should not be entirely rejected because of what he characterized as the record's minor technical shortcomings. The court rejected Renard's claims, but the judges who evaluated Abbot Durand's claims were more inclined to compromise. Basing their decision on the richness of the see's written proofs and the unconvincing signature on the abbot's charter, the judges awarded the disputed church to the see, but the court also ruled that Durand's record was invalid only insofar as it pertained to the disputed property: "The document of donation that Count Ermengol, son of Borrell, had made to the monastery was judged invalid only in the place where the tithes and first fruits of Castellono applied. However, in all other places, it is firm and to be honored." The abbot's record was thus invalid in some places and valid in others. A flawed document was, it seems, better than no document at all.

The motivations behind such ambivalent decisions are not always clear. A rigorous process of investigation, which included the submission of several written proofs and their comparison in terms of content and formal features, was followed by a decision which found the abbot's document lacking, but not altogether invalid. Disputants and judges guarded vigilantly against forgeries and written proofs that did not meet their standards for legal validity, but despite their caution and their enthusiasm for properly executed documents, individual cases show that even rejected documents were still useful to disputants. Some charters were rejected as utterly false and their rejection undermined a disputant's claims altogether. In other cases, an ambiguity or technical flaw in a written proof made it less convincing or less authoritative, but the flaw did not eliminate the document's probatory value altogether.

PROBLEMS WITH WRITTEN PROOFS II: LOST DOCUMENTS

Although judges often expressed a cheery confidence that this profusion of writing would make for better law, clearer memory, and greater stability, the warm attachment to written proofs entailed distinctive problems. In practice, the relationship between memory, property, and writing was more complex than the judges' confident assertions might suggest. Judges devoted considerable attention to ferreting out illegitimate documents, but forgeries were not the only or even the most serious difficulty they encountered when they relied on written proofs. Courts also had to deal with the problem of lost records. Documents could only discharge their vaunted mnemonic function—could only ward off oblivion—if people were able to hold onto them. The sheer abundance of documents in Catalonia and Languedoc shows that the inhabitants of the region were, in fact, gifted at both creating and retaining records, but lost documents still often provoked problems.

During a dispute at Agde, the presiding judges asked the canons of Saint Stephen whether they had charters to support their claim to a disputed property. The canons replied weakly that they had lost it, but for all the apparent weakness of their admission, the canons did not believe that their negligence vitiated their claim.[29] In a dispute involving the monastery of Santa Cecilia de Montserrat, one disputant reported having lost a comital donation.[30] During a 1027 dispute, a castellan similarly reported that he had lost a comital charter through neglect.[31] In 1011, the Count of Barcelona renewed a grant made by his parents to the monastery of Sant Cugat. The count's scribe wrote pointedly that the original had been "lost through negligence," a charge which must have been especially galling to Sant Cugat's monks, whose normal zeal for record-keeping must have flagged momentarily.[32]

This handful of cases suggests that the question of how to deal with lost documents often arose during disputes. But the best way to explore the implications of lost records is to examine two catastrophic events that destroyed hundreds of documents: a flood in the valley of the Tet river in the 870s and the sack of Barcelona in 985. The late ninth-century flood of the Tet predates the tenth- and eleventh-century disputes that are the subject of this book, but the monks' response to the flood provides valuable background for understanding how institutions protected their property by creating records and by training the memories of their neighbors.

The monastery of Eixalada-Cuixà was founded around 840 and grew quickly. Under the guidance of several dynamic abbots, the monastery acquired a great deal of property throughout Cerdanya, especially along the

---

29. *Agde* 330.
30. *Santa Cecília* 184.
31. ACA Berenguer Ramon I, 56.
32. *Sant Cugat* 436.

valley of the River Tet.[33] Under the lavish patronage of Cerdanya's comital dynasty, the monastery eventually became one of Catalonia's most important.

The monks of Cuixà did not achieve this distinction without overcoming considerable challenges. In the early autumn of 878, the River Tet flooded. One especially shrill account reported (wrongly) that the flood destroyed the monastery's site and killed every member of the community. This account exaggerated the flood's death toll, but the consequences of the flood were grave. It seems likely that more than a dozen monks perished.[34] The record of the flood in Cuixà's documents is one of the earliest accounts of the life-threatening floods in the river valleys of Roussillon. Throughout the Middle Ages and even as late as 1940, the recurrent flooding of the Tet and Tech Rivers took lives in exactly the areas inhabited by the monks of Cuixà in the ninth century.[35]

The devastating flood convinced the surviving monks to move their foundation to a safer location upstream. The physical relocation of the community was one component of a well-organized and carefully executed plan to reconstruct the monastery after the flood's devastation.

The second component of the reconstruction program was not physical, but textual. The monks began to reconstitute the precious documents which the Tet's unruly waters had obliterated. Between November 878 and February 879, the monastery's monks created five remarkable documents.[36] These documents recorded how Cuixà's monks assembled witnesses who testified about the monastery's lost charters. The first of these transactions involved fifteen witnesses who testified about sales, donations, and exchanges made before the flood. In this case, the witnesses chiefly remembered gifts that they had themselves made to the monastery—memories which were duly recorded. On 29 January 879, the monastery's advocate, Borrell, gathered another group of seven witnesses in the presence of judges and *boni homines*: "The witnesses . . . testified in the presence of these judges about the lost documents of sale and royal diplomas—documents which were lost at Eixalada

33. See Pierre Ponsich, "Le domain foncier de Saint-Michel de Cuxa aux IX, X, XI siècles," *Etudes Roussillonaises* 2 (1952): 67–100.

34. Ramon d'Abadal i de Vinyals, "Com neix i com creix un gran monestir pirinenc abans de l'any mil: Eixalada-Cuixa," *Analecta Montserratensia* 8 (1954–55): 125–337, especially, 148–50. See also R. B. H. Bautier, "Notes historiques sur le Marche d'Espagne: Le Conflent et ses comtes au IXe siècle," *Mélanges Félix Grat* (Paris, 1946), I: 210–22.

35. Jean-Marc Antoine, Bertrand Desailly, and Jean-Paul Métaille, "Les Grand *Aygats* du XVIIIe siècle dans les Pyrénées," *Les Catastrophes naturelles dans l'Europe médiévale et moderne*, ed. Bartolomé Bennassar (Toulouse, 1996), 243–60.

36. *Cuixà* 57, 58, 59, 60, 61.

during the flood of the River Tet."[37] Unlike the first group of witnesses, these testified not about their own previous gifts but about transactions with which they were familiar: "We witnesses know and truly understand, our eyes saw, our ears heard, and we were present in the *villa* Ascaro when Count Miro commended to Abbot Baro and the monk Protasius these documents of sale and this royal privilege; we saw these documents read and reread, and we are familiar with the entire group of these documents. . . ." After the witnesses described the contents of the documents they knew so well, the judges accepted their testimony. Two days later, six of the same witnesses, joined by four others, participated in an assembly which restored another group of lost documents.[38] Again, the ten witnesses testified about documents which they had seen and heard read aloud. The judges again approved their testimony and the documents were restored. The monastery's advocate was reportedly delighted to have received the court's justice, but he took no time to celebrate his accomplishment. Ten days later, Borrell was in another *villa* organizing another judicial assembly with an almost entirely new list of witnesses.[39]

In the months following the traumatic flood, the monastery's representatives canvassed the countryside, asking dozens of neighbors to testify about their knowledge of lost documents. The monks of Cuixà lost their original deeds, but by spring they had created an authoritative catalog of their property rights from the testimony of their neighbors. The monks had good reason to be concerned about their property. Some of their more aggressive neighbors evidently saw the flood as an opportunity to encroach on the monastery's land. Within a few weeks of the flood, the monastery was involved in a dispute with a neighboring property-holder.[40] The encounter must have reinforced the monks' conviction that the community was vulnerable without thorough and well-publicized written records of its property rights.

When they set out to reconstruct their archive, the monks were fortunate to have neighbors with prodigious memories. In some cases, testimony was given by original donors about transactions only a few years old. But in many others, witnesses testified to their detailed knowledge of many transactions, some of which had occurred decades earlier. During the second assembly, in January 879, for example, witnesses remembered in detail sixteen different transactions dating from 840 to 876; some of the lost documents they remembered so vividly were nearly forty years old. The boundaries of vineyards and fields and the identity of their owners is, of course, the type of

37. *Cuixà* 57.
38. *Cuixà* 58.
39. *Cuixà* 59, 60.
40. *Cuixà* 55; and Abadal i de Vinyals, "Com neix i com creix," 403.

information least likely to be forgotten in small agricultural communities, but one still cannot help wondering what it was exactly that all these witnesses remembered. Some lost documents seem to have been remembered, in Patrick Geary's phrase, with "more than total recall."[41]

It is possible that all of the monastery's neighbors remembered in detail a complicated array of transactions from the 840s and 850s without any external aids, but in this case their memories were no doubt helped along by some of Cuixà's activities prior to the flood. In 876, two years before the flood, the monastery held assemblies attended by many neighboring property-holders at which the monastery's records and privileges were read aloud. The monks could not have anticipated that the Tet would swallow up these same documents two years later, but they rightly thought that training their neighbors' memories was a worthwhile project.

The monks of Cuixà were creative, but they did not invent from whole cloth these procedures for reconstituting lost documents. The *Visigothic Code* provided for people who lost documents. A rule in the *Code's* seventh book outlined penalties for those who had forged, destroyed, or stolen documents.[42] Nobles who did so lost a quarter of their property; people of lesser rank were whipped and reduced to slavery. The same rule also allowed destroyed, stolen, or missing documents to be reconstituted through a procedure called *reparatio scripturae* (restoration of records). When ninth-, tenth-, and eleventh-century judges borrowed from the *Code*, they did so selectively, and their use of this rule is no exception. Legal professionals and disputants enthusiastically adopted one part of the rule while they ignored other parts. Despite the considerable number of cases involving forged documents, the *Code's* carefully stipulated sanctions for this crime were never mentioned in later records. The section of the rule related to the restoration of lost documents, on the other hand, became a valuable tool for judges, disputants, and for the monks of Cuixà.

According to the *Code*, if someone destroyed a record and subsequently admitted their misdeed, they could testify regarding the destroyed document's contents. If this testimony were corroborated by other witnesses, the collective testimony would have the same legal force as the original document. A similar process could be used for lost documents. If one of the original act's subscribers testified to the act's contents, this testimony could stand in the place of the document itself. If none of the original act's subscribers were available, other witnesses who were familiar with the missing document

---

41. Patrick J. Geary, *Furta Sacra: Thefts of Relics in the Central Middle Ages* (Princeton, 1978), 85.
42. *Leges Visigothorum*, VII.5.2.

could testify at a public inquest that they had seen it and were acquainted with its contents. This testimony would be treated as if it were the original document.[43] The transactions of fall 878 and winter 879 which reconstituted Cuixà's archive thus had a foundation in Visigothic law. In every case, when the judges heard the testimony pertaining to the lost documents, they cited the Visigothic rule which, in effect, converted memories into documents.[44] In doing so, the judges introduced a procedure that enjoyed popularity from the ninth to early thirteenth centuries in cases of disastrous loss and those of minor negligence.[45] Their use of the procedure for *reparatio scripturae* is testimony to the dynamism of Cuixà's monks and their enthusiasm for written records. After all, these were the same monks who were the first in the region to seek and acquire papal confirmations of their property rights.

Relying on a Visigothic legal procedure and the well-tutored collective memory of their neighbors, the monks of Cuixà reconstituted their records and thereby protected their patrimony. A century later, individual property-holders turned to the same procedure in the wake of a different disaster: the sack of Barcelona in 985. In that year, the military leader of al-Andalus undertook one of his customary summer raids on the Christian kingdoms perched precariously in the northern Iberian Peninsula. The Andalusi army met with little effective resistance and, after a short siege, sacked the city. Many of Barcelona's citizens were killed; many others were taken to Córdoba in captivity. For decades after al-Mansur's raid, charters lamented the destruction of the city, the slaughter of many of the city's inhabitants, and the captivity of many others. Pious donations often included provisions regarding the long-awaited return of heirs from al-Andalus.[46]

In addition to human costs, there were documentary costs. References to the loss of family members and loved ones were accompanied by grim as-

---

43. The *Visigothic Code* was not the only medieval code to make provisions for lost documents. The Aragonese *Vidal Mayor* (III, 45) included provisions for lost records. Tilander, ed., *Vidal Mayor*, 2:244. Rosamond McKitterick discusses lost documents in the law of the Alamans in *The Carolingians and the Written Word*, 67. See also Ian Wood, "Disputes in Late Fifth- and Sixth-Century Gaul," in *Settlement of Disputes*, ed. Davies and Fouracre, 13.

44. *Cuixà* 57.

45. A short note by José Ríus Serra includes two early thirteenth-century references. See "Reparatio Scripturae," *AHDE* 5 (1928): 246–53. The provision was also invoked in León, although less often than in Catalonia. In 1007, privileges destroyed by fire were restored through the Visigothic procedure. See "Colección Diplomática de Alfonso V," in *León y su historia: Miscelanea historica* V, ed. José María Fernández del Pozo (León, 1984), doc. 6.

46. See Rovira i Solà, "Notes documentals sobre alguns efects"; and Zimmerman, "La prise de Barcelone par al-Mansur," 195.

sessments of the documentary implications of the raid. A 992 document from Barcelona's cathedral began:

> In the year of the Lord 985 ... armies advanced. ... Devastating all the land, they seized Barcelona. They depopulated the city and overwhelmed it with a great fire, so that all that was gathered there burned. Whatever escaped the fire, they took away: the spoils of booty—documents and charters and various volumes of books—in part consumed by the fire, and in part taken back to their land. Among these perished the charters of donation, gift, exchange, sale, and a booklet of royal privileges.[47]

Fortunately for surviving property-holders, judges in Barcelona knew their *Visigothic Code* every bit as well as the monks of Cuixà had. Courts, judges, and property-holders faced with this crisis of records turned to the *Code*. Charters bemoaning the destruction of Barcelona and its many documents cited the rule for *reparatio scripturae* as a way of restoring the region's past:

> These judges ... found the decree of the law in Book VII, title 5, chapter 2 of the *Visigothic Code*. ... The law does not ambivalently but very clearly instructs that if someone should lose a document through whatever accident, he should have the right to prove it by a public court, by the investigation of judges, by his own oath, and by the oaths of legitimate and knowledgeable witnesses who say that they themselves saw and knew the [missing] document. This testimony restores the truth of the lost document.[48]

Similar laments and similar invocations of the Visigothic rule appeared in other records that strove to restore the truth of lost documents. In 987, two years after the raid, a woman named Dulcidia sought the help of Judge Orús in Barcelona because her titles had been destroyed. The judge's assessment of her situation began with an account of the raid:

> Barcelona was besieged by Saracens and, with God willing because of our sins, it was captured on the sixth day of the same month. All who had stayed there at the command of Count Borrell to keep and defend the city were killed or captured. All of their substance also perished. Of those who were there, both books and royal privileges and all of those documents made in whatever way, by which they held their alods and possessions between them and their ancestors for the past 200 years, [were lost]. Among these were lost the documents of a man named Adam and his wife Dulcidia.[49]

---

47. Zimmerman, "La Catalogne," in *Les sociétés méridionales*, ed. Zimmerman, app. 1, 163–65. See also *Barcelona* 261.

48. Zimmerman, "La Catalogne," 163–64.

49. *Barcelona* 172.

With the judge's guidance, Dulcidia's witnesses testified about their knowledge of several documents she had possessed before the raid. The judge accepted their testimony and ruled: "These documents were lost on the day of Barcelona's fall. Today, according to the order of the law, the same written text of these documents is restored."

There was a resurgence in the use of the Visigothic rule for restoring lost documents immediately after the 985 raid. Once judges and litigants had rediscovered the pleasures of turning testimony about lost documents into documents themselves, there was no turning back.[50] Throughout the eleventh century, shrewd disputants, learned judges, and witnesses with impressive recall restored "lost" documents. In 1020, Bishop Oliba of Vic used the procedure to restore the endowment of the church of Manresa.[51] In this case, the documents to be reconstituted had allegedly been destroyed in a Muslim raid in 1003: "Be it known to all that the persecutions of the pagans took place in the time of Count Ramon, and the city of Manresa was laid waste by them. The churches were destroyed and torn out by the roots, so that neither books nor any charter instruments remained."[52] The testimony of six witnesses, described as having detailed knowledge of the church's property, traced the limits of the original endowment and the boundaries of the parish by referring to dozens of landmarks.

Oliba's use of the rule for restoring documents at Manresa is a testament to his creativity and erudition. In addition to being bishop of Vic, Oliba was also abbot of the monastery of Sant Miquel de Cuixà, a position that would have made him familiar with the documents reconstituting the monastery's patrimony after the flood of the Tet.[53] Although most people used the rule to restore records related to individual transactions, Oliba reckoned from what he saw in Cuixà's archive that the procedure for *reparatio* could be put to much broader use. Brandishing the *Code*, one could not only restore a lost charter recording the sale of a particular alod; one could reconstruct an entire monastic or ecclesiastic patrimony.

A 1032 dispute provides a final example of how complicated the process of *reparatio* sometimes became. Abbot Guitard of the monastery of Sant Cugat and Mir Geribert each claimed fortifications (including buildings, lands, and fishing rights) south of Barcelona. Abbot Guitard had been litigating aggressively and successfully on Sant Cugat's behalf for decades. Mir Geribert,

---

50. See García López, *Estudios Críticos*, 81–82.

51. See Ramon d'Abadal i de Vinyals, "L'abat Oliba i la seva època," in *Dels Visigots als Catalans*.

52. *Oliba* 63.

53. Oliba also would have known two ninth-century examples of *reparatio scripturae* in Vic's archive, *Vic* 27 and 28.

a magnate with ties to Barcelona's vicecomital family, was a worthy opponent for the shrewd abbot. He was one of the engines of the unrest that plagued the county of Barcelona between 1040 and 1060; and this dispute with Sant Cugat in the early 1030s can be seen as one of the early skirmishes in a more protracted conflict. The dispute took place in the context of an ongoing struggle over control of *castra* on the frontier and of the lucrative trade route to Tortosa.[54]

Mir claimed that the disputed properties belonged to his son because his son's great grandfather (Galindo) had established rights through *aprisio* (cultivation and long-term possession). The abbot replied that he knew nothing about this *aprisio*, but he did know that Frankish kings and counts of Barcelona had confirmed the property into the monastery's possession with royal and comital privileges. Guitard also claimed that the monastery had established rights to the property by bringing it into cultivation, despite the difficulties and dangers posed by the property's location on the Muslim-Christian frontier. Guitard thus based his claim both on written proofs and on having developed the land.

However, the royal privilege which Guitard invoked as the centerpiece of his case no longer existed. Instead of presenting this record, Guitard said that he could present witnesses who knew about the (now missing) document and its contents:

> Although Mir wanted to prove his *aprisio*, the judges preferred to receive the abbot's witnesses rather than Mir's, because the opinion of the decree (which Louis, king of the Franks, father of King Lothar, made of these churches to Sant Cugat by *aprisio*, and which the petitioner claimed were made by Galindo the great grandfather of this Galindo) was anterior. Since this order was destroyed in the sack of the city of Barcelona, witnesses testified on Guitard's behalf for the restoration of the lost document. They said that they had seen it and heard it read. Among other things, they heard it indicated that the property from which this conflict springs was a possession of the church of Sant Cugat for sixty years and more.[55]

Rejecting the judges' decision in favor of Sant Cugat, Mir left the court and appealed to another judge, Bonfill Marc. To this judge, he attacked the credibility of Sant Cugat's witnesses. He claimed that the first of these had apostatized, abandoned his monastic habit, sought out concubines, and conceived

---

54. Bonnassie, *Catalogne*, 543–44, 625.

55. *Sant Cugat* 527. For examples of disputants making similar claims, see ACA Monacals Sant Llorenç del Munt 182; *Barcelona* 261; ACB Diversorum B 1697; ACB Lib. Ant. IV, f. 155, doc. 365; *Notes hist.* 545; *Guissona* 3; and Eduardo Corredera Gutierrez, *El Archivo de Ager y Caresmar* (Balaguer, 1978), no. 5.

children with them. The second witness, in Mir's account, had committed adultery. The abbot's third witness had, according to Mir, deviated from the Christian faith, imitating the Muslim faith by performing circumcision.[56]

After hearing this assault on the monastery's witnesses, the judge, perhaps thinking that there could be little in the way of written proof for such failings, asked Mir if he had witnesses who could verify these accusations. Mir claimed that he could produce such witnesses, but in the meantime he asked the judge to verify his claim to the disputed property and presented two witnesses to testify that it was rightly his. Judge Bonfill was willing to entertain the notion that Sant Cugat's witnesses were ineligible to testify, but he was going to follow procedural rules scrupulously.[57] He told Mir that he would consider testimony about the unreliability of Sant Cugat's witnesses, but refused to issue a decision in favor of Mir's claim and offered two reasons for his refusal. The first was procedural: disputants could pursue only one complaint at a time, while Mir was trying to prove both that Sant Cugat's witnesses were unreliable and that his own claim was legitimate. The judge would not entertain Mir's claims about *aprisio* until he had presented the witnesses that would allegedly discredit Sant Cugat's witnesses. The judge's second reason was that he had reservations about the reliability of Mir's own witnesses, one of whom was "gravely oppressed with infirmity," while the other was "decrepit with age."

Judge Bonfill decided to leave the case open until further proofs could be gathered and all witnesses heard. The abbot protested that Mir had forfeited any right to further litigation by allowing too much time to elapse. Despite the judge's delay, Mir failed to materialize with the witnesses he promised who would prove that the monastery's witnesses were lecherous apostates. The judge awarded the disputed property to Sant Cugat, basing his decision in large part on written proofs that no longer existed.

Here, as in other cases involving *reparatio scripturae*, lost documents still had value as proofs. The Visigothic rule dictating procedure for the restoration of lost documents allowed litigants to argue claims using documents that "existed" only in the memory of witnesses. Disputants tried to present witnesses who could talk about lost documents consistently and in detail. Lost documents were a special form of proof. Like any other type of written proof, they had certain forensic strengths and weaknesses.

These re-creations of lost documents reflect a certain anxiety about writ-

56. *Sant Cugat* 527.
57. On infamy disqualification, see Jeffrey A. Bowman, "Infamy and Proof in Medieval Spain," in *Fama: The Politics of Talk and Reputation in Medieval Europe*, ed. Thelma Fenster and Dan Smail (Ithaca, N.Y., 2003).

ten records which sprang from a paradoxical combination. Disputants, donors, and judges operated in a legal environment that emphasized the importance of written proofs in holding, exchanging, and fighting over property. This legal environment, however, was occasionally compromised by disasters—military, hydrological, or personal—which destroyed records. Documents were repeatedly described as guarantees of stability, coherence, and continuity, but these guarantees of permanence kept getting lost, stolen, or destroyed. Litigation in these conditions demanded a certain amount of legal creativity, which could embrace both the importance of written evidence and the fact that many transactions (including very recent ones) left no records or left records that vanished.

These collected examples of written proofs in all their variety (charters and privileges, legitimate and forged, lost and restored) suggest some general conclusions about the place of documents in medieval courts. The first and most general conclusion is that written proofs played a prominent role in the assessment of competing claims. Legal professionals insisted on the importance of written records. Large institutions and individual property-holders alike created, kept, and used written records. During disputes, litigants constructed their cases around documents they presented in court—documents which judges examined with care and sophistication. Written records were vastly more important as proofs than judicial ordeals.

Attitudes toward written proofs further confirm the importance of written law in this region. Scribes regularly repeated the idea that property transactions should be recorded in writing, and property-holders heeded this advice. Moreover, a particular rule from the *Visigothic Code* informed the way people held and fought over land. The *Visigothic Code*'s provision for *reparatio scripturae* is yet another example of the way in which Visigothic law, although not uniformly enforced, exercised considerable influence even when used in ways that may have surprised Visigothic legislators. The *Code*'s provision for *reparatio scripturae* allowed individuals and institutions to reconstitute the past—to argue claims using documents that existed only in the memory of neighbors. The rule allowed them to remain energetically attached to written records, even when those records were burned by marauding armies, had floated downstream, or were lost through mundane carelessness. In some cases, presenting a written proof was not so much a matter of being able to display a physical document as it was of being able to describe a missing document persuasively. Lost documents were not non-evidence in these courts; they were a special subcategory of written proof. A seventh-century rule thus informed how people litigated and how they remembered well into the late eleventh century.

The integrity of documents was vital to the integrity of institutions. The loss of whole archives in catastrophes left individuals and institutions vulnerable. The unscrupulous were not above exploiting the instability caused by lost documents. When faced with record-keeping disasters, monasteries and cathedral chapters quickly set about reconstituting records of their property rights and their ties to donors. But just as there are always those who will exploit misfortune, so too there are those who will exploit rules. The rule allowing people to reconstitute records was doubtless a boon to people who had suffered much, but after reading a certain number of early eleventh-century records, one begins to suspect that some of the putatively destroyed documents never really existed.

Catastrophes invited a sort of hypermemory. Sociologists, psychologists, and historians have long acknowledged that memory is, in some important sense, social and collective.[58] Memory was, in the Middle Ages as it is today, fluid and subject to constant renegotiation. Catastrophes, large and small, inspired projects of collective memorialization. The examples I have discussed were principally concerned with the interrelated question of property rights and social relations, but one finds corroborating evidence by looking at how narrative history has engaged the same events. The 985 sack of Barcelona is often viewed as a crucial turning point in the history of this region—as the birth of an independent Catalonia. The earliest examples of narrative history in the region, which were significantly indebted to charter material, consecrate the sack of Barcelona as the fundamental moment in the crystallization of a regional identity.[59] If one remembers how thoroughly charters recorded the capture of Barcelona, the murder of its inhabitants, and the destruction of its documents, a historiographic irony emerges: the destruction of the re-

58. Maurice Halbwachs' writings on collective memory effectively founded the field of research, which has drawn the attention of historians during the past two decades. For an overview of scholarship, see the forum on collective memory in the *American Historical Review* 102 (1997). See also Fentress and Wickham, *Social Memory*; Patrick J. Geary, *Phantoms of Remembrance: Memory and Oblivion at the End of the First Millennium* (Princeton, 1994); and Clanchy, *From Memory to Written Record: England, 1066–1303* (Cambridge, 1979).

59. Miquel Coll i Alentorn, "La historiografia de Catalunya en el període primitiu," *Estudis Romànics* 3 (1951–52): 145–46; Paul Freedman, "Symbolic Interpretations of the Events of 985–988," *Symposium Internacional Sobre els Orígens de Catalunya (segles viii–xi)* (Barcelona, 1991), 117–29. The short chronicle of Sant Pere de les Puelles stressed the loss of books and documents. Miquel Coll i Alentorn, "La Crònica de Sant Pere de les Puelles," *I Col.loqui d'Història del Monaquisme Català, Santes Creus, 1966* (Santes Creus, 1969), 2: 35–50. The millennium of al-Mansur's raid was celebrated with great pomp in 1985. On a humbler scale, testimony often centered witnesses' memories around personal triumphs and disasters (e.g., broken arms, the burial of a favorite horse). See John Bedell, "Memory and Proof of Age in England, 1272–1327," *Past and Present* 162 (1999): 3–27.

gion's written history (charters, privileges, and books) became enshrined as the birth of the region's history. One cannot help but wonder whether all the records destroyed in floods and raids were not, ultimately, better remembered, more richly documented, more carefully recorded, and more abundantly witnessed than they would have been had the Tet stayed within its banks and had al-Mansur chosen to pummel León one more time rather than set his sights on Barcelona.

A final conclusion to be drawn from the cases involving documents relates to conceptions of proof in medieval courts more generally. The examples of lost documents reconstituted through witness testimony dramatize how different types of proof were interdependent. Historians' discussions of proof in medieval courts too often suggest that the distinctions between written proofs, oral proofs, and ordeals were more absolute than they actually were.[60] The procedure for *reparatio scripturae* blurred distinctions between oral and written proofs; witness testimony was treated as if it were a document.[61] Even before the flood, the monks of Cuixà orchestrated performances of their documents and they expected witnesses to remember these performances. The see of Urgell's canons also understood the value of instructing the community's memory and arranged for the count of Urgell to read in court a record of one of his gifts. At a later date, when the count's memory of his own benevolence faltered, the canons were able to call upon many people who remembered the count's performance and his gift.[62] Allowing records to gather dust until needed was not the most profitable way to use them. The public presentation of documents was one way to help witnesses absorb a written record's contents.

Judges in Catalonia often began their investigations into disputed property rights by asking litigants whether they had either documents or witnesses to support their claims; in practice, these two types of proof often became indistinguishable. The examples of the different varieties of proof from this region are distinctive, but elsewhere—Normandy, England, the Poitou, Italy—a similar interdependence of proofs is apparent.[63] The dis-

60. See, for example, R. van Caenegem, "The Law of Evidence in the Twelfth Century: European Perspective and Intellectual Background," *Proceedings of the Second International Congress of Medieval Canon Law* (Vatican City, 1965), 297–310; Jean-Philippe Lévy, "La Preuve, des origines à nos jours," *Recueils de la société Jean Bodin* 17 (1965): 9–70; and Duby, "The Evolution of Judicial Institutions," 51–53.

61. See, for example, HGL 194; Agde 323; and *Béziers* 44.

62. *Urgellia* 416. Michael Clanchy discusses the ways in which documents were frequently read aloud in court in *From Memory to Written Record*, 215.

63. See Jane Martindale's discussion of disputes near Poitou, "'His Special Friend?'" 44–45; Bedell, "Memory and Proof of Age in England"; and Emily Zack Tabuteau, *Transfers of Property in Eleventh-Century Normandy* (Chapel Hill, N.C., 1988), 212.

pute between Sant Cugat and Mir Geribert began as a case turning on written proofs, but eventually centered on the reliability of several different groups of witnesses. The case thus serves not only as an apt conclusion to a discussion of how disputants used written proofs, but also as a rich introduction to the place of witness testimony in property disputes.

CHAPTER SEVEN
COMMUNITY, MEMORY, AND PROOF: THE PLACE OF WITNESS TESTIMONY

The dispute between Mir Geribert and Sant Cugat discussed in the last chapter came to be dominated by conflicting witness testimony. Although the earliest recorded phase of the conflict centered on Sant Cugat's royal privilege, three different groups of witnesses eventually played roles, whether by their presence or absence. One group testified on the monastery's behalf in order to restore a privilege allegedly destroyed in the sack of Barcelona. According to Mir, these witnesses were "fornicators" and "apostates." A second group of witnesses testified that Mir's ancestor had established rights to the disputed property by *aprisio*. These witnesses were, in one judge's opinion, unreliable because of their advanced age and infirmity. Mir promised to present a third group to confirm his accusations about the shortcomings of the first, but these witnesses never materialized. The case involved attacks on the moral qualities and mental capabilities of different witnesses—attacks which raise the question of how courts evaluated witnesses and their testimony. The three witness groups in this case afford an introduction to the range of troubles which courts and disputants encountered when they relied on testimony. The memory of witnesses might be faulty; witnesses might be partial and dishonest; and it was not always easy to get witnesses to appear in court.

Judge Pons Bonfill Marc expressed concern when he wondered what Mir's witnesses could possibly remember about a claim of *aprisio* they had heard many years earlier, but a generous amount of elapsed time did not always provoke such skepticism. Although Mir questioned the morals and orthodoxy of

Sant Cugat's witnesses, neither he nor the judges hearing the case questioned the validity of their testimony on the grounds that they were testifying about their vivid memory of a record that had been destroyed forty-eight years earlier. Like Mir's own witnesses, Sant Cugat's witnesses were old. Mir did not, however, challenge their testimony on those grounds. Instead, he accused them of adultery and apostasy—athletic failings for such an aged trio and failings that would render them *infames* ("infamous") according to the *Visigothic Code*. The judge was willing to consider Mir's allegations about Sant Cugat's witnesses, but he would not disqualify their testimony until Mir substantiated his claims about their past. As the court proceedings increasingly focused on the reliability of different witnesses, the question of the original royal privilege faded from view. In this case, a lost document provided the framework for discussing the history of a disputed property, but the evidence the court actually examined was entirely oral. Although they disagreed about the relative merits of the witnesses who offered testimony, all the participants seemed to have agreed that the value of witness testimony varied considerably. The witnesses called to provide testimony in the case were, depending on whom one listened to, adulterous or chaste, pious or apostasizing, feeble or sound.

Despite complications like these, disputants often used witness testimony to substantiate property claims. Judges and scribes insisted on the importance of written records in sifting competing claims, but in practice the outcomes of many cases were determined by witness testimony alone rather than by, or in addition to, written proofs. Even the manner in which judges began investigations reflects the fact that written documents and witness testimony enjoyed a dual dominance as modes of proof; judges often asked disputants whether they had either *testes vel scriptis* (i.e. witnesses or documents)—to support their claims.

Those who offered testimony in tenth- and eleventh-century courts were usually witnesses rather than the oath-helpers that featured prominently in many early medieval courts. Witnesses testified about their first-hand knowledge of particular events or transactions rather than offering their general solemnized support for one of the litigants. Unlike a witness, an oath-helper swore an oath in support of a disputant and in so doing invoked God's participation in an earthly contest. In its reliance on divine participation in human struggles, the judicial logic of oath-helping resembled the logic of judicial ordeals. Witness testimony in this region, on the other hand, was not assessed by God but by earthly judges according to earthly criteria. Witnesses were useful to the court because they had seen and heard particular transactions or were familiar with longstanding patterns of behavior. In this respect, judicial practice in the tenth and eleventh centuries departed from Visigothic legislation which made the swearing of oaths a key form of proof.[1]

Throughout Europe, the distinction between oath-helpers offering their solemnized support and witnesses offering their knowledgeable testimony was not always clear.[2] But if in general disputants and judges did not always distinguish neatly between the two forms of proof, in the Province of Narbonne, courts were strongly inclined toward witness testimony. Judges paid attention to the *Visigothic Code*'s rules regarding testimony, but rarely relied on oaths as proofs. In this respect, judges in this region acted much like their counterparts in other parts of Christian Spain. The 1055 Council of Coyanza promulgated rules stipulating that witnesses were not to be accepted in court unless they had direct knowledge about the subject of their testimony. Documents from the nearby monasteries suggest that such legislation had practical effects on the ways proofs were assessed.[3] In Catalonia as well, most witnesses claimed to have direct knowledge of the facts about which they testified.[4]

Witnesses usually testified in groups. Ordinarily, these groups consisted of two or three people, although occasionally they might swell to twenty. Most witnesses were men, but it was not uncommon for women to testify.[5] Witness groups included both clergy and laity.[6] Usually when a large pool of possible witnesses was available to testify, two or three members of this larger group were selected.[7] Broadly speaking, tenth- and eleventh-century practice thus corresponded to a range of earlier legal authorities stipulating that in criminal cases and in property disputes a single witness was insufficient proof. Scripture provided one of the foundations for this idea. Two passages in *Deuteronomy* demanded that important offenses be judged only if two or

1. Alvarado Planas, "Ordalias y derecho," 492. For compurgation in a later period, see Richard Helmholz, "Crime and Compurgation in the Courts of the Medieval Church," *Law and History Review* 1 (1983): 1–26.

2. Davies and Fouracre, conclusion to *Settlement of Disputes*, 221.

3. See also García Gallo, "El concilio de Coyanza: Contribución al estudio del derecho canónico en Alta Edad Media," *AHDE* 20 (1950): 298; and Saturnino Ruiz de Loizaga, *Iglesia y Sociedad en el Norte de España: Iglesia Episcopal de Valpuesta, Alta Edad Media* (Burgos, 1991), 200.

4. On Visigothic law's contribution to legal prescriptions on hearsay evidence, see Frank R. Hermann, "The Establishment of a Rule against Hearsay," *Virginia Journal of International Law* 36 (1995): 1–51.

5. See, for example, *Santa Anna* 76. On women testifying in courts elsewhere, see Elisabeth van Houts, "Gender and Authority of Oral Witnesses in Europe (800–1300)," *TRHS*, 6th series, 9 (1999): 201–20.

6. *Urgellia* 252; *Oliba* 69; *Oliba* 83.

7. ACB Lib. Ant. IV, f. 34, doc. 1000.

three witnesses were available.[8] In *Matthew*, Jesus advises the disciples to rely on two or three witnesses to resolve tenacious conflicts: "Moreover if thy brother shall trespass against thee, go and tell him his fault between thee and him alone: if he shall hear thee, thou hast gained a brother. But if he will not hear thee, then take with thee one or two more, that in the mouth of two or three witnesses every word may be established."[9] In *John* too, Jesus mentions approvingly Mosaic law regarding the need for two or more witnesses.[10] In addition to such scriptural guidance on the question of testimony, judges could turn to earlier secular legislation which also mandated multiple witnesses. Justinianic legislation echoed this idea with the maxim, *testis unus testis nullus*.[11] The *Visigothic Code* required at least two witnesses before a judge was permitted to base a decision on testimony.[12]

Judges and disputants knew that not all witnesses were equally reliable and well-informed, and they devoted some attention to evaluating prospective witnesses. Records usually describe witnesses as qualified, lawful, or truthful (*idoneus, legitimus,* or *veridicus*). Such terms provide little insight into how members of a court determined that a particular witness was acceptable, but they do suggest that testimony was not accepted indiscriminately. Witnesses had to enjoy a certain reputation within the community.[13] The use of such general terms of approbation of certain witnesses is a small, but not insignificant, indicator that judges were aware of the dangers of bad witnesses. If their own experience or common sense did not adequately instruct them, Visigothic legislation included a number of rules that warned against false testimony. Judges may also have been familiar with Carolingian capitularies that lamented the poor quality of witnesses who were allowed to testify and stipulated stringent punishments for perjury.[14]

Although witness groups were composed of several people, they did not aspire to any diversity of opinion. On the contrary, groups testified as a single collective witness, or at least that is the manner in which judges understood and scribes recorded their testimony. A case from Agde notes a judge's

---

8. Deuteronomy 17:6 and 19:15. See also David Daube, *Witnesses in Bible and Talmud* (Oxford, 1986).

9. Matthew 18:15–16.

10. John 8:17. See also 2 Corinthians 13:1 and 1 Timothy 5:19.

11. Jean-Philippe Lévy, "Le problème de la preuve dans les droits savants du moyen âge," *RSJB* 17 (1965): 151.

12. *Leges Visigothorum,* II.1.25 and II.4.3.

13. The terms are sufficiently general that their use does not demand any special legal explanation, but it is worth noting that the *Visigothic Code* described desirable witnesses as *idoneus* or *legitimus*; *Leges Visigothorum,* II.4.6; II.4.7; II.5.12; III.2.3; VI.5.5.

14. Olivier Guillot, "Le Duel Judiciaire: Du Champ Legal (Sous Louis le Pieux) au Champ de la Pratique en France (XIe s.)," *La giustizia nell'alto medioevo (secoli IX–XI),* 731.

approval of unified, unvarying testimony: "When the judge heard these witnesses testifying well and without variation, but offering one testimony all together, he entered with them into the church of Saint Stephen, and they put their hands over the most holy altar."[15] A case in Urgell similarly involved three witnesses testifying with one voice: "In their presence, Salla presented his proof [*testimonia*]: that is [the witnesses] Guillem of Ripella, . . . Odo, . . . and Arnold, . . . who with one mouth acknowledged that they had seen the transfer or gift of this *castrum* into the power of the above-mentioned Bishop Salla through the handing over of a ring."[16] Witnesses may have disagreed with one another and there may have been discrepancies in their memories, but judges and scribes effaced any traces of disagreement and uncertainties from the record.

This emphasis on the uniformity of testimony suggests something about how courts approached oral proofs. The court's goal in hearing witness testimony seems not to have been the reconstruction of events from the fragmentary knowledge of a range of different witnesses, each of whom might be expected to present discrete and possibly conflicting accounts. Instead, witnesses were expected to testify about a particular well-defined question and to do so in harmony. In this sense, judges did not approach witness testimony with the same attitude they displayed toward written proofs. When examining records, judges searched for irregularities in form and content. When listening to witness testimony, they elided differences and tried instead to formulate a single, unified testimony. That is the most common way in which charters record witness testimony, but not all judges agreed that this was the most fruitful way to examine witnesses. In his copy of the *Visigothic Code*, Judge Bonhom remarked that witnesses should be examined separately, presumably because they might have different knowledge of the events in question and might influence each other.[17]

In court, witnesses testified about their knowledge of three things: particular transactions, long-term possession, and the boundaries defining different properties.

15. *Agde* 323.
16. *Urgellia* 278.
17. Escorial z.II.2, f. 3r. Bonhom's suggestion is in keeping with the lessons taught by the *Book of Susannah*, in which the heroine rebuffs the sexual advances of two lecherous men who spied on her. The jilted elders accuse her of adultery, and she is very nearly convicted—until Daniel suggests that the accusers be questioned separately. The inconsistencies in their separate testimony convince the court that Susannah is innocent and that her accusers have committed perjury. Both the *Usatges of Barcelona* and the *Siete Partidas* required that witnesses be heard separately. *Usatges* 99; *Siete Partidas* III.xvi.26. In one case, witnesses were questioned separately and this procedure was described as customary (*sicut mos est*). See *HGL* 175.

Most witness groups testified that they had seen a disputant enjoy undisturbed possession of a disputed property for a prolonged period of time, usually thirty years. The idea that long-term occupation generated unshakeable property rights conformed both to Visigothic law and to Carolingian rules regarding *aprisio* grants.[18] The *Visigothic Code* forbade legal actions concerning transactions that had taken place thirty years or more in the past. Even to seventh-century legislators, the notion seemed hallowed by time. In one rule, Reccesvind insisted that the period of thirty years seemed determined not by human institution but by nature itself (*natura*).[19] The existence of and respect for such rules was, of course, a boon to disputants who lacked written proofs to show how they had acquired their rights. Even without such records, they might substantiate their claim by presenting witnesses who testified that they or their predecessors had held the same rights for three decades without challenge. A 997 case included testimony related to long-term tenure: "We, the above-mentioned witnesses, know and recognize fully in truth, and we saw with our own eyes, these tithes being held and possessed by the see of Saint Mary for thirty years and more."[20] Disputes at Elne, Girona, Barcelona, Sant Cugat, and elsewhere involved similar testimony.[21] Testimony affirming that a disputant had possessed property rights without challenge for a long time was the most common variety.

Witnesses also offered testimony about transactions, describing how they had been present at and remembered particular sales or donations. In 1030, a dispute centered on the earlier donation of property by a man named Eldo to a woman named Trudlend and her three daughters. To substantiate her claim, Trudlend presented five people who testified that they had witnessed the original donation.[22] In a case at Vic, the chapter's archdeacon produced witnesses to show that his opponents had unjustly alienated the same property twice, first to the see and then to another party.[23]

Since disputes often began in challenged bequests, it is not surprising that witnesses were frequently called to testify about the contents of testaments. When asked to do so, witnesses not only described the provisions of those

18. André Dupont, "Considération sur la colonisation et la vie rurale dans le Roussillon et le March d'Espagne au IXe siècle," *AMidi* 67 (1955): 223–45.

19. *Leges Visigothorum*, X.2.3; X.2.4. See also King, *Law and Society*, 101. The Fourth Council of Toledo (633) ruled that boundaries unchallenged for thirty years should remain so.

20. *Urgellia* 252.

21. *HGL* 175; *Girona* 100; *Sant Cugat* 317; *Notes hist.* 209; ACB Lib. Ant. III, f. 5, doc. 14; ACA Berenguer Ramon I, 13; *Oliba* 95; and *Sant Cugat* 577.

22. *Urgellia* 438.

23. ACV Calaix 6, 1833. For a 1042 case see ACB Lib. Ant. IV, f. 155, doc. 365.

testaments, but also their memories of the conditions under which the testaments had been dictated.[24] When they described the provisions included in testaments, witnesses often affirmed the coherence of testators when they dictated their testaments.[25]

Somewhat less often, witnesses testified about boundaries. In 994, a judicial assembly resolved a conflict by seeking knowledgeable witnesses from the area surrounding a disputed property. Countess Ermengard of Cerdanya presided over a court accompanied by her son, Bishop Berenguer of Elne. The abbot of the monastery of Saint Mary at Arles complained that several people had been infringing on the boundaries of a *villa* belonging to the monastery. The abbot insisted that no one could legitimately cultivate land, construct buildings, or harvests crops within the boundaries of the *villa* without the monastery's permission and claimed that some malefactors were guilty of doing just such things. He further complained that people in the surrounding communities had not been eager to help the monastery safeguard its property.

The countess listened carefully to the abbot's complaint, and then asked the two judges and attending magnates how the court might resolve such a serious problem. The judges cited a popular passage from the *Visigothic Code* which stated that suppressing the truth was as great a crime as contriving falsehood and prescribed penalties for those who testified falsely or concealed their knowledge. The court then undertook an investigation of the limits of the *villa*, which involved finding witnesses who knew the traditional boundaries of properties in the area:

> When the countess and the magnates heard the counsel that the law instructed, they ordered that all proven observers who were born in Tapias and Furchas or who were raised there should come into their presence. Whoever should be the oldest and should best know the truth about these boundaries should swear not to conceal the truth and not to tell lies. When all the inhabitants of these *villas* heard about this judgement from the judges and magnates, it pleased them. They gathered in front of the church of Saint Martin, which is within the alod of Tordarias, and they chose from among themselves three witnesses who would swear an oath in the church of Saint Martin with their hands over the altar of the holy martyrs Abdon and Sennen. Their names were Sigfred, Stephen, and Altimir. The witnesses left the church and went up to the ridge that is above the church, where the two routes join together, that which comes from Saint Peter and that footpath which comes from Saint Stephen.[26]

24. *Oliba* 99.
25. *Agde* 323; *HGL* 193–194.
26. *Marca* 143.

As in other cases, a small group of witnesses was selected from a larger available pool. Although age was sometimes a liability, in this case the court sought out older witnesses. The witnesses, accompanied by members of the court and a crowd of onlookers, circumambulated the limits of the *villa* in a jerky but precise fashion. The three long-time residents walked through fields, gardens, hills, and streams, noting which properties were owned by whom. After describing dozens of landmarks, they stopped: "They went down by the garden in the forest which is beneath the house made by Bonfilius. . . . From there the witnesses did not walk any further. Instead, they said that they did not know anything more about defining these alods." Although their local knowledge (and perhaps their stamina, for they were old and their itinerary involved a considerable amount of clambering up and down hills) had a limit, the witnesses agreed about a long list of landmarks which the scribe fixed in writing. Although the witnesses quit their tour near the garden by the house Bonfilius constructed, their testimony about the long-known borders of different properties sufficed for the court's immediate purpose of responding to the abbot's complaint.

Bishop Oliba of Vic's 1020 restoration of the endowment of the diocese of Manresa relied on his appeal to the Visigothic procedure of *reparatio scripturae* and on witness testimony: "They sought out old boundary observers, as the authority of the law teaches, now lost because of the persecutions. They identified the limits of the parish of Saint Mary, as they were indicated in the endowment, which more than thirty years earlier had been drafted by Bishop [Gregory]."[27] The restoration mentioned lost documents and proceeded to explain how witnesses described landmarks indicating the limits of the church's property. In these cases and others, courts resolved disputes and prepared for future conflicts by appealing to the collective memory of senior members of the community. Rather than seeking witnesses who remembered isolated transactions, courts sought witnesses who reconstructed the landmarks which distinguished one property from another. There was a foundation for such procedures in a short title in the tenth book of the *Visigothic Code, De Terminis et limitibus,* that specified that if there were uncertainty about the boundaries of a disputed property, a judge could request the testimony of local elders (*certiores vel seniors*) to determine established limits.[28]

With its reliance on the collective wisdom of a group's *certiores vel seniores*—evident in Countess Ermengard's examination of those who had been born and raised near the disputed *villa* Tordarias—testimony about boundaries involved the participation of the broader community to a greater extent

27. *Oliba* 63. See also *Cart. rous.* 43.
28. *Leges Visigothorum*, X.3.5.

than other forms of testimony. The decisions reached were shaped to a large extent by collective activity. In chapter 3, I noted that accounts of judicial assemblies usually focus on the activities of judges and disputants. Occasionally, however, documents reveal broader collective responses to conflict. These responses might take the form of *boni homines* who encouraged parties to reconsider claims they found unreasonable or testimony about boundaries. The description of the tracing of the limits of Tordarias, for example, dramatizes the public and collective nature of some testimony. Litigants, judges, witnesses, and spectators paraded through the fields, gardens, and vineyards of numerous property-holders. In such cases involving boundaries, one can most clearly detect collective efforts to restore fractured peace. Judicial professionalism and collective action were not necessarily antithetical.[29]

Witness testimony thus provided judicial assemblies with information that neither written proofs nor judicial ordeals could. The documents used as proofs during disputes usually commemorated particular transactions by which property relations were altered. Witness evidence related *both* to particular transactions and to witnesses' memory of enduring situations. In some cases, witnesses testified because they had been present when a testament had been drafted or when a donation was read aloud. More often, they testified that a particular disputant and his family had occupied the same vineyard for thirty years or that the boundary between one disputant's vineyard and another's was widely known to be a particular boulder or road.

CHALLENGED TESTIMONY

Testimony was not without its own limitations. Just as written proofs might be lost, destroyed, or inconclusive, witnesses could be unreliable, forgetful, or dishonest. Judges and litigants recognized these difficulties and, as I have already suggested, they did not rely on witness testimony indiscriminately. The now-familiar case of Mir Geribert and Guitard provides one vivid example of how two disputants suspected (or at least accused) each other of producing deceptive and unreliable witnesses. Theatrical accusations of the sort Mir Geribert leveled at Sant Cugat's witnesses were rare, but disputants and judges often voiced more mundane reservations about the reliability of witness testimony.

The abbot of Sant Cugat, for example, insisted that Mir's own witnesses

29. In general, see Susan Reynolds, *Kingdoms and Communities*, especially chapter 1, "Collective Activity in Traditional Law, 900–1140."

were too old to be reliable. So too the testimony provided by witnesses in the restoration of documents at Cuixà might provoke raised eyebrows. Describing records lost in the flood of the Tet, witnesses recalled their detailed knowledge of five documents of sale or exchange. They remembered twelve different donors or sellers, the dates on which the transactions took place, the properties in question, the terms of the agreements, and the names of the scribes.[30] In another procedure of *reparatio scripturae*, witnesses remembered the details of twelve different documents involving dozens of participants and properties.[31] Some of these transactions had taken place thirty-eight years earlier. The restoration of Manresa raises similar questions about the function of testimony. Bishop Oliba's stated goal was the restoration of the diocese and its patrimony, a goal which he claimed was complicated by the destruction of all written records related to the diocese in a Muslim raid. Most of the lost documents Oliba referred to were created in the 930s. When the bishop organized witnesses to restore these documents, they testified about transactions that had taken place ninety years earlier, the records of which had been destroyed more than fifteen years earlier. Sometimes medieval disputants raised questions about the quality of witness testimony; at other times, even if the testimony was uncontested, the modern reader must wonder what precisely was being remembered and how clearly.

The cases at Cuixà and Manresa were extraordinary in that they dealt with the wholesale reconstruction of a monastic and an ecclesiastic patrimony relying on witness testimony. But the question of witness reliability came up in relatively modest disputes as well. Judges often asked disputants if they had any objections to the witnesses their opponents presented. In some cases, both parties presented witnesses and one party withdrew its claim altogether upon hearing the opposition's testimony.[32] In a 1029 dispute, Judge Guifré of Vic asked one disputant, Bernat, whether he had objections to his opponent's witnesses. Bernat conceded that he could say nothing against them.[33]

Such docile responses were not, however, the norm. Disputants often refused to accept testimony offered by their opponents' witnesses, claiming that the testimony provided was untruthful or irrelevant. In 997, Judge Guifré presented several witnesses to support the see of Urgell's claim to certain tithes. Segar, who had challenged the see's claim, refused to accept their testimony: "Judge Guifré presented himself with his legitimate witnesses

30. See chapter 6 above.
31. *Marca* 40.
32. *HGL* 175.
33. *Oliba* 95.

[*testibus legitimis*] before us in this court, but Segar did not want to receive them and instead abandoned the court."[34] In another case sixteen years later, a disputant named Guitard followed Segar's uncooperative example: "Then when Guitard should have accepted these proofs, he left without the judge's consent and he did not want to accept [them]."[35] A woman named Bonadonna did the same after her opponent's witnesses testified—a decision which the scribe openly criticized: "Although Bonadonna should have accepted these proofs, she left [the court] and did not want to accept the proofs [*noluit recipere ipsas provas*]."[36] In 1051, one set of disputants refused to accept witness testimony even though the judge had given them the opportunity to question the witnesses' reliability and the three disputants had admitted that they had no objections:

> Before receiving the testimony, they spoke to the litigants Dalmaç, Guillem, and Adalbert. They asked them if there were any grounds by which they could reasonably contradict these witnesses because of their infamy. They said that there was nothing that they could object to. So they were informed by the judges that they should accept the testimony of the witnesses, which they refused to receive; and they contemptuously withdrew from court.[37]

There were legitimate reasons that one might have challenged witness testimony. As some of the above cases have shown, judges often invited disputants to question the reliability of witnesses. Dalmaç, Guillem, and Adalbert were asked whether they could reject the witnesses through any charge of infamy. The judge was doubtless thinking of rules in the *Visigothic Code* which disqualified certain people from giving testimony. Major criminals (killers, poisoners, sorcerers, perjurers, and those who had violated religious vows) were branded with *infamia* and disqualified. Aside from these exceptions, Visigothic law allowed any free person of rational mind over the age of fourteen to testify.[38]

Dalmaç, Guillem, and Adalbert were not the only disputants to offer no reason for rejecting witness testimony. In the 1018 dispute between Countess Ermessenda and Count Hug of Empúries, Hug refused to accept Ermessenda's witnesses. Hug's representative offered excuses for his refusal that were described as "trifling and ridiculous."[39] The dispute between Abbot Guitard and Mir Geribert, in which Mir accused the abbot's witnesses of a

---

34. *Urgellia* 252.
35. *Urgellia* 539.
36. *Urgellia* 398.
37. ACV Calaix 9, Episcopologio II, 51.
38. *Leges Visigothorum*, II.4.1; and King, *Law and Society*, 103.
39. *Oliba* 56.

host of dramatic failings, was, in its specificity, an exception to the rule.[40] Usually, when disputants rejected their opponents' witnesses, they offered no explanations for why they did so—or at least none that scribes considered worth recording.

When disgruntled disputants abandoned hearings, the judicial process usually faltered for only a moment. Cases in which disputants abandoned hearings—usually because they objected to testimony—all ended in more or less the same way: the judges hearing the case conferred and decided to accept the challenged testimony. Judges usually justified their decision to do so by citing a passage from the *Visigothic Code* which supported judicial discretion in accepting or rejecting controversial testimony. The practice of overriding protests and accepting challenged testimony was one of the most important powers judges possessed. Judges tried to ensure that all parties accepted the testimony of every witness, but in cases where one party refused to do so, judges decided the case over the protests (or despite the absence) of uncooperative disputants.

Judges firmly believed in their ability to adjudicate cases in this manner. In the case involving the tithes of Aiguatèbia, Judge Guifré cited this rule when Renard failed to show for the third hearing at Ripoll. Although in this particular case Judge Sendred's client was unsuccessful, Sendred himself was especially enthusiastic about the notion of a judge's discretion regarding witness testimony. In an earlier transaction, Sendred, invoking the *Visigothic Code* and the presiding count's instructions, had accepted witness testimony over the objections of one disputant.[41] Sendred further stated that it would not be permitted for disputants who left court to produce any witnesses to testify on their behalf—a notion of disqualification echoed in other cases.[42] A few years later, he cited the same rule from the *Code* in another dispute, noting that he accepted the witnesses according to the *Code*'s guidance and at the command of the presiding countess.[43] Other judges often cited the same rule.[44]

Despite Sendred's apparent enthusiasm, accepting testimony over the protest of one disputant was an extreme step, one that judges usually took reluctantly—only when they were convinced that they had exhausted alternatives. Judges might consult at some length about the best course of action: "We judges debated about this among ourselves, and we found in Book II [of

40. *Sant Cugat* 527.
41. *Urgellia* 398.
42. *Sant Cugat* 496; ACB Lib. Ant. IV, f. 110, doc. 279.
43. *Urgellia* 539.
44. *Sant Cugat* 496; *Sant Cugat* 529; ACV Calaix 9, Episcopologio II, 51; *Oliba* 56; *Oliba* 95.

the *Visigothic Code*] this decision: If by order of the judge one party will produce witnesses and it is fitting that the other party should receive them, but instead [that party] leaves the hearing without the consent of the judges, it is allowed for the judges to accept the witnesses."[45] Even when judges are not described as poring over copies of the *Code* for guidance, descriptions of litigants leaving court and of subsequent judicial decisions to accept challenged testimony echo the language of the *Code*. Scribes and judges were clearly uncomfortable with such situations and tried to show that their decisions conformed to the conditions described in the *Code*. They noted, for example, that the uncooperative disputant should have accepted the testimony. In Bonadonna's case, the record insists that her objections to her opponent's witnesses were not legitimate. Hug's reservations about his opponent's witnesses were dismissed as *inanes et superfluas*.[46] Records also emphasize that judges encouraged uncooperative disputants to accept the testimony. Judges usually claimed that they had exhausted alternatives before they accepted testimony that was sure to alienate one of the disputants.

THE INTERDEPENDENCE OF PROOFS

The most interesting feature of the constellation of written records, witness testimony, and the ordeal was their practical interdependence. No rigid hierarchy of proofs existed, and disputants often relied on more than one type of proof. Boundaries between written and oral, rational and irrational, were porous. The popular reliance on the Visigothic procedure of *reparatio scripturae* for restoring lost documents through witness testimony affords one example of the complicated interplay of different proofs. The flood of the Tet and the flurry of transactions in the decades after the sack of Barcelona testify to the importance of this procedure in defining property relations and, for individual litigants, in winning disputes. Extraordinarily popular among judges and property-holders, the procedure does not conform neatly to categories like "written" or "oral." The evidence produced by *reparatio scripturae* was, in the logic of eleventh-century courts, to be treated like written proof even if the information had been gathered through the oral examination of witnesses.

The procedure for restoring lost documents produced an especially interesting form of hybrid proof, but this was not the only type of proof which

45. *Urgellia* 252.
46. *Oliba* 56.

combined features of oral and written, rational and irrational, individual and collective. In 956, a dispute over an alod erupted between a woman named Bonafilia and the canons of Agde. The bishop of Agde and several canons brought their complaint before a court and claimed that a woman named Fachilo had drafted a document which gave the contested alod to her husband Pons. Fachilo had specified that if their daughter did not attain majority, Pons would enjoy the use of the alod for life. After his death, the property would go to the cathedral church of Saint Stephen at Agde. The canons complained that Bonafilia had contravened the conditions of Fachilo's gift and had taken the alod from them. Presented with a dispute that emerged in part from the terms of this *scriptura*, it is not surprising that the judge asked the canons to submit the record whose conditions they had so carefully explained:

> The judge asked the bishop and the canons of Saint Stephen if they had this document. They answered that they did not because they had lost it. The judge then asked them if they had any witnesses who had read it or heard it read out. The bishop and canons responded with one voice that they had enough true witness testimony for us. The witnesses came into this presence, and their names were Dodbert and Artald: "For we are witnesses that we saw this document and we heard it read how Fachilo gave with a document of donation to her daughter and her husband Pons the alod in the *villa* Fornellus.[47]

The testimony of Dodbert and Artald about their knowledge of the record convinced the court of the canons' right to the disputed property. The canons won the case with proofs that were neither purely written nor purely oral.[48] In many cases, disputants' arguments in court relied on witness testimony about absent written proofs. Canons, bishops, and monks from Agde to Barcelona found ways to wield the legitimacy of written titles without actually producing them in court. Instead they orchestrated oral performances of absent, but allegedly well-remembered, documents.

In other cases, legitimate written proofs were available, but they were considered insufficient. In the 1040s, the canons of Urgell presented a testament to support their claim to the disputed alod of Nocholo. They explained that a sickly Erimam had come to the cathedral and had stated that upon his (rapidly approaching) death, the canons would receive this alod. Erimam ordered that a document recording this bequest be made. Erimam's brother, Arnau, was extremely displeased by this arrangement. He insisted that the document which the canons presented was not the truth (*non erat veritas pre-*

47. *Agde* 330.
48. See also ACB Lib. Ant. IV, f. 155, doc. 365.

fata scribtura).[49] Arnau's indignation got the better of him. He took matters into his own hands and pillaged the disputed property. The bishop and the judge hearing the case ordered the canons to present witnesses who could vouch for the legitimacy of their document: "The judge judged that these canons should give witnesses that the document was true and authentic [*idonea*]." Arnau relented and accepted the canons' witnesses. The judge only made his decision and Arnau only abandoned his claim after the canons had provided both written evidence *and* witness testimony corroborating the legitimacy of the document. Written proofs alone did not suffice. Erimam's testament and witness testimony about his document worked in concert. In a similar case at Vic, judges accepted a testament as a valid proof only after the chapter had produced witnesses supporting their case.[50]

In a 1030 case mentioned above, Eldo named Trudlend and her daughters the beneficiaries of his testament. During a later dispute with the see of Urgell, Trudlend presented Eldo's testament in court. The document— properly dated, witnessed, and signed—corroborated her claims. But the notation of the original judge, no less than Guifré of Vic, caused the presiding judge some concern. When the judge asked Trudlend if she could produce witnesses who would vouch for the validity of the testament, she replied that she could:

> In order to prove this, she brought worthy witnesses . . . who testified on oath saying thus: "We witnesses swear by God, almighty Father, and Jesus Christ his son and by the Holy Spirit . . . that we saw and it was transacted in our presence, when the priest Eldo transferred and donated this document of donation which he made to Trudlend and to her daughters, into the hand of Trudlend . . . according to the law of gifts. The handing over of the document took place in our presence and in the presence of Judge Isarn and many other witnesses, in the place above the lands where Eldo lived. We know what we say to be right and true; no fraud or scheming effects our testimony, but we promise it is true and say so by the above oath in the Lord." Judge Bonfill received this testimony for the confirmation of the charter of donation, and in his court and in the presence of other worthy men, the daughter of Trudlend received those things given to her.[51]

Here too, a document with all possible signs of legitimacy was not enough to substantiate Trudlend's claim. The circumspect judge required her to present five witnesses to confirm the document's validity before he would acknowledge Eldo's gift.

49. *Urgellia* 612.
50. ACV Calaix 9, Episcopologio II, 51.
51. *Urgellia* 438.

Written proofs and witness testimony were almost always complementary parts of the discovery process, and judges saw this interdependence of proofs as a fundamental aspect of judicial practice. In 981, Count Roger of Carcassonne prefaced a donation to Saint-Hilaire by insisting on the joint necessity of documents and witnesses to confirm the transactions recorded in them.[52] This reliance on multiple forms of proof was not restricted to one type of disputant. The literate judges of Barcelona, Vic, and Urgell appealed to oral evidence, and groups of relatively humble lay litigants presented documents. The interdependence of oral and written forms is one of the distinguishing features of courts in this region, but similar dynamics informed the social and legal world of Europe more generally in this period. The complex interplay of oral and written is also evident in the courts of Provence and Italy, in the making of the Domesday book, and in Breton hagiography.[53] This interaction of varieties of proof occasionally caused trouble elsewhere, just as it did in Catalonia and Languedoc. Michael Clanchy discusses a twelfth-century dispute over investiture in England which pitted Anselm of Canterbury against Henry I. The dispute turned on whether to accept written proofs— in this case, an impressive papal bull shown by Anselm's monks—or the testimony of three bishops. The bishops dismissed Anselm's bull as mere sheepskin "blackened with ink and weighted with a little lump of lead."[54] Even in a world where documents were commonly used and widely respected, detractors argued that memory was more reliable than the written word.

The *Visigothic Code* acknowledged that records and testimony might be at odds. The *Code* stipulated punishments for testators who made written testaments and oral bequests which contradicted each other. In such cases, the *Code* indicated that the written testament was to be honored and that judges were not to accept oral testimony regarding other bequests.[55] The Visigothic legislators' preference for the written will in such cases was never invoked in tenth- and eleventh-century disputes, although Judge Bonfill Marc cited part of the rule.[56] Judges paid attention to the *Code's* observation that two forms of proofs might contradict each other, but they do not seem to have accepted the hierarchy of proofs that the *Code* proposed. A clear judicial preference for

52. *HGL* 134.

53. Geary, "Living with Conflicts in a Stateless France"; Bougard, *La justice dans le royaume d'Italie*, 224; Robin Fleming, "Oral Testimony and the Domesday Inquest," *Anglo-Norman Studies* 17 (1994): 101–22; Julia M. H. Smith, "Oral and Written: Saints, Miracles, and Relics in Brittany, 850–1250," *Speculum* 65 (1990): 311; and Nick Everett, "Literacy and Law in Lombard Government," *Early Medieval Europe* 9 (2000): 118.

54. Clanchy, *From Memory to Written Record*, 233.

55. *Leges Visigothorum*, II.5.18.

56. *Urgellia* 438. See also García López, *Estudios Críticos*, 489.

written proofs over witness testimony grew on the Iberian Peninsula only during the twelfth and thirteenth centuries.[57]

In practice, the arguments made by disputants and assessed by courts were based on amalgams of different mutually reinforcing proofs. Judges expressed great trust in documents, but they frequently relied on witness testimony to stand in place of lost documents, to discredit faulty documents, and to corroborate legitimate ones. In both comital courts and in more modest assemblies, disputants relied on complicated admixtures of the written, the oral, and, occasionally, the divine to prove their claims.

The flexibility of courts in terms of proofs and the lack of any clearly articulated hierarchy for evaluating proofs does not indicate that courts were indiscriminate in what they considered persuasive evidence. On the contrary, judges subjected proofs to intense scrutiny. They rejected documents for a variety of reasons: missing signatures, boundary clauses that did not correspond to other clauses, a signature that did not match, or failure to conform to Visigothic procedural rules. In other words, judges evaluated written evidence with considerable legal, diplomatic, and historical rigor. Similarly, witnesses were challenged because they were too old, too young, too immoral, or too uninformed. In many cases, the variety of proofs afforded judges considerable discretion. They were able to exploit diverse sources of information about disputed properties (and property-holders) and to test proofs against one another.

Each form of proof had strengths and limitations. Written records might be lost or forged, but they were not subject to the contingencies of fallible memory. Judicial ordeals afforded divine direction, but the forms that direction took were difficult to interpret. Judges could question witnesses about their testimony, but those witnesses might be misinformed or dishonest. Judges understood these advantages and limitations, and so did disputants. As judges faced the task of weighing proofs, disputants confronted the challenge of shaping proofs into persuasive arguments. In court, they strove to show that their own proofs were clear and compelling while their opponents' were defective. With varying degrees of success, disputants crafted strategies for navigating the constellation of proofs. Clever disputants did not let documents languish unread and unremembered. Instead they orchestrated performances of their records, knowing that neighbors with well-tutored memories were an asset in court. Successful litigants shaped the reception of

57. See, for example, R. I Burns' discussion of proofs in *Siete Partidas* (III, xx) and Pere Benito i Monclús, "El plet dels homes francs de Sarrià (1258) Crisi i pervivència de l'alou pagès a la Catalunya medieval," in *Les sociétés méridionales à l'âge féodal (Espagne, Italie et sud de la France, X–XIIIe s), Hommage à Pierre Bonnassie*, ed. Hélène Débax (Toulouse, 1999), 71–79.

their proofs before, during, and after actual judicial assemblies. In court, disputants disagreed about how proofs should be assessed. Some argued that venerable royal privileges should trump other claims; others suggested that such privileges were too vague to resolve difficult cases. Some argued with eloquence and conviction that thirty-years' tenure, witnessed by neighbors, established rights which could not be challenged by documents of any sort. Others countered that a clear, written title was more compelling than any amount of witness testimony regarding uninterrupted possession. Just as they strove to discredit their opponents' written proofs, so too disputants tried to undermine the authority of their opponents' witnesses, pointing out inconsistencies in their testimony or suggesting reasons that they should be excluded from testimony.

Some disputants made their arguments methodically, others recklessly. Some were honest, others unscrupulous. Some litigants knew a great deal about the rules and norms that governed proofs; others fared poorly because they were confused and ill-informed. There were patterns to the ways in which courts evaluated proofs, but success or failure often depended as much on how one used the proofs that were available as it did on the quality of the proofs themselves.

PART III

ENDINGS AND CONTEXTS

CHAPTER EIGHT
WINNING, LOSING, AND
RESISTING: HOW DISPUTES
ENDED

The first two parts of this book explored the resources communities possessed for addressing conflict and the ways disputants tried to substantiate their claims to disputed property. Lay and ecclesiastic magnates presided over judicial assemblies at which professional judges evaluated cases with frequent (but selective) appeals to written law and to ritual sanctions. Courts relied on different types of proof to sift conflicting claims, and disputants displayed a formidable range of abilities in presenting proofs. The exploration of courts, codes, proofs, and strategies in preceding chapters reveals a great deal about property and conflict during the central Middle Ages, but so far I have left unexamined questions about how disputes ended. This chapter addresses questions such as: Did these courts resolve disputes? When did disputants stop fighting and why? Were courts able to enforce their decisions? How long did resolutions endure?

The nature of surviving sources is a particularly acute problem in discussing how disputes ended. In those rare instances when documentation is especially rich, it is possible to trace the contours of a dispute or the history of a particular property. But in most cases, surviving records are fragmentary, and it is possible to catch only a brief glimpse of one moment in a dispute which may have affected several generations of property-holders. In most cases, it is difficult to say with confidence whether court-issued decisions resolved conflicting claims permanently, temporarily, or not at all. Many disputes surfaced again in one form or another, whether in judicial assemblies, informal negotiations, violent confrontations, or chronic rancor.

A second difficulty is that records vary greatly in the amount of information they provide. Some monasteries and cathedral chapters had scribal traditions of recording arguments and decisions in considerable detail. The resulting documents record disputants' proofs, judges' decisions, and gifts or payments from winners to losers. Many records are less complete and include only a judge's decision or a quitclaim. The brevity of such records suggests that some of the conditions of a settlement (such as gifts to a losing party or a losing party's objection to the settlement) went unrecorded. In other words, although two disputes may have reached similar ends, they may look quite different on parchment.

The final, and perhaps most intractable, challenge is one I have pointed to in the introduction and elsewhere above: the opinions of some litigants are recorded more thoroughly and sympathetically than others. A significant number of disputants rejected judicial decisions and abandoned the courts that issued them. The authority of magnates, the erudition of judges, and the encouragement of neighbors did not convince them that justice was being done. In some cases disputants rejected decisions simply because their ambitions were thwarted, but in others they had coherent and thoughtful reasons for doing so—reasons that are unfortunately represented very poorly in records. The voices, however faint, of property-holders like Renard and Geriberga are still worth listening for.

For these reasons, conclusions about how disputes ended must be more speculative than conclusions about other elements of the legal world of the Province of Narbonne. It is easier to understand the process of disputing—how disputants argued and how they understood proofs—than it is to grasp how, when, and whether disputes were "settled." One of the ironies of these sources is that the phase of the dispute process which was of the keenest interest to the litigants themselves (the outcome) is the most obscure to historians.

THREE TYPES OF SETTLEMENT

Courts responded with creativity to the challenges before them and formulated decisions that responded to the particularities of different disputes. For this reason, any categorization of decisions will not do justice to the nuanced solutions crafted by judges, bishops, countesses, and *boni homines*. A typology of decisions can, however, provide some rough sense of the types of settlement courts issued. Settlements in this region might be divided into three broad categories. The first (and most common) type of decision was one in which a court decided unequivocally in favor of one disputant. The second category includes cases in which an unequivocal decision in favor of one party was followed by some sort of compensation to the losing party. In decisions of the third type, courts proposed compromise settlements, usually dividing the disputed property equally among disputants. Of 161 disputes with clearly described decisions, 98 record unequivocal decisions in favor of one disputant. In 37 cases, unequivocal decisions were accompanied by some compensation to the losing party. In 26 cases, courts opted for compromise decisions.

The most common type of decision requires the least comment. In these cases, judges and magnates assessed proofs offered by contending parties and determined that one party's claim was clearly superior. These cases often ended with the losing parties acknowledging the superiority of their opponents' case and renouncing future claims to disputed properties.

The second type of settlement, in which winning parties made payments, gifts, or concessions to losers, admitted more variation. There were two main types of remuneration. In many cases, victorious parties gave one-time gifts of produce, livestock, or money to losing parties. In other cases, defeated parties were granted circumscribed property rights. A court might, for example, award the disputed property to one disputant and instruct the victor to grant a life-tenure or rights of usufruct to the defeated party. A few examples can show how such decisions unfolded in practice. In 1008, two groups of cousins quarreled over a salt pan near Narbonne before an assembly composed of the abbot of a nearby monastery and a group of *boni homines*:

> These men, hearing this argument and seeing the truth of the matter, separated them [the disputants] and gave them useful advice. They recognized that they had no right [to the property] because they were not legitimate heirs, and that they should make an agreement with their kindred, which they did. So that things should be better . . . Esteve and his sisters gave their cousins three Narbonne *solidi*, and they accepted them. Then Pons and his sisters ordered their cousins to make this quitclaim or security, that from that day on they would not interfere with this alod.[1]

In another case, the count and countess of Barcelona presided over a court in which a group of peasants claimed that the count himself had mistakenly appropriated their field. The count and countess promised to hear the group's claims openly and honestly, and to respond "just like other people." Submitting to the decision of their magnates and judges, who decided in the peasants' favor, the count and countess surrendered the field and received a countergift of "thirty of the best and fattest rams."[2] A disputant named Lu-

1. *HGL* 166.ii.
2. ACA Ramon Borrell 104.

pus abandoned his claim to some property when he received a horse and other movables worth fifty *solidi* from Cuixà's monks.[3] Losing litigants often received countergifts like these from their opponents, and such compensation may well have been more common than surviving records indicate. Such transactions doubtless made it considerably easier for some litigants to accept defeat. At the same time, countergifts signaled the finality of agreements. Once a defeated litigant publicly accepted a gift in exchange for her quitclaim, it would be much harder to renew claims to disputed properties.[4]

The resolutions reached in these cases could be still more complicated. Some victors affirmed their legal victory but immediately granted restricted property rights to their defeated opponents. Rather than severing ties with losing disputants or offering losers a horse for their quitclaims, winners granted losers life-tenures. While a court had decided that the disputed alod or *castrum* rightly belonged to a given monastery or cathedral chapter, the losing disputant would, according to the terms of the new agreement, occupy the property until his or her death. Such arrangements appealed to both parties for several reasons. A victorious church or monastery gained explicit recognition of its proprietary rights to disputed property. A partial grant to the defeated party provoked only a minimal disruption in the exploitation of the land. The landlord continued to enjoy rents and payments without having to establish a new tenant on the property. The losing disputant, on the other hand, retained some interest in the disputed property (albeit as a tenant rather than freeholder). Tenants also enjoyed the benefits of affiliation with monastic communities and their holy patrons. When Jofre Maier abandoned his claim because of the sentence of excommunication that had been imposed on him, his quitclaim did not mark the end of his relationship with the monastery but rather its intensification:

> I came before Count Ramon and Countess Valentia in the castle Mur and I quit myself of that *condamina* into the hand of Abbot Arnau in such a way that neither I nor any of my progeny will demand it. After this the count and the abbot approved that I should come to the monastery of Gerri and to the monks, and I came into their presence and I gave [the *condamina*] up over the altar of the blessed Mary. Then the abbot and the monks gave me this land by their hands— except for the tithes. In this agreement, I accepted that I should hold it com-

3. BNF coll. Doat 82, f. 335.

4. For other cases that ended with unequivocal decisions followed by some sort of compensation to the losing party, see ACA Ramon Berenguer 62; ACV 6, 1406; *HGL* 207.v; ACB Lib. Ant. I, f. 175, d. 461; ACB Lib. Ant. II, f. 190, doc. 568; ACA Berenguer Ramon I, 101; *HGL* 370; and *Béziers* 66. On the difficulty of identifying such gifts in records, see Patrick Wormald, "Giving God and King Their Due: Conflict and Its Regulation in the Early English State," in *La Giustizia nell'alto medioevo (secoli IX–XI)*, 549–92.

pletely during my lifetime. After my death it will freely and completely transfer to the monastery without any restrictions. Because of the gift that they made me, I make a gift in memory of the blessed Mary such that each year I will give twenty loaves of bread [*fogasas*] and the meat of one pig . . . and two *sesters* of wine and one quarter of oats.[5]

Although both parties acknowledged the superiority of the monastery's claim, both received something and the ties between Jofre and the monastery were strengthened.

The dispute over the tower of Moja recorded in Sant Cugat's cartulary was similarly resolved with a concession to the losing party. The monks and Geribert disagreed about who owned the tower. The court awarded the tower and property attached to it to the monastery. Abbot Guitard, claiming to have been inspired by divine mercy, granted partial rights to Geribert, allowing him to work the property and including several restrictions—notably that "both he and his children should make a gift of the tithes and the rents of this alod faithfully and sincerely to the monastery."[6] The agreement also stipulated that Geribert could not sell, trade, or give away any part of the rights he had received. The abbot's grant of usufruct to Geribert was hedged with restrictions designed to prevent any confusion about the monastery's ultimate rights to Moja. Geribert's annual gift to the monastery would serve as a regular reminder to Geribert and his family that they were Sant Cugat's tenants.

Such arrangements were usually designed to remind holders of usufruct grants that their rights were limited.[7] Unlike one-time payments to defeated disputants, arrangements like these enmeshed disputing parties in long-term relationships, and because of this they also posed challenges for everyone involved.[8] No matter how emphatically agreements stressed the limited scope of tenants' rights, tenants' understanding of their rights tended to swell over time. Because of this tendency, settlements that involved usufruct or life-tenure often ran amok. For example, Igiga left an alod to Sant Cugat on the condition that her son would enjoy rights of usufruct. As a reminder of the terms of the agreements, her son was required to pay ten *solidi* each year to the monastery. Despite this annual prod to his memory, Igiga's son did not

5. *Gerri* 4. On the sentence of excommunication, see chapter 2 above.

6. *Sant Cugat* 438. See also *Sant Cugat* 542.

7. See, for example, *Adge* 330; *Barcelona* 224; *Lézat* 478; *Urgellia* 535; *Sant Cugat* 612 and 613; *Sant Cugat* 623; and *Oliba* 130 and 131.

8. Barbara Rosenwein has shown how Cluny's friends and Cluny's enemies were the same people; they cycled through rhythmic periods of concord and antagonism which strengthened their ties to the monastery. See Head, Rosenwein, and Farmer, "Monks and their Enemies," 772.

maintain a clear sense of how limited his rights were. Misunderstanding (or disregarding) the status of the property, he sold part of it to a third party, Rossello. When the monastery's abbot came looking for Igiga's son (perhaps in search of Sant Cugat's annual payment), he found instead the industrious Rossello hard at work developing the property.[9] The abbot struck the same deal with Rossello that he had with Igiga. Rossello, after all, was doing more to make the monastery's property productive than Igiga's apparently lazy son ever had. Rossello, for his part, was probably eager to avoid a confrontation in court with Abbot Guitard—a confrontation which Rossello almost certainly would have lost. Both the monastery and Rossello seemed content with the solution, but the case highlights the problems that emerged with such agreements. Ecclesiastic and monastic landlords strove to remind tenants that their property rights were limited. Despite these reminders, tenants often "forgot" the terms of agreements or thought of those agreements as open to constant renegotiation. Decisions involving one-time payments allowed for a cleaner break between disputants. Decisions in which the losing party received some limited property rights allowed for warmer relations between disputants but at the same time sowed the seeds of future misunderstanding.

One-sided payments generally involved conditions which softened the loser's defeat. These gifts and concessions were sometimes so generous that one-sided decisions begin to look more like compromises; the victor's victory begins to ring a bit hollow. Nevertheless, it is important to distinguish between one-sided victories with concessions to losers, on the one hand, from explicit gifts or payments, on the other. Even if an agreement involved significant concessions to the defeated party, the winning party still emerged with a written record vindicating his or her claim. Given the importance of written proofs in upholding property rights, such a record would have been of considerable value in defending the property from subsequent challenges.

The third type of decision was compromise. In these cases, courts divided property rights between contending parties. In 987, two brothers, Vivas and Ugbert, brought a disagreement about their inheritance before a court presided over by the bishop of Barcelona. The bishop, a judge, an archdeacon, and several others decided that the two brothers should divide equally the property which included an alod, cows, sheep, grain, and wine.[10] In 1024, several brothers quarreled over their shares of an inheritance. In this case as well, a disputed alod and *castrum* were, at the instruction of two judges, di-

9. *Sant Cugat* 479.

10. *Archivo Condal* 207. Pierre Bonnassie places this dispute in the context of several generations of this family's economic activities. See his "Une famille de la campagne barcelonaise."

vided.[11] In a 1013 dispute between Sant Cugat and Adalaiz, a comital court issued the following decision:

> When both parties had in turn argued vehemently about this, the count and countess, with the group of priests and nobles and the approval of the judges, gave and imposed the following decision between the two parties: Since they were not able to disentangle in strict ownership whose right was greater, and since it was difficult for one family to exploit this place and to bring it into cultivation and to construct a fortified tower, and since no small number of neighbors gather in shelter from the approach of the yoke of the Saracens, they would make two equal portions out of these lands, and they would similarly build one tower together, and one half would be given to Sant Cugat, the other half conveyed to Adalaiz. They would construct this tower together, and they would possess it together happily [cum felicitate] and they would take fish together from these ponds, and those fish they would collectively divide in half. Adalaiz and her children will faithfully make a donation to the monastery of one tenth of the fish which God should provide from fishing there.[12]

The count, countess, and judges were apparently not altogether comfortable with compromise and felt compelled to provide several discrete justifications for this patchwork solution: the obscurity of earlier transactions, the difficulty of exploiting this particular property, and the necessity of providing a refuge for the area's inhabitants. The decision reflects the court's desire both to end strife between the disputants and to bolster regional security.

Courts in the Province of Narbonne varied in organization. There are some general patterns in the relationship between different types of organization and types of settlements reached. Judicial assemblies in which *boni homines* played a prominent role were more likely to recommend compromise solutions.[13] Although *boni homines* were often taciturn witnesses to judicial proceedings, in compromise decisions they intervened more directly. They advised disputants about which solutions to pursue and which to avoid. Given the importance of such groups, it is not surprising that this advice was often persuasive. Prudent disputants would have thought it foolish to flout the forcefully expressed advice of the *boni homines*. Although there are numerous cases in which disappointed disputants rejected judges' decisions, there are none in which disputants rejected the guidance of a group of *boni homines*. When *boni homines* did assume more prominent roles, they tended to be more compromise-oriented than professional judges. This tendency

---

11. *Guissona* 1.

12. *Sant Cugat* 452.

13. See Pierre Toubert on the role of *boni homines* in Latium. *Les structures du Latium médiéval*, 2 vols. (Rome, 1973), 1229–54.

should not, however, be mistaken for a rigid rule. Professional judges in comital courts also ordered compromise decisions.[14]

Some compromise decisions resulted from the difficulties judges encountered in evaluating contradictory or confusing proofs. Despite their careful examination of records and witnesses, they simply could not untangle which disputant's claim was superior. In other cases, the problem of insufficient evidence was accompanied by the normative idea that compromises were desirable because they reflected a spirit of peace and equity. In other words, some courts formulated compromise decisions not only because they lacked adequate proofs to resolve conflicting claims, but because they saw some intrinsic merit in doing so.[15] They divided disputed property not only because the proofs were unclear but also, as neighbors advised two disputants in 1046, *pro causa amoris.*[16]

PENALTIES, PROMISES, AND BOUNDARIES: MAKING DECISIONS WORK

The region's courts were, in many ways, remarkably strong. Judges were carefully trained and performed their duties with careful attention to written law. Counts, countesses, and bishops played important roles in administering justice. Property-holders relied on a variety of proofs to establish their property rights. The community at large had some voice in the settlement of disputes through the participation of *boni homines.* Despite these strengths,

14. *Archivo Condal* 207; ACA Berenguer Ramon 13; and *Sant Cugat* 452.

15. In a 1032 case, Bishop Oliba stated that his decision was guided in part by his long-term care for Vic's cathedral chapter. See *Oliba* 105. Claudie Duhamel-Amado describes the rhetoric of compromise that informs many eleventh-century records in "La famille aristocratique languedocienne: Parenté et patrimoine dans les vicomtés de Béziers et Agde (900–1170)," Thesis presented for doctorat d'Etat, Université de Paris IV, 1994," vol. I, 204–5. See also Cheyette, "Suum cuique tribuere"; and White, "'*Pactum Legem Vincit et Amor Judicium.*'" Michael Clanchy discusses legal traditions juxtaposing law and love, or formal pleadings and informal negotiation, an opposition summed up in the twelfth-century *Leges Henrici Primi*: "pactum legem vincit et amor judicium." *Lex* and *amor* were seen as contrary ways of achieving a solution, and many documents voiced a preference for the latter over the former. Michael Clanchy, "Law and Love in the Middle Ages," in Bossy, *Disputes and Settlements,* 47–67. Unlike the tradition described by Clanchy, documents from the Province of Narbonne did not portray *placita* as things to be avoided.

16. *Santa Anna* 54; For other compromises and divisions of property, see ACV 6, 2155; *Santa Cecília* 96; *Marca* 204; *Lézat* 721; ACB Diversorum B 134; APO Fossa 12J24 n. 11; *HGL* 206; *Girona* 78; BNF coll. Baluze 117, f. 282–3; *Urgellia* 599; and *Roses* 8.

courts often lacked formal means to enforce their decisions. Courts often managed to make their decisions stick, but the mechanisms of enforcement were informal, irregular, and frequently ineffective. A judge's decision, a disputant's quitclaim, or an agreement arrived at through the intervention of *boni homines* often provided a respite from the hostilities between disputants. Such decisions and agreements, however, often failed to put a decisive and final end to disputes.

Courts took measures to ensure the stability of the agreements they formulated, and these enjoyed mixed success. One step was to threaten violators of agreements with penalties. The *si quis* clauses that stipulated the penalties incumbent on anyone who contravened the terms of an agreement usually included more than one type of sanction. In addition to the curses and threats of excommunication discussed in chapter 2 above, they often included financial penalties. The simplest of these were monetary fines. The two brothers who divided their inheritance in 987 agreed that they were obligated to pay fifty *solidi* if they violated the terms of the agreement.[17] In other cases, disputants were threatened with payments to the injured party ranging from ten to five hundred *solidi* if they reneged on an agreement or renewed a dispute.[18] Other agreements stipulated fines and penalties in quantities of gold, ranging from one pound to forty.[19]

Other *si quis* clauses linked the size of the penalty to the value of the disputed property. Violators of a court decision were obligated to compensate the injured party two, three, or four times the value of the property involved. Some penalty clauses referred to the *Visigothic Code* as the foundation for these penalties.[20] The two types of financial penalty were often combined. Violators were threatened with fines of a particular amount and some factor of compensation: a pound of gold and double compensation, five pounds of gold and triple compensation, or ten pounds of gold and quadruple compensation.[21] Such sanctions sealed a court's decision with a sense of finality (however deceptive that sense may have been) and impressed upon participants the costs of violating an agreement.

Understanding the practical implications of these financial penalties is

17. *Achivo Condal* 207. On these fines, see also Kosto, *Making Agreements*, 48.

18. ACB Lib. Ant. IV, f. 34, d. 100 (10 *solidi*); *Sant Cugat* 479 (100 *solidi*); *Urgellia* 380 (100 *solidi*); *Barcelona* 329 (300 *solidi*); and *Sant Cugat* 452 (500 *solidi*).

19. For example, ACA Berenguer Ramon 13 (one pound); *Santa Anna* 54 (one pound); *Viage* 15, 34 (two pounds); *Sant Cugat* 597 (two pounds); *Sant Cugat* 317 (ten pounds); *Nîmes* 104 (ten pounds); ACB Lib. Ant. I, f. 232, d. 630 (twenty pounds); BNF coll. Baluze 117, ff. 282–83 (thirty pounds); and BNF coll. Moreau 19, ff. 87–88 (forty pounds).

20. *Oliba* 56. See also *Urgellia* 372; *Urgellia* 425; and *Sant Cugat* 263.

21. *Guissona* 1; *Oliba* 99; and *Oliba* 95.

nearly as difficult as understanding the practical significance of the ritual sanctions in the same *si quis* clauses. The foremost interpretive challenge is that, although the threat of financial penalties no doubt encouraged disputants to take agreements seriously, there is no evidence that such sanctions were ever enforced. There are instances of violators of agreements compensating injured parties, but there are none in which a judge referred to an earlier sanction clause and ruled that a violator should pay the specified fine. Many transactions and negotiations doubtless went unrecorded, but it seems unlikely that such sanctions could have been applied regularly without leaving any trace, especially since judges, disputants, and advocates often referred to earlier agreements and written records during hearings.

A second difficulty is that payments in the amounts stipulated were all but impossible. Despite the growing flood of Andalusi gold, fines in sanction clauses were absurdly large. After 990, references to gold in sales and exchanges reflect new prosperity at all levels of society, but fines of ten and twenty pounds of gold in sanction clauses were entirely unrealistic. The fines were stipulated not only in impossible amounts, but also in curious units. While some sanction clauses specified payments in *solidi*, many others specified fines in units of weight or currency that were extremely uncommon. The units of exchange most often used in sales, contracts, and other property transactions rarely appeared in sanction clauses.[22]

In short, the financial penalties stipulated in sanction clauses do not seem to have been applied in any literal sense. That is not to say that such sanctions were pointless or ineffective, but rather that their significance seems to have been largely symbolic. The threat of such sanctions would have impressed disputants with the weight of courts' decisions and possibly deterred would-be violators. Sanction clauses surrounded the violation of an agreement with costly consequences, financial and ritual, but the fines in *si quis* clauses served more as a method of signaling the finality of a settlement than as a practical means of penalizing those who had second thoughts.

Courts took other, more concrete, measures to guarantee the stability of agreements. In some cases, disputants formalized the boundaries of disputed properties by walking around their limits, discussing landmarks, and agreeing on which landmarks determined the boundaries. These collective agree-

---

22. See, for example, ACA Berenguer Ramon I, 101; ACA Ramon Borrell 114; *Sant Cugat* 437; Gaspar Feliu Montfort, "Las ventas con pago en moneda en el condado de Barcelona hace el año 1010," *Cuadernos de historia economica de Catalunya* 5 (1971): 9–41; Jorge Rius Cornadó, "Dato sobre la economía monetaria en Cataluña durante el siglo XI," *Cuadernos de historia economica de Catalunya* 9 (1973): 15–68; and Lluís To Figueras, *El monestir de Santa Maria de Cervià i la pagesia: Una ànalisi local del canvi feudal* (Barcelona, 1991): 57–63; Bonnassie, *Catalogne*, 372–98; and Farías Zurita, "Compraventa de Tierras."

ments were committed to writing. Circling properties in a group allowed judges and the community to survey collective knowledge about the rights of different property-holders. The practice had been used in the Province of Narbonne to address property disputes since at least the ninth century.[23] Some courts erected markers to commemorate newly established boundaries, as in a 1037 case between the monastery of Sant Cugat and a lay disputant named Bernat:

> Therefore, I, Bernat Hodger, who had petitioned about this, abandon any claim, as was determined and walked-off [*sicut piduatum vel definitum fuit*] on the last day of this hearing, where the cross was made in the stone that is there, and down to Paladol and through to the Calcada or to the river where the mark was made in the large stone and to the plain, and from there by signs and letters to the top of Mount Kalafell and down by marks and signs [*per notas vel signas*] to the sea.[24]

After some investigations, boundaries between properties were newly marked with stones and crosses.[25] Judges and surveyors also marked trees to indicate boundaries. Some courts drew on two rules from the *Visigothic Code* which prescribed the use of X-shaped marks, called *decurias*, to demarcate property divisions.[26] Some judges also consulted geometry texts that allowed them better to mark and record boundaries.[27]

Walking as a group around the limits of a property enabled the court to gather information and to achieve a collective commitment to respect boundaries. The function of circumambulation was thus twofold: it gathered evidence and created a record of the established boundaries that would prevent future conflict. The practice codified information about the past and, at the same time, generated consensus regarding the limits of a *villa* or vineyard that would, at least in theory, make future disagreements less likely. Walking the limits of a disputed property and marking its boundaries was a concrete way

23. *HGL* II, 150; *HGL* 18; and *Nîmes* 20. See Wendy Davies, "Disputes: Their Settlement and Their Conduct," 301; and Roger Collins, "Disputes in Early Medieval Spain," in *Settlement of Disputes*, ed. Davies and Fouracre, 88, 100.

24. *Sant Cugat* 545.

25. *Cart. Rous.* 32. See also *Sant Cugat* 470; *Oliba* 63; *Sant Cugat* 509; and *Nîmes* 20.

26. *Guissona* 2. For Visigothic legislation about boundary markers, see *Leges Visigothorum*, X.3.3, VIII.6.1. For a ninth-century case mentioning *decurias*, see *Girona* 9. See also Pierre Portet, "Le règlement des conflits de bornage en Catalogne, Languedoc et Provence (IXe-Xe siècles)," in *Les sociétés méridionales à l'âge féodal*, ed. Débax, 59–61.

27. Bonhom's copy of the *Visigothic Code* includes a geometry treatise, which Bonhom suggests might be useful for resolving disputes between neighbors. Escorial z.ii.2, f. 4r. On the use of practical texts for surveying, see McKitterick, *The Carolingians and the Written Word*, 244.

of engaging the memory of the community.[28] Such procedures stored information about the resolution of conflicting claims in the minds of neighboring landholders. Courts strove to record and to inscribe these collective agreements in several places: on parchment, in the memory of the area's inhabitants, and on the landscape itself. Circumambulations are another example of how public opinion played a role in stabilizing agreements.

The important role played by witnesses in supporting the longevity of agreements is clear not only in boundary investigations but also in the witness lists that accompanied virtually every agreement. When losing disputants abandoned their claims, they often swore oaths that they would never again trouble the disputed property and its rightful owners. The court's decision or the disputant's quitclaim were followed by a sanctification of the new agreement. Disputants exchanged oaths over altars with the reconciled disputants cradling relics.[29] All of this was witnessed by members of the community who affixed their names to agreements. The public avowal of settlements encouraged disappointed litigants to confront the reality of their own defeat and also disseminated information about the terms of a settlement to the wider community. In doing so, they functioned much in the same way that circumambulations did. When disputants swore to uphold an agreement, they sent messages both to themselves and to the wider community about the newly ordered or restored property relations. Disputes usually pitted individuals or small groups against each other, but judicial assemblies rarely consisted only of disputants and judges. Records of disputes usually indicate that courts were, in fact, crowded. Scribes regularly listed more than a dozen people who witnessed proceedings and then remarked that it would be tedious to try to record the names of all those present. Courts were often populated by dozens of people—men and women, lay and clergy, magnates and peasants, many of whom signed the decisions.[30] Witnesses were guarantees that the terms of a resolved dispute enjoyed broad support and that knowledge of those terms would remain available.

Witnesses and concerned neighbors often influenced disputants. Some disputants were persuaded to alter the proofs they presented or the terms of an agreement through the intervention of their neighbors. The role of *boni homines* in formulating compromises shows that such groups did indeed pressure disputants. In signing agreements, witnesses recognized some measure

28. For examples elsewhere, see Hudson, *Land, Law, and Lordship,* 159; and Geary, "Land, Language, and Memory," 179–82.

29. See, for example, *Adge* 323; *Barcelona* 172; *HGL* 149; *Urgellia* 252; ACB Lib. Ant. IV, f. 34, doc. 100; *HGL* 175; *Oliba* 83; *Cart. Rous.* 33.

30. The number of signatories to agreements varied considerably, but many decisions were signed by a dozen or more witnesses.

of responsibility for enforcing the terms of agreements or, at the very least, for encouraging disputants to adhere to agreements. Witnesses to quitclaims or court decisions, like donors to churches or monasteries, assumed some responsibility for the future health of agreements.[31] At times, *boni homines* appear in records advising disputants to compromise; often they must have advised property-holders in other ways. *Boni homines* may have dissuaded certain litigants from pursuing cases before these even reached court. The influence that witnesses used to maintain agreements is the sort that left few traces in surviving documents; conclusions about their role must be speculative. Nevertheless, documents emphasize that large audiences heard disputes and scribes took pains to record the approval of prominent witnesses. In the absence of more formal mechanisms of enforcement, the memory of witnesses played a significant role in making the decisions of courts durable.

CHRONIC PROBLEMS AND RESISTANCE TO SETTLEMENTS

The decisions reached by courts often established only a fragile peace. A by-now familiar case from Sant Cugat shows that court-issued decisions did not necessarily settle disputes permanently. In 1013, a widow named Adalaiz claimed a property called Caldarium, which was also claimed by Sant Cugat. In a comital court, the monastery's abbot presented royal privileges (reconstituted through *reparatio scripturae*), while Adalaiz claimed that the property belonged to her by *aprisio*. The judges hearing the dispute formulated a compromise solution that allowed each party partial rights. But even a court presided over by the count and countess of Barcelona and staffed by professional judges attained only a modest degree of success in crafting a lasting settlement. Four years after the court issued its decision, the abbot and the widow again complained to a comital court—repeating the same conflicting claims. The judges admitted weakly that they were unable to sort out who was the rightful owner. Because of their uncertainty, the judges handed the property over to the count of Barcelona, who asserted comital rights to unowned property. The count retained rights to Caldarium but turned control of the property over to Sant Cugat.[32]

31. Some records specifically mentioned the responsibility of the donor to ensure the durability of a gift. See *Sant Cugat* 439; *Lézat* 721. Compare Antoni Udina i Abelló's description of the role of witnesses and executors in guaranteeing respect for testaments, *La successió testada*, 143.

32. *Sant Cugat* 452; *Sant Cugat* 464.

Many disputes dragged on for years and even decades. A dispute between the canons of Agde and the monastery of Saint-Victoire de Marseilles over the church of Saint-André just outside of Agde's walls occupied the better part of a century.[33] In the early tenth century, a disputant petitioned the bishop of Nîmes numerous times over the course of three years before his claim was heard.[34] The struggle over the titles of Gurb near Vic erupted intermittently between 990 and at least 1164.[35] A 1087 decision issued in a dispute near Elne sketched the troubled history of a property which shuttled jerkily back and forth between Elne's chapter and several generations of related claimants who repeatedly gave the alod to the church and reclaimed it.[36] Some properties were chronic problems.

Shrewd disputants recognized the often ephemeral character of agreements and anticipated their collapse. A series of records from Urgell provides a valuable example of how experienced property-holders saw litigation over property as an ongoing process rather than an isolated event. In 1024, Abbot Durand of the monastery of Saint Cecilia and the see of Urgell brought a dispute over the churches of Curticita and Castellono before Count Ermengol II of Urgell. Both sides presented written proofs. After evaluating the donation presented by Durand and the various royal and papal privileges presented by the see's representative, Judge Pons declared Durand's document a fake and awarded the property to the see.[37]

The see had proven its claim to the judge's satisfaction, but the hearing was not over. Up to this point, Count Ermengol played little recorded role in the hearing. Once the judge had presented his decision, the count came forward: "When all of these things were done, the humble and devoted Count Ermengol, in whose presence this took place, came before the altar of the see and ordered that the testaments of his grandfather, Count Borrell, and his father, Count Ermengol, be read out before him." There is no explanation as to why the teenage count was seized by the desire to hear a performance of his ancestors' last wishes. Whatever the reason, the court indulged his desire. The testaments were read, and passages from them were grafted into the record of the dispute between the see of Urgell and Abbot Durand. Among other things, Count Ermengol heard that his grandfather

33. André Castaldo, *L'Église d'Agde (X–XIII siècles)* (Paris, 1970), 30–34. See also Magnou-Nortier, *Société laïque*, 495–6.

34. *Nîmes* 20.

35. Freedman, *Diocese of Vic*, 129–30. See also Odilo Engels, "Episkopat und Kanonie in Mittelalterlichen Katalonien," *Reconquista und Landherrschaft: Studien zur Rechts' und Verfassungsgeschichte Spaniens im Mittelalter* (Paderborn, 1979), 152–53.

36. *HGL* 370.

37. On the use of written proofs in this case, see chapter 6 above.

had given the see a *villa* called Tuixén—a property unrelated to those claimed by Abbot Durand. When Count Ermengol's father's testament was read aloud, it too referred to Tuixén. The count learned that his father had at one time unjustly taken the property from the see, but had realized his error and had returned it. Inspired by the reading of the wills at the altar, the count said that he would do justice (*justitiam facere*) to the see by confirming a wide range of the see's property rights. The count gave or restored to the see the (disputed) church of Curticita, the (disputed) tithes from Castellono, and the *villa* of Tuixén: "Recognizing myself to be of legitimate age, having reached fourteen years and more, all of this I give and render to the Holy See of Saint Mary in the city of Urgell into the hand of Bishop Ermengol, so that he and his successors might do with these as it is the custom of bishops to do with other gifts given to the church."[38]

The see's dispute with Abbot Durand had become more than a simple defense of one beleaguered portion of the see's patrimony. The judicial hearing regarding Curticita became an opportunity to present a catalog of troubled properties before a large audience. Determining the superiority of the see's claims to Curticita had been an easily accomplished task, but the see's advocate and the judges were not content merely to send Abbot Durand away empty-handed. Drawing on a range of disparate authorities, they built global claims about the authorities of bishops over suffragan churches. They used their dispute with Abbot Durand as the occasion to strengthen their grip on other properties. The ill-equipped Abbot Durand stumbled into playing a small and unrewarding role in a public celebration of the see's wealth and power. The see presented a daunting collection of royal and papal privileges before a host of lay magnates, who themselves might pose a threat to the see's property. The see not only recovered the disputed property, but also gave its potentially aggressive neighbors a memorable lesson in episcopal authority.

The see's motivation for all this ceremony was simple: lay magnates had short memories. Four years after the dispute involving Abbot Durand, Count Ermengol, having reached the age of nineteen, complained to Bishop Ermengol that the see was unjustly holding the *villa* of Tuixén; the count claimed that Tuixén rightly belonged to him. Ambivalence about whether or not the see of Urgell should hold Tuixén was, it seems, a recurrent problem for members of Urgell's comital dynasty. When the bishop responded to the count's complaint, he was no doubt reassured by the fact that at least five people in the assembly had been members of the court or signatories to the count's renunciation of any interest in Tuixén four years earlier. Count Ermengol complained that he had a charter proving his right to Tuixén. The bishop replied

38. *Urgellia* 390.

that he had records issued by the count's father and his grandfather granting the *villa* to the see. Finally, the bishop prodded the count's memory:

> Indeed you yourself were in this holy seat during the feast of All Saints with your magnates after you had turned fourteen years old, giving in divine mercy, for the divine love of the Heavenly Father and for fear of the horrible pains of Gehenna, you acknowledged that which your ancestors had done, and you made a document of donation or recognition of those *villae* to the Lord God and to the holy see of Saint Mary in perpetuity.[39]

At the bishop's prompting, laced with threats of eternal suffering and appeals to the count's illustrious ancestors, the count remembered the gift that he, his father, and his grandfather had each given. For the second time in four years, Count Ermengol II abandoned his claim to Tuixén.

The bishop's strong defense of the see's property in this case should be remembered alongside his dispute over the tithes of Aiguatèbia with his sister and her husband two years later. Bishop Ermengol adroitly fended off those he viewed as threats to the see's property (counts, abbots, sisters) by turning moments of crisis into pageants of episcopal power. The bishop and his representatives used public hearings not only to defend challenged rights but also to prepare for future challenges. They anticipated that properties like Tuixén would continue to be objects of conflict. Disputes over relatively insignificant properties became social and political dramas whose implications extended well beyond the terms of the original conflict. The dispute with Abbot Durand became an opportunity to catalog property, codify relations between the count and the see, and display the see's collection of comital, royal, and papal privileges. The bishop chose his proofs carefully. When fighting with the abbot of Saint Cecilia, he relied on royal privileges and papal bulls. When fighting with the count of Urgell, he used documents drafted by the count's ancestors. Disputants had long memories for the land their ancestors had cultivated and for lost documents regarding their property rights, but they had short memories for agreements in which they had alienated property. The see of Urgell took measures to ensure that such agreements would not be forgotten, just as the monks of Cuixà regularly reminded their neighbors of the monastery's rights.[40]

Because of the fragmentary nature of surviving evidence, one usually can see only isolated moments in these processes of getting and keeping property. Usually, the only moment accessible to historians is one during which

39. *Urgellia* 425; Borrell Travalens, Guillem Lavanciensi, Isarn de Caupdiaz, Viscount Guillem, Arnau de Tost, and probably others attended both hearings.

40. See the discussion of lost documents in chapter 6 above.

claims were made about the establishment of a peace. In cases where documentation allows a fuller reconstruction of the events surrounding a dispute, it is clear that such assertions of restored harmony were often optimistic. Courts made clear decisions and they deployed a range of mechanisms for promoting the stability of those decisions. These mechanisms were not, however, adequate to the task of ensuring that disputes once settled would remain settled. A court's decisions might result in a renewed peace for several days, several years, or for a generation. But, as the cases of Tuixén, Caldarium, and Gurb show, court-issued decisions might resolve conflicts temporarily, but the same conflicting claims might emerge later with renewed ferocity.[41]

Although conflicts often rose again to the surface gradually, in many cases it was not long-festering discontent and fading memories which unsettled the decisions issued by courts, but explicit resistance to a court's decisions. Many disputants rejected courts' authority and abandoned judicial hearings altogether. These sudden departures were often precipitated by judges' decisions regarding proofs. When judges agreed to hear challenged testimony, the challenging disputants sometimes left court. In 997, a court in Urgell reached a decision only after one of the disputants had abruptly left the proceedings: "Segar did not want to accept these witnesses, but instead he removed himself from the court."[42] In 1025 at Sant Cugat, a litigant left for the same reason: "When these men had testified, . . . he saw himself defeated by his own failure and did not want to accept these witnesses but took himself from the court."[43] During the 1018 dispute between Count Hug of Empúries and Countess Ermessenda of Barcelona, Hug's representative refused to accept the countess's witnesses and offered inadequate (even, according to the scribe, ridiculous) explanations for this refusal.[44] Disputants who abandoned courts challenged both the legitimacy of their opponents' proofs, the authority of judges, and, in some cases, procedural norms. In cases like these, judges may have resolved thorny legal questions to their own satisfaction, but they failed to bring at least one of the disputants to peace. Such cases further illustrate the limited coercive force that courts exercised. Counts, bishops, and judges were respected and powerful, but disgruntled and uncooperative disputants often simply walked away if things were not to their liking.

Aside from dramatizing the limits of courts' power, these cases suggest re-

41. Patrick Geary rightly suggests that we should pay attention to the entire process of a dispute rather than focusing narrowly on settlements. See Geary, "Living with Conflicts in Stateless France," 139.

42. *Urgellia* 252.

43. *Sant Cugat* 496.

44. *Oliba* 56. For similar cases, see *Lézat* 409; *Urgellia* 398; *Urgellia* 539; ACV 9, 51; ACV 6, 2155; and *Girona* 78.

current tensions between the institutions that administered justice and the litigants who moved within those institutions. Records of the decisions issued by courts usually suggest that the disputants who abandoned hearings did so because their claims were groundless. Scribes described Bonadonna, Renard, and Mir Geribert as uncooperative, lawless troublemakers. We should not, however, accept these characterizations too quickly.

Taken case by case, litigants who abandoned courts could be dismissed as lawless thugs who resisted widely respected institutions. If, however, we view such disputants collectively, it becomes somewhat harder to see them in this exclusively negative light. The frequency with which disputants rejected judicial decisions and removed themselves from proceedings requires explanations that do more than simply dismiss them as scofflaws and their cases as oddities. Abandoning a court could be motivated by the simple frustration of losing a claim. But the same action might also be prompted by an informed conviction that courts did not generate fair decisions, that they were biased in favor of some disputants, or that they operated according to rules which distorted (rather than remedied) the just distribution of property. In other words, most disputants who abandoned judicial assemblies had, at least in their own minds, legitimate reasons for doing so. On the one hand, such disputants can be seen as truculently refusing to respect the authority of the courts, the opinions of judges, or the rules of the law. On the other hand, they might be thought of as defying a judicial system which favored some disputants over others and which applied one set of rules while ignoring legitimate alternatives.

To reconcile these two conflicting views of disputants who abandoned judicial proceedings, we should try to establish what motivated these disputants to take such drastic actions. Unfortunately, evidence for motivations is scanty. Judges and scribes were understandably eager to discredit disputants who flouted the authority of the courts. When scribes noted the departures of these disputants, they characterized those who left as uncooperative and wrong-headed. Descriptions of disputants who abandoned courts thus assumed a formulaic quality: "Although Segar should have done thus, instead he did so." Surviving records thus do not offer sympathetic accounts of the motivations and attitudes of those who resisted the authority of the courts. James Scott's observations about the limitations of the public transcript might be usefully applied to these disappointed medieval litigants: "The fact is that power-laden situations are nearly always inauthentic; the exercise of power nearly always drives a portion of the full transcript underground."[45]

45. James Scott, *Weapons of the Weak: Everyday Forms of Peasant Resistance* (New Haven, Conn., 1985), 286.

Tenth- and eleventh-century courts were indeed power-laden situations, and when a disputant abandoned a hearing, a portion of the full transcript was driven underground. When disputants removed themselves from court, they also removed themselves from the historical record. The attitudes and ambitions of disputants who rejected or questioned the system are thus extremely difficult to reconstruct. Despite these difficulties, it is still worth trying to account for these disputants, if only to be able to trace the contours of a particularly lamentable gap in our understanding.

The 1018 dispute between Count Hug of Empúries and Countess Ermessenda of Barcelona is particularly well-documented and affords the opportunity to examine a disputant who refused to cooperate. Several years before the dispute began, Hug had sold a *villa* called Ullastret to Count Ramon Borrell of Barcelona. The count died in 1017 and his son, Count Berenguer Ramon I, inherited Ullastret. The young count's mother, Countess Ermessenda, widow of the former count, acted on her son's behalf. Hug claimed that the original sale was invalid because it had been executed when he was a minor; he demanded that Ermessenda return the *villa* to him. The countess assured Hug that she was ready to do whatever was right according to the law and that she would adhere to a court's decision in the matter. Hug rejected her suggestion and proposed an unconventional alternative. He suggested that they resolve their claims through a judicial combat in which he would fight against a champion chosen by the countess.[46]

Hug and Ermessenda disagreed about the desirability of bringing their disagreement to court, but both litigants had an idea of what going to court meant and an understanding of the likely implications of such a choice. For the countess, a judicial assembly operating with professional judges under the auspices of a count or bishop was a place of justice; Hug saw the same court as an arena of prevarication. He explained his rejection of the countess's offer by saying that he was eager to avoid the ambiguity that would, he was sure, attend a settlement reached in court. The countess, who over the course of several decades showed herself to be a tireless and shrewd proponent of Visigothic legal procedure, replied that Hug's proposal of a trial by combat was unacceptable because it contravened Visigothic law. Unshaken by the countess's refusal to appoint a champion and unimpressed by her legal erudition, Hug resorted to self-help. He seized the disputed *villa*, prompting the scribe to note priggishly that this seizure also violated Visigothic law.

Suspecting that further negotiation with Hug would be fruitless, the

---

46. *Oliba* 56. Ferran Valls i Taberner rightly identifies Hug's proposal as a particularly early reference to judicial combat. "Notes sobre el duel judicial a Catalunya," in *Obras Selectas* (Madrid-Barcelona, 1954), 2:249.

countess sought outside intervention. A dispute between magnates of this caliber generated a court composed of similarly impressive magnates. Count Bernat of Besalú and Bishop Oliba of Vic jointly presided over the deliberations of three judges (Guifré of Vic among them) and a host of *boni homines*.[47] Hug's impatience with formal legal solutions did not diminish once the countess had brought her complaint before this assembly. He showed his qualified indifference by sending a representative rather than appearing in court himself. Perhaps sensing that a claim to Ullastret based on Hug's minority was winning few adherents, Hug's advocate, Berenguer, adjusted the count's claim. Instead of trying to vacate the original sale, Berenguer argued that the *villa* was rightly Hug's because it was within the county of Empúries and, in that county, Hug exercised all the power that had formerly pertained to Frankish kings. Hug's representative thus transposed the original claim about the validity of the sale into a question of comital authority. The conflict was no longer about Hug's age at the time of the transaction, but was instead about rulership.

The court examined proofs but, in a rare omission for such a detailed record, there is no description of the proofs that Hug and Ermessenda offered to support their claims. The record states only that the judges discussed the proofs and decided that Hug's claims were not valid since Count Ramon Borrell had clearly enjoyed some powers in Ullastret which Hug had claimed were his alone. Thus, when Hug's representative shifted the terms of his client's claim, the court responded to the new claim. The judges did not address the question of Hug's minority and the validity of the original sale until later. They devoted the bulk of their energies to refuting Hug's more inflammatory claim about holding Ullastret as a sovereign prince. They rejected this claim, insisting that Ramon Borrell had held Ullastret with princely authority, and so should Ermessenda and the young Count Berenguer Ramon I. The judges ruled that Hug had no legitimate claim to Ullastret.

Just as the court seemed to be rolling gently toward a decision, the real trouble began. Count Bernat, one of the court's co-presidents, was unhappy with the court's decision against Hug and had to be persuaded to accept it.[48] Hug's representative, Berenguer, initially swore that his client would abide

47. The co-presidency of Bernat and Oliba reflects both the intimate ties of comital and episcopal authority in administering justice and the close cooperation within aristocratic families in the region: Bernat and Oliba were brothers, both sons of Oliba Cabreta of Cerdanya.

48. What becomes of Bernat's discontent is not specified. He may have been persuaded by the other members of the court, or he may have grudgingly gone along with a decision that did not please him.

by the court's decision, but Berenguer shared Hug's own mercurial temperament. When the judges asked whether Berenguer was willing to accept the witnesses presented by Countess Ermessenda to prove that her husband had ruled over Ullastret, he not only refused to accept them but left the assembly without the permission of the judges. Berenguer's hasty departure meant that one of the parties to the dispute was absent and unrepresented. Hug's lack of representation did not, however, stop the court from doing its work. Just as Judge Guifré would issue a decision about the tithes of Aiguatèbia in 1027 despite the absence of Renard and Judge Sendred, so too the judges in this case were unhindered by Berenguer's flight. Citing the same Visigothic rule that Guifré would, they insisted on their authority to accept the countess's witnesses. Eight witnesses testified that they had seen Count Ramon holding Ullastret, receiving its customary dues, and maintaining judges and *saiones* there. Each of these points in their testimony helped to establish that the count had exercised the rights of a prince in Ullastret. The judges proclaimed that Ullastret should be returned to the countess and her son.

When they had formally returned the disputed property to the countess, the judges scrupulously recorded each step in the legal reasoning that had led to their decision: "So that this judgment may remain undisturbed, we strengthened it step by step with the decrees of the laws." They invoked a number of rules from the *Visigothic Code*, and noted how Hug had violated each of them. They dismissed Hug's original claim that he had sold the *villa* while a minor, not because the claim was untrue but because the claim was never formally examined in court. The judges invoked rules from the *Visigothic Code* which protected the orderly succession of the property of the dead. Presumably referring to Hug's seizure of the disputed property, they cited a rule stipulating that the transfer of property without a clear title was illegal. Finally, they cited a rule specifying that any invader of property was required to compensate the rightful owner double or triple the value of the property. Their decision not only upheld the countess's claims, it also indicted Hug's every step. There is no indication of how the court planned to enforce its decision or to help the countess recover Ullastret.

Hug abandoned proceedings twice (once in person, once by proxy), and the machinery of the court rolled on resolutely without him. Despite Hug's unvarnished contempt for the court and its procedures, the judges continued to enumerate the ways in which he had violated rules culled from the *Visigothic Code*. Hug's reaction to the court's decision is not recorded, but it seems unlikely that he would have docilely embraced the decision of a court whose authority he so clearly did not acknowledge.[49]

49. Such disputes could also come to abrupt (and undocumented) ends. The year af-

Hug was temperamental, but his actions were not senseless. Initially, he was willing to negotiate with the countess about how they might resolve their differences. He even proposed his own method of adjudication. Trial by combat was an unconventional way of determining right, and one that was entirely out-of-step with prevalent understandings of proof, but the proposal was not a refusal to find some means of adjudicating their differences. Moreover, Hug voiced lucid reasons for not wanting to go to court. He wanted to avoid the ambiguity that attended the decisions issued by judges. Courts usually issued unequivocal decisions in favor of one disputant, but Hug was right to suggest that these decisions did not always resolve disputes. Hug never imagined that the decision of a court, however carefully framed within the traditions of Visigothic law, was a solution. As the hearing moved forward, Hug's concerns, at least in his own eyes, were fully justified. The judges ignored his representative's complaints about the countess's witnesses. Berenguer's reasons for questioning their testimony may have been, as the scribe suggests, trivial, but Hug was not the only disputant to believe that judges could be unjust and arbitrary in accepting challenged testimony. Indeed, in this case, Berenguer's concerns about the judges' decision seem to have been shared, at least in part, by one of the court's presidents, Count Bernat.

The countess's desire to have her son's claim adjudicated according to Visigothic law was motivated by more than her enthusiasm for venerable legal traditions. The countess also had personal reasons for preferring Visigothic law, professional judges, and formal courts. On numerous occasions, she had shown herself deft in the use of the written law. Visigothic law was thus not only a widely distributed cultural resource, it was also one of the countess's particular strengths. For Hug, Visigothic law did not guarantee justice; it simply meant that Ermessenda would have a sort of home-court advantage and that a decision in her favor was more likely. Visigothic law was, of course, widely respected and most litigants accepted its authority, but Hug's skepticism about the justice and efficiency of the law was not his alone. Other litigants suggested that they did not want their disputes adjudicated according to the rules of the *Code*, and some courts even accommodated their requests. Hug's suspicions about this particular assembly were probably further exacerbated by the appointment of Bishop Oliba as one of the court's two presidents, since the bishop and the countess were close friends.[50]

---

ter this dispute, Hug was alongside Countess Ermessend and Count Berenguer Ramon at the restoration of canonical life in Gerona. See *España Sagrada: Teatro geográfico-histórico de la Iglesia de España*, ed. Henrique Florez et al., 52 vols. (Madrid, 1746–1918), 43:427. The quondam opponents also presided over a judicial hearing several years later (*Sant Cugat* 496).

50. Ramon Abadal i de Vinyals, "L'abat Oliba i la seva època," 207. See also Santiago Sobrequés i Vidal, *Els grans comtes de Barcelona* (Barcelona, 1961), 40–41.

In other words, Hug's distrust of the courts makes him stand out some-what, but his concerns were not groundless. His motivations and attitudes are difficult to reconstruct, but his responses to the court and its decisions are suggestive. While the countess remained firmly committed to written law and a judicial hearing, Hug clumsily but energetically shifted from one strat-egy to the next. At times he played along with the court's procedural man-dates (basing his original claim on the age of minority in Visigothic law), at times he proposed alternatives (trial by combat), at times he rejected the court's authority altogether. Finally, he resorted to force, seizing the disputed *villa*. The record portrays him as a swaggering, violent renegade, and other evidence tends to corroborate this portrait of Count Hug as aggressive.[51] But the unresolved and escalating hostilities in the conflict with Countess Er-messenda resulted both from Hug's bellicose temper and from Ermessenda's inflexible attachment to a legal system which served her interests very well but which Hug saw as a tool for prevaricators. The procedural rules which the countess and the court invoked so reverently and deployed so deftly only further alienated litigants like Hug. While the judges cited Visigothic rules condemning Hug's allegedly unjust invasion of the count's property, and while the court's scribe dutifully described Hug's unjust seizure of the dis-puted property, we can be confident that Hug would have described his own actions in very different terms. The alleged violence, invasion, and force might, in this case, have amounted to little more than Hug's ongoing ex-ploitation of the disputed land.

The lesson to be drawn from this case and others like it is fairly straight-forward, although often overlooked: litigants and judges did not necessarily see law, property, and justice in the same way. A decision carefully crafted by pro-fessional judges with scrupulous reference to written rules may have satisfied fastidious fellow judges. But the same decision could appear quite differently to individual property-holders. Some disputants simply did not trust courts, written law, or professional judges. Just as the inhabitants of the region differed in the ways they understood inheritance and alienability, so too they disagreed about whether courts were instruments of justice or tools of exploitation which worked only in the interest of certain property-holders. Many property-hold-ers, even those more cooperative than Hug, probably shared his skepticism.

51. Several years prior to the dispute over Ullastret, Hug seized the county of Rous-sillon from his young nephew. In 1021, Pope Benedict VII identified Hug as one of the *in-vaders* of the property of the monastery of Sant Pere de Roda and threatened Hug with excommunication if he refused to return to the monastery everything he had taken un-justly. *Papsturkunden*, ed. Zimmerman, no. 531. On the monks' complaint, see *Oliba* 72. On Hug's career, see Francisco Montsalvatje y Fossas, *Los Condes de Ampurias Vindicados* (Olot, 1917), especially, 58–60.

Litigants had legitimate and varied reasons to question the desirability of going to court. In addition to the concerns Hug expressed, lay property-holders had to assess the likelihood of failure. Most recorded disputes were between a lay person or group of lay people, on the one hand, and a monastery or cathedral chapter, on the other. In these conflicts, lay disputants usually lost. Cathedral chapters, bishops, and monasteries won unequivocal victories in roughly three-quarters of such cases. Of the remaining cases, some ended in compromises and others did not leave clearly recorded outcomes. The disproportionate success rate of clerical and monastic disputants is even more striking in records drawn from particular institutions. The monastery of Sant Cugat was involved in nineteen disputes, eighteen of which were decided in the monastery's favor. Compromises, agreements, and payments occasionally followed some of these decisions, but the monastery was a remarkably successful litigant by any standard. The see of Urgell's success rate was only slightly less impressive; the see won clear-cut victories in twelve out of fifteen cases.

Figures like these are only suggestive. The surviving evidence does not precisely reflect the medieval reality. It seems at first glance as if monasteries and cathedral chapters almost always won property disputes. The appearance of success is due in part to distortions in the survival of evidence. Records were expensive to create and difficult to store. Monasteries and cathedral chapters reevaluated which records in their archives were useful and which might be scraped and reused. Records of disputes in which churches and monasteries lost were less valuable than those which supported an institution's claims. Although original tenth- and eleventh-century documents from Urgell, Vic, and Barcelona exist, many records are extant only in thirteenth-century cartularies, the compilation of which almost certainly involved editing out failures. When the canons of Urgell or the monks of Sant Cugat composed cartularies that were intended to catalog and defend their patrimony, records of defeat were unappealing candidates for inclusion.[52]

These distortions in the evidence do not, however, entirely account for the dramatic discrepancies in success rates between individual lay disputants and large institutional disputants. Although the surviving evidence is thus somewhat deceptive, the unavoidable conclusion is that large churches and monasteries enjoyed distinct advantages in court. The professional judges

52. Chris Wickham, "Land Disputes and Their Social Framework," 105; and Paul Fouracre, "Carolingian Justice," 785. Despite this process of erasure, some cases survive from the Province of Narbonne in which, against all odds, disputants overcame the vast resources of an ecclesiastic institution or a count, *and*, against all odds, the record of their victory has survived. See *Santa Cecília* 96; ACA Ramon Borrell 114; ACB Lib. Ant. I, f. 175, doc. 461; *Oliba* 130; and *Guissona* 12.

who decided winners and losers were not always above the fray. Having been trained in cathedral chapters and monastery schools, they were often personally attached to the litigants who appeared before them. Monasteries and cathedral chapters possessed superior legal and ritual resources. They usually had greater experience in litigating than their opponents, and experience was a great advantage then, just as it is today.[53] With some notable exceptions, monks and clerics were more adept than lay disputants at defending their interests in courtrooms. They knew how to cite law codes, how to marshal and coach teams of convincing witnesses, and how to create, store, and forge written records. They often enjoyed intimate ties to the magnates who presided over judicial assemblies. Judges favored interpretations of Visigothic law that made it especially difficult for lay disputants to win against churches and monasteries.[54] The selective application of Visigothic law favored ecclesiastic disputants at the expense of kin groups and contrary to other long-standing understandings of property and inheritance.

These advantages became even more pronounced in light of particular political situations. In several cases in the years following 1010 related to land to the south and west of Barcelona, the monastery of Sant Cugat enjoyed vast superiority in terms of legal expertise and also benefited from its ties to Barcelona's comital family. The count of Barcelona and the abbot of Sant Cugat formed an alliance to secure and develop the frontier by building and maintaining fortifications.[55] Sant Cugat was an integral part of the count of Barcelona's military and economic program. Landholders who disturbed the monastery's progress probably had little chance of receiving a sympathetic hearing in a comital court.

Moreover, Abbott Guitard and his monks were professional disputants. They would have been more at ease in court than landholders from the newly incorporated regions. Many of these property-holders had chosen to live in an relatively undeveloped and sparsely populated area. Most of them must have been uncomfortable with litigating in formal courts, and they made their discomfort known by leaving them. The disputants who abandoned courts were partly lawless thugs and partly dissenters, distrustful of a legal system which, with great ceremony and erudition, served the interests of powerful institutional property-holders.

Cases in which disputants expressed dissatisfaction with law, judges, and courts are forceful reminders that we should be attentive to imbalances in

---

53. Marc Galanter, "Why the 'Haves' Come Out Ahead: Speculations on the Limits of Legal Change," *Law and Society Review* 9 (1974): 95–160.

54. See chapter 2 above.

55. See Kosto, *Making Agreements*, 180.

power and resources when examining disputes. Disparities in social, political, and economic power between disputants conditioned the ways in which hearings were conducted and the outcomes that were generated.[56] Judicial assemblies were carefully ordered and often conformed to written rules, but they did not always afford a level playing field.

Moreover, the gap in economic, cultural, and political resources between disputants could be enormous. A rich, well-endowed monastery closely tied to Barcelona's comital family and lavishly supplied with legal experts was not an even match for a frontier widow, however clever and tenacious she might be. In his copy of the *Visigothic Code*, Judge Bonhom noted that judges had a special responsibility to protect the interests of the powerless. Bonhom knew that social and legal realities were messier than law codes, so while he instructed judges to protect the weak, he also acknowledged that many judges failed to do so. Judges corrupted by power and wealth were, in Bonhom's eyes, like wolves at sundown. The bellicose Count Hug did not share Bonhom's poetic temperament, but he may well have shared the sentiment.

56. Maureen Cain and Kalmar Kulcsar, "Thinking Disputes: An Essay on the Origin of the Dispute Industry," *Law and Society Review* 16 (1982): 397.

CHAPTER NINE
JUSTICE AND VIOLENCE IN
MEDIEVAL EUROPE

When they fought over property, litigants in the Province of Narbonne relied on a range of interrelated proofs. They argued their cases with greater or lesser finesse and they encountered different obstacles. The preceding chapters have anatomized the resources that communities used and have traced the contours of the dispute process. In this chapter, I situate these judges, property-holders, and courts within broader contexts. For example, property disputes can teach us lessons about the coherence of public institutions, the continuity of legal practices, and violence in Catalonia and Septimania during the tenth and eleventh centuries. It is also revealing to compare property disputes in this region with conflicts elsewhere in Europe. Although the ways in which judges and property-holders fought over property were particular to this region, some features of this legal world had important analogs throughout Christian Spain, Francia, Italy, England, and Bavaria. The disputes that have been at the core of preceding chapters serve here as a point of departure for a broader examination of the dynamics of conflict, justice, and violence in the tenth and eleventh centuries.

VIOLENCE AROUND THE YEAR 1000

I have already suggested that the study of disputes sheds light on broad questions of peace and violence around the year 1000. Historians once confidently presented a chronology of the decay of the political world of Latin Europe during the central Middle Ages: the Carolingian order frayed and crumbled during the late tenth century; unrest and violence followed in the eleventh. A complex of social and political changes, described as the Feudal Revolution, took place around the turn of the millennium. In this revolution, the free peasantry lost its vitality as new varieties of servitude proliferated. A new class of lay lords pillaged the countryside and oppressed humbler classes with impunity. Public authority eroded in the tenth century; an age of independent, and often oppressive, lords followed in the eleventh. These political transformations provoked popular responses, such as the Peace of God councils at which churchmen and the peasantry joined forces to resist the endemic violence.

The Feudal Revolution has proven an influential historical framework, shaping the research agenda of medievalists since the 1950s. Over the past decade, however, some historians have challenged the model that yokes together these varied phenomena and describes them as a feudal revolution. They have asked whether ruptures in social, political, and religious life were really so dramatic, and even whether they took place at all.

These debates about change and continuity, about order and violence, pose fundamental questions about how to periodize the Middle Ages. What continuities linked Carolingian and Capetian Francia? What continuities linked Antiquity and the Middle Ages? Did the most significant realignments of the medieval social and political order occur in the late ninth century, around the year 1000, or in the early thirteenth century? Are the depredations and *malae consuetudines* of lay lords which recur in eleventh-century records signs of fractured governance, moribund justice, and widespread instability, or were they rhetorical, stylized laments which indicate no significant changes in the relations between lay lords, on the one hand, and peasants and clerics, on the other?

Property disputes illuminate these questions in several ways. The administration of justice has long been an important element of scholarship related to the Feudal Revolution. Scholars like Pierre Bonnassie view the degradation of comital courts as one of the key features of the political transformations of the early eleventh century. Those who challenge the model of the Feudal Revolution also point to property disputes, suggesting that anthropological approaches to dispute settlement allow us to trace the inner logic of conflicts and to see long-term continuities. In other words, property disputes and courts play major roles in scholarship on all sides of the Feudal Revolution debate.[1]

1. Duby, "The Evolution of Judicial Institutions." See also Toubert, *Structures du*

Moreover, the Province of Narbonne has achieved a curious prominence in discussions of the Feudal Revolution. Pierre Bonnassie's study of Catalonia is among the most influential of the numerous regional studies suggesting that a Feudal Revolution affected much of western Europe. Bonnassie has argued for a sudden, fundamental, and widespread rupture in social, political, and economic life. Others have followed Bonnassie's lead. The most comprehensive synthetic description of the Feudal Revolution (Poly and Bournazel's *The Feudal Transformation*) often relies on Bonnassie's study to support its claims about the period's violence. Catalonia has become one of the crucial laboratories for examining feudal societies both because of the relative abundance of surviving sources and because of the research of Bonnassie and others.[2] If classic feudalism once lived between the Rhine and the Loire, the Feudal Revolution now seems to have come in its most virulent form between the Tet and the Llobregat.

Finally, disputes are relevant to this debate because differing interpretations of the Feudal Revolution often touch on the question of how anthropological insights might be used when interpreting medieval sources. Dominique Barthélemy, the Feudal Revolution's most vociferous critic, acknowledges important debts to legal anthropology. He regularly refers to the work of anthropologists and of historians who have relied on anthropological models. Barthélemy insists that there were types of self-regulation which traditional models of political history might neglect, but which an anthropological perspective allows us to see.[3]

This ongoing discussion about social and political order in medieval Europe thus hinges on how to interpret records of property disputes. Did the decisions issued by courts reflect fragmentation? Did once "public" courts slide irrevocably toward anarchy? Were late eleventh-century courts less effective than their tenth-century precursors? Were eleventh-century disputes more violent that ninth- or tenth-century disputes?

The examination of courts, codes, proofs, and strategies in the Province of Narbonne affords partial answers to these questions. Disputes allow us to see that the administration of justice and the practice of disputing did not change during this period as dramatically as some have argued. Property dis-

---

Latium, 2:1274, 1280–81; Jean-Pierre Poly and Eric Bournazel, *Feudal Transformation*, *900–1200* (New York, 1991), 18–19; and Dominique Barthélemy, "La mutation féodale a-t-elle eu lieu?" in *Annales: Economies, sociétés, civilisations* (hereafter *AESC*) 47 (1992): 772.

2. Bisson's work, for example, relies heavily on documents from Catalonia. See "The 'Feudal Revolution.'"

3. Barthélemy, "La mutation féodale," 773; and idem., "Encore le débat," 356–57; Bisson argues (rightly, I think) that Barthélemy interprets the conclusions reached by Geary and White too liberally. "The 'Feudal Revolution,'" 41 n. 119.

putes also enable us to trace with greater subtlety the putative transition from public to private. Here too, attention to the micropolitical and microsocial factors at play suggests that this transition is neither as abrupt nor as clearcut as some have argued. When examining tenth- and eleventh-century courts, public and private may simply be anachronistic categories. Finally, this group of disputes serves as a useful lens through which to examine the overall coherence of the model of the Feudal Revolution, which links together a variety of social, political, and religious changes. In practice, these different elements of change were not always so firmly welded to each other.

The first question to address is whether the administration of justice changed and, if so, how dramatically. In Bonnassie's account of the Feudal Revolution in Catalonia, prior to 1020 public tribunals formulated judicial decisions. After that time, violence became widespread, counts and judges lost their power to impose decisions, and unofficial compromises became more common. In other words, the system of justice moved from public to private.[4]

Bonnassie and others point to the use of written law as an index of an enduring public order. Citations of written codes are seen as markers of the coherence of Romano-Visigothic traditions of public authority that are swept away after 1020.[5] If citations of Visigothic law are taken as signs of an enduring public order, the collapse of that order should be manifested in a drop in the number of such citations. Visigothic law did not, however, vanish. Enthusiasm for written law continued unabated into the late eleventh century. Aquilino Iglesias Ferreirós catalogs 142 references to Visigothic law in records from Catalonia between 1050 and 1100.[6] Relying on some of the same evidence from Catalonia, Michel Zimmerman catalogs nineteen references to the *Visigothic Code* between 950 and 1000, fifty-eight between 1000 and 1050, and fifty-six between 1050 and 1100.[7] Neither scholar reports a significant disruption in the use of written law during the eleventh century. There is little difference between the quantity of citations during the first and second halves of the eleventh century. Written law did not fizzle and die between 1020 and 1060.

4. "From the beginning of the eleventh century, the courts were no longer orderly and justice became a veritable free-for-all." Bonnassie, "From the Rhône to Galicia," 118; *Catalogne*, 565

5. "The phenomenon of continuity, of the survival of very ancient structures, visible in Catalonia is to be found in all of these countries. The most obvious sign was their common attachment to Romano-Visigothic traditions; from the Rhône to Galicia, the *lex Visigothorum* still retained all its prestige and vigour in the tenth century. . . . The sway of Gothic law . . . was universal." Bonnassie, "From the Rhône to Galicia," 111–12; See also Magnou-Nortier, *Société laïque*, 270–72.

6. Iglesia Ferreirós, "Creación del derecho," 99–423.

7. Zimmerman, "L'usage du droit wisigothique," 247.

Of course, the number of citations provides at best a crude index of the coherence of legal procedures. What mattered in court was not so much whether written law was cited, but in what manner litigants used written law. The nature of judicial assemblies might have changed considerably while scribes continued to cite the same rules. Here we would do well to remember again the dispute over the tithes of Aiguatèbia that pitted Bishop Ermengol of Urgell against his sister, Geriberga, and her husband, Renard, in the autumn of 1027. Renard had presented a written record substantiating his claim to the property; Ermengol rejected the proof. The dispute dragged on through several hearings—Renard finally failed to appear at a hearing at Ripoll.

Pierre Bonnassie presents this case as a sure sign of the breakdown of public courts and the degradation of the judicial system.[8] For Bonnassie, these judges are not defenders of public order; they twist legal traditions for their own good. His treatment of the case shows how difficult it is to interpret citations of written law. In some cases, citations are signs of coherent public courts; in other cases, they are signs of sophistry and judicial disarray. In some cases, they reflect the coherence of public authority, and in others they indicate the corruption of that order. One cannot help but share Bonnassie's frustration with the machinations of the two judges dragging the proceedings up and down the valley of the Tet and over the Pyrenees. But the manipulation of written law was nothing new in 1027. Well before 1020, litigants had abandoned courts that did not generate hoped-for responses. Disputants forged or manipulated proofs. These machinations are apparent both in the records of property transactions and in the work of writers in the centuries leading up to the year 1000 who deplored such abuses. In the ninth century, Hincmar lamented that litigants often exploited the plurality of legal rules. In order to avoid their own national laws, some litigants, in Hincmar's memorable phrase, "fled to the capitularies."[9] Theodulf of Orléans, like Bonhom of Barcelona, complained bitterly about the ways in which the administration of justice was perverted.

Citations of written law were, in other words, always selective and frequently manipulative. The application of the *Visigothic Code* was always and everywhere partial, creative, and interested. Rules that were useful to clerical disputants defending property were often repeated. Written law did not preclude appeals to other discourses or reliance on other strategies. Disputants often invoked both written law and ritual sanctions. Litigants saw no

8. Bonnassie, *Catalogne*, 561.

9. Simeon Guterman, *The Principle of the Personality of the Law in the Germanic Kingdoms of Western Europe* (Frankfurt-am-Main, 1990), 112.

contradiction in pursuing their claims across distinct legal and ritual discourses.

In other words, the use of written law in this region did not change fundamentally during the eleventh century. Throughout the tenth and eleventh centuries, disputants, judges, and advocates referred to the *Visigothic Code* and, less often, to other legal texts. They did so because the *Code* was widely considered authoritative and because they felt the invocation of particular rules would advance their own causes. Whether invoked in the middle of the tenth century or the middle of the eleventh, rules were both reflections of collective legal understanding and tools deployed with particular goals in mind—tools which some disputants used more skillfully than others. Citations of law signal the ongoing importance of the Visigothic legal tradition in the eleventh century, but they do not reflect the unshakable coherence of that tradition. Nor do they prove that courts were free of manipulation, exploitation, or self-interest. In 1027, Judge Sendred and Judge Guifré may have relied on especially sophisticated varieties of manipulation, but finessing the law was nothing new.

Written law thus affords little evidence of fundamental shifts in the administration of justice. But proponents of the Feudal Revolution have also detected other changes in the ways in which disputes were processed. Some argue that the decay of comital courts entailed a shift in the types of proofs used by disputants from a system that relied predominantly on written proofs to one in which less "formal" proofs (witness testimony) and less "rational" proofs (judicial ordeals) became more important.[10] Here, the evidence suggests some modest changes over the course of the eleventh century.

Judicial ordeals appear so infrequently that it is impossible to chart any meaningful trends in their use. The handful of cases involving ordeals are distributed across the entire period, from the Sant Cugat case in 988 into the later eleventh century. There is a small increase in the use of the ordeal after 1060, but the ordeal was used so rarely that this modest increase does not constitute a significant reordering of the ways in which courts processed proofs. Ordeals throughout the entire period were highly idiosyncratic forms of proof.

Trends in the two more conventional varieties of proof, written records and witness testimony, are slightly more revealing. Both forms of proof were common throughout the tenth and eleventh centuries. Tenth-century courts that took place well before the social upheaval described by Bonnassie often involved informal proofs. A 987 hearing relied for evidence only on one disputant's account of what happened.[11] In Barcelona in 989 and 990, disputants

10. Bonnassie, *Catalogne*, 562. See also Ourliac, "Notes sur les actes," 251.
11. *Viage* 13, 20.

relied on no proofs other than one disputant's account (*narratio*) of the conflict.[12] A 996 dispute involving the bishop of Girona was resolved by the two disputants gathering groups of witnesses to testify.[13] On the other hand, disputes that occurred during the years Bonnassie identifies as particularly troubled (1020–1060) maintained important features of earlier courts. After 1020, professional judges still relied on written proofs to resolve competing claims. Throughout the 1030s and 1040s, in Girona, Barcelona, and Urgell professional judges examined written proofs and referred to Visigothic law when making decisions about proofs.[14]

Although no sudden breaks are apparent in the variety of proofs used in court, some gentle trends do emerge. Between 980 and 1020, written proofs were mentioned in 55 percent of all property disputes. The figure drops to 40 percent between 1020 and 1060. There is a noticeable reduction in the prevalence of written proofs, but documents were by no means replaced by other forms of proof. The most important feature of the forensic procedure in these courts was not the preference for one variety of proof, but the practical interdependence of different varieties.

Gradual changes are also apparent in the roles played by the professional judges who were such a vital feature of the legal landscape of the region. In sheer numbers, the presence of judges remained nearly constant between 985 and 1060. Between 980 and 1020, 64 percent of recorded property disputes were heard in the presence of a judge; between 1020 and 1060, this figure dropped very slightly to 61 percent. Professional judges were active in the region after 1060 as well.[15] The ways in which judges worked changed during the eleventh century. In the early eleventh century, two- or three-judge panels often heard disputes together. This sociability was one of the distinctive features of legal procedures in the region around the year 1000. Over time, this professional network frayed. Judges still participated in the adjudication of disputes, but lone judges became the rule after 1040. The prevalence of these solitary judges clearly represents some erosion in the co-

---

12. *Archivo Condal* 218; *Barcelona* 201.

13. *Sant Cugat* 317. See also ACB Lib. Ant. IV, f. 34, d. 100.

14. *Girona* 100; *Urgellia* 438; *Urgellia* 539; *Urgellia* 560; ACB Lib. Ant. IV, f. 155, d. 365; ACA Berenguer Ramon I, 101; BNF coll. Doat 71, ff. 295–7; *Oliba* 130; *Santa Anna* 54; and *LFM* 590.

15. See, for example, *Girona* 143 (1075), 148 (1080), 154 (1084), 160 (1089); *Santa Anna* 114 (1078 or 1079); *Viage* 15.17; *Roses* 8, 4; APO Fossa 12J25 n. 239; HGL 370; ACA Monacals Santa Cecilia de Montserrat 75; *Guissona* 42, 57; *Cart. Rous.* 64, 65; *Santa Anna* 64, 67; HGL 370; *Cartas de población y franquicia de Cataluña*, ed. Josep Maria Font Ruis (Barcelona 1969), 22; ACB Lib. Ant. II, f. 115, doc. 344; and ACA Monacals Sant Llorenç del Munt 111, 128, 159, 166.

herence of the judicial profession. In the decades around the year 1000, judges worked together on cases, drafted legal codices, and shared similar training. The vitality and sophistication of the courts was due in part to this corps of talented, hardworking, and closely connected jurists. In the second half of the eleventh century, judges continued to draft testaments, to hear disputes, and to witness property transactions, but they forged few of the enduring working relationships that had been so important to their predecessors.

Subtle changes are also evident in court presidencies. After 1020 counts and countesses are recorded less often presiding over judicial assemblies. Between 980 and 1020, a count, countess, or viscount presided at over 55 percent of recorded judicial assemblies hearing property disputes. Between 1020 and 1060, the figure drops to 44 percent.[16] From the 1040s and 1050s, counts and countesses less often presided jointly over assemblies with bishops. The reduction in the prominence of comital presidencies is noteworthy, but such a reduction does not indicate the total collapse of comital authority.

Although the changes in judges' activities, proofs, and comital authority during the eleventh century were not drastic, it is worth asking whether the gradual modifications altered the types of outcomes generated by courts. According to some scholars, the erosion of comital authority compelled courts to moderate their ambitions. Rather than issuing judge-made decisions, courts were forced to strive for more informal settlements. According to this model, compromise settlements should become more common in the post-transformation world.[17] For disputes with clearly recorded outcomes, there is a small increase in the popularity of compromise decisions and gifts or payments to losing parties. Between 985 and 1034, roughly 65 percent of all disputes with clearly recorded endings resulted in unequivocal victories for one disputant. After 1035, that figure drops slightly to 55 percent. There were gradual changes in the administration of justice, but no dramatic ruptures. Just as courts often relied on both written proofs and witness testimony, so too they often involved both the official decisions of judges and the inter-

---

16. Bonnassie describes a reduction in comital courts in Barcelona. The figures he provides are, however, subject to alternative interpretations. He describes a precipitous drop in the number of public pleas: eight between 1011–1020, three from 1021 to 1030, and only one in each of the following two decades (*Catalogne*, 562). But the figures for the earliest of these decades are skewed. Of the eight pleas he cites between 1011 and 1020, six were related to the same two complicated disputes—both of which involved the monastery of Sant Cugat and property on the southern frontier. In other words, the relative richness of public pleas between 1011 and 1020 has less to do with the coherence of the count's court than it does with the flurry of litigation by Sant Cugat's abbot.

17. See, for example, Duby, "The Evolution of Judicial Institutions," 19.

vention of *boni homines*.[18] Comital courts with professional judges did not issue only one-sided, authoritative decisions; they sometimes crafted compromises. Particular types of courts were not rigidly linked to particular types of decision.

Changes in eleventh century courts are often described as shifts from public to private. The Feudal Revolution has been seen as, among other things, a bumpy slide from public order to private anarchy.[19] For many scholars, the endemic violence of the Feudal Revolution springs from the loss of something importantly public.[20] Sharp distinctions between public and private are, however, difficult to trace in this period. In the introduction, I pointed to a case involving the monastery of Serrateix that dramatizes the difficulties inherent in this distinction. In January 1020, the abbot of the monastery of Serrateix appeared before a comital court, presided over by Count Guifré of Cerdanya. The count was attended by two viscounts, several *nobili viri*, and Judge Sendred. The abbot's representative petitioned a woman named Emo who, he claimed, unlawfully held an alod called Pujol. The abbot claim that this property rightly belonged to Serrateix and presented a record of donation to the court to prove his claim. The judge read the abbot's record and found it legitimate and truthful. The judges then questioned Emo about why she was holding the property. She explained that she and her husband, Arnau, had purchased Pujol from a man named Ardoman. The judge questioned Ardoman, who corroborated Emo's account and explained that he had purchased the property from Oliba, son of the former count, before Oliba had become a monk at Ripoll. Having heard these witnesses and examined written proofs, the judge ruled that the monastery's document was older and therefore superior. Citing a rule from the *Visigothic Code* regarding the irreversibility of gifts to churches, Judge Sendred ordered Emo to relinquish Pujol to the monastery.[21]

As I have described it, the record of this dispute is one that might inspire great confidence in the coherence and public nature of early eleventh-century comital courts. A public authority—Count Guifré—presided over a widely attended judicial assembly at which a professional judge evaluated a variety of proofs in accordance with the written law of the *Visigothic*

18. Settlements and decisions could involve both judge-based adjudication and more informal intervention at the same time, despite Bonnassie's claim that ". . . the compromise negotiated between families little by little replaced the sentence of the judge." See his "Feudal Conventions in Eleventh-Century Catalonia," in *From Slavery to Feudalism*, 188.

19. Bonnassie, *Catalogne*, 556; and Bisson, "The 'Feudal Revolution,' " 9.

20. Bisson, "The 'Feudal Revolution,' " 18, 19.

21. *Oliba* 62.

Code.[22] On closer scrutiny, however, the "public" quality of the proceedings becomes less clear. The presiding count was Oliba's brother. According to Ardoman's testimony (which no one challenged), Oliba had sold him Pujol before becoming a monk sometime around 1002.[23] By the time of the hearing in 1020, Oliba was abbot of Ripoll, abbot of Sant Miquel de Cuixà, and bishop of Vic. Count Guifré and Bishop Oliba sprang from a comital dynasty dominating the counties of Besalú, Berga, and Cerdanya. In responding to the abbot's complaint, Count Guifré was tidying up what could be seen as his brother Oliba's youthful mistake and he was doing much more at the same time.

Guifré and Oliba's family had patronized Serrateix for decades. In 983 or 984, their father, Count Oliba Cabreta, accompanied by two of his four sons (Berengar and the twelve-year-old Oliba), confirmed the monastery's rights to the disputed alod.[24] In 988, Oliba Cabreta and Countess Ermengard donated another alod to the monastery. Oliba himself made a gift to the monastery in 1003.[25] In 993, the countess, accompanied by her sons Guifré, Bernat, and Oliba, attended and approved the election of the monastery's abbot.[26] Count Guifré was the head of a dynasty with a rich history of both familial cooperation and monastic patronage.[27] The intimate ties between the presiding count and the plaintiff monastery surely blurs any clear boundary between public and private. Given the longstanding ties which linked Serrateix to Cerdanya's comital dynasty, to say that the count acted as a public

22. Bisson notes with reference to this record: "Moreover virtually the only conspicuous events of this age, including the hypothetically troubled years 975–1035, were public convocations and courts: vicarial tribunals in the Mâconnais; great pleas and trials in Francia and the Spanish March; coronations and synods, the latter mostly in north Frankland, but including the early assemblies to secure the Peace in some regions extending from Picardy to the Pyrenees." See "The 'Feudal Revolution,' " 10.

23. For Oliba's career, see the introduction to *Diplomatari i Escrits Literaris de l'Abat i Bisbe Oliba*, ed. Eduard Junyent (Barcelona, 1992), ix–xxii; and Anselm M. Albareda, *L'Abat Oliba: Fundador de Montserrat (971?–1046), Asseig biogràfic* (Abadia de Montserrat, 1931; reprint, 1972).

24. *Oliba* 7. See also Ramon Ordeig i Mata, "Dades referents al comte Oliba Cabreta," *Miscel.lània Ramon d'Abadal: Estudis d'Història Oferts a Ramon d'Abadal i de Vinyals en el centenari del seu naixement*, ed. Jaume Sobrequés i Callicó and Sebastià Riera i Viader (Barcelona, 1994), 25–40.

25. *Oliba* 32.

26. BNF coll. Moreau 14, 62–63; *Oliba* 15.

27. Serrateix was, in the words of Ramon Abadal, one of ". . . les grans fundacions monacals que són l'ornament religiós de la casa comtal . . ." See his "L'Abat Oliba i la seva època," 155, 164. See also Peter Linehan, "The Church and Feudalism in the Spanish Kingdoms in the Eleventh and Twelfth Centuries," *Miscellanea del Centro di studi medioevali* 14 (1995): 306–7.

authority when he presided over this assembly fails to account for the many affective, micropolitical factors that governed the way this dispute unfolded. At the same time Count Guifré was discharging a public office in administering justice, he was also acting as the head of a family that had cultivated close ties to the plaintiff monastery for generations. He was not only dispensing justice and defending public order; he was also fostering his family's relations with Serrateix's monks and saintly patrons. Guifré was a public authority, but he was also the monastery's protector.[28]

Similar entanglements and relations informed other "public" courts. In 1010 and 1026, the monastery of Sant-Miquel de Cuixà brought disputes before judicial assemblies presided over by the same Count Guifré.[29] Members of the count's family had been the monastery's patrons and protectors for nearly 150 years.[30] Guifré was indeed the embodiment of a longstanding tradition of public, comital authority which rested on Visigothic law and Carolingian ideas of order. Perhaps even more vividly, he knew himself to be the representative of a family that had built, patronized, and protected Sant-Miquel de Cuixà for five generations. The strands of public justice, ritual commemoration, private patronage, and affective affiliation were impossible to disentangle; public and private were inextricable because indistinguishable. Count Guifré of Cerdanya is a good example of the complex allegiances, duties, and traditions that pervaded comital courts. Connections of the sort which tied Guifré to Serrateix and Cuixà bound other counts and viscounts to other institutions.

The monastery of Sant Cugat was a particular favorite of Barcelona's comital family, and the counts and countesses regularly heard the monastery's property litigation in their courts. The countess of Carcassonne presided over courts in which the abbot of Saint-Hilaire strove to protect and enlarge the monastery's patrimony. The countess, her husband, and others in the family had been patrons of the monastery and beneficiaries of the saint's protection. To label these comital courts "public" is to emphasize one institutional aspect of their character but to neglect the ongoing ties which linked aristocratic families to churches, monasteries, and cathedral chapters—ties which lay magnates cultivated with care and energy. In these cases, counts and countesses were not only exercising public authority; they were also

28. Abadal, "L'Abat Oliba i la seva època," 185 n. 20. For the "dynastic and family dimension" of dispute settlement in western France, see Martindale, "His Special Friend?' " 54–55.

29. *HGL* 168; *Oliba* 87.

30. See *Cuixà* 64, 68, 75, 77, 85, 89, 92, 94. I trace the ties between the monastery and Cerdanya's comital dynasty in "Councils, Memory, and Mills: The Early Development of the Peace of God in Catalonia," *Early Medieval Europe* 8 (1999): 99–130.

sculpting their family's relations with a saint and his community. This is not to suggest that the decisions issued by courts like Guifré's were crudely unfair, although it stretches the imagination to think of the monastery's patron as disinterested. Nor does it mean that such courts were *already* privatized or *already* feudalized. Emphatic distinctions between public and private simply do not do a very good job of accounting for the complexity of the situation. Comital, public procedures were not segregated from the private, ritual concerns of kin groups.[31]

The schematic juxtaposition of public and private thus distorts our understanding of the administration of justice. At the same time, the public-private opposition invites narratives of disruption and discontinuity. Models that posit stark distinctions between public and private usually emphasize change while obscuring continuities. Proponents of the Feudal Revolution devote considerable attention to such institutional transformations—from comital courts to informal assemblies, from public to private—but these transformations alone are perhaps not the most important changes of the eleventh century. Such transformations are of interest in their own right, but the model of the Feudal Revolution insists on connections between institutional changes, on the one hand, and dramatic social and political upheaval, on the other. Alongside accounts of the fragmentation of comital courts, descriptions of the Feudal Revolution place parallel accounts of cataclysmic eruptions of violence. As comital courts weakened, the argument goes, churches, monasteries, and peasants increasingly suffered from the depredations of lay lords. Public courts were no longer able to protect the poor and the clergy who suffered at the hands of oppressive lords. Counts and bishops were no longer able to restrain the rapacity of marauding bands of armed men.

Violence there certainly was, but the evidence for newly disruptive forms of violence emerging in the early eleventh century is equivocal. Over the course of several decades, Bishop Oliba of Vic regularly complained that the

31. "L'idée d'une 'privatisation' de la justice 'publique' post carolingienne n'a aucune pertinence, en fait; ces catégories modernes se révèlent inopérantes." Barthélemy, *La société dans le comté de Vendôme,* 654. Elsewhere, Barthélemy cautions against overemphasizing the "public" character of tenth-century assemblies. See *L'an mil et la paix de Dieu,* 281. For other reservations about the value of this distinction, see Patrick J. Geary, "Moral Obligations and Peer Pressure: Conflict Resolution in the Medieval Aristocracy," in *Georges Duby: L'écriture de l'histoire,* ed. Claudie Duhamel-Amado and Guy Lobrichon (Bruxelles, 1996)," 221, 222; Claudie Duhamel-Amado, "La famille aristocratique languedocienne," volume 1, book 1, 99; Paul Fouracre, "Carolingian Justice," 790–91; José María Mínguez, "Justicia y Poder en el Marco de la Feudalización de la Sociedad Leonesa," *La Giustizia nell'alto medioevo (secoli IX–XI)* 491–95, 506; Kosto, *Making Agreements,* 14; Bougard, "La justice dans le royaume d'Italie," 138; and Brown, *Unjust Seizure,* 192.

see of Vic and the monasteries over which he presided at Ripoll and Cuixà suffered from the usurpations of avaricious laymen. Oliba's complaints to the Council of Vic in 1022 and to a synod in Narbonne in 1043 are excellent examples of his attempts to secure ecclesiastic and monastic property against lay competitors.[32] Oliba also was an innovator, and he used Peace and Truce councils to protect the churches and monasteries in his care. But if Oliba's efforts show an enterprising churchman struggling to protect monastic and ecclesiastic property rights, it is harder to say whether his efforts signal new threats to those churches and monasteries. There are, after all, tenth-century precedents for complaints of the sort Oliba regularly made. In 991, Bishop Salla of Urgell excommunicated two dioceses because certain laymen had disturbed the see's property. The bishop communicated his decree to neighboring bishops and asked for their support in thwarting these lay depredations.[33] The alleged perpetrators were, incidentally, close allies of Oliba's mother. A 979 papal letter complained of usurpations of church property from the see of Elne and the monastery of Sant Pere de Roda. In 1001, the bishop of Barcelona appealed to the pope for help in his struggles against the city's viscount.[34] The aggression of lay magnates was a serious problem for some property-holders, but it was not a new problem.[35]

Property disputes in the Province of Narbonne thus yield at best mixed evidence for profound transformations during the early eleventh century. Some gradual changes in the administration of justice occurred, but important continuities also existed. Relations between counts and countesses, on the one hand, and courts, on the other, changed. After the middle of the eleventh century, counts and countesses presided less frequently over judicial assemblies. The competencies and jurisdictions of different courts had long been poorly defined. During the eleventh century, the number of courts multiplied further and counts less-often presided over them. Comital and episcopal courts surrendered some of their authority to vicarial, abbatial, and seigneurial assemblies. Judges still played an important role in the adjudication of property disputes, but they failed to maintain the dynamism and rigor that distinguished their predecessors. And a modest change occurred in the types of decisions courts formulated. These changes are certainly worth noting, but they do not indicate widespread upheaval; the diminished prominence of comital courts did not lead inevitably to violence and disorder.

The equation of strong public authorities and social order is not one to

32. *Oliba* 149, 68.
33. *Urgellia* 225.
34. Zimmerman, *Papsturkunden, 896–1046*, t. II, doc. 252, 395.
35. For other examples, see *Urgellia* 286; *HGL* 134; and *Girona* 100.

take for granted. Peace and order were not necessarily by-products of the strength of traditional, so-called public institutions such as comital courts. Mechanisms other than comital courts could process conflicts with similar degrees of success. A case from the monastery of Santa Maria de Lavaix provides a useful illustration. In July 1063, the monastery's abbot brought a complaint before a court composed a judge, a *saio*, and a handful of local notables. The abbot complained that one Bradila had taken a church that belonged to the monastery. Bradila responded that he did not hold the church unjustly. He explained that his parents built the church, had it consecrated, and endowed it with property, books, and liturgical paraphernalia. On their deaths, Bradila insisted, the church passed to him. The abbot conceded that much of what his opponent said was true. But he added that after his father's death, Bradila had joined his mother and his brother in giving the church to the monastery. The abbot presented a record to the court by which Bradila, his mother, and his brother had transferred the disputed church to one of the abbot's predecessors. Judge Peter asked Bradila whether he had, as the abbot claimed, approved of this donation. Bradila admitted that he could not deny the document's authenticity. The judge, with a vague reference to the rules governing church property, decided that the church should be returned to the monastery. Bradila abandoned his claim and the merciful abbot allowed him to hold the church on the monastery's behalf.[36]

The case includes several of the standard indices of the decay of public justice. No count, countess, viscount, or bishop presided over the hearing. A motley collection of lesser notables and *boni homines* heard the dispute. Peter still bore a judge's title, but his gestures to written law were unconvincing; he was no Bonhom of Barcelona. The dispute might also be used as an example of how churches and monasteries struggled to defend their property rights from lay aggression. The context might even be called violent with some degree of linguistic precision: the record twice mentions that Bradila took the disputed church violently (*violenter*), although it is hard to know exactly what that means.

However, despite these possible intimations of decaying justice and growing violence, the more powerful impression this record gives is one of a modest, but well-ordered, collective mechanism for reconciling competing property claims. There were admittedly differences between an assembly like this one and a comital court in Barcelona around the year 1000, but there were a good number of similarities as well. The abbot formally accused a layman before a court which included a judge and a *saio*. The judge and other members of the court evaluated written proof alongside witness testimony.

36. *Lavaix* 27.

The judge referred (admittedly vaguely) to written rules. The court finally issued an unequivocal decision in favor of one disputant. After the court issued its decision, the disputants themselves carved out a more accommodating arrangement.

More significant than the fleeting reference to the law or the presence of legal professionals is the fact that both disputants appealed to coherent normative frameworks that are by now familiar to readers.[37] The abbot insisted on the superiority of written proofs and the irrevocability of gifts to churches. Bradila based his claim on his family's development of and long-term possession of the disputed property. He did not seize the church randomly; he thought that the church was his and he had reasons for thinking so. Finally, the court was able to formulate a clear decision as well as to sanction a workable compromise. Judge Peter's court admittedly does not look like a tenth-century comital court, but it hardly qualifies as anarchy.[38]

The degeneration of comital justice did not necessarily lead to violent disruptions of social and legal order. This case and others like it suggest that communities processed disputes and orchestrated some degree of order without the participation of "public" lords.[39] Less formal courts displayed important continuities with earlier courts. Judges and disputants continued to rely (selectively) on written law. Lay and clerical litigants argued with reference to long-standing norms, presenting written records and witnesses to substantiate their claims. Judges evaluated proofs and issued decisions. Many procedural elements were present in the modest, non-comital courts of the mid- and late eleventh century. Courts might become—as some would have it—more private, without provoking explosions of violence. Violence there was, but it was not always senseless. It took place within coherent normative frameworks; claims and counterclaims could be antagonistic without being anarchic.[40]

The disruptions in the legal and social world of the eleventh century were neither as abrupt nor as total as they have been described. That is not to deny

37. See chapter 2 above and Stephen White's discussion of normative frameworks in "Debate," 214.

38. As Patrick Geary suggests: "The decline of comital courts may have meant less the transformation of conflict resolution than a change of its locus." "Moral Obligations and Peer Pressure," 221.

39. For other examples, see *Girona* 100; *Santa Anna* 54; *Santa Anna* 76; *Viage* 9, 12; *Santa Anna* 114; and *Santa Cecília* 186. On long-term continuities in the administration of justice, see Janet Nelson, "Kings with Justice, Kings without Justice," 819; and Barthélemy, *L'an mil et la paix de Dieu*, 510.

40. Compare David Nirenberg's treatment of violence toward minorities in the Crown of Aragon during the fourteenth century, *Communities of Violence: Persecution of Minorities in the Middle Ages* (Princeton, 1996).

that there were changes in social, economic, and political structures during the first half of the eleventh century. After all, the mechanisms for administering justice constitute only one component of the Feudal Revolution. If there were certain legal continuities, there were also notable changes. The early decades of the eleventh century witnessed an economic takeoff, fueled by the influx of gold from al-Andalus and the implementation of new technologies (such as water mills), the growth of a monetary economy, and the development of mechanisms of credit. New tools for mediating social and political relations, such as the *convenientiae*, emerged.[41] These agreements did not sweep aside judicial assemblies and courts, but they did provide alternative means of regulating potentially antagonistic relationships. In some parts of the Province of Narbonne, the structure of families also changed during the eleventh century.[42] New opportunities for castellans and knights (*milites*) arose.[43] Peace councils were a new forum for public legislation and they served some of the same functions that earlier courts had in terms of articulating norms, protecting ecclesiastical property, and restraining seigneurial rapacity.[44] Continuities in the administration of justice or the processing of disputes do not minimize the importance of changes like these. The continuities in law, courts, and normative frameworks do, however, suggest that linkages between the different components of the Feudal Revolution should be scrutinized carefully.

Justice, power, ritual, and property could be related in unpredictable ways, and the model of the Feudal Revolution does not always appreciate the unpredictability of these connections. The Feudal Revolution has proven an appealing model for describing the social and political world of the eleventh century because it explains a wide range of phenomena: changes in the administration of justice, varieties of land tenure, social ties, political structures, and military organization can all be seen as symptomatic of a greater transformation. Understanding change in this period may involve dismantling the many elements of social, political, and legal history that have been so firmly fused together in descriptions of the Feudal Revolution.

Regional studies treating the tenth, eleventh, and twelfth centuries confirm that whatever transformation took place was marked by a high level of local particularity. In the Anjou, for example, the trajectory of change does

41. See Kosto, *Making Agreements*.

42. Bonnassie, *Catalogne*, 544–49; and Lydia Martínez i Teixidó, *Les famílies nobles dels Pallars en els segles XI i XII* (Lleida, Spain, 1991).

43. Bonnassie, "The Formation of Catalan Feudalism," 160.

44. See Gener Gonzalvo i Bou, *La Pau i la Treva a Catalunya: Origen de les Corts Catalanes* (Barcelona, 1986); Freedman, *Origins of Peasant Servitude*, 83–85; and Bonnassie, *Catalogne*, 654–62.

not resemble the one described by Duby for the Mâconnais. Comital power and the prestige of Carolingian institutions suffered only minor degradations in the Anjou, and then not until after 1060.[45] Elsewhere, the Count of Angoulême's authority was solid until 1030, and Peace councils were signs of the strength of lay magnates rather than of their weakness.[46] In Picardy, comital power was largely untroubled as late as 1120.[47] In Berry, the degradation of comital power did not correspond closely to the emergence of a powerful knightly class.[48] Around Chartres, the proliferation of castles reflected the consolidation of comital authority rather than its breakdown.[49] Similarly, in Champagne, castellans were agents of comital power rather than threats to it.[50] In Portugal, the "privatization" of justice did not occur until as late as the thirteenth century.[51] These few examples show what a range of conclusions might be reached by regional studies with regard to only one element (comital power) of the Feudal Revolution.

In Catalonia, peasants were subjected to increased seigneurial pressures during the eleventh century, but these did not have immediate and sweeping results. Oppressive exactions did not multiply until after 1060. Peasant communities developed strategies to resist assaults on their independence. Many peasants managed to retain the favorable tenures that characterized the tenth century. The transition from a free to a subject peasantry took centuries rather than decades, and often times that transition did not begin in earnest until the middle of the twelfth century.[52] In Catalonia, each of the putative elements of the Feudal Revolution (the fraying of comital power, the proliferation of new forms of servitude, shifts in land tenure, the emergence of new

45. Olivier Guillot, *Le comte d'Anjou et son entourage au XIe siècle* (Paris, 1972), 353, 431–33.

46. André Debord, *La société laïque dans les pays de la Charente, Xe–XIIe s* (Paris, 1984), 107, 113, 124.

47. Robert Fossier, *La terre et les hommes en Picardie jusqu'à fin du XIIIe siècle* (Paris, 1968), 2:488.

48. Guy Devailly, *Le Berry du Xe siècle au milieu du XIIIe. Etude politique, religieuse, sociale, économique* (Paris, 1973), 196.

49. André Chédeville, *Chartres et ses campagnes, XIe–XIIe siècles* (Paris, 1973), 271, 287.

50. Michel Bur, *La formation du comté de Champagne, v. 950–1150* (Nancy, France, 1977), 402, 452, 501.

51. Robert Durand, *Les Campagnes portugaises entre Douro et Tage aux XIIe et XIII siècles* (Paris, 1982), 470. For Castile, see Ignacio Álvarez Borge, *Poder y relaciones sociales en Castilla en la Edad Media: Los territorios entre el Arlanzón y el Duero en los siglos X al XIV* (Salamanca, 1996), 127–30.

52. The *incastellamento* in Old Catalonia did not disrupt older parish networks. See Freedman, *Origins of Peasant Servitude*, 40, 204–5; and Manuel Riu, "El Feudalismo en Cataluña," *En Torno al Feudalismo Hispanico: I Congreso de Estudios Medievales* (Avila, 1989), 377–79, 390–91.

knightly classes, changes in the administration of justice) followed its own logic. Whatever revolutions, transformations, or ruptures occurred during the eleventh century displayed a dizzying degree of local variation. Descriptions of the Feudal Revolution often obscure these local subtleties.

Significant changes took place in the Province of Narbonne during the eleventh century, but treating these changes as a coherent, monolithic package has obscured what was genuinely new in the *convenientiae*, Peace councils, or in eleventh-century courts. The model of the Feudal Revolution has too firmly welded together discrete social and political innovations. The eleventh century was indeed tumultuous. Disputes over property rights are themselves excellent windows on the competitive aspects of medieval society. Competition should not, however, be mistaken for chaos. Disputes emerged most often not from the absence of rules or norms but from conflicts between different, coherent normative frameworks.

OTHER VINEYARDS, OTHER COURTS: JUSTICE IN WESTERN EUROPE

Certain features of the legal world of the Province of Narbonne were peculiar to this region, while other characteristics of the disputing process were more broadly distributed. Legal practice in Barcelona found occasional echoes in Braga, Lucca, and Blois. Susan Reynolds suggests that some of the rules, attitudes, and practices which dominated disputing were present throughout the post-Carolingian world:

> Before the twelfth century . . . legal procedures and the ideas they embody seem to have been very similar in England, France, Germany, and at least the northern part of Italy. Thereafter the legal systems which developed within the emerging political units began to diverge like species on slowly separating continents. . . . That is not to argue for a moment either that local variations were insignificant or that the ideas I detect were universally accepted or were the only important ideas around. It was an essential feature of medieval institutions that they tolerated a high degree of local autonomy and variety. But all this was part of the common culture.[53]

These "local variations," such as the importance of the *Visigothic Code* and the use of particular procedures related to proof (e.g., *reparatio scripturae*), are extremely important. At the same time, elements of the administration of jus-

53. Reynolds, *Kingdoms and Communities*, 8–9.

tice looked similar in many parts of Europe between 900 and 1100. In the final pages of this book, I explore the ways in which the experiences of counts, bishops, judges, and disputants in the Province of Narbonne resembled the experiences of their contemporaries throughout Europe.

Disputes in the Province of Narbonne unfolded in recurrent patterns. The most common type of dispute was a challenged bequest in which a lay person or group of lay people tried to reclaim property from a church or monastery. The church or monastery claimed to have received the property as a bequest; and lay challengers argued that the same property was rightfully theirs by inheritance. The death of a property-holder, the departure of a property-holder on pilgrimage, or any other minor social transition might bring these conflicting claims to the surface.[54]

The same basic pattern was common throughout Europe. Challenged gifts which pitted lay and clerical litigants against one another were the chief source of legal conflict from the ninth to the twelfth century.[55] In the Vendômois, kin groups were often angered by monastic claims to part of their *hereditas*. Courts in Burgundy and Provence often devoted their attention to disputes that emerged when lay property-holders challenged the property claims of churches and monasteries. Analogous disputes arose throughout Christian Spain, Francia, England, Bavaria, and Italy. Disputes over personal status, in which a person was alleged to be servile, occurred regularly in some parts of Europe, but these were absent in the Province of Narbonne.[56] There

54. In Provence, Patrick Geary notes that new eruptions of conflict corresponded to moments of transition, such as deaths or marriages, that is, ". . . points in the aristocratic life cycle when relationships had to be spelled out and property holdings had to be clarified." See his "Living with Conflicts in Stateless France," 141.

55. Penelope Johnson, *Prayer, Power, and Patronage: The Abbey of La Trinité de Vendôme, 1032–1187* (New York, 1981), 91–93; Brown, *Unjust Seizure*, 143; Barthélemy, *La Société dans le comté de Vendôme*, 653; Stephen Weinberger, "Les conflits entre clercs et laïcs dans la Provence médiévale," *AMidi* 92 (1980): 269–79. For Burgundy, see Duby, "The Evolution of Judicial Institutions," 20; Nelson, "Dispute Settlement in Carolingian West Francia," 55; Le Jan, "Justice Royale et pratiques sociales," 83; Timothy Reuter, "Property Transactions and Social Relations," in *Property and Power in the Early Middle Ages*, ed. Davies and Fouracre, 185; and Hudson, *Land, Law, and Lordship*, 196. However, eleventh-century disputes in northern Francia described by Geoffrey Koziol differed significantly from those in the Province of Narbonne. Disputes in the north often centered on questions of jurisdiction and customary duty. See Koziol, *Begging Pardon and Favor*, appendix 1.

56. For examples in Italy, Francia, and England, see Balzaretti, "The Monastery of Sant' Ambrogio and Dispute Settlement"; Wickham, "Land Disputes and Their Social Framework," 118; Guillot, *Comte d'Anjou*, vol. 2, no. C67; Patrick Wormald, *The Making of English Law: King Alfred to the Twelfth Century*, vol. 1, *Legislation and Its Limits* (Oxford, 1999), 76–80; Nelson, "Dispute Settlement in Carolingian West Francia"; Paul Hyams, "The Proof of Villein Status in the Common Law," *English Historical Review* 89 (1974):

were, of course, always unpredictable contingencies that might provoke property disputes—such as the 972 dispute in León which erupted because litigants were drunk—but property disputes in many places followed similar patterns.[57]

Although the general pattern of the challenged bequest was widespread, there were important regional variations in how such disputes unfolded. Distinct rules, norms, and habits inflected how disputants in different regions articulated their claims. Disputants widely scattered throughout Francia, Italy, and Iberia, for example, argued that members of kin groups had certain unquestionable rights to a patrimony or *hereditas*, but only disputants in Catalonia and Languedoc supported these claims by appealing to Carolingian rules governing *aprisiones*. Churchmen throughout Europe argued that gifts to churches were irrevocable, but only in Christian Spain and some parts of Mediterranean France did they invoke rules from the *Visigothic Code* to bolster their claims.

Larger social, political, and military movements at times influenced the trajectory of property disputes. The shifting southern border between the county of Barcelona and the caliphate of Córdoba was also the boundary between Latin Christendom and the Muslim world. Political and territorial conflict on this frontier often affected individual property-holders. In the wake of the 985 sack of Barcelona, disputes over property arose because many property-holders were captives in al-Andalus. For decades, courts wrestled with the question of how to handle disputes centered on proofs that had been destroyed in the sack of Barcelona. Disputants who had no written proof to support their claims quickly learned that they might invoke missing proofs, whether or not such proofs had ever really existed. After 1010, the political situation improved for the Christian principalities of northern Spain. The counts of Barcelona led raids into al-Andalus in 1010, 1013, and 1017. The rulers of Catalonia, Castile, Galicia, and Asturias made effective and lasting gains of land to the south. By 1040 the taifa kingdoms of al-Andalus were making tribute payments to the count of Barcelona. The increased security of the frontier affected property-holders and inflected disputes, just as the sack of Barcelona had done thirty years earlier.

The military unrest which unsettled property relations in certain parts of

721–49. For disputes over status elsewhere on the Iberian Peninsula, see Reyna Pastor, *Resistencias y luchas campesinas en la época de crecimiento y consolidación de la formación feudal* (Madrid, 1980), 25, 33–34; and *Colección de Documentos de la Catedral de Oviedo*, ed. Santos Garcia Larragueta (Oviedo, 1962) (hereafter *Oviedo*), 53. For a ninth-century case from the Province of Narbonne, see *Marca* 34.

57. Justo Perez de Urbel, *Sampiro, su cronica y la monarquia leonesa en el siglo X* (Madrid, 1952), appendix 2, doc. 1.

Catalonia did the same in other parts of Christian Spain. Property-holders throughout the region confronted similar difficulties as the inhabitants of Barcelona, who struggled with lost documents, and property-holders south of the Llobregat River, who dealt with claims complicated by long abandonment.[58] The eleventh century was a turbulent period for those on the frontier between the Christian and Muslim worlds. Knights and clerics began to move into the Iberian Peninsula in large numbers. Tribute money flowed from tributaries in al-Andalus to kings, counts, and monasteries in northern Spain and beyond. The Christian capture of the ancient Visigothic capitol Toledo in 1085 was a blow to Andalusi confidence and heralded a new period of aggressive intervention in the Iberian Peninsula by both Christians from Latin Europe and Almoravids. The annual military campaigns undertaken by Christians and Muslims and the influx of fortune-seekers had dramatic effects on the ways in which people held, cultivated, and fought over land. In frontier zones, monastic and ecclesiastic patrimonies grew at the expense of established settlers.[59]

The situation on the Iberian Peninsula was especially dramatic, but such energies and conflicts were apparent in other parts of the Mediterranean. As al-Andalus reeled under internal strife and the unprecedented vitality of Christian aggression, so too Muslim Sicily and Apulia fell gradually to Norman invaders. The stirring of bands of European warriors throughout the Mediterranean during the eleventh century almost inevitably disrupted or complicated property relations. In the year 1000, one of Barcelona's property-holders, Matrona, returned after fifteen years in captivity in Córdoba to discover that her brother had appropriated her property. Matrona was not the only property-holder to deal with border crossings, confused titles, and litigation over property. The new century that Matrona witnessed would see an unprecedented number of European property-holders wrestling with larger political and military movements. The century that began with Matrona's return to Barcelona after a long captivity drew to a close with the conquest of cities at opposite ends of the Mediterranean (Toledo in 1085, Jerusalem in 1099), reflecting the expansion of Latin Christendom.

These conquests had important echoes in the humbler world of vineyards, mills, and fields. The monastery of Sant Cugat displayed a keen interest in land south of the Llobregat after 1010, and frequently brought other prop-

58. See, for example, José Maria Mínguez Fernández, ed., *Colleción diplomática del monasterio de Sahagún (857–1230)*, vol. 1, siglos IX y X (León, 1976), 340; and María Isabel Pérez de Tudela y Velasco, "Guerra, violencia y terror: La destrucción de Santiago de Compostela por Almanzor hace mil años," *en La España Medieval* 21 (1998): 9–28.

59. See, for example, José Avelino Gutiérrez González, "El Páramo Léones. Entre la Antigüedad y la Alta Edad Media," *Studi Historica, Historia Medieval* 14 (1996): 47–96.

erty-holders to court. This campaign to expand the monastery's patrimony may have been, in part, the product of Abbot Guitard's idiosyncrasies and ambitions. But the monastery's policy and practice can also be understood as early tremors of a century of European territorial, economic, and cultural expansion—expansion which on the local level prompted property disputes.[60]

In the Province of Narbonne, written law played an important role in determining how people fought over property. Frequent references to the *Visigothic Code* reflect the enthusiastic, but selective, application of Visigothic law. Reliance on the *Code* is more amply documented in Catalonia than elsewhere, but records from some other regions also reflect the use of Visigothic law during the tenth and eleventh centuries. In other parts of Christian Spain, judges and scribes used the *Code* to determine inheritance portions, dowries, and testamentary procedure.[61] Fernando I of León invoked Visigothic law in 1046 when he punished a group of peasants (*rusticani*) who had killed one of his representatives.[62] The same king invoked Visigothic law when he made donations to churches.[63] Visigothic rules popular in the Province of Narbonne which proclaimed the irrevocability of gifts to churches, the sanctity of ecclesiastical property, and the right of a property-holders to alienate also appeared in other regions.[64] Rules asserting the right to alienate property were especially popular around Braga and Coimbra.[65] Transactions undertaken as a result of violence, fear, or intimidation were disqualified.[66] As many as 150 references to Visigothic law survive from the kingdom of León

60. In 1063, a woman sold land in order to pay her brother's ransom to the Normans. Around the same time, the abbot of a monastery in Naples complained that monks had fled because of the Norman siege. Patricia Skinner, "When Was Southern Italy 'Feudal,'" *Settimane* 47 (2000): 330.

61. For testamentary procedure, see *Oviedo* 71. For dowry, see *Cartulario de Santa Cruz de la Serós*, ed. Antonio Ubieto Arteta, Textos Medievales, 19 (Valencia, 1966), no. 11, 1009; Justiniano Rodríguez Fernández, *El monasterio de Ardón* (León, 1964), doc. 81. See also *Liber Fidei Sanctae Bracarensis Ecclesiae*, ed. Pe. Aveline de Jesus da Costa, 2 vols. (Braga, 1965–78) (hereafter *LFSB*), 110, 112; and *Cartulario de San Vicente de Oviedo, 781–1200*, ed. D. Luciano Serrano (Madrid, 1929), no. 67.

62. Justiniano Rodríguez Fernández, "El Ordenamiento Juridico Leones en la Edad Media," *León Medieval: Doce Estudios* (León, 1978), 69–81; Juan José Larrea, "Villa Matanza," in *Les sociétés méridionales à l'âge féodal*, ed. Débax, 223–28.

63. *España Sagrada: Teatro geográfico-histórico de la Iglesia de España*, ed. Henrique Florex, et al. (Madrid, 1746–1918), vol. 36, ap. 22.

64. *LFSB*, 201, 238; *Cartulario de San Vicente de Oviedo, 781–1200*, no. 48, no. 87.

65. Claudio Rodiño Caramés, "A Lex Gótica e o Liber Iudicum no Reino de León," *Cuadernos de Estudios Gallegos* 44 (1997): 29. See also Durand, *Campagnes portugaises*, 45–47. For examples, see *LFSB* 22, 159, 173.

66. *Cartulario de San Vicente de Oviedo*, no. 38.

between the ninth and twelfth centuries.[67] Invocations and citations of Visigothic law were usually related to a core of common themes, but there was still a degree of regional variety in how judges and disputants used the *Code*. On at least two occasions, judges in the court of Alfonso V of León appealed to a rule from the *Code* that judges in the Province of Narbonne ignored altogether.[68] Courts and litigants throughout the Iberian Peninsula drew from the *Code* some of the same lessons their contemporaries in the Province of Narbonne did.

The intense attachment to written law in Christian Spain is noteworthy, but some other parts of Europe displayed a similar enthusiasm. Legal procedure in ninth-, tenth-, and eleventh-century Italy was often indebted to written law. Litigants and judges relied both on law codes, such as the *Lombard Laws*, and on Carolingian capitularies.[69] The closest counterparts to the judges of Catalonia were to be found elsewhere on the Iberian Peninsula and in Italy. Like their counterparts in Catalonia, these judges often issued decisions with reference to written law. Thus in 998, a judge Uberto in Rome consulted the written law when adjudicating a dispute. Judges in the Kingdom of Italy, like those in the Province of Narbonne, formed an important, prosperous, subaristocratic class.[70] In Italy, as in northern Spain, different legal traditions were often combined. Just as judges in eleventh-century Barcelona might rely on the *Visigothic Code*, scripture, and canon law, judges in Italy invoked both Lombard law and Carolingian legislation. Even regions especially attached to particular law codes still showed flexibility in their application. In a case near Mantua in 1045, litigants claimed they were subject to Visigothic law and judges accepted their claim. Litigants in ninth-century

67. Rodiño Caramés, "A Lex Gótica e o Liber Iudicum"; Collins, "Visigothic law and Regional Custom"; José Ángel García de Cortázar, "La formación de una sociedad feudal," *Settimane* 47 (2000): 525–28. For Castile, see Ernesto Pastor Díaz de Garayo, *Castilla en el Tránsito de la Antigüedad al Feudalismo: Poblamiento, poder político y estuctura social. Del Arlanza al Duero (siglos VII–XI)* (Vallodolid, Spain, 1996), 186, 222.

68. "Colección Diplomática de Alfonso V," ed. Fernández del Pozo, docs. 26, 31.

69. See, for example, C. Manaresi, ed. *I placiti del "Regnum Italiae,"* Fonte per la storia d'Italia 92 (Rome, 1955), 145; Raffaello Volpini, "Placiti del 'Regnum Italiae' (secc. IX–XI). Primi contributi per un nuovo censimento," *Contributi dell'Instituto di storia medioevale*, ed. Piero Zerbi (Milan, 1975), vol. 3, nos. 15, 29, 32, 33; Wickham, "Lombard-Carolingian Italy, 700–900," 114; and Padoa Schioppa, "Aspetti della giustizia," 24. For the use of capitularies, see Bougard, *Justice dans le royaume d'Italie*, 46–53. For the application of written law, see Everett, "Literacy and Law in Lombard Government."

70. See Wickham, "Justice in the Kingdom of Italy," 227; Bougard, *Justice dans le royaume d'Italie*, 281–89; and idem., "La Justice dans le royaume d'Italie aux Ixe–Xe siècles," *La giustizia nell'alto medioevo (secoli IX–XI)*, 133–76.

Italy appealed to the *lex baiuvariorum*.[71] The meaning of *lex* or *leges* in Merovingian Gaul was similarly diffuse, referring to Alaric's Breviary, Salic law, canon law, or even a widely accepted body of custom.[72] In Bavaria, the terms *lex, ritus, mos,* and *usus* were used almost interchangeably.[73] Certain parts of western Europe were attached to the use of written legal traditions, but these legal traditions remained elastic. The importance of written law has in general been underestimated during this period, but the degree of attachment to written law varied widely by region. Some regions, even those with highly developed conceptions of justice and effective means for resolving disputes, saw very few references to written law.[74]

The legal pluralism apparent in Francia, Italy, and Christian Spain can be explained, in part, by the fact that litigants and judges were always adapting law codes to particular needs. Judges and the presidents of courts often accepted a range of different written authorities, but these were almost always shaped by contemporary exigencies. In the Province of Narbonne, for example, judges passed over in silence rules from the *Code* that protected the property rights of kin groups. A similar process of selective application of the law is apparent wherever written law was used. In western and northern Francia, capitularies that prohibited giving property to churches without the consent of those who might be disinherited were ignored by clerical and monastic property-holders whose cases would suffer from the rigorous application of those rules.[75] At the same time, clerical and monastic litigants invoked rules which supported the right of property-holders to alienate their property without hindrance. In other words, although the particular corpus of rules available varied from one region to the next, the instrumental appeal of the written law for disputants was often the same. Ecclesiastical litigants in Burgundy did not rely on the *Visigothic Code* as their contemporaries in

71. Franca Sinatti d'Amico, *Le prove giudiziarie nel diritto longobardo. Legislazione e prassi da Rotari ad Astolfo* (Milan, 1968), 43–44; and Delogu, "La Giustizia nell'Italia Meridionale Longobarda," *La giustizia nell'alto medioevo (secoli IX–XI)*, 295. For the Mantuan appeal to Visigothic law, see Bougard, *Justice dans le royaume d'Italie*, 295; Carl I. Hammer, "*lex scripta* in Early Medieval Bavaria: Use and Abuse of the *lex baiuvariorum*," in *Law in Medieval Life and Thought*, ed. Edward B. King and Susan J. Ridyard, Sewanee Medieval Studies 5 (Sewanee, 1990), 195.

72. Guillot, "Justice dans le royaume franc," 660; and Fouracre, "Disputes in Later Merovingian Francia," 33.

73. Brown, "The Use of Norms in Disputes," 22.

74. Brittany, for example, was such a region. See Wendy Davies, *Small Worlds: The Village Community in Early Medieval Brittany* (London, 1988); and Wormald, *Making of English Law*, 1:85.

75. Reynolds, *Fiefs and Vassals*, 105.

Catalonia did, but they were still most interested in rules that emphasized the alienability of property.[76]

Throughout the post-Carolingian world, those who administered justice and recorded property transactions strove to do so in accordance with written law. The frequent use of written law during the tenth and eleventh centuries is apparent not only in the record of sales, gifts, and disputes. Bonhom's copy of the *Code* is a particularly rich example of a manuscript that affirms the importance of written law, but many copies of the *Code* were produced and circulated during this period. Records from Oviedo, Braga, Sahagún, Celanova, and León mention copies of the *Visigothic Code*.[77] The production of legal manuscripts, whether Bonhom of Barcelona's legal compendium or Abbo of Fleury's *collectio canonum*, shows that written legal traditions were understood as vital tools, suitable for reconciling differences, maintaining peace, and protecting property rights. Under the leadership of Abbo, the monks of Fleury relied heavily on their library to defend their monastery from aggressive neighbors.[78] The same interest in written law is also apparent in episcopal letters. Bishop Oliba of Vic, for example, invoked *lex* when he tried to dissuade King Sancho of Navarre from contracting a marriage which Oliba considered incestuous. Bishop Fulbert of Chartres, Oliba's contemporary, similarly drew on the *Theodosian Code* when he wrote letters to magnates offering guidance and threatening correction.[79]

The discourse of law was often fused with the discourse of ritual. Throughout Europe, to varying degrees, monasteries and churches relied both on rules culled from Roman vulgar law or Germanic codes, on the one hand, and excommunications, curses, and the humiliation of relics on the other. Some of the same vivid curses and the same ritual affiliation with scriptural villains, like Dathan and Abiron, appear, for example, in charters from other regions of Christian Spain.[80] Learned law and ritual sanctions were not in-

76. See, for example, *Cluny* 1088, 447.

77. *Oviedo* 50; García Lopez, *Estudios Criticos*; Collins, "Visigothic Law and Regional Custom," 104; and Gibert, *Enseñanza del derecho*, 33.

78. On Abbo's use of written law, see Jean-Pierre Poly, "Le procès de l'an mil ou du bon usage des *Leges* en temps de désarroi," *La giustizia nell'alto medioevo (secoli IX–XI)*, 39; and Rosenwein, Head, and Farmer, "Monks and Their Enemies," 872–74.

79. *Letters and Poems of Fulbert of Chartres*, ed. Behrends, p. xxiv. English courts provide a contrast. No surviving record of Anglo-Saxon litigation cites any Anglo-Saxon law code. Alan Kennedy, "Law and Litigation in the *Libellus Athelwoldi episcopi*," *Anglo-Saxon England* 24 (1995): 175, 183.

80. See, for example, a record which describes Dathan and Abiron as lawbreakers, in *Oviedo* 111; and Saturnino Ruiz de Loizaga, *Iglesia y Sociedad en el Norte de España*, especially the section entitled, "El Espiritu de Justicia en Santa Maria de Valpuesta." For the

compatible. In the context of litigation, these two discourses shared one very important characteristic: both afforded distinct advantages to ecclesiastic and monastic disputants.

Around the year 1000, a legal culture especially devoted to written law and fostered by legal professionals was most apparent in Catalonia and Septimania, on the periphery of Latin Europe. There, written law played a more important role than in the courts of England or Francia. The sophistication of these courts is apparent not only in the use of written law but also in the activities of the professional judges who were largely responsible for the law's preservation, interpretation, and application. Prominent members of society, these judges cooperated closely, studying the law, adjudicating disputes, and supervising other transactions. The judges of Barcelona, Vic, Urgell, and Girona were the most impressive such group of legal professionals in eleventh-century Europe, but there were analogs in other regions. Judges adjudicated disputes and applied the law in other parts of Christian Spain. A 1025 document from León described the duties of judges with reference to the *Visigothic Code*.[81] Judges in Braga, Coimbra, and Oviedo occasionally consulted the *Visigothic Code* and cited its rules when adjudicating disputes, although their training and expertise is more obscure than that of their contemporaries in Barcelona.[82] These judges had some responsibility for applying the law of the *Visigothic Code*, but, on the whole, the image of judges in other parts of Christian Spain is less vivid. Although it is possible to trace the careers of a handful of judges in other parts of the Iberian Peninsula over the course of many years, these other judges did not form the professional networks that judges in Catalonia did.[83]

The closest contemporary analogs to the judges of the Province of Narbonne were in Italy. In northern Italy, judges played an important role in the administration of justice and occupied prominent social and economic positions, like their contemporaries in Vic and Barcelona. They enjoyed wealth, advantageous marriages, and clerical preferment.[84] Judges studied the written law, adjudicated disputes, witnessed property transactions, and consulted

---

association of law and ritual in Italy, see Wickham, "Justice in the Kingdom of Italy," 194. For curse clauses in England, see Hudson, *Land, Law, and Lordship,* 167.

81. "Colección Diplomática de Alfonso V," ed. Fernández del Pozo," doc. X. In *Oviedo* 42, the grant of the Fuero of León in July 1017 mentions royally appointed judges.

82. *Oviedo* 74; Minguez, "Justicia y Poder en el Marco," 512–15. See also Justo Pérez de Urbel, "Cardeña y sus escribas durante la primera mitad del siglo X," in *Bivium: Homenaje a Manuel Cecilio Díaz y Díaz* (Madrid, 1983), 217–37.

83. A Judge Adaiub, for example, presided over at least five transactions near the monastery of Sahagún during the mid tenth century. *Colección diplomática del monasterio de Sahagún* 88, 145, 146, 147, 159; and Collins, "Disputes in Early Medieval Spain," 95.

84. Bougard, *Justice dans le royaume d'Italie,* 281–89.

each other in confusing cases. Occasionally, they represented lay and clerical litigants in court.[85] Some Italian judges were, like Sendred or Bonhom of Barcelona, quasi-itinerant.[86] Carolingian traditions of comital responsibility for the administration of justice also remained alive in Italy, and judges often served by comital appointment, like their counterparts in Barcelona or Cerdanya.[87]

With some notable exceptions, the role of court presidents in the Province of Narbonne in questioning disputants, assessing proofs, and issuing decisions was less active (and less fully described) than that of judges. Merovingian and Carolingian precedents, both theoretical and practical, provided the foundation for the organization of tenth- and eleventh-century courts.[88] Comital and episcopal responsibility for the administration of justice was a well-established principle in much of western Europe by the tenth century. In practice, comital and episcopal jurisdictions often blended into one another and bishops and counts often jointly administered justice.[89] The shared responsibility of secular and ecclesiastical magnates, the learned professionalism of the judges, and the communal participation of the *boni homines* allowed for great flexibility in practice. As in the status and role of judges, so too in the organization of courts, the Province of Narbonne more closely resembled Italy and other parts of Christian Spain than anywhere else. In northern Italy, Castile, and Catalonia, traditions of comital and episcopal responsibility for rendering justice remained more compelling than in other parts of the post-Carolingian world.[90]

In other parts of Europe, the organization of courts was less standardized. Away from the shores of the Mediterranean, those who organized courts and adjudicated property disputes were more likely to be men (and occasionally

85. Patricia Skinner, *Family Power in Southern Italy: The Duchy of Gaeta and Its Neighbours, 850–1139* (Cambridge, 1995), 93–94, 193–97. For *iudices* acting as advocates, see Volpini, "Placiti del 'Regnum Italiae,'" nos. 8, 12, 30; and Wickham, "Justice in the Kingdom of Italy," 225. For judges consulting about the law in a confusing case, see Volpini, "Placiti del 'Regnum Italiae,'" no. 29. For the study of law, see Gian Paolo Massetto, "Gli studi di diritto nella Lombardia del secolo XI," *Italia Sacra* 51 (1993): 61–116.

86. Schioppa, "Aspetti della giustizia," 15.

87. See, for example, Bougard, "Justice dans le royaume d'Italie," 170–72. see also Jean-Marie Martin, "Le juge et l'acte notarie en Italie meridionale," in *Scrittura e Produzione*, 287–301.

88. For Merovingian Gaul, see Luce Pietri's discussion of justice in Gregory of Tours, "Grégoire de Tours et la justice dans le royaume des Francs," *La Giustizia nell'alto medioevo (secoli v–viii)*, 478.

89. Bougard, *Justice dans le royaume d'Italie*, 239. For two cases during the 1040s in which a bishop and a count presided jointly, see Guillot, *Le comte d'Anjou*, 1:247; 1:268. See also Chédeville, *Chartres et ses campagnes*, 288.

90. For Castile, see Díaz de Garayo, *Castilla en el Tránsito de la Antigüedad al Feudalismo*, 184–85, 195.

women) who enjoyed some widely recognized, but unofficial, regional prominence and had ties to the disputants. In many places, informal arbiters—possessing neither office nor legal expertise—played important roles.[91]

The Province of Narbonne remained attached to the notion that counts, countesses, viscounts, and bishops had some responsibility for presiding over courts and to the notion that professional judges should issue decisions in property disputes. In practice, however, these ideas were extraordinarily flexible. Even in fairly traditional courts, there were ample opportunities for the broader participation of the community. Throughout medieval Europe, *boni homines* played important, though ill-defined, roles in processing disputes. They strove to resolve conflicts by pressuring disputants to compromise or to accept decisions of judges or arbiters.[92] The *boni homines* bore a greater burden of responsibility for maintaining order in those regions with weak courts and without some variety of professional judges or experienced arbiters. But even in regions where judges were relatively strong and courts well-ordered, *boni homines* played a vital role in the resolution of disputes. The strength of presiding counts and the erudition of professional judges did not, in other words, preclude the vital participation of *boni homines*. Comital courts staffed with professional judges often worked in concert with the more informal pressures community members brought to bear.[93] The *boni homines*, though usually silent in surviving records, expressed a collective interest in resolving differences, keeping the peace, and supporting the decisions of legitimate courts.

In the Province of Narbonne, courts devoted considerable attention to sifting the probative value of different proofs: written records, witness testimony, and, on rare occasions, judicial ordeals. Some of the dynamics of proof and strategy were intensely regional; only in Catalonia and Septimania, for example, did litigants make claims by *aprisio* or try to restore lost records through *reparatio scripturae*. Other parts of the forensic landscape resembled practices elsewhere. In general, written proofs were extremely important in medieval courts. In Merovingian Gaul, documents were an "integral part of customary procedure" and were often used (along with oath-helping and

91. White, "Inheritances and Legal Arguments," 66, 83; Cheyette, "Suum cuique tribuere," 292; and Davies, "Dispute in Ninth-Century Brittany," 83.

92. Benoît Cursente, "Entre parenté et fidélité: les 'amis' dans le Gascogne des XIe et XIIe siècles," in *Les sociétés méridionales à l'âge féodal*, ed. Débax, 285–92; Cheyette, "Suum cuique tribuere," 292; and White, "Inheritances and Legal Arguments," 66–68.

93. Geary, "Moral Obligations and Peer Pressure," 217–21; Toubert, *Les structures du Latium*, 1229–54; Minguez, "Justicia y Poder en el Marco," 542; Ourliac, "Juges et Justiciables au XI siècle"; and Nelson, "Dispute Settlement in Carolingian West Francia," 58–59.

oath-swearing) to resolve property disputes.[94] In Carolingian west Francia, written proofs, witness testimony, and invocations of the thirty-year rule were the most common forms of proof.[95] Anglo-Saxon courts frequently relied on written proofs.[96] The situation in Italy is, again, perhaps the closest analog to that in Catalonia. In the ninth century, written proofs and witness testimony were the most common forms of proof. Two-thirds of northern Italian cases between 700 and 900 involved charters as proofs.[97] This pattern continued into the tenth and eleventh centuries with some modifications. Courts in southern Italy, for example, grew increasingly attached to written proofs during the eleventh century.[98] As in Catalonia, some judicial hearings in Italy involved the examination of numerous written proofs. Powerful institutions, like the monastery of Sant' Ambrogio, kept archives of old documents, including records of sales, Carolingian diploma, and papal privileges, which they used during litigation.[99] During a 999 dispute near Benevento in which Lombard law was cited, disputants presented ten written proofs.[100]

Judges and disputants were especially enthusiastic about written proofs, but there was no rigid hierarchy mandating that records were always superior to witness testimony. In court, testimony about long-term possession could defeat otherwise impressive documents.[101] In Italy, as in the Province of Narbonne, written proofs and witness testimony were in practice interdependent. Courts and judges often relied on more than one variety of proof. They might, for example, ask witnesses to confirm the validity of a document. Together, written proofs and witness testimony were the most important forms of proof in many parts of Europe.[102]

Less frequently, courts relied on judicial ordeals and judicial duels. In

94. Fouracre, "Disputes in Later Merovingian Francia," 35–36; and Guillot, "Justice dans le royaume franc," 730–31.

95. Nelson, "Dispute Settlement in Carolingian West Francia," 50–56.

96. Bruce O'Brien, *God's Peace and King's Peace: The Laws of Edward the Confessor* (Philadelphia, 1999), 14–16; and Wormald, "Disputes in Anglo-Saxon England," 157.

97. Wickham, "Land Disputes and their Social Framework," 114. On the predominance of written proofs, see also Schioppa, "Aspetti della giustizia," 18; and Bougard, *Justice dans le royaume d'Italie*, 222–29.

98. Skinner, *Family Power in Southern Italy*, 21–22, 193.

99. On the use of Carolingian diploma, see Ross Balzaretti, "The monastery of Sant' Ambrogio." On Monte Cassino, see Skinner, *Family Power in Southern Italy*, 186.

100. Volpini, "Placiti del 'Regnum Italiae,'" no. 15.

101. Wickham, "Land Disputes and Their Social Framework," in *Settlement of Disputes*, 109.

102. Oath-helping played little or no role in property disputes in Septimania and Catalonia, although it was important elsewhere, as in Merovingian Gaul and Anglo-Saxon England. See Wood, "Disputes in Late Fifth- and Sixth-Century Gaul," in *Settlement of Disputes*, 15–16; and Kennedy, "Law and Litigation."

practical terms, these were the least important varieties of proof.[103] Courts and litigants appealed to them only in extraordinary circumstances. The results were often unsatisfactory. Although there are only a handful of references to ordeals in the Province of Narbonne, these cases often reflect fault lines in the ways judges and disputants understood proof. Judge Bonhom, for example, accepted Sentemir's proposed ordeal as a proof in the 988 dispute with Sant Cugat, but years later when he compiled his copy of the *Visigothic Code*, he omitted the *Code's* rule relating to judicial ordeals. Bonhom saw the ordeal as a proof that might be more easily manipulated than others.

Judicial ordeals rarely resolved property disputes, but they can help dramatize important questions about proof. In many respects, attitudes toward judicial ordeals and duels in this region resembled those elsewhere. Throughout Europe, ordeals were much less popular than documents, witness testimony, or oath-helping. They were rarely proposed and even less frequently executed. In eleventh-century Anjou-Touraine, for example, of the fourteen recorded judicial duels, only one seems to have determined the outcome of a conflict. In ten cases, the prospect of a duel led people to make peaceable settlements before the duel began. In three others, a solution emerged after the duel began but before it had reached a conclusion.[104] From the tenth to the twelfth centuries, very few cases were settled by "irrational proofs" in Aquitaine. In Castile, written proofs were common, while appeal to judicial ordeals was not, and there were no judicial duels.[105] As in the Province of Narbonne, judicial ordeals and duels were proposed only when a disputant was, at least in the eyes of the court, particularly belligerent, underhanded, or uncooperative.[106]

Ordeals were uncommon, but they nevertheless served as a safety valve for courts and a refuge for desperate disputants. Judges and the communities they served throughout Europe regarded judicial ordeals with deep ambivalence. Many invocations of ordeals were strategic; parties who proposed ordeals often had little real expectation of actually undergoing a trial. They tended to appear only during particularly acrimonious disputes when the reputation of at least one of the disputants was uncertain.[107]

No variety of proof—controversial or otherwise—could be profitably used by courts without interpretation. Judges, counts, bishops, disputants, and

---

103. Martindale, "'His Special Friend?'" 49; Bougard, *Justice dans le royaume d'Italie*, 222–29; and Wickham, "Justice in the Kingdom of Italy," 181, 197.

104. Guillot, "Le duel judiciaire," 750–51.

105. Díaz de Garayo, *Castilla en el Tránsito de la Antigüedad al Feudalismo*, 184–85.

106. Brown, *Unjust Seizure*, 207. See also Martindale, "'His Special Friend?'" 47–48; Kennedy, "Law and Litigation," 166–70; and Devailly, *Le Berry*, 201.

107. White, "Proposing the Ordeal and Avoiding It," 102.

boni homines throughout Europe did not blindly accept proofs. They subjected them to intense scrutiny and often developed sophisticated criteria to determine their value. Courts in many places confronted the same challenges as those confronted by judges in Barcelona, Béziers, and Elne. Documents were supposed to preserve memory and to ensure the stability of agreements. Sometimes instead of doing so, they provoked controversy or afforded opportunities for deception. Judges rejected some documents as inauthentic.[108] Underhanded disputants in England and León stole documents,[109] and litigants in Italy and France conspired to destroy them.[110] Litigants throughout post-Carolingian Europe accused their opponents of presenting inaccurate or forged records.[111] Judges cultivated diplomatic and paleographic skills by which they might detect forgeries and exclude illegitimate documents.

Missing or destroyed records were a persistent problem that went hand-in-hand with widespread reliance on written proofs. Disputants in Italy lost important documents which they asked courts to replace. During a 962 case—in the course of which Lombard law was cited—disputants claimed that they had a legitimate record, but not with them.[112] A case in León involved royal privileges which had been replaced after the originals were destroyed in a fire.[113] Judges and litigants in other regions may have been less fortunate than the monks of Saint-Miquel de Cuixà or the inhabitants of Barcelona, who could rely on the procedure for *reparatio scripturae*, but they nevertheless had to grapple with the difficulties arising from written proofs that had been lost or destroyed. Disputants and courts often had to improvise means of replacing lost proofs, but the *Visigothic Code* was not the only body of legislation to include provisions for lost documents. A sixth-century

108. *Oviedo* 74, 83.

109. Wormald, "Disputes in Anglo-Saxon England," 158–61; and *Tumbos del monasterio de Sobrado de los Monjes* (Madrid, 1976), vol. 1, doc. 130.

110. Wickham, "Land Disputes and Their Social Framework," 116; Davies and Fouracre, *Settlement of Disputes*, 213 n. 32; and Gregoria Cavero Dominguez and Encarnación Martin López, eds., *Colección Documental de la Catedral de Astorga*, vol. 1 (León, 1999) no. 361.

111. Volpini, "Placiti del 'Regnum Italiae,'" no. 10; François Bougard, "'*Falsum Falsorum Judicum Consilium*': L'Écrit et la justice en Italie centro-septentrionale au XI siècle," *BEC* 155 (1997): 299–314; and Nelson, "Dispute Settlement in Carolingian West Francia," 56.

112. F. Calasso, "Accertamento negoziale e processuale di diritti nell'alto medio evo," *Annali di Storia del diritto* 9 (1965): 199.

113. Patricia Skinner mentions the 994 record of a lost charter, *Family Power in Southern Italy*, 193. See also "Colección Diplomática de Alfonso V," doc. 6. 1007, app. 23. For records destroyed by fire in Italy, see *I diplomi di Berengario I*, ed. Luigi Schiaparelli (Rome, 1903), no. 135.

Merovingian formulary provided guidance for dealing with lost documents; so too did some other law codes.[114]

Just as the interpretation of written proofs involved certain challenges, so too did the interpretation of witness testimony. Courts, judges, and litigants confronted numerous problems in evaluating testimony. Who could legitimately testify in court? What happened if a disputant challenged the testimony of his opponent's witnesses? What if written proofs and witness testimony conflicted? In some areas, the testimony of serfs was challenged or disqualified. In the 1050s, the monks of Saint-Germain-des-Prés sought a royal privilege that would legitimate their serfs as witnesses. They presented three forged charters suggesting that the same privilege had been extended by earlier monarchs.[115] Courts from León to Lombardy tried to assess the reliability of witness testimony.[116] In some cases, bodies of legislation established guidelines for who could offer testimony. A capitulary of 816, for example, stipulated that a witness in a property dispute must reside in the county in which the disputed property was located.[117] Even when guidelines about residency, age, or status were clear, litigants tried to convince courts that their opponents' witnesses were misinformed, lying, or ineligible to testify.

The main forms of proofs throughout Europe were thus written records and witness testimony. The ways in which courts and disputants used these proofs and argued with them in court varied. Some regions showed a more programmatic attachment to written proofs. More important than the type of proofs used is the fact that courts, whenever possible, relied on multiple forms of proof. Judges and *boni homines* saw that proofs could be mutually illuminating—that the testimony of two or three witnesses could, for example, shed light on the validity of a written record. In twelfth- and thirteenth-century Portugal, oaths were used to confirm witness testimony.[118] In Anglo-Saxon

114. Wood, "Disputes in Fifth- and Sixth-Century Gaul," 13; McKitterick, *The Carolingians and the Written Word*, 67. See also *El Fuero de Jaca: Edición Critica*, ed. Mauricio Molho (Saragossa, 1964) 598.

115. Pierre Pétot "Serfs d'Église habilités à témoigner en justice," *CCM* 3 (1960): 191–94.

116. "Colección Diplomática de Alfonso V," doc. X. In one Italian case, the testimony of a group of witnesses was not accepted because they were not property-holders. See Schioppa, "Aspetti della giustizia," 21–22. For a witness who admitted to giving false testimony, see *Becerro Gótico de Cardeña* 98. For a 1025 case near Braga, which included the balancing of written proofs and the testimony of witnesses with citations of Visigothic law, see *LFSB* 22.

117. Nelson, "Dispute Settlement in Carolingian West Francia," 47.

118. Durand, *Campagnes portugaises*, 160.

England, written proofs and oaths were seen as mutually corroborating.[119] In northern France, the written word was supported by the spoken.[120] In Castile and León, judges and disputants relied on both documents and testimony about earlier transactions or about long-term occupation.[121] In Italy, witness testimony confirmed the validity of written proofs.[122] The boundary clauses in a record of sale might corroborate the testimony of a disputant's neighbor. Relying on different interdependent varieties of proof in this fashion was no simple task. Reconciling and interpreting different varieties of proof was among the most difficult challenges confronted by courts.

Given the complexity of these questions about proof, it is not surprising that medieval courts often proved creative in formulating, issuing, and enforcing decisions. Any discussion of the proofs used in medieval courts leads almost inevitably to a discussion of how disputes ended. It is difficult to understand the logic of proofs in medieval courts or to grasp the strategies by which disputants tried to win their cases, but tracing the resolutions of disputes poses even greater interpretive difficulties. Historians are on shakier ground when describing how disputes ended than when trying to describe the ways in which judges thought, courts functioned, and disputants argued. From Galicia to Bavaria, from Gaeta to the Danelaw, the evidence for how disputes ended is distorted. Surviving records suggest that churches and monasteries were all but invincible in courts throughout Europe. However, one of the reasons that ecclesiastical institutions seem invariably to have won is that these same institutions created and kept the records of these disputes,[123] and in fact monopolized certain skills for the creation and maintenance of written records. This fact has important consequences for modern historians, and it had important consequences for medieval litigants. The clerical monopoly on these skills distorts the pool of available evidence; certain

---

119. "The one broad conclusion which might with some hesitation be offered about documentary title in litigation is that it does not appear even in late Anglo-Saxon England that documents in themselves could alone be probative in the ordinary course. As a class of evidence they were firmly locked into the wider complex of oral procedures and, it would seem, treated essentially as another witness to the worth of the claims in whose support they were produced." Kennedy, "Law and Litigation," 172–73.

120. Laurent Morelle, "Les chartes dans la gestion des conflits (France du nord, XI–début XII siècle)," *BEC* 155 (1997): 290.

121. Díaz de Garayo, *Castilla en el Tránsito de la Antigüedad al Feudalismo*, 184–85; See, for example, *Oviedo* 53, 58, 74.

122. See, for example, Manaresi, *I placiti del "Regnum Italiae,"* 145.

123. Wickham, "Land Disputes and Their Social Framework," 105; and Wormald, "Disputes in Anglo-Saxon England," 151.

records were preserved while others were not. At the same time, the clerical monopoly on these skills gave churchmen a real edge in property disputes. They were usually better able to shape normative traditions to fit their own interests. Enthusiasm for written proofs offered advantages to ecclesiastical and monastic disputants who more deftly deployed written proofs.

This is not to suggest that no lay property-holders understood, used, and argued with written proofs. On the contrary, some lay litigants kept careful records and knew how to use them in court. The widow Adalaiz, wrangling with Abbot Guitard, is a fine example, and there were others like her. But wherever written proofs were important, churches, monasteries, and cathedral chapters enjoyed advantages when fighting over property. Lay people in many regions challenged donations to churches and monasteries as illegal alienations of family patrimonies. They often lost in court because they lacked the written proofs that clerical disputants were often better able to present.[124]

Caution is thus warranted in discussing how disputes ended, but it is possible to make general observations about outcomes. Courts in the Province of Narbonne tended to issue unequivocal decisions in favor of one litigant. This tendency distinguishes these courts and judges from those in other parts of Europe, which were more inclined to settle disputes by issuing compromise decisions. These general tendencies do not, however, mean that particular types of judicial institutions invariably generated the same type of decision. In other words, no rigid equation links the formal elements of the administration of justice (judges, courts, and law) to particular varieties of settlement.[125]

Judges, court presidents, *boni homines*, and disputants found compromise settlements and concessions to losing parties attractive for many reasons. In some cases, compromises were inspired by principle. Legal professionals and disputants invoked norms suggesting that resolutions which acknowledged both parties' rights were especially desirable. The most concise formulation of this ideal was *pactum legem vincit et amor judicium*. Concord and peace were to be preferred to law and justice. Other compromises were motivated less by ideals than by a court's inability to sort out conflicting claims. The proofs offered were ambiguous, or both parties were equally convincing. Judges and members of the community were unable to disentangle the complicated history of the disputed property; they saw compromise as the only way to pro-

124. Le Jan, "Justice Royale," 83–84; and Weinberger, "Les conflits entre clercs et laïcs," 270.

125. For a 999 example from Italy, see Skinner, *Family Power in Southern Italy*, 91. See also White, "Inheritances and Legal Arguments," 68.

ceed. Finally, compromise decisions were sometimes motivated by the practical recognition that a unilateral decision might be especially hard to enforce.

Courts throughout Europe often marked the resolution of disputes in similar ways. Disputants were required to swear that they would not challenge the agreed-upon settlement. Boundaries were newly recorded and affirmed. Members of the court often circumambulated disputed properties to show their general agreement about their boundaries.[126] Losers from Lombardy to Normandy received payments, gifts, or grants after having been defeated in court. Sometimes, these concessions were explained by the fact that the victorious parties were inspired by love; judges from Bavaria to León found themselves moved by mercy.[127]

These steps doubtless contributed to the lasting stability of settlements but, in general, the ability of courts to enforce judicial decisions lagged far behind their ability to generate thoughtful decisions. Courts in the Province of Narbonne and elsewhere often formulated decisions with admirable clarity and resolve. But there is little evidence that any of these courts possessed any systematic means of enforcing their decisions, however carefully crafted these may have been. Even courts replete with counts, bishops, professional judges, and written law often lacked means of enforcing their decisions. In Catalonia, and elsewhere in Spain, *saiones* had some responsibility for executing court decisions, but their participation was irregular and evidence for their effectiveness is slim.

The courts of Christian Spain were not unique in this regard. Courts often lacked the wherewithal to make their decisions stick. In many cases, the only ways in which courts could encourage disputants to accept their decisions involved informal pressures. They might impress upon a disputant the legal rectitude of the decision, pointing to the *Visigothic Code*, the *Lombard Laws*, or synodal decrees. In such cases, courts tried to persuade disappointed disputants that they had lost for a reason. Courts also relied on the pressure that could be brought to bear by the *boni homines* attending the court and by other members of the community.

The effectiveness of these informal pressures is difficult to gauge. To be sure, such pressures worked in many cases far better than modern historians can easily understand. At the same time, there is ample evidence that such

126. For a 940 example, see Emilio Sáez and Carlos Sáez, eds. *Colección diplomática del monasterio de Celanova (842–1230)* (Alcalá, 1996) vol. 1, no. 62. On perambulation in León, see Collins, "Visigothic Law and Regional Custom," 88.

127. *Tumbos del monasterio de Sobrado de los Monjes* (Madrid, 1976), vol. 1, doc. 130; *Oviedo* 58, 87; *LFSB* 21; Brown, "The Use of Norms in Disputes," 30; Wickham, "Land Disputes and Their Social Framework," 120; and Tabuteau, *Transfers of Property*, 29–30.

solutions to the problem of enforcement often were only temporary. Many litigants flatly refused to participate in judicial hearings, even when these were sanctioned by impressive authorities.[128] Some disputants in the Province of Narbonne simply refused to come to court, and others elsewhere did the same. For example, litigants called to the bishop of Lucca's court in 897 refused to attend.[129] Disputants reluctant to appear in court also troubled eleventh-century Italian courts.[130] Some chose to stay away because they actively wanted to impede the courts' deliberations, others because they were occupied with other concerns. Fulbert of Chartres described some of these difficulties to Archbishop Gauzlin of Bourges. Fulbert had summoned some people to a hearing, but "they replied that it was harvest time and they were too busy to be involved in lawsuits at present."[131] Other disputants participated in judicial hearings only until they began to suspect that they would not win the victories they had hoped for. These widespread incidents in which litigants refused to cooperate are a telling index of the fragility of court-issued decisions. Even in those corners of Europe where courts were sophisticated and coherent, they often lacked the means to enforce decisions.[132]

Courts possessed few potent tools to deal with uncooperative litigants. Such troublesome disputants reveal weaknesses in the abilities of courts to enforce their decisions, but they also may be seen in a more positive light. Some uncooperative disputants were governed by base self-interest; they would not participate in the administration of justice because they knew that justice would serve them poorly. But other uncooperative litigants show signs of more principled resistance. They refused to attend courts or to adhere to court decisions, because they saw courts as unjust, biased, or corrupt. Some of the disputants in the Province of Narbonne, for example, rejected the law of the *Visigothic Code*, because they saw it as unfair. Similar incidents of resistance occurred elsewhere.[133] Given the extremely selective ways in which the *Code* was applied, the feelings of frustrated property-holders and their refusal to participate were not unreasonable. It is hard to interpret resistance to the authority of the courts, but it is safe to say that some disputants were

128. Fouracre, "Disputes in Later Merovingian Francia," 38, 43.

129. Wickham, "Land Disputes and Their Social Framework," 119.

130. Volpini, "Placiti del 'Regnum Italiae,'" nos. 29, 32, 33.

131. Behrends, *Letters and Poems of Fulbert*, no. 74. See also, no. 3, in which Fulbert notes the difficulties of setting a day for a *placitum*.

132. For examples of people not cooperating with court orders or failing to appear, see Volpini, "Placiti del 'Regnum Italiae,'" no. 33; and Wickham, "Land Disputes and Their Social Framework," 123.

133. See, for example, *Oviedo* 73.

motivated not by their own recalcitrance but instead by their clearheaded decision not to comply with legal procedures which, to them, appeared unjust.

The people of tenth- and eleventh-century Europe thought long and hard about the interlocking problems of law, justice, property, and community. The administration of justice in this period was more sophisticated than is often acknowledged. In many places, impressive institutions that combined community involvement and legal professionals administered justice. Courts displayed an admirable ability to maintain traditions, while at the same time adapting legal traditions and combining different modes of settlement. At times, these strengths became weaknesses. The flexibility of many courts allowed disputants to propose idiosyncratic proofs and unworkable solutions. Many of the resolutions forged by learned judges and thoughtful *boni homines* were extremely fragile. This fragility sprang in part from the fact that courts often lacked the power to enforce decisions. But it also resulted from the fact that many disputes sprang from deep structural conflicts that no single judicial decision could resolve. Many property disputes arose not from disagreements about who sold what to whom, but from the clash of fundamentally different notions of how property rights were configured. The ways in which people acquired, owned, and fought over property were informed by venerable legal traditions, but these traditions did not always offer unified and coherent answers to the questions that were most pressing to judges and property-holders.

Property disputes afford a valuable window onto both the political structures and the intellectual world of the Middle Ages. But they do more than allow us to trace transformations in institutions, such as comital courts, or to chart the vitality of legal traditions, such as the *Visigothic Code*. The greatest interest of these disputes may be in the fact that they allow us to see the people of the tenth- and eleventh-centuries struggling to reconcile these traditions with the mundane demands of daily life. In property disputes, we see law being transformed through the concrete engagement of lords, judges, disputants, and members of the community. We can see monks, such as those at Sant Miquel de Cuixà, formulating impressive accommodations of Visigothic law and scriptural curses; sophisticated judges, such as Bonhom of Barcelona, writing an essay that impresses upon his fellow-judges their responsibilities toward the poor and humble; tenacious widows, like Adalaiz, trying to recover her vineyards from powerful institutions; and, finally, disaffected brothers-in-law, like Renard, walking away from a system that he clearly felt did not always function well.

WORKS CITED

UNPUBLISHED PRIMARY SOURCES

ARXIU CAPITULAR DE VIC (VIC)
Calaix 6
Calaix 9

ARXIU CAPITULAR D'URGELL
Pergamins

ARXIU DE LA CATEDRAL DE BARCELONA (BARCELONA)
Libri Antiquitatum I–IV
Series Diversorum B
Series Diversorum C

ARXIU DE LA CORONA D'ARAGÓ (BARCELONA)
Cancelleria reial
   Pergamins Borrell II
   Pergamins Ramon Borrell
   Pergamins Berenguer Ramon I
   Pergamins Ramon Berenguer I

Ordes religiosos (Monacals)
   Pergamins Santa Cecilía de Montserrat

Pergamins Sant Benet de Bages
Pergamins Sant Llorenç del Munt
Pergamins Sant Pere de Besalú

ARCHIVES DÉPARTMENTALES DES PYRÉNÉES-ORIENTALES (PERPIGNAN)
Séries H
Séries J (Fonds Fossa)

ARCHIVES DÉPARTMENTALES DE L'AUDE (CARCASSONNE)
Séries G
Séries H

BIBLIOTHÈQUE NATIONALE (PARIS)
Collection Baluze
Collection Doat
Collection Moreau
MS Latin 6
MS Latin 2528
MS Latin 4404
MS Latin 4418
MS Latin 4667
MS Latin 4668
MS Latin 4670
MS Latin 5211 D

REIAL MONASTERIO DEL ESCORIAL (MADRID)
MS d. I. 1
MS z. II. 2

PUBLISHED PRIMARY SOURCES

Abadal i de Vinyals, Ramon. *Catalunya Carolingia II: El Diplomes Carolingia à Cata-lunya*, part 3, vol. 2, *Els comtats de Pallars i Ribagorça*. Barcelona, 1955.
———. "Com neix i com creix un gran monestir pirinenc abans de l'any mil: Eixalada-Cuixà." In *Analecta Montserratensia* 8 (1954–55): 139–338.
Alart, Bernard, ed. *Cartulaire roussillonnais*. Perpignan. 1880.
Altés i Aguilo, F. X. "El diplomatari del monestir de Santa Cecília de Montserrat I, anys 900–999," *Studia monastica* 36 (1994): 225–302.

——. "El diplomatari del monestir de Santa Cecília de Montserrat II, anys 1000–1077," *Studia monastica* 37 (1995): 301–94.

Alturo i Perucho, Jesús. *Diplomatari de Polinyà del Vallès. Aproximació a la història d'un poble del segle X al XII.* Bellaterra, 1985.

——. ed. *L'arxiu antic de Santa Anna de Barcelona del 942 al 1200 (Aproximació històrico-lingüística)*, 3 vols. Barcelona, 1985.

Andrew of Fleury. *Vie de Gauzlin, Abbé de Fleury / Vita Gauzlini Abbatis Floriacensis monasterii.* Ed. Robert-Henri Bautier and Gillette Labory. Paris, 1969.

Baraut, Cebrià. *Les actes de consagracions d'esglésies de l'antic bisbat d'Urgell, segles IX–XII.* La Seu d'Urgell, 1986.

——. *Cartulari de la vall d'Andorra, segles X–XIII*, 2 vols. Andorra, 1990.

——. ed. "Els documents del segles IX–XI conservats a l'Arxiu Capitular de la Seu d'Urgell," *Urgellia* 2 (1979): 7–145; 3 (1980): 7–166; 4 (1981): 7–186; 5 (1982): 7–158; 6 (1983): 7–244; 7 (1984–85): 7–220; 8 (1986–87): 7–150.

Barrau Dihigo, Louis, and Jaume Massó i Torrents eds. *Gesta comitum Barchinonensium*, Chroniques Catalanes II. Barcelona, 1925.

Bastardas, Joan. "Doc Judicis Antics, s. IX i XI." In *Documents Jurídics de la Història de Catalunya*, ed. Iago de Balanzó i Sala, 23–30. Barcelona, 1992.

——. ed. *Usatges de Barcelona: El codi a mitjan segle XII.* Barcelona, 1984. [English trans. Donald J. Kagay. *Usatges of Barcelona: The Fundamental Law of Catalonia.* Philadelphia, 1994.]

Bernard of Angers. *Liber Miraculorum sancte Fidis.* Ed. Auguste Bouillet. Paris, 1897.

Bofarull y Mascaró, Prospero de et al., eds. *Colección de documentos inéditos del Archivo de la Corona de Aragón*, 42 vols. Barcelona, 1847–1973.

Brutails, Jean-Auguste. "Extraits de quelques documents de Saint-Martin du Canigou." *Bulletin Historique* (1879): 251–55.

Cassan, L., and E. Meynial eds. *Cartulaire des abbayes d'Aniane et Gellone.* Montpellier, 1898–1900.

Cavero Dominguez, Gregoria, and Encarnación Martín López, eds. *Colección documental de la Catedral de Astorga.* León, 1999.

Constans i Serrats, Lluís G. ed. *Diplomatari de Banyoles*, vol. 1. Banyoles, 1985.

de Clercq, Carol, ed. *Concilia Galliae A. 511 – A. 695.* Corpus Christianorum, Series Latina 148A. Tournhout, 1963.

Desjardins, Gustave, ed. *Cartulaire de l'abbaye de Conques en Rouergue.* Paris, 1879.

España Sagrada: Teatro geográfico-histórico de la Iglesia de España. Ed. Henrique Florez et al., 52 vols. Madrid, 1746–1918.

Fàbrega i Grau, Angel, ed. *Diplomatari de la Catedral de Barcelona. Documenys dels anys 844–1260*, vol. 1. Barcelona, 1995.

Fernández del Pozo, José María, ed. "Colección Diplomática de Alfonso V." In *León y su historia: Miscelanea historica* V, 163–264. León, 1984.

Fischer Drew, Katherine, trans., *The Lombard Laws.* Philadelphia, 1973.

Font Ruis, Josep Maria, ed. *Cartas de población y franquicia de Cataluña*, vol. 1. Barcelona, 1969.

Formulae Merowingici et Karolini Aevi. Ed. Karl Zeumer. Monumenta Germaniae Historica, Legum sectio V. Hanover, 1886.

Fulbert of Chartres. *The Letters and Poems of Fulbert of Chartres.* Ed. Frederick Behrends. Oxford, 1976.

Garcia Larragueta, Santos, ed. *Colección de Documentos de la Catedral de Oviedo*. Oviedo, 1962.

Garrido Garrido, José Manuel, ed. *Documentación de la Catedral de Burgos (804–1143)*. Burgos, 1983.

Gerbert of Aurillac. *Lettres de Gerbert, 983–997*. Ed. Julien Havet. Paris, 1889.

——. *The Letters of Gerbert with His Papal Privileges as Sylvester II Translated with an Introduction*. Trans. H. P. Lattin. New York, 1961.

Germer-Durand, E., ed. *Cartulaire du chapitre de l'église Notre-Dame de Nîmes, 876–1156*. Nîmes, 1872–1874.

Gonsalvo i Bou, Gener, ed. *Les constitucions de Pau i Treva de Catalunya, segles XI–XIII*. Barcelona, 1994.

Gros, M. "L'arxiu del monestir de Sant Joan de las Abadesses: Notícies històriques i regeste del documents dels anys 995–1115." In *II Col.loqui d'història del monaquisme català*. Poblet, 1974.

Histoire Générale de Languedoc. Ed. Claude Devic and J. J. Vaissette, 2nd. ed. 16 vols. Toulouse, 1872–1904.

Junyent, Eduard, ed. *Diplomatari de la Catedral de Vic, segles IX–X*, 4 fascicles. Vic, 1980.

——. *Diplomatari i escrits literaris de l'abat i bisbe Oliba*. Barcelona, 1992.

Kehr, Paul. *Die ältesten Papsturkunden Spaniens*. Berlin, 1926.

Lacarra, José María, ed. "Documentos para el estudio de la reconquista y repoblación del Valle del Ebro." *Estudios de Edad Media de la Corona de Aragon* 2 (1946): 269–574; 3 (1947–48): 499–727; 5 (1952): 511–668. [Reprinted in *Textos medievales* 62–63 (1982–83).]

Leges Visigothorum. Ed. Karl Zeumer. Monumenta Germaniae Historica, Leges I. Hanover, 1902. [English trans. Samuel P. Scott. *The Visigothic Code*. Boston, 1910.]

Liber Feudorum Maior: Cartulario real que conserva en el Archivo de la Corona de Aragón. Ed. Francisco Miquel Rosell, 2 vols. Barcelona, 1945–47.

Liber Fidei Sanctae Bracarensis Ecclesiae. Ed. Pe. Aveline de Jesus da Costa, 2 vols. Braga, 1965–78.

Llorens, Antoni. "El documents dels segles x i xi de l'Arxiu Capitular de Solsona." *Urgellia* 11 (1992–93): 301–486.

Manaresi, C., ed. *I placiti del 'Regnum Italiae.'* Fonte per la storia d'Italia 92. Rome, 1955.

Mansi, Giovanni, ed. *Sacrorum Conciliorum Nova et Amplissima Collectio*, 31 vols. Venice and Florence, 1759–98.

Marquès i Planagumà, Josep María. *Pergamins de la Mitra (891–1687): Arxiu Diocesà de Girona*. Girona, 1984.

——. ed. *El Cartoral de Santa Maria de Roses, segles x–xiii*. Barcelona, 1986.

——. ed. *El Cartoral dit de Carlemany, del bisbe de Girona*, 2 vols. Barcelona, 1993.

Martin, E., ed. *Cartulaire de la ville de Lodève*. Montpellier, 1901.

Mas, Josep. "Rúbriques del 'Libri Antiquitatum' de la Sèu de Barcelona." *Notes històriques del Bisbat de Barcelona*, vol. 9–10. Barcelona, 1914–15.

Mínguez Fernández, José Maria, ed. *Colección Diplomática del monasterio de Sahagún (857–1230)*, vol. I, siglos IX y X. León, 1976.

Molho, Mauricio, ed. *El Fuero de Jaca: Edición Critica*. Saragossa, 1964.

Montsalvatje y Fossas, Francisco. *Noticias históricas*, 26 vols. Olot, 1889–1910.

Ourliac, Paul, and Anne-Marie Magnou, eds. *Cartulaire de l'abbaye de Lézat*. 2 vols. Paris, 1984–87.

Perez de Urbel, J. *Sampiro, su Crónica y la Monarquia Leonesa en el siglo X.* Madrid, 1952.

Pérez i Gómez, Xavier, ed. *Diplomatari de la cartoixa de Montalegre (segles X–XII).* Barcelona, 1998.

Petrus de Marca and Etienne Baluze. *Marca Hispanica sive limes Hispanicus.* Paris, 1688; Reprint, Barcelona, 1972.

Pons i Guri, Josep M., ed. "Diplomatari del Monestir de Sant Pol de Mar (segles X–XII)." In *Recull d'estudis d'història juridica Catalana*, 3:363–412. Barcelona, 1989.

Puig i Ferreté, Ignasi M., ed. *El Cartoral de Santa Maria de Lavaix: El Monestir durant els segles XI–XIII.* La Seu d'Urgell, 1984.

———. *El monestir de Santa Maria de Gerri (segles xi–xiv) colleció diplomàtica.* Barcelona, 1991.

Puig i Puig, Sebastian. *Episcopologio de la Sede Barcinonense: Apuntes para la historia de la iglesia de Barcelona y de sus prelados.* Barcelona, 1929.

Puig i Ulstrell, Pere, ed. *Pergamins del Priorat de Santa Maria de Terrassa, anys 977–1633.* Terrassa, 1979.

Riu, Manuel, ed. "Diplomatari del Monestir de Sant Llorenç de Morunys, 971–1613." *Urgellia* 4 (1981): 187–259.

Rius Serra, José, ed. *El Cartulario de "Sant Cugat" del Vallés*, 3 vols. Barcelona, 1946.

Roquette, J-B. *Cartulaire de Béziers (Livre Noir).* Paris and Montpellier, 1918–1922.

———. *Le livre noir de Maguelone.* Montpellier, 1922.

Sáez, Emilio, and Carlos Sáez, eds. *Colección Diplomática del monasterio de Celanova (842–1239)*, vol. 1. Alcalá, 1996.

Sangés, Domènec. "Recull de documents del segle XI referents a Guissona i la seva Plana." *Urgellia* 3 (1980): 195–305.

Soler García, Josefina, ed. *Cartulario de Tavernoles.* Castellón de la Plana, 1964.

Terrin, Odile, ed. *Cartulaire du chapitre d'Agde.* Nîmes, 1969.

Theodulf of Orleans. *Paraensis ad Iudices*, in MGH Poetae Latini I, *Versus Teudulfi episcopi contra iudices*, no. 28, 493–517.

Tilander, Gunnar, ed. *Vidal Mayor: Traducción Aragonesa de la Obra* in excelsis dei thesauris *de Vidal de Canellas.* Leges Hispanicae Medii Aevi. Lund, 1956.

Udina Martorell, Federico, ed. *El Llibre Blanch de Santas Creus.* Barcelona, 1947.

———. ed. *El archivo Condal de Barcelona en los siglos ix–x: Estudio crítico de sus fondos.* Barcelona, 1951.

Valls i Taberner, Ferran, *Privilegis i ordinacions de les valls pyrenenques*, 3 vols. Barcelona, 1915–20; reprint of vol. 3, Saragossa, 1990.

Villanueva, Jaime, and Joaquin Lorenzo Villanueva. *Viage literario a las Iglesias de España*, 22 vols. Madrid-Valencia, 1803–1902.

Volpini, Rafaello, ed. "Placiti del 'Regnum Italiae' (secc. IX–XI). Primi contributi per un nuovo censimento." In *Contributi dell'Instituto di storia medievalae*, vol. 3, ed. P. Zerbi, 245–520. Milan, 1975.

Zimmerman, Harald, ed. *Papsturkunden, 896–1046*, vol. 2. Vienna, 1985.

Abadal i de Vinyals, Ramon d'. "A propos du legs visigothique en Espagne." *Settimane di studio del centro italiano di studi dell'alto medioevo* 5 (1958): 541–86.

——. "La fundació del monestir de Ripoll." *Analecta Montserratensia* 9 (1962): 187–97.

——. "A propos de la 'domination' de Barcelone sur le Midi français." *Annales du Midi (Amidi)* 76 (1964): 315–45.

——. *Dels Visigots als Catalans*, 3d ed., 2 vols. Barcelona, 1986.

Abel, Richard L. "A Comparative Theory of Dispute Institutions in Society." *Law and Society Review* 8 (1973): 217–347.

Albareda, Anselm M. *L'Abat Oliba: Fundador de Montserrat (971?–1046), Asseig biogràfic.* Abadia de Montserrat, 1931. Reprint, Barcelona, 1972.

Alexandrenko, Nikolai A. "The Poetry of Theodulf of Orleans: A Translation and Critical Study." Ph.D. Diss. Tulane University, 1970.

Alvarado Planas, Javier. "Ordalías y Derecho en la España Visigoda." In *De la Antigüedad al Medievo, siglos IV–VIII: III Congreso de Estudios Medievales*, 437–540. Avila, 1993.

Álvarez Borge, Ignacio. *Poder y relaciones sociales en Castilla en la Edad Media: Los territorios entre el Arlanzón y el Duero en los siglos X al XIV.* Salamanca, 1996.

Antoine, Jean-Marc, Bertrand Desailly, and Jean-Paul Métaille. "Les Grand *Aygats* du XVIIIe siècle dans les Pyrénées." In *Les Catastrophes naturelles dans l'Europe médiévale et moderne*, ed. Bartolomé Bennassar, 243–60. Toulouse, 1996.

Araguas, Philippe. "Les châteaux des marches de Catalogne et Ribagorce 950–1100." *Bulletin monumental* 137 (1979): 205–24.

Asad, Talal. "Notes on Body Pain and Truth in Medieval Christian Ritual." *Economy and Society* 12 (1983): 283–327.

Aubenas, Roger. "Quelques réflexions sur le problème de la pénétration du droit romain dans le Midi de la France au Moyen Age." *AMidi* 68–69 (1964): 371–78.

Aurell i Cardona, Martí. *Les noces du comtes: Mariage et pouvoir en Catalogne, 785–1213.* Paris, 1995.

Bachrach, Bernard. *Fulk Nerra, the Neo-Roman Consul, 987–1040: A Political Biography of the Angevin Count.* Berkeley, 1987.

Baist, G. "Ritual de pruebas judiciales tomado de un códice del Escorial." *Boletín Histórico* (1880): 136–40, 153–55, 172–73.

Balari y Jovany, D. José. *Orígenes Históricos de Cataluña.* Barcelona, 1899.

Baldwin, John W. "The Intellectual Preparation for the Canon of 1215 against Ordeals." *Speculum* 36 (1961): 613–36.

Balzaretti, Ross. "The Monastery of Sant' Ambrogio and Dispute Settlement in Early Medieval Milan." *Early Medieval Europe* 3 (1994): 1–18.

Baraut, Cebrià. "L'evolució política de la senyoria d'Andorra des dels orígens fins al pariatges (segles IX–XIII)." *Urgellia* 11 (1992–93), 225–99.

Barbero, Abilio, and Marcelo Vigil, eds. *La formación del feudalismo en la península ibérica.* Barcelona, 1978.

Barral i Altet, Xavier. *Le paysage monumental de la France autour de l'an mil.* Paris, 1987.

Barral i Altet, Dominique Iogna-Prat, Anscari Manuel Mundó, Josep Maria Salrach,

Michel Zimmerman, eds. *Catalunya i França meridional, a l'entorn de l'any mil — La Catalogne et la France méridionale autour de l'an mil.* Barcelona, 1991.

Barthélemy, Dominique. "Présence de l'aveu dans le déroulement des ordalies, IXe–XIIIe siècles." In *L'Aveu: antiquité et moyen-âge*, 191–214. Rome, 1986.

——. "Diversité des ordalies médiévales." *Revue Historique* 280 (1988): 3–25.

——. "La mutation féodale a-t-elle eu lieu?" *Annales: Economies, sociétés, civilisations (AESC)* 47 (1992): 767–77.

——. *La société dans le comté de Vendôme: de l'an mil au XIVe siècle.* Paris, 1993.

——. "Encore le débat sur l'an mil." *Revue historique de droit français et étranger* 73 (1995): 349–60.

——. *L'an mil et la paix de Dieu: La France chrétienne et féodale, 980–1060.* Paris, 1999.

Barthélemy, Dominique, and Stephen D. White. "Debate: The 'Feudal Revolution.'" *Past and Present* 152 (1996): 196–223.

Bartlett, Robert. *Trial by Fire and Water: The Medieval Judicial Ordeal.* Oxford, 1986.

——. *The Making of Europe: Conquest, Colonization, and Cultural Change 950–1350.* Princeton, 1993.

Bartlett, Robert, and Angus Mackay, eds. *Medieval Frontier Societies.* Oxford, 1989.

Bassols de Climent, Mariano, and J. Bastardas Parera, eds. *Glossarium mediae latinitas Cataloniae.* Barcelona, 1960–1976.

Bastier, Jean. "Le testament en Catalogne du IXe au XIIe siècle: Une survivance wisigothique." *RHDFE* 51 (1973): 373–417.

Battle i Gallard, Carme. *Els origens medievals de la Seu d'Urgell.* Barcelona, 1979.

Bäuml, Franz H. "Varieties and Consequences of Medieval Literacy and Illiteracy." *Speculum* 55 (1980): 237–65.

Baudreu, D. "*Villa, vicaria, castrum.* Aux origines d'un village du Bas-Razès: Malviès (Aude) au XI siècle." *AMidi* 99 (1980): 495–511.

Bautier, Robert-Henri. "Notes historiques sur la Marche d'Espagne: Le Conflent et ses comtes au IXe siècle," *Mélanges Félix Grat*, I: 210–222. Paris, 1946.

——. "L'historiographie en France en Xe et XIe siècles (France du Nord et de l'Est)." *Settimane di studio del centro italiano di studi dell'alto medioevo* 17 (1970): 793–855.

Bedell, John. "Memory and Proof of Age in England, 1272–1327." *Past and Present* 162 (1999): 3–27.

Beer, Rudolf. *Die Handschriften des Kloster Santa Maria de Ripoll.* Vienna, 1907.

Benet i Clara, Albert. "Immigració ultrapirenenca a Catalunya en l'Edat Mitjana (ss. IX–XII)." In *Actas del Congreso Internacional "Historia de los Pireneos" Cervera 1988*, vol. 2, 121–42. Madrid, 1991.

Benito i Monclús, Pere. "El plet dels homes francs de Sarrià (1258) Crisi i perivència de l'alou pagès a la Catalunya medieval." In *Les sociétés méridionales à l'âge féodal (Espagne, Italie et sud de la France X–XIIIe s): Hommage à Pierre Bonnassie*, ed. Hélène Débax, 71–79. Toulouse, 1999.

Bensch, Stephen P. *Barcelona and Its Rulers, 1096–1291.* Cambridge, 1995.

Bishko, Charles Julian. *Studies in Medieval Spanish Frontier History.* London, 1980.

Bisson, Thomas N. *The Medieval Crown of Aragon: A Short History.* Oxford, 1986.

——. "L' Essor de Catalogne: Identité, pouvoir et idéologie dans une société du XII siècle." *AESC* 39 (1984): 454–79. Reprinted as "The Rise of Catalonia: Identity, Power, and Ideology in a Twelfth-Century Society." In *Medieval France and her Pyrenean Neighbours: Studies in Early Institutional History*, 215–36. London, 1989.

——. "The 'Feudal Revolution.'" *Past and Present* 142 (1994): 6–42.

——. *Tormented Voices: Power, Crisis, and Humanity in Rural Catalonia, 1140–1200.* Cambridge, Mass., 1998.

——. ed. *Cultures of Power: Lordship, Status, and Process in Twelfth-Century Europe.* Philadelphia, 1995.

Bloch, Marc. *Feudal Society.* Trans. L. A. Manyon, 2 vols. London, 1961.

Blok, D. P. "Les formules de droit romain dans les actes du haut Moyen Age." In *Miscellania Mediaevali in Memoriam Jan Frederik Niermeyer*, 17–28. Groningen, 1967.

Bolòs i Masclans, Jordi. "L'evolució del domini del monestir de Sant Llorenç prop Bagà durant els segles IX–XII," *Acta historica et archaeologica mediaevalia* 1 (1980): 65–73.

Bongert, Yvonne. *Recherches sur les cours laïques du Xe au XIIIe siècle.* Paris, 1949.

Bonnassie, Pierre. "Une famille de la campagne barcelonaise et ses activités économiques aux alentours de l'an Mil," *AMidi* 76 (1964): 261–303.

——. *La Catalogne du milieu du Xe à la fin du XIe siècle: Croissance et mutations d'une société*, 2 vols. Toulouse, 1975–1976.

——. "Feudal Conventions in Eleventh-Century Catalonia." In *From Slavery to Serfdom in Southwestern Europe*, 170–94. Cambridge, 1991. Originally published as, "Les conventions féodales dans la Catalogne du XIe siècle." *AMidi* 89 (1968): 529–61.

——. "From the Rhône to Galicia: Origins and Modalities of the Feudal Order." In *From Slavery to Serfdom in Southwestern Europe*, 104–31. Cambridge, 1991. Originally published as "Du Rhône à la Galice: genèse et modalités du régime féodale." In *Structures féodales et féodalisme dans l'Occident méditerranéan, Xe–XIIIe siècles*, 17–56. Rome, 1980.

——. "The Formation of Catalan Feudalism and Its Early Expansion (to c. 1150)." In *From Slavery to Serfdom* 149–69. Originally published as "Sur la formation du féodalisme catalan et sa prémière expansion (jusqu'à 1150 environ)." In *La formació del feudalisme*, 7–21.

——. "The Survival and Extinction of the Slave System in the Early Medieval West, Fourth to Eleventh Centuries." In *From Slavery to Serfdom*, 1–59. Originally published as "Survie et extinction du régime esclavagiste dans l'Occident du haut moyen âge, IV–XI s." *CCM* 28 (1985): 307–43.

Bonnassie, Pierre, and Jean-Pascal Illy. "Le clergé paroissal aux IXe–Xe siècles dans le Pyrénées orientales et centrales." In *Le Clergé rural dans l'Europe médiévale et moderne*, ed. Pierre Bonnassie, 153–66. Toulouse, 1995.

Borafull y Mascaró, Prospero de. *Los condes de Barcelona vindicados y cronología de los reyes de España considerados soberanos independientes de su Marca.* Barcelona, 1836.

Bossy, John, ed. *Disputes and Settlements: Law and Human Relations in the West.* Chicago, 1983.

Bouchard, Constance. "The Origins of the French Nobility: A Reassessment." *American Historical Review* 86 (1981): 501–32.

Bougard, François. *La justice dans le royaume d'Italie de la fin du VIIIe siècle au début du XIe siècle.* Rome, 1995.

——. "La Justice dans le royaume d'Italie aux IXe–Xe siècles." In *La Giustizia nell'alto medioevo (secoli IX–XI)*, 133–76.

——. "'*Falsum Falsorum Judicum Consilium*' : L'Écrit et la justice en Italie centro-septentrionale au XI siècle." *Bibliothèque de L'École des Chartes (BEC)* 155 (1997): 299–314.

Bourdieu, Pierre. *Outline of a Theory of Practice.* Cambridge, 1977.

——. *The Logic of Practice.* Stanford, Calif., 1990.

Bourin-Derruau, Monique. *Villages médiévaux en Bas-Languedoc: Genèse d'un sociabilité, Xe–XIVe siècle,* 2 vols. Paris, 1987.

Bowman, Jeffrey A. "Councils, Memory, and Mills: The Early Development of the Peace of God in Catalonia." *Early Medieval Europe* 8 (1999): 99–130.

——. "Infamy and Proof in Medieval Spain." In *Fama: The Politics of Talk and Reputation in Medieval Europe,* ed. Thelma Fenster and Daniel Lord Smail, 95–117. Ithaca, N.Y., 2003.

Brand, Paul. "'Time Out of Mind': The Knowledge and Use of the Eleventh- and Twelfth-Century Past in Thirteenth-Century Litigation." *Anglo-Norman Studies* 16 (1994): 37–54.

Brooke, C. N. L. "Approaches to Medieval Forgery." In *Medieval Church and Society: Collected Essays,* 100–20. London, 1971.

Brown, Elizabeth A. R. "The Tyranny of a Construct: Feudalism and Historians of Medieval Europe." *American Historical Review* 79 (1974): 1063–88.

——. "*Falsitas pia sive reprehensibilis*: Medieval Forgers and Their Intentions." In *Fälschungen in Mittelalter,* Monumenta Germaniae Historica, Schriften 33, vol. 1, 101–20. Hannover, 1988.

Brown, Peter. "Society and the Supernatural. A Medieval Change." *Daedalus* 104 (1975): 133–51. Reprinted in *Society and the Holy in Late Antiquity,* 302–32. Berkeley, 1982.

Brown, Warren. *Unjust Seizure: Conflict, Interest, and Authority in an Early Medieval Society.* Ithaca, N.Y., 2001.

Brugières, Marie-Bernadette. "Réflexions sur la crise de la justice en Occident à la fin de l'Antiquité: L'apport de la littérature." In *La Giustizia nell'alto medioevo (secoli V–VIII),* 165–218.

Brunel, Clovis. "Les juges de la paix en Gévaudan au milieu du XIe siècle." *BEC* 109 (1951): 32–41.

Bruyning, L. F. "Law Court Procedure in the Lombard Kingdom." *Journal of Medieval History* 11 (1985): 193–214.

Buc, Philippe. *The Dangers of Ritual: Between Early Medieval Texts and Social Scientific Theory.* Princeton, 2001.

Bur, Michel. *La formation du comté de Champagne, v. 950–1150.* Nancy, 1977.

Cain, Maureen, and Kalmar Kulcsar. "Thinking Disputes: An Essay on the Origins of the Dispute Industry." *Law and Society Review* 16 (1982): 375–402.

Calasso, F. "Accertamento negoziale e processuale di diritti nell'alto medio evo." *Annali di Storia del diritto* 9 (1965): 168–203.

Carlin, Marie-Louise. *La pénétration du droit romain dans les actes de la pratique provençale, Xie–XIIIe siècle*. Paris, 1967.

Carreras i Candi, Francesch. "Lo Montjuích de Barcelona." *Memorias de la Real Academia de Buenas Letras de Barcelona* 8 (1906): 197–450.

Castaldo, André. *L'église d'Adge, Xe–XIIIe siècle*. Paris, 1970.

Catafau, Aymat. "Une famille Roussillonnaise du Xeme siècle." *Etudes Roussillonaises* 12 (1993): 91–108.

———. *Les celleres et la naissance du village en Roussillon (Xe–XVe siècles)*. Perpignan, 1998.

Caucanas, Sylvie. *Les ressources hydraliques en Roussillon du IXe au début du XIVe siècle*. 1988.

Chandler, Cullen. "Between Court and Counts: Carolingian Catalonia and the *aprisio* Grant, 778–897." *Early Medieval Europe* 11 (2002): 19–44.

Chédeville, André. *Chartres et ses campagnes, XIe–XIIe siècles*. Paris, 1973.

Cheyette, Fredric L. "Suum cuique tribuere." *French Historical Studies* 6 (1970): 287–99.

Clanchy, Michael T. *From Memory to Written Record: England, 1066–1307*. Cambridge, 1979.

———. "Law and Love in the Middle Ages." In *Disputes and Settlements: Law and Human Relations in the West*, ed. John Bossy, 47–67. Cambridge, 1983.

Coll i Alentorn, Miquel. "La historiografia de Catalunya en el període primitiu." *Estudis Romànics* 3 (1951–52): 139–96.

———. "La Crònica de Sant Pere de les Puelles." *I Col.loqui d'Història del Monaquisme Català, Santes Creus, 1966*, 2:35–50. Santes Creus, 1969.

Collins, Roger. "Charles the Bald and Wifred the Hairy." In *Charles the Bald, Court and Kingdom*, ed. Janet Nelson and M. T. Gibson, 169–88. Oxford, 1981.

———. "*Sicut Lex Gothorum continet:* Law and Charters in Ninth and Tenth-Century Léon and Catalonia." *English Historical Review* 396 (1985): 490–512.

———. "Visigothic Law and Regional Custom in Disputes in Early Medieval Spain. In *The Settlement of Disputes*, ed. Davies and Fouracre, 85–104.

———. "Literacy and the Laity in Early Medieval Spain." In *The Uses of Literacy in Early Medieval Europe*, ed. R. McKitterick. Cambridge, 1990.

Colman, Rebecca. "Reason and Unreason in Early Medieval Law." *Journal of Interdisciplinary History* 4 (1974): 571–91.

Comaroff, John L., and Simon Roberts, eds. *Rules and Processes: The Cultural Logic of Dispute in an African Context*. Chicago, 1981.

Constable, Giles. "Forgery and Plagiarism in the Middle Ages." *Archiv für Diplomatik* 29 (1983): 1–41.

Cover, Robert M. "The Supreme Court, 1982 Term. Foreword: *Nomos* and Narrative." *Harvard Law Review* 97 (1983): 4–68.

———. "Violence and the Word." *Yale Law Journal* 95 (1986): 1601–29.

———. *Narrative, Violence, and the Law: The Essays of Robert Cover*, ed. Martha Minow, Michael Ryan, and Austin Sarat. Ann Arbor, Mich., 1992.

Cowdrey, H. E. J. "The Peace and Truce of God in the Eleventh Century." *Past and Present* 46 (1970): 42–67.

Cuadrada, Coral. *El Maresme medieval: Les jurisdiccions baronals de Mataró i Sant Vincenç / Vilassar (hàbitat, economia i societat, segles X–XIV)*. Barcelona, 1988.

Cursente, Benoît. "Entre parenté et fidélité: Les 'amis' dans le Gascogne des Xie et XIIe siècles." In *Les sociétés méridionales à l'âge féodal (Espagne, Italie et sud de la France X–XIIIe s): Hommage à Pierre Bonnassie*, ed. Hélène Débax, 285–92. Toulouse, 1999.

Da Rosa Pereira, I., "Livros de direito na idade media." *Lusitania Sacra* 7 (1964–66): 7–60; 8 (1970): 81–96.

Daube, David. *Witnesses in Bible and Talmud*. Oxford, 1986.

Davies, Wendy. "Property Rights and Property Claims in Welsh 'Vitae' of the Eleventh Century." In *Hagiographie Cultures et Sociétés, IVe–XIIe siècles*, ed. Pierre Riché and Evelyn Patlagean, 515–33. Paris, 1981.

———. "Disputes: Their Conduct and Settlement in the Village Communities of Eastern Brittany in the Ninth Century." *History and Anthropology* 1 (1985): 289–312.

———. *Small Worlds: The Village Community in Early Medieval Brittany*. London, 1988.

Davies, Wendy, and Paul Fouracre, eds. *Property and Power in the Early Middle Ages*. Cambridge, 1995.

———. *The Settlement of Disputes in Early Medieval Europe*. Cambridge, 1986.

de Arvizu, Fernando. "Las causes de desheredación en el derecho altomedieval de Aragón y Navarra." *Mélanges offerts à Jean Dauvillier*, 1–14. Toulouse, 1979.

Debax, Helène, ed. *Les Sociétés meridionales à l'age féodal (Espagne, Italie et sud de la France, Xe–XIIIe s.): Hommage à Pierre Bonnassie*. Toulouse, 1999.

Debord, André. *La société laïque dans les pays de la Charente, Xe–XIIe s*. Paris, 1984.

Delcor, Mathias. "Ermengol évêque d'Urgell et son oeuvre (1010–1035) de l'histoire à l'hagiographie." *Cahiers de Saint-Michel de Cuxa* 20 (1989): 161–90.

Delogu, Paolo. "La Giustizia nell'Italia Meridionale Longobarda." In *La Giustizia nell'alto medioevo (secoli IX–XI)*, 257–308.

Deswartes, Thomas. "Rome et la spécificité catalane. La papauté et ses relations avec la Catalogne et Narbonne (850–1030)." *Revue Historique* 294 (1995): 3–43.

Devailly, Guy. *Le Berry du Xe siècle au milieu du XIIIe. Etude politique, religieuse, sociale, économique*. Paris, 1973.

Díaz de Garayo, Ernesto Pastor. *Castilla en el Tránsito de la Antigüedad al Feudalismo: Poblamiento, poder político y estucura social. Del Arlanza al Duero (siglos VII–XI)*. Vallodolid, 1996.

Díaz y Díaz, Manuel C. "La circulation des manuscrits dans la Péninsule Ibérique du VIIIe au XIe siècle." *CCM* 12 (1969): 219–40, 383–92.

———. "La Lex Visigothorum y sus manuscritos: Un ensayo de reinterpretación." *Anuario de historia del derecho español (AHDE)* 46 (1976): 163–224.

———. *Codices Visigoticos en la Monarquia Leonesa*. León, 1983.

Donahue, Charles. "Proof by Witnesses in the Church Courts of Medieval England: An Imperfect Reception of Learned Law." In *On the Laws and Customs of England*, ed. M. S. Arnold et al., 127–58. Chapel Hill, N.C., 1981.

Duby, Georges. "The Evolution of Judicial Institutions." In *The Chivalrous Society*, trans. Cynthia Postan, 15–58. Berkeley, 1977. Originally published as "Recherches sur l'évolution des institutions judiciaires pendant le Xe et le XIe siècle dan le Sud de la Bourgogne." *Le Moyen Age* 52 (1946): 149–95.

———. *La société au XIe et XIIe siècles dans la région mâconnaise*. Paris, 1953.

DuCange, Charles Dufresne. *Glossarium mediae et infimae Latinitatis,* 10 vols. Niort, 1883–1887.

Duhamel-Amado, Claudie. "Les pouvoirs et les parents autour de Béziers (980–1100)." *AMidi* 189–90 (1989): 309–18.

——. "L'alleu paysan a-t-il existé en France méridionale autour de l'an Mil?" In *La France de l'an Mil,* ed. Robert Delort, 142–61. Paris, 1990.

——. "La famille aristocratique languedocienne. Parenté et patrimoine dans les vicomtés de Béziers et Agde (900–1170)." Thesis presented for doctorat d'Etat. Université de Paris IV. Paris, 1994.

Dupont, André. "Considérations sur la colonisation et la vie rurale dans le Roussillon et le March d'Espagne au IXe siècle." *AMidi* 67 (1955): 223–45.

——. "L'aprision et le régime aprisionaire." *Le Moyen Age* 71 (1965): 179–213, 375–99.

Durand, Aline. *Les paysages médiévaux du Languedoc (Xe–XIIe siècles).* Toulouse, 1998.

Durand, Robert. *Les Campagnes portugaises entre Douro et Tage aux XIIe et XIII siècles.* Paris, 1982.

Ellickson, Robert C. *Order without Law: How Neighbors Settle Disputes.* Cambridge, Mass., 1991.

Engels, Odilo. *Schutzgedanke und Landesherrschaft im östlichen Pyrenäenraum, 9–13. Jahrhundert.* Munster, 1970.

——. *Reconquista und Landherrschaft: Studien zur Rechts- und Verfassungsgeschichte Spaniens im Mittelalter.* Paderborn, 1979.

Everett, Nick. "Literacy and Law in Lombard Government." *Early Medieval Europe* 9 (2000), 118.

Farías Zurita, Víctor. "Problemas cronológicos del movimiento de Paz y Tregua catalán del siglo XI." *Acta historica et archaeologica mediaevalia* 14–15 (1993–94): 9–37.

——. "Compraventa de tierras: Circulación monetaria y sociedad campesina en los siglos X y XI. El ejemplo de Goltred de Reixac." *Anuario de Estudios Medievales* 29 (1999): 269–99.

Feliu Montfort, Gaspar. "Las Ventas con pago en moneda en el condado de Barcelona hasta el año 1010." *Cuadernos de historia económica de Cataluña* 5 (1971): 9–43.

——. "El condado de Barcelona en los siglos IX y X: Organizacíon territorial y económico-social." *Cuadernos de historia económica de Cataluña* 7 (1972): 9–32.

——. "El Patrimoni de la Seu de Barcelona durant el pontificat del bisbat Aeci (995–1010)." In *Miscel.lània Ramon d'Abadal: Estudis d'Història Oferts a Ramon d'Abadal i de Vinyals en el centenari del seu naixement,* ed. Jaume Sobrequés i Callicó and Sebastià Riera i Viader, 51–68. Barcelona, 1994.

——. "La pagesia catalana abans de la feudalització." *Anuario de Estudios Medievales* 26 (1996): 19–41.

Felstiner, William L. F., R. L. Abel, and Austin Sarat. "The Emergence and Transformation of Disputes: Naming, Blaming, Claiming." *Law and Society Review* 15 (1980–81): 631–54.

Fischer-Drew, Katherine. *Law and Society in Early Medieval Europe.* London, 1988.

Flach, Jacques, "Le droit romain dans les chartres du IXe au XIe siècle." In *Mélanges Fitting,* 1:383–422. Montpellier, 1908.

Fleming, Robin. "Oral Testimony and the Domesday Inquest." *Anglo-Norman Studies* 17 (1994): 101–22.

Font Rius, José María. "Entorn a la figura de Ponç Bonfill Marc, jutge comtal de Barcelona." *Boletim da Faculdade de Direito* 68 (1982): 377–95.

———. "Les modes de détention de châteaux dans la 'vielle Catalogne' et ses marches extérieures du début du IXe au début du XIe siècle." *Les structures sociales de l'Aquitaine, du Languedoc et de l'Espagne au premier âge féodal*, 63–77. Paris, 1969.

Fontaine, Jacques. *Isidore de Seville et la culture classique dans l'Espagne wisigothique*, 2 vols. Paris, 1959.

Fossier, Robert. *La terre et les hommes en Picardie jusqu'à fin du XIIIe siècle*. Paris, 1968.

Fouracre, Paul. "Carolingian Justice: The Rhetoric of Improvement and Contexts of Abuse." In *La Giustizia nell'alto medioevo (secoli V–VIII)*, 771–803.

Freedman, Paul H. *The Diocese of Vic: Tradition and Regeneration in Medieval Catalonia*. New Brunswick, N.J., 1983.

———. "Cowardice, Heroism, and the Legendary Origins of Catalonia." *Past and Present* 121 (1988): 6–28.

———. "Le pouvoir épiscopale en Catalogne au Xe siècle." In *Catalunya i França meridional, a l'entorn de l'any mil*, ed. Barral i Altet et al., 174–80. Barcelona, 1991.

———. *The Origins of Peasant Servitude in Medieval Catalonia*. Cambridge, 1991.

———. "Symbolic Interpretations of the Events of 985–988." In *Symposium Internacional Sobre els Orígens de Catalunya (segles viii–xi)*, 117–29. Barcelona, 1991.

Freeman, Ann. "Theodulf of Orleans: A Visigoth at Charlemagne's Court." In *L'Europe Héritière de l'Espagne Wisigothique*, ed. Jacques Fontaine and Christine Pellistrandi, 185–94. Madrid, 1992.

Galanter, Marc. "Why the 'Haves' Come Out Ahead: Speculations on the Limits of Legal Changes." *Law and Society Review* 9 (1974): 95–148.

Gallanis, Thomas. "The Rise of Modern Evidence Law." *Iowa Law Review* 84 (1999): 499–560.

Ganshof, François. "Charlemagne et l'administration de la justice dans la monarchie franque." In *Karl der Grosse: Lebenswerk und Nachleben*, ed. H. Beumann, 1:394–419. Düsseldorf, 1965.

———. "La Preuve dans le droit franc." *Recueils de la sociéte Jean Bodin pour l'histoire comparative des institutions (RSJB)* 17 (1965): 71–98.

Garaud, Marcel. "Le droit romain dans les chartes poitevines au XIe siècle." In *Mélanges de droit romain dédiés à Georges Cornil*, 1:399–424. Ghent, 1926.

———. *Les châtelains de Poitou et l'avènement du régime féodale, XIe au XIIe siècles*. Poitou, 1967.

García de Cortázar, José Ángel. *La sociedad rural en España medieval*. Madrid, 1988.

———. "Estructuras sociales y relaciones de poder en León y Castila en los siglos VIII a XII: La formación de una sociedad feudal." *Il Feudalismo nell-alto medioevo Settimane (de studi soll'alto medioevo)* 47 (2000): 497–563.

García Gallo, Alfonso. "El concilio de Coyanza: Contribución al estudio del derecho canónico en Alta Edad Media," *AHDE* 20 (1950): 275–633.

———. "Consideraciones críticas de los estudios sobre la legislación y la costumbre visigoda." *AHDE* 44 (1974): 343–464.

García López, Yolanda. "La Tradicion del Liber Iudiciorum: Una Revisión." In *De la*

Antigüedad al Medievo, siglos IV–VIII: III Congreso de Estudios Medievales, 383–416. Avila, 1993.

——. *Estudios Críticos de la 'Lex Wisigothorum.'* Memorias del Seminario de Historia Antigua V. Alcalá, 1996.

Garí, Blanca. "Las *querimoniae* feudales en la documentación catalana del siglo XII, 1131–1178." *Medievalia* (1984): 7–49.

Gaudemet, Jean. "Survivance romaines dans le droit de la monarchie francque de Ve au Xe siècles," *Tidjschrift voor Rechtsgeschiednis* 23 (1955): 149–206.

——. "Les ordalies au Moyen Age: Doctrine, législation et pratique canoninques." *RSJB* 17 (1965): 99–135.

——. "Le droit romain dans la pratique et chez les docteurs aux XIe et XIIe siècles." *CCM* 8 (1965): 365–80.

Gautier-Dalché, J. "Moulin à eau, seigneurie, communauté rurale dans le nord de l'Espagne, IX–XII siècles." In *Mélanges R. Labande: Etudes de Civilisation Médiévale IX–XII s.*, 337–49. Poitiers, 1974.

Geary, Patrick J. *Furta Sacra: Thefts of Relics in the Central Middle Ages.* Princeton, 1978.

——. "Humiliation of Saints." In *Saints and Their Cults: Studies in Religious Sociology, Folklore, and History*, ed. Stephen Wilson, 123–40. Cambridge, 1983.

——. "Living with Conflicts in Stateless France: A Typology of Conflict Management Mechanisms, 900–1200." In *Living with the Dead in the Middle Ages*, 125–60. Ithaca, N.Y., 1994. Originally published as "Vivre en conflit dans une France sans état: Typologie des mécanismes de réglement des conflits, 1050–1200." *AESC* 41 (1986): 1107–33.

——. *Phantoms of Remembrance: Memory and Oblivion at the End of the First Millennium.* Princeton, 1994.

——. "Extra-Judicial Means of Conflict Resolution." In *La Giustizia nell'alto medioevo (secoli V–VIII)*, 570–601.

——. "Moral Obligations and Peer Pressure: Conflict Resolution in the Medieval Aristocracy." In *Georges Duby: L'écriture de l'histoire*, ed. Claudie Duhamel-Amado and Guy Lobrichon, 217–22. Bruxelles, 1996.

——. "Land, Language, and Memory in Europe, 700–1100." *Transactions of the Royal Historical Society*, 6th series, 9 (1999): 169–84.

Gibert, Rafael. *Enseñanza del derecho en Hispania durante los siglos vi a xi.* Ius Romanum Medii Aevi (IRMA) I, b, cc. Milan, 1967.

Giordanengeo, G. *Le droit féodal dans le pays de droit écrit: L'exemple de la Provence et du Dauphiné, XIIe–début du XIVe siècle.* Rome, 1988.

——. *La giustizia nell'alto medioevo (secoli V–VIII)*, 2 vols. Settimane di studio del Centro italiano di studi sull'alto medioevo 42. Spoleto, 1995.

——. *La giustizia nell'alto medioevo (secoli IX–XI)*, 2 vols. Settimane di studio del Centro italiano di studi sull'alto medioevo 44. Spoleto, 1997.

Gluckman, Max. "The Peace in the Feud." In *Custom and Conflict in Africa*, 1–26. New York, 1956.

——. *Politics, Law, and Ritual in Tribal Society.* Chicago, 1965.

Goetz, Hans Werner. "Serfdom and the Beginnings of a 'Seigneurial System' in the Carolingian Period: A Survey of the Evidence." *Early Medieval Europe* 2 (1993): 29–51.

Gonzalvo i Bou, Gener. *La pau i la treva a Catalunya: Origen de corts Catalanes.* Barcelona, 1986.

Gouron, André. *La Science juridique française aux xie et xiie siècles.* IRMA I, 4, d–e. Milan, 1978.

———. *La science du droit dans le Midi de la France au Moyen Age.* London, 1984.

Gramain, Monique. "La composition de la cour vicomtale de Narbonne aux XIIe et XIIIe siècles." *AMidi* 81 (1969): 121–39.

———. "*Castrum*, structures féodales et peuplement en Bitterois au XIe siècle." *Structures féodales et féodalisme dans l'Occident méditerranéan, Xe–XIIIe siècles,* 119–34. Rome, 1980.

Grassotti, Hilda. *Las instituciones feudo-vassaláticas en León y Castilla,* 2 vols. Spoleto, 1969.

Guglielmi, Nilda. "La figura del juez en el concejo (León-Castilla, siglos XI–XIII)." In *Mélanges offertes à Réne Crozet,* 1003–24. Poitiers, 1966.

Guillot, Olivier. *Le comte d'Anjou et son entourage au XIe siècle.* Paris, 1972.

———. "La participation au duel judiciaire de témoins de conditions serve dans l'Ile-de-France du XIe siècle: Autour d'un faux diplôme de Henri Ier." In *Droit privé et institutions régionales: Etudes historiques offertes à Jean Yver,* 345–60. Paris, 1976.

———. "Justice dans le royaume franc a l'époque merovingienne." In *La Giustizia nell'alto medioevo (secoli V–VIII),* 653–731.

———. "Le Duel Judiciaire: Du champ legal (sous Louis le Pieux) au champ de la pratique en France." In *La Giustizia nell'alto medioevo (secoli IX–XI),* 715–85.

Gulliver, P. H., ed. *Disputes and Negotiations: A Cross-Cultural Perspective.* New York, 1979.

Guterman, Simeon L. *The Principle of the Personality of the Law in the Germanic Kingdoms of Western Europe from the Fifth to the Eleventh Century.* Frankfurt-am-Main, 1990.

Gutiérrez González, José Avelino. "El Páramo Léones. Entre la Antigüedad y la Alta Edad Media." *Studi Historica, Historia Medieval* 14 (1996): 47–96.

Guyotjeannin, Olivier. "L'épiscopat dans le domaine capétien, Xe–XIIe s." In *Pouvoirs et libertés aux temps des premiers Capétiens,* 97–108. Paris, 1993.

Guyotjeannin, Olivier, Jacques Pycke, and Benoît-Michel Tock. *Diplomatique Médievale,* L'Atelier du Médiéviste 2. Brepols, 1993.

Hammer, C. I. "*Lex scripta* in Early Medieval Bavaria: Use and Abuse of the *Lex Baiuariorum.*" In *Law in Medieval Life and Thought,* Sewanee Medieval Studies 5, 185–95. Sewanee, 1990.

Harries, Jill. *Law and Empire in Late Antiquity.* Cambridge, 1999.

Head, Thomas F. *Hagiography and the Cult of the Saints: the Diocese of Orléans, 800–1200.* Cambridge, 1990.

Head, Thomas F., Barbara Rosenwein, and Sharon Farmer. "Monks and Their Enemies: A Comparative Approach." *Speculum* 66 (1991): 764–96.

Head, Thomas F., and Richard Landes, eds. *The Peace of God: Social Violence and Religious Response in France around the Year 1000.* Ithaca, N.Y., 1992.

Helmholz, Richard. "Crime, Compurgation, and the Courts of the Medieval Church." *Law and History Review* 1 (1983): 1–26.

———. "Excommunication in Twelfth-Century England." *Journal of Law and Religion* 11 (1994–1995): 235–53.

Herman, Frank. "The Establishment of a Rule against Hearsay." *Virginia Journal of International Law* 36 (1995): 1–51.

Hinojosa, Eduardo de. "La réception du droit romain en Catalogne." In *Mélanges Fitting*, vol.2: 393–408. Montpellier, 1908.

———. "L'admisión del derecho romano en Cataluña." *Boletin de le Real Academia de Buenas Letras de Barcelona* 5 (1909–1910): 209–21.

Hoffman, Hartmut. *Gottesfriede und Treuga Dei.* Monumenta Germaniae Historica Schriften 20. Stuttgart, 1964.

Hudson, John. *Land, Law, and Lordship in Anglo-Norman England.* Oxford, 1994.

———. "Anglo-Norman Land Law and the Origins of Property." In *Law and Government in Medieval England and Normandy: Essays in Honor of Sir James Holt*, 198–222. Cambridge, 1994.

Hyams, Paul. "The Proof of Villein Status in the Common Law," *English Historical Review* 89 (1974): 721–49.

———. "Trial by Ordeal: The Key to Proof in the Early Common Law." In *On the Laws and Customs of England: Essays in Honor of Samuel E. Thorne*, ed. Morris S. Arnold, Thomas A. Green, Sally A. Scully, and Stephen D. White, 90–126. Chapel Hill, N.C., 1981.

———. "The Charter as a Source for the Early Common Law." *The Journal of Legal History* 12 (1991): 173–91.

Iglesia Ferreirós, Aquilino. "La creación del derecho en Cataluña," *AHDE* 47 (1977): 99–423.

———. "El proceso del Conde Bera y el Problema de las ordalias," *AHDE* 51 (1981): 1–221.

Innes, Matthew. "Memory, Orality, and Literacy in an Early Medieval Society." *Past and Present* 158 (1998): 3–36.

Johnson, Penelope. *Prayer, Power, and Patronage: The Abbey of La Trinité de Vendôme, 1032–1187.* New York, 1981.

Jornet, Núria. "Les femmes catalanes à travers leurs testaments, 938–1131." In *La femme dans l'histoire et la société méridionales (IXe–XIXe s.)*, 91–101. Montpellier, 1995.

Junyent, Eduard. "Le rouleau funéraire d'Oliba, abbé de Notre-Dame de Ripoll et de Saint Michel de Cuixa, évêque de Vich." *AMidi* 63 (1951): 249–62.

———. "La biblioteca de la Canónica de Vich en los siglos X–XI." *Gesammelte Aufsätze zur Kulturgeschichte Spaniens* 21 (1963): 136–45.

Just, Peter. "History, Power, Ideology, and Culture: Current Directions in the Anthropology of Law." *Law and Society Review* 26 (1992): 373–411.

Kelleher, Marie. "Boundaries of Law: Code and Custom in Legal Practice in Early Medieval Catalonia." *Comitatus* 30 (1999): 1–11.

Kennedy, Alan. "Law and Litigation in the *Libellus Athelwoldi episcopi*." *Anglo-Saxon England* 24 (1995): 131–83.

———. "Disputes about *bocland*: The Forum for Their Adjudication." *Anglo-Saxon England* 14 (1985): 179–95.

Kerr, Margaret E., Richard K. Forsyth, and Michael J. Plyley. "Cold Water and Hot Iron: Trial by Ordeal in England." *Journal of Interdisciplinary History* 22 (1992): 573–96.

Kienast, Walther. "Das Fortleben des gotischen Rechts in Südfrankreich und Katalonien." In *Studien über die französichen Völkstamme des Frühmittelalters*, 151–70. Stuttgart, 1968.

King, P. D. *Law and Society in the Visigothic Kingdom*. Cambridge, 1972.

Koch, A. "L'origine de la haute et de la moyenne justice dans l'Ouest et le Nord de la France," *Tijdschrift voor Rechtgeschiednis* 21 (1953): 42–58.

——. "Continuité ou rupture? De la justice domaniale et abbatiale à la justice urbaine et comtale à Arras." *Revue du Nord* 40 (1958): 289–96.

Kosto, Adam J. *Making Agreements in Medieval Catalonia: Power, Order, and the Written Word, 1000–1200*. Cambridge, 2001.

Koziol, Geoffrey. *Begging Pardon and Favor: Ritual and Political Order in Early Medieval France*. Ithaca, N.Y., 1992.

Lacarra, Jose Maria. "Les Ville-frontières dans l'Espagne des XIe et XIIe siècles." *Le Moyen Age* 18 (1963): 205–22.

Larrea, Juan José. "Villa Matanza." In *Les sociétés méridionales à l'âge féodal (Espagne, Italie et sud de la France X–XIIIe s): Hommage à Pierre Bonnassie*, ed. Hélène Débax, 223–28. Toulouse, 1999.

Larson, Laurence M. "Witnesses and Oath Helpers in Old Norwegian Law." In *Anniversary Essays in Medieval History by Students of Charles Homer Haskins*, 133–56. Boston, 1929.

Lauranson-Rosaz, Christian. *L'Auvergne et ses marges (Velay, Gévaudan) du VIIIe au XIe siècle: Le fin du monde antique?* Le-Puy-en-Velay, 1987.

——. "La romanité du Midi de l'an Mil (le point sur les sociétés méridionales)." In *Le France de l'an Mil*, ed. Robert Delort, 49–73. Paris, 1990.

L'environnement des églises et la topographie religieuse des campagnes médiévales, ed. M. Fixot and E. Zadora-Rio. Documents d'archéologie française 46. Paris, 1994.

LeGoff, Jacques. "The Symbolic Ritual of Vassalage." In *Time, Work, and Culture in the Middle Ages*, trans. Arthur Goldhammer, 237–87. Chicago, 1980.

Lehfeldt, Elizabeth A. "Convents as Litigants: Dowry and Inheritance Disputes in Early Modern Spain." *Journal of Social History* 33 (2000): 375–84.

LeJan, Régine. "Justice Royale et pratiques sociales dans le Royaume Franc au IXe siècle." In *La Giustizia nell'alto medioevo (secoli IX–XI)*, 47–85.

Lemarignier, Jean-François. "A propos de deux textes sur l'histoire du droit romain au moyen âge, 1008 et 1308." *BEC* 101 (1940): 157–68.

——. "La dislocation du 'pagus' et le problème des 'consuetudines,' X–XI siècles." In *Mélanges d'histoire du moyen âge dédiés à la mémoire de Louis Halphen*, ed. Charles-Edmond Perrin, 401–10. Paris, 1951.

——. *Le gouvernement royal aux premier temps capétiens, 987–1106*. Paris, 1965.

Lemesle, Bruno. *La société aristocratique dans le Haut-Maine (XIe–XIIe siècles)*. Renne, 1999.

Levy, Ernst. "Reflections on the First 'Reception' of Roman Law in Germanic States." *American Historical Review* 48 (1942): 20–29.

Lévy, Jean-Phillipe. "La formation de la théorie romaine des preuves." In *Studi in onore di Siro Solazzi*, 418–38. Naples, 1948.

——. "L'evolution de la preuve des origines à nos jours. Synthèse générale." *RSJB* 17 (1965): 9–70.

———. "Le problème de la preuve dans les droits savants du moyen âge." *RSJB* 17 (1965): 137–67.

Lewis, A. R. *The Development of Southern French and Catalan Society, 718–1050.* Austin, Tex. 1965.

———. "Land and Social Mobility in Catalonia, 778–1213." In *Geschichte in der Gesellschaft: Festschrift für Karl Bosl zum 65. Geburtstag,* 312–23. Stuttgart, 1974.

Linehan, Peter. *History and Historians of Medieval Spain.* Oxford, 1993.

———. "The Church and Feudalism in the Spanish Kingdoms in the Eleventh and Twelfth Centuries." *Miscellanea del Centro di studi medioevali* 14 (1995): 303–29.

Little, Lester K. *Benedictine Maledictions: Liturgical Cursing in Romanesque France.* Ithaca, N.Y., 1993.

López, Ortiz, J. "El proceso en los reinos asturianos de nuestra reconquista antes de la recepció ramano-canónica." *AHDE* 14 (1942–43): 184–226.

Lot, Ferdinand. *Etudes sur le règne de Hugues Capet et la fin de Xe siècle.* Paris, 1903.

Magnou-Nortier, Elisabeth. *La société laïque et l'église dans la province ecclésiastique de Narbonne.* Toulouse, 1974.

———. "La terre, la rente et le pouvoir dans les pays de Languedoc pendant le haut Moyen Age." *Francia* 9 (1981): 79–115; 10 (1982): 21–65.

———. "A propos de la *villa* et du manse dans les sources méridionales du Haut Moyen Age." *AMidi* 96 (1984): 85–91.

———. "*Lex et consuetudo*: Enquête dans les sources législative carolingienne," *Recueil de mémoires et travaux publié par la société d'Histoire de Droit et des institutions des Anciens Pays de Droit écrit* 14 (1987): 197–207.

———. "Recherches sur la fiscalité foncière durant le haut Moyen Age: Premiers résultats." In *Historia económica y de las instituciones financieras en Europa: Trabajos en homenaje de Ferran Valls i Taberner,* ed. Manuel J. Peláez Barcelona, 1989.

———. "Note sur l'expression 'justitiam facere' dans les capitulaires carolingiennes." In *Haut Moyen Age, Culture, Education, et Société: Etudes offertes à Pierre Riché,* ed. M. Sot, 249–64. Paris, 1990.

———. "The Enemies of the Peace: Reflections on a Vocabulary, 500–1100." In *The Peace of God: Social Violence and Religious Response in France around the Year 1000,* ed. Thomas Head and Richard Landes, 58–79. Ithaca, N.Y., 1992.

Maire Vigueur, J. C. "Gli 'iudices' nella città comunali: Identità culturale ed esperienze politiche." In *Federico II e le città italiane,* ed. Pierre Toubert and A. Paravicini Bagliani, 161–76. Palermo, 1994.

Martí, Ramon. "La integració a l'alou feudal' de la seu de Girona de les terres beneficiade pel 'règim dels hispans': Els casos de Bàscara." In *La formació del feudalisme,* 49–62.

Martin, Jean-Marie. "Le juge et l'acte notarié en Italie méridionale du VIIIe au Xe siècle." In *Scrittura e produzione documentaria nel mezzogiorno longobardo. Atti del Convegno internazionale di studi (Badia di Cava, ottobre 1990),* ed. G. Vitolo and F. Mottola, 287–300. Badia di Cava, 1991.

Martindale, Jane. " 'His Special Friend.' Dispute Settlement and Political Power within the French Kingdom from the Tenth to the Twelfth Centuries." *Transactions of the Royal Historical Society,* 6th series, 5 (1995): 21–57.

Martínez Catherine, and Nicole Rossignol. "Le peuplement du Rossillon, du Conflent et du Vallespir aux IXe et Xe siècles." *AMidi* 87 (1975): 139–56.

Martínez Díez, G. "Un nuevo Codice del 'Liber iudiciorum' del siglo XII." *AHDE* 31 (1961): 651–94.

Martínez i Teixidó, Lydia. *Les famílies nobles del Pallars en els segles XI i XII*. Lleida, 1991.

Massetto, G. P. "Gli studi di diritto nella Lombardia del secolo XI." In *Lanfranco di Pavia e l'Europa del secolo XI = Italia Sacra* 51, ed. G. Onofrio, 61–116. Rome, 1993.

Mateu y Llopis, Mateu. "Los fragmentos del *Forum Iudicum* de Ripoll." *Analecta Montserratensia* 9 (1962): 199–205.

Mattoso, Jose. "Sanctio (875–1100)." In *Religião e cultura no Idade Média Portuguesa*, 394–440. Lisbon, 1982.

McCrank, Lawrence. "The Cistercians of Poblet as Landlords: Protection, Litigation, and Violence on the Medieval Catalan Frontier." *Citeaux: commentarii cistercienses* 26 (1975): 255–83.

McKitterick, Rosamond. "Some Carolingian Law-Books and Their Function." In *Authority and Power: Studies on Medieval Law and Government Presented to Walter Ullmann on his Seventieth Birthday*, ed. Brian Tierney and Peter Linehan, 13–27. Cambridge, 1980.

———. "Knowledge of Canon Law in the Frankish Kingdoms before 789: The Manuscript Evidence." *Journal of Theological Studies* 36 (1985): 97–117.

———. *The Carolingians and the Written Word*. Cambridge, 1989.

———. "Perceptions of Justice in Western Europe in the Ninth and Tenth Centuries." In *La Giustizia nell'alto medioevo (secoli IX–XI)*, 1073–1102.

Merry, Sally Engle. "Legal Pluralism." *Law and Society Review* 22 (1988): 869–96.

Miller, William Ian. *Bloodtaking and Peacemaking: Feud, Law, and Society in Saga Iceland*. Chicago, 1990.

Mínguez, José María. "Justicia y Poder en el Marco de la Feudalicazión de la Sociedad Leonesa." In *La Giustizia nell'alto medioevo (secoli IX–XI)*, 491–546.

Miret i Sans, Joaquim. "Los vescomtes de Cerdanya, Conflent y Bergadà." *Memorias de la Real Academia de Buenas Letras de Barcelona* 8 (1906): 113–75.

Monod, Gabriel. "Les moeurs judiciaires au VIIIe siècle d'après la 'Paraenesis ad Judices' de Theodulf." *Revue Historique* 35 (1887): 1–20.

Montsalvatje y Fossas, Francisco. *Los Condes de Ampurias Vindicados*. Olot, 1917.

Moore, R. I. "Family, Community, and Cult on the Eve of the Gregorian Reform." *Transactions of the Royal Historical Society*, 5th series, 30 (1980): 49–69.

Moore, Sally Falk. *Law as Process*. London, 1978.

———. *Social Facts and Fabrications: "Customary" Law on Kilimanjaro 1880–1980*. Cambridge, 1986.

Mor, C. G. "En torno a la formación de los 'Usatici Barchinonae,'" *AHDE* 37–38 (1957–58): 413–59.

Morelle, Laurent. "Les chartes dans la gestion des conflits (France du nord, XI–début XII siècle)." *BEC* 155 (1997): 267–98.

Morris, Colin. "Judicium Dei: The Social and Political Significance of the Ordeal in the Eleventh Century." *Studies in Church History* 12 (1975): 95–111.

Mundó, Anscari M. "Entorn de les famílies dels bisbes Oliba de Vic i Oliba d'Elna." *Boletín de la Real Academia de Buenas Letras de Barcelona* (1959–60): 169–78.

——. "La datació de documents pel rei Robert (966–1031) a Catalunya." *Anuario de Estudios Medievales* 4 (1967): 13–34.

——. "Domains and Rights of Sante Pere de Vilamajor (Catalonia): A Polyptych of c. 950 and c. 1060." *Speculum* 49 (1974): 238–57.

——. "Monastic Movements in the East Pyrenees." In *Cluniac Monasticism in the Central Middle Ages*, ed. Noreen Hunt, 98–122. London, 1979.

——. "Els manuscrits del 'Liber Iudiciorum' en les comarques gironines." *La formació del feudalisme*, 77–86.

——. "El 'Liber Iudiciorum' a Catalunya." In *Documents Jurídics de la Història de Catalunya*, ed. Iago de Balanzó i Sala, 13–22. Barcelona, 1992.

——. "El jutge Bonsom de Barcelona, cal·lígraf i copista del 979 al 1024." In *Scribi e Colofoni: Le sottoscrizioni di copisti dalle original all'avvento della stampa*, ed. Emma Condello and Giuseppe de Gregorio, 269–88. Spoleto, 1995.

Nader, Laura, and Harry F. Todd Jr., eds. *The Disputing Process: Law in Ten Societies.* New York, 1978.

Nelson, Janet. *Politics and Ritual in Early Medieval Europe.* London, 1986.

——. "The wary widow." In *Property and Power in the Early Middle Ages*, ed. Davies and Fouracre (Cambridge, 1995), 82–113.

——. "Kings with Justice, Kings without Justice." In *La Giustizia nell'alto medioevo (secoli IX-XI)*, 797–823.

O'Brien, Bruce. *God's Peace and King's Peace: The Laws of Edward the Confessor.* Philadelphia, 1999.

Ordeig i Mata, Ramon. "Dades referents al comte Oliba Cabreta." In *Miscel·lània Ramon d'Abadal: Estudis d'Història Oferts a Ramon d'Abadal i de Vinyals en el centenari del seu naixement*, ed. Sobrequés i Callicó, and Jaume and Sebastià Riera i Viader, 25–40. Barcelona, 1994.

Orlandis, José. "Huellas visigóticas en el derecho de la Alta Edad Media." *AHDE* 20 (1950): 5–49.

Ourliac, Paul. "La '*Convenientia.*'" *Etudes d'histoire du droit médiéval*, 243–52. Paris, 1979.

——. "Notes sur les actes français et catalans du Xe siècle." In *Les pays de Garonne vers l'an mil: La société et le droit: recueil d'études*, 239–56. Toulouse, 1993.

——. "Juges et justiciables au XIe siècles, les *boni homines.*" *Recueil de mémoires et travaux publié par la Société d'histoire du droit et des institutions des anciens pays de droit écrit* 16 (1994): 17–33.

Parisse, Michel. *Noblesse et chevalerie en Lorraine médiévale: Les familles nobles du XIe au XIIIe siècle.* Nancy, 1982.

Pastor, Reyna. *Resistencias y luchas campesinas en la época de crecimiento y consolidación de la formación feudal.* Madrid, 1980.

Pérez de Benavides, Manuel de. *El testamento visigótico: Una contribución al estudio del derecho romano vulgar.* Granada, 1975.

Pérez de Tudela y Velasco, María Isabel. "Guerra, violencia, y terror: La destrucción de Santiago de Compostela por Almanzor hace mil años." *En la España Medieval* 21 (1998): 9–28.

Pérez de Urbel, Justo. "Cardeña y sus escribas durante la primera mitad del siglo X." In *Bivium: Homenaje a Manuel Cecilio Díaz y Díaz*, 217–37. Madrid, 1983.

Peters, Edward. "The Death of the Subdean: Ecclesiastical Order and Disorder in Eleventh-Century Francia." In *Law, Custom, and the Social Fabric of Medieval Europe: Essays in Honor of Bryce Lyon*, ed. Bernard Bacrach and David Nichols, 51–72. Kalamazoo, Mich., 1990.

Petit, Carlos. "Iustitia et Judicium en el Reino de Toledo: Una estudio de teología visigoda." In *La Giustizia nell'alto medioevo (secoli V–VIII)*, 843–932.

——. "De Negotiis Causarum, I." *AHDE* (1985): 161–67.

——. "De Negotiis Causarum, II." *AHDE* (1986): 5–165.

Pétot, Pierre. "Serfs d'Église habilités à témoigner en justice." *CCM* 3 (1960): 191–94.

Pietri, Luce. "Grégoire de Tours et la Justice dans le royaume des Francs." In *La Giustizia nell'alto medioevo (secoli V–VIII)*, 475–569.

Pilarczyk, Ian C. "Between a Rock and a Hot Place: The Role of Subjectivity in the Medieval Ordeal by Hot Iron." *Anglo-American Law Review* 25 (1996): 87–112.

Platelle, E. *La justice seigneurial de l'abbaye de Saint-Amand: Son organisation judicaire, sa procédure et sa compétence du XIe au XVIe siècle*. Louvain, 1965.

——. "La violence et ses remèdes en Flandre au XIe siècle." *Sacris Erudiri: Jaarboek voor Godsdienstwetenschappen* 20 (1971): 101–73.

Poly, Jean-Pierre. "Les légistes provençaux et la diffusion du droit romain dan le Midi." In *Recueil de mémoires et travaux publié par la Société d'histoire du droit et des institutions des anciens pays de droit écrit* 9 (1974): 613–35.

——. *La Provence et la société féodale, 879–1166. Contribution à l'étude des structures dites féodales dans le Midi*. Paris, 1976.

——. "Le procès de l'an mil ou du bon usage des *Leges* en temps de désarroi." In *La Giustizia nell'alto medioevo (secoli IX–XI)*: 9–40.

Poly, Jean-Pierre, and Eric Bournazel. *The Feudal Transformation, 900–1200*. New York, 1991.

——. "Post-Scriptum." *RHDFE* 73 (1995): 361–62.

Ponsich, Pierre. "Le Conflent et ses comtes du IXe au XIIe siècle." *Etudes Roussillonnaises* 1 (1951): 241–344.

——. "Le domain foncier de Saint-Michel de Cuxa aux IX, X, XI siècles." *Etudes Roussillonnaises* 2 (1952): 67–100.

——. "Les problèmes de Saint-Michel de Cuxa d'après les textes et les fouilles," *Etudes Roussillonaises* 2 (1952): 21–66.

——. "Le table de l'autel." *Cahiers de Saint-Michel de Cuxa* 6 (1975): 41–65.

Portella i Comas, Jaume, ed. *La formació i expansió del feudalisme Català, = Estudi General: Revista del Col.legi Universitari de Girona* 5–6. Girona, 1985–1986.

Portet, Pierre, "Le règlement des conflits de bornage en Catalogne, Languedoc et Provence (IXe–Xe siècles)." In *Les sociétés méridionales à l'âge féodal (Espagne, Italie et sud de la France X–XIIIe s): Hommage à Pierre Bonnassie*, ed. Hélène Débax, 59–61. Toulouse, 1999.

Poumarède, J. *Recherches sur les successions dans le Sud-Ouest de la France au Moyen Age*, 2 vols. Toulouse, 1972.

Powers, James F., trans. *The Code of Cuenca: Municipal Law on the Twelfth-century Castilian Frontier*. Philadelphia, 2000.

Prieto, Morera, A. *El reino de León en la Alta Edad Media, II: Ordenamiento jurídico del reino*. León, 1992.

Radding, Charles M. "Superstition to Science: Nature, Fortune, and the Passing of the Medieval Ordeal." *American Historical Review* 84 (1979): 945–69.

Rappaport, Roy. "The Obvious Aspects of Ritual." In *Ecology, Meaning, and Religion*, 173–222. Richmond, Calif., 1979.

Remensnyder, Amy. *Remembering Kings Past: Monastic Foundation Legends in Medieval Southern France*. Ithaca, N.Y., 1995.

Reuter, Timothy. "Property Transactions and Social Relations between Rulers, Bishops and Nobles in Early Eleventh-Century Saxony." In *Property and Power in the Early Middle Ages*, ed. Wendy Davies and Paul Fouracre, 165–99. Cambridge, 1995.

———. "Debate: The Feudal Revolution." *Past and Present* 155 (1997): 177–95.

Reynolds, Susan. *Fiefs and Vassals: The Medieval Evidence Reinterpreted*. Oxford, 1994.

———. *Kingdoms and Communities in Western Europe, 900–1300*. Oxford, 1984.

Riché, Pierre. *Enseignement du droit en Gaule du VIe au XIe siècle*, IRMA I, 5, b, b. Milan, 1965.

———. *Education and Culture in the Barbarian West, Sixth through Eighth Centuries*. London, 1993.

Riu, Manuel. "Formación de las zonas de pastos veraniegos del monasterio de Sante Creus en el Pirineo, durante el siglo XI." *Boletin del archivo bibliographico* 14 (1961): 137–53.

———. "Hipòtesi entorn dels origens del feudalisme a Catalunya," *Quaderns d'Estudis Medievals* 2 (1981): 195–208.

———. "El Feudalismo en Cataluña." In *En Torno al Feudalismo Hispanico: I Congreso de Estudios Medievales*, 373–91. Avila, 1989.

Rius Cornadó, Jorge. "Dato sobre la economía monetaria en Cataluña durante el siglo XI." *Cuadernos de historia económica de Cataluña* 9 (1973): 15–68.

Ríus Serra, José. "El derecho visigodo en Cataluña." *Gesammelte Aufsätze zur Kulturgeschichte Spaniens* 8 (1940): 65–80.

———. "Reparatio Scripturae." *AHDE* 5 (1928): 246–53.

Roberts, Simon. *Order and Dispute: An Introduction to Legal Anthropology*. New York, 1979.

Rodiño Caramés, Claudio. "A Lex Gotica e o Liber Judicum no reino de León." *Cuadernos de Estudios Gallegos* 109 (1997): 9–45.

Rodríguez Fernández, Justiniano. *El Monasterio de Ardón*. León, 1964.

———. "El Ordenamiento Juridico Leones en la Edad Media." In *León Medieval: Doce Estudios*, 69–81. León, 1978.

Rosenwein, Barbara. "Feudal War and Monastic Peace: Cluniac Liturgy as Ritual Agression." *Viator* 2 (1971): 129–57.

———. *To Be the Neighbor of Saint Peter: The Social Meaning of Cluny's Property, 909–1049*. Ithaca, N.Y., 1989.

———. *Negotiating Space: Power, Restraint, and Privileges of Immunity in Early Medieval Europe*. Ithaca, N.Y., 1999.

Rosenwein, Barbara, and Lester Little, eds. *Debating the Middle Ages: Issues and Readings*. Malden, Mass., 1998.

Rouche, Michel. "Les survivances antiques dans trois cartulaires du sud-ouest de la France aux Xe et XIe siècles." *CCM* 23 (1980): 93–108.

Rouland, Norbert. "Histoire du droit et anthropologie juridique." *Droit et cultures* 18 (1989): 193–223.

Rovira i Solà, Manuel. "Notes documentals sobre alguns efecte de la presa de Barcelona per al-Mansur." *Acta historica et archaeologica medievalia* 1 (1980): 31–53.

Ruiz de Loizaga, Saturnino. *Iglesia y Sociedad en el Norte de España: Iglesia Episcopal de Valpuesta, Alta Edad Media.* Burgos, 1991.

Ruiz Doménec, José Enrique. "Las estructuras familiares catalanas en la alta edad media." *Cuadernos de Arqueología* 16 (1975): 265–324.

——. "The Urban Origins of Barcelona: Agricultural Revolution or Urban Development?" *Speculum* 52 (1977): 265–86.

——. "Las prácticas judiciales en la Cataluña feudal." *Historia. Instituciones. Documentos* 9 (1983): 245–72.

——. *L'estructura feudal: sistema de parentiu i teoria de l'aliança en la societat catalan, c. 980–1220.* Sant Boi de Llogebrat, 1985.

Salrach i Marés, Josep Maria. "La societat i el govern de Catalunya a l'alta edat mitjana, segles IX–XII." *Cuadernos de historia económica de Cataluña* 18 (1978): 22–37.

——. *El procés de feudalització, segles III–XII.* Vol. 2 of *Història de Catalunya,* ed. Pierre Vilar. Barcelona, 1987.

——. "El comte-bisbe Miró Bonfill i l'acta de consagració de Cuixà de l'any 974." *Acta historica et archaeologica Mediaevalia* 10 (1989): 107–24.

——. "Conqesta de l'espai agrari i conflictes per la terra a la Catalunya carolíngia i comtal." *Catalunya i França meridional, a l'entorn de l'any mil,* ed. Xavier Barral i Altet et al., 203–11. Barcelona, 1991.

——. "Formació, organització i defense del domini de Sant Cugat en els segles X–XII." *Acta historica et archaeologica mediaevalia* 13 (1992): 127–73.

——. "Agressions senyorials i resistències pageses en el procés de feudalització." In *Revoltes populars contra el poder de l'Estat.* Barcelona, 1992.

——. "Violència feudal, violència contra qui?" In *Les sociétés méridionales à l'âge féodal (Espagne, Italie et sud de la France X–XIIIe s): Hommage à Pierre Bonnassie,* ed. Hélène Débax, 207–13. Toulouse, 1999.

——. "Práticas judiciales, transformación social y acción política en Cataluña (siglos IX-XIII)." *Hispania* 57 (1997): 1009–48.

Sánchez Albornoz, Claudio. "Documentos solore el juicio del Libro en León durante el siglo X y un feudo en castellano de XIII." *AHDE* 1 (1924): 382–90.

——. "Notas para el estudio del sayón en el reino Asturleonés." *Boletim da Faculdade de Direito* 68 (1982): 949–53.

Scales, Peter. *The Fall of the Caliphate of Córdoba: Berbers and Andalusis in Conflict.* Leiden, 1994.

Schioppa, Paolo. "Aspetti della giustizia milanese nell'età carolingia." *Archivio Storico Lonmbardo* 114 (1988): 9–25.

Scott, James. *Weapons of the Weak: Everyday Forms of Peasant Resistance.* New Haven, Conn., 1985.

Sénac, Philippe. *Frontières et Espaces Pyrénéens au Moyen Age.* Perpignan, 1992.

——. ed. *Histoire et archéologie des terres Catalanes au Moyen Age.* Perpignan, 1995.

Shideler, John C. *A Medieval Catalan Noble Family: The Montcadas, 1000–1230*. Berkeley, 1983.

Sicard, Germain. "L'organisation judiciaire en Languedoc." *Etudes historiques à la mémoire de Noël Didier* (1960): 293–99.

Sinatti d'Amico, Franca. *Le prove giudiziarie nel diritto longobardo*. Legislazione e prassi da Rotari ad Astolfo. Milan, 1968.

Skinner, Patricia. *Family Power in Southern Italy: The Duchy of Gaeta and Its Neighbours, 850–1139*. Cambridge, 1995.

———. "When Was Southern Italy 'Feudal'?" *Il Feudalismo nell'alto medioevo Settimane di studio sull'alto medioevo* 47 (2000): 309–45.

Smith, Julia M. H. "Oral and Written: Saints, Miracles, and Relics in Brittany, c. 850–1250." *Speculum* 65 (1990): 309–43.

Sobrequés Vidal, Santiago. *El grans comtes de Barcelona*. Barcelona, 1961.

Starr, June and Jane Collier, eds. *History and Power in the Study of Law: New Directions in Legal Anthropology*. Ithaca, N.Y., 1989.

Stock, Brian. *The Implications of Literacy: Written Language and Models of Interpretation in the Eleventh and Twelfth Centuries*. Princeton, 1983.

Sutherland, J. N. "Aspects of Continuity and Change in the Italian Placitum, 962–972." *Journal of Medieval History* 2 (1976): 89–118.

Tabuteau, Emily Zack. *Transfers of Property in Eleventh-Century Norman Law*. Chapel Hill, N.C., 1988.

Taverner, J. de. "Historia de los condes de Empurias y Perelada." *Revista de Ciencias Históricas* 3 (1881): 548–69; 4 (1886): 37–71, 97–119.

Taylor, Nathaniel Lane. "The Will and Society in Medieval Catalonia and Languedoc, 800–1200." Ph.D. Diss., Harvard University, 1995.

To Figueras, Lluís. "El comte Bernat I de Besalú i el seu testament sacramental." In *Amics de Besalú i el seu comtat: IV Assemblea d'Estudis sobre el Comtat de Besalú: Camprodon, 1980*, 117–28. Olot, 1983.

———. "El marc de les comunitates pageses: *villa* i parròquia en les diòcesis de Girona i Elna, final del segle IX–principi de l'XI." In *Catalunya i França meridional, a l'entorn de l'any mil*, ed. Xavier Barral i Altet et al., 212–39. Barcelona, 1991.

———. *El monestir de Santa Maria de Cervià i la pagesia: Una ànalisi local del canvi feudal*. Barcelona, 1991.

Toubert, Pierre. *Les structures du Latium médiéval*, 2 vols. Rome, 1973.

Treschow, Michael. "The Prologue to Alfred's Law Code: Instruction in the Spirit of Mercy." *Florilegium* 13 (1994): 79–110.

Trubek, David M. "Studying Courts in Context." *Law and Society Review* 14 (1980–81): 485–501.

Udina i Abelló, Antoni. *La successió testada a la Catalunya altomedieval*. Barcelona, 1984.

———. "L'administració de justícia en els comtats pirinencs, segles ix–xii." In *Miscel.lània Homenatge a Josep Llandonosa*, 129–45. Lleida, 1992.

———. "'Mitto in Baialia' les solidaritats familiars i feudals a la Catalunya medieval, s. x–xii." *Medievalia* 11 (1994): 65–79.

Udina Martorell, Federico. "El sedimento visigodo en la Cataluña condal (a propósito del artículo 'L'usage du drois wisigothique en Catalogne' de Zimmerman)." *Revista de Archivos, Bibliotecas y Museos* 77 (1974): 565–81.

Valls i Taberner, Ferràn. "El 'liber iudicum popularis' de Homobonus de Barcelona." *AHDE* 2 (1925): 200–12.

——. "La cour comtale Barcelonaise." In *Obras Selectas*, II:258–75. Madrid, 1954.

van Caenegem, R. C. "The Law of Evidence in the Twelfth Century: European Perspective and Intellectual Background." In *Proceedings of the Second International Congress of Medieval Canon Law*, 297–310. Vatican City, 1965.

——. "La Preuve dans le droit du moyen âge occidental—Rapport de synthèse." *RSJB* 17 (1965): 691–753.

——. "Methods of Proof in Western Medieval Law." *Mededelingen van de Kon. Acad. voor Wetenschappen van België Academiae Analecta, Kl. Letteren* 45 (1983): 85–127.

——. "Reflexions on Rational and Irrational Modes of Proof in Medieval Europe." *Tijdschrift voor Rechtsgeschiedenis* 58 (1990): 263–79.

van Houts, Elisabeth. "Gender and Authority of Oral Witnesses in Europe (800–1300)." *TRHS*, 6th series, 9 (1999): 201–20.

van Kleffens, Eelco Nicolaas. *Hispanic Law until the End of the Middle Ages*. Edinburgh, 1968.

Vilar, Pierre. *La Catalogne dans l'Espagne moderne: Recherches sur les fondements économiques des structures nationales*, 3 vols. Paris, 1962.

Vinogradoff, Paul. *Roman Law in Medieval Europe*. Oxford, 1909.

Vodola. Elisabeth. *Excommunication in the Middle Ages*. Berkeley, 1986.

Wallace-Hadrill, J. M. "The Bloodfeud of the Franks." In idem, *The Long-Haired Kings*, 121–47. Toronto, 1982.

Weinberger, Stephen. "Les conflits entre clercs et laïcs dans la Provence du XIe siècle." *AMidi* 92 (1980): 269–79.

Werner, Karl Ferdinand. "Missus—marchio—comes." In *Histoire comparée de l'administration, VIe–XVIIIe siècles. Francia* Beiheft 9, ed. Werner Paravicini and Karl Ferdinand Werner, 191–239. Munich, 1980.

——. "Observations sur le rôle des évêques dans le mouvement de la paix au Xe et XIe siècles." In *Mediaevalia Christiana XIe–XIIe siècles: Hommages à Raymonde Foreville*, ed. Coloman Viola, 155–95. Paris, 1989.

White, James Boyd. *The Legal Imagination: Studies in the Nature of Legal Thought and Expression*. Boston, 1973.

——. *Heracles' Bow. Essays on the Rhetoric and Poetics of the Law*. Madison, Wisc., 1985.

White, Stephen D. "'*Pactum Legem Vincit et Amor Judicium*': The Settlement of Disputes by Compromise in Eleventh-Century Western France." *American Journal of Legal History* 22 (1978): 281–308.

——. "Feuding and Peace-Making in the Touraine around the Year 1100." *Traditio* 42 (1986): 195–263.

——. "Inheritances and Legal Arguments in Western France, 1050–1150." *Traditio* 43 (1987): 55–103.

——. *Custom, Kinship, and Gifts to Saints. The Laudatio Parentum in Western France, 1050–1150*. Chapel Hill, N.C., 1988.

——. "Proposing the Ordeal and Avoiding It: Strategy and Power in Western French

Litigation, 1050–1110." In *Cultures of Power: Lordship, Status, and Process in Twelfth-Century Europe*, ed. Thomas N. Bisson, 89–123. Philadelphia, 1995.

———. "Debate: The Feudal Revolution." *Past and Present* 152 (1996): 205–23.

Wickham, Chris J. *The Mountains and the City. The Tuscan Appennines in the Early Middle Ages.* Oxford, 1988.

———. "Justice in the Kingdom of Italy." In *La Giustizia nell'alto medioevo (secoli IX-XI)*, 179–250.

———. "Land Disputes and Their Social Framework in Lombard-Carolingian Italy, 700–900." In *The Settlement of Disputes*, ed. Davies and Fouracre, 105–24.

———. "Gossip and Resistance among the Medieval Peasantry." *Past and Present* 160 (1998): 3–24.

Wickham, Chris, and James Fentress. *Social Memory.* Oxford, 1992.

Wolff, Philippe. "Quidam homo nomine Roberto negociatore." *Le Moyen Age* 69 (1963): 129–39.

Wood, Ian. "Disputes in Late Fifth- and Sixth-Century Gaul: Some Problems." In *The Settlement of Disputes*, ed. Davies and Fouracre, 7–22.

Wormald, Patrick. "Lex scripta and Verbum Regis." In *Early Medieval Kingship*, ed. P. H. Sawyer and I. N. Wood, 105–38. Leeds, 1977.

———. "Giving God and King Their Due: Conflict and Its Regulation in the Early English State." In *La Giustizia nell'alto medioevo (secoli IX–XI)*, 549–92.

———. *The Making of English Law: King Alfred to the Twelfth Century.* Vol. 1, *Legislation and Its Limits.* Oxford, 1999.

Yngvesson, Barbara, and Lynn Mather, "Language, Audience, and the Transformation of Disputes." *Law and Society Review* 15 (1980–81): 775–821.

Zimmerman, Michel. "L'usage du droit wisigothique en Catalogne du IXe au XIIe siècle: Approches d'une signification culturelle." *Mélanges de la Casa de Velázquez (MCV)* 9 (1973): 233–81.

———. "La prise de Barcelone par al-Mansur et la naissance de l'historiographie catalane." *Annales de Bretagne et des Pays de l'Ouest* 87 (1980): 191–218.

———. "Un formulaire du Xe siècle conservé à Ripoll." *Faventia* IV/2 (1982): 25–86.

———. "L'image du monde musulman et son utilisation en Catalogne du IXe au XIIe siècle." In *Minorités et marginaux en Espagne et dans le midi de la France, VIIe-XVIIIe siècles.* Actes du Colloque de Pau, 27–29 Mai 1984, 471–96. Paris, 1986.

———. "Naissance d'une principauté: Barcelone et les autres comtés catalans aux alentours de l'an mil." In *Catalunya i França Meridional a l'entorn de l'any mil*, ed. Xavier Barral i Altet et al., 111–35. Barcelona, 1991.

———. ed. *Les sociétés méridionales aux alentours de l'an mil: répertoire des sources et documents commentés.* Paris, 1992.

———. "Le vocabulaire latin de malédiction du IXe au XIIe siècle: Construction d'un discours eschatologique." *Atalaya, Revue Française d'Etudes Médiévales Hispaniques* 5 (1994): 37–55.

———. "Langue et lexicographie: L'apport des actes catalans." *BEC* 155 (1997): 185–205.

INDEX

Abbo of Fleury, 235
Adelaide (countess of Carcassonne), 108
Advocates. *See* Legal representatives
Agobard of Lyons, 121
al-Andalus, 16, 19, 21, 24, 27, 50, 194,
    226, 230–31
Alcuin of York, 88
Alfonso V (king of León), 233
Alienability of property, 35, 39–42, 47–
    48, 52, 232, 234
al-Mansur, 19, 156, 163
Anjou, the, 226
Anselm of Canterbury, 180
Aprisio, 47, 50–51, 159–60, 165, 170, 197,
    230, 238
Apulia, 231
Architectural remains, 79–80
Arles-sur-Tech (monastery), 143
Arnold (bishop of Maguelonne), 74
Arnulf (bishop of Vic), 149
Arxiu Capitular d'Urgell, 3
Arxiu de la Corona d'Aragó, 3
Asturias, 230
Atto of Vercelli, 121

Barcelona, 23
    sack of, 27, 144, 152, 156, 162, 177,
    230
Barthélemy, Dominique, 213
Bavaria, 229, 234

Bequests and gifts, challenged, 14–15,
    42–43, 170, 229–30
Berenguer (bishop of Elne), 149, 171
Berenguer Ramon I (count of Barcelona),
    203–5
Bernard (bishop of Béziers), 74
Bernat (count of Besalú), 108, 204–6
Bernat Tallaferro (count), 102
Berry, 227
Bishops, 16, 49
    collaboration of, 16, 70–73
    role in administering justice, 100–108,
    115, 237
    Visigothic rules related to, 44–45
    See also individual bishops
Bisson, Thomas N., 7–9
Bonhom (judge), 52, 84–98, 102, 122–25,
    131–33, 138–39, 148, 169, 210, 215,
    224, 237, 240, 247
Boni homines, 100, 103, 111–12, 114, 125,
    136, 173, 186–87, 191–92, 196–97,
    204, 224, 237–38, 242, 244, 247
Bonnassie, Pierre, 7–9, 58, 110, 212–17
Borrell (bishop of Vic), 100, 149
Borrell II (count of Barcelona), 19–20,
    104, 150
Boundaries, testimony related to, 169–73
Boundary clauses, 144–45, 243
Boundary markers, 194–95, 245
Bourdieu, Pierre, 76

Bournazel, Eric, 213
Brittany, 81–82
Burgundian Code, 89
Burgundy, 81, 227, 229, 234

Canon law, 34, 53–54, 105
Canons. *See* Cathedral chapters
Capetians, 19, 212
Capitularies, 168, 233, 242
Carolingians:
　legal institutions, 87–88, 102, 237
　privileges issued by, 25, 50, 142, 230
　public order, 7, 56–57, 212
　See also Capitularies
Cartularies, 3–4, 52, 97, 138
Castile, 230, 237, 243
Cathedral chapters, 143
　of Agde, 178
　of Béziers, 48, 74
　of Elne, 124–25
　of Nîmes, 63, 69
　of Urgell, 63, 105, 114, 178–79
　of Vic, 170
Charlemagne, 25, 50, 87
Charles the Bald (king of the West
　　Franks), 142
Charles the Simple (king of the West
　　Franks), 103
Chartres, 227
Clanchy, Michael, 180
Cluny, 21, 59
Compensation to losing parties, 186–87
Compromise, 10, 98, 112–13, 187, 190–
　92, 244
Convenientiae, 226, 228
Córdoba, 19, 24, 96, 148, 230–31
Counts and countesses, 3, 8–9, 100–108,
　112–15, 218–19, 226–27, 237
　of Angoulême, 227
　of Barcelona, 16, 100–103, 221, 230
　of Carcassonne, 103, 221
　of Cerdanya, 16, 91, 103, 152–53, 219–
　21
　cooperation with bishops, 98, 106, 115,
　237
　monastic patronage, 79, 209, 220–22
　of Urgell, 16
　See also individual counts
Courts. *See* Judicial assemblies
Cover, Robert, 77–78

Coyanza, Council of, 167
Criminal law, 129–30, 137
Curses, 56, 60–69, 235. *See also* Ritual
　sanctions
Custom, 33, 42, 119

Dathan and Abiron, 61–63, 66–68, 76,
　235
Decurias, 195
Deusdé (bishop of Barcelona), 100
Durand (abbot of Saint Cecilia), 198–
　200

Egica (king), 36
England, 163, 229, 239, 242–43
Ermengard (countess of Cerdanya), 71,
　107, 171–72, 220
Ermengol (bishop of Urgell), 1–2, 4–6,
　9–10, 15, 91, 149–50, 199–200, 215
Ermengol I (count of Urgell), 150–51
Ermengol II (count of Urgell), 102, 198–
　200
Ermessenda (countess of Barcelona), 91,
　107–8, 111, 126, 187, 201, 203–7
Ervig (king), 35
Ervig Marc (judge), 91
Excommunication, 20, 56, 58–60, 65–66,
　69–75, 129–30. *See also* Ritual sanc-
　tions

Fernando I (king of León), 232
Feudal Revolution, 7–8, 212–28
Floods, 152–55
Force, disqualifying sales and exchanges,
　37–39
Forgeries, 147–51, 241
Forum Iudicum. See Visigothic Code
Fourth Lateran Council, 121, 133
Frankish kings, 19–20, 50. *See also individ-
　ual kings*
Frujà (bishop of Vic), 149
Fueros, 89
Fulbert (bishop of Chartres), 72, 235, 246

Galicia, 134, 140, 230
Geary, Patrick, 59, 155
Gold, 21–22, 194, 226
Gondemar (bishop of Barcelona), 122–23
Gothic identity, 19, 87
Gregorian Reform, 19–21, 104–5

Guifré (archbishop of Narbonne), 16, 20, 74–75
Guifré (count of Cerdanya), 8, 102, 219–21
Guifré (judge), 1, 5–6, 10, 83, 91–93, 96–98, 100–101, 146, 174, 176, 179, 204–5, 216
Guifré the Hairy (count of Barcelona), 16
Guisla (viscountess of Conflent), 1, 6, 15–16, 19, 81
Guitard (abbot of Sant Cugat), 26, 101, 107, 126, 144, 158–59, 165–66, 173–74, 189, 209, 232, 244

Henry I (king of England), 180
Hincmar of Rheims, 65
Hispani, 50
Hug (count of Empúries), 108, 111–12, 175, 201, 203–7, 210
Hugh Capet, 19–20

Iglesias Ferreirós, Aquilino, 214
Infamy, 166. See also Reputation
Inheritance, 23, 27, 39–40, 47–50, 98, 120. See also Bequests
Isidore of Seville, 35, 84
Italy, 163, 180, 229, 233–34, 236–69
Ivo of Chartres, 121
Iudex. See Judges

Judges, 6, 11, 51, 54, 59, 64, 81–99, 109, 120, 208–9, 217–18, 244
   appointment, training, and careers of, 90, 96–97, 102
   collaboration among, 91–92, 98, 217
   corruption among, 87–89
   different types of, 81–82
   in other regions, 236–38
   questioning witnesses and evaluating proofs, 106, 127, 138–39, 145–51, 160, 166, 176–77
Judicial assemblies, 4, 8–9, 59, 98, 100–115, 181, 196, 210, 237–38
   competencies and jurisdictions of, 103–7, 114
   enforcement of decisions, 246–47

Lauranson-Rosaz, Christian, 57, 76
Law codes, 33–36, 53, 57–58, 62, 120
   judges' study of, 83–86
selective citation of, 33–47, 52–55
   See also Fueros, Lombard Laws, Theodosian Code, Usatges of Barcelona, and Visigothic Code
Legal representatives, 111
León, 140, 163, 232, 235–36, 243
Leovgild (king), 35
Lézat, 97, 150
Liber Iudiciorum. See Visigothic Code
Little, Lester, 60
Lombard Laws, 89, 233, 239, 245
Lombardy. See Italy
Lost records, 151–64, 177–78, 231, 241–42
Lothair (king of the Franks), 20
Louis the Pious (king of the Franks), 142

Magnou-Nortier, Elisabeth, 57–59
malae consuetudines, 212
mallus publicus, 102
Manresa, 158, 172, 174
Memory, 112, 154–55, 162, 168–72, 189–90
Mir Geribert, 20, 158–60, 164–66, 173–75, 202

Nicaea, Council of, 53
Normandy, 163

Odo (abbot of Sant Cugat), 122–23
Oliba (bishop of Vic), 70–71, 92, 102, 148–49, 158, 172, 174, 204, 206, 219–23, 235
Oliba Cabreta (count of Cerdanya), 220
Ordeals, judicial. See Proofs
Orléans, Council of, 105, 114
Orús (judge), 93, 96–97, 157

Peace and Truce of God, 21, 57–58, 106, 129–30, 134, 137, 226
Penalties for violating agreements, 61–75, 192–95
Pere (bishop of Girona), 100
Picardy, 227
Placita. See Judicial assemblies
Poly, Jean-Pierre, 57, 213
Pons Bonfill Marc (judge), 91–92, 94–98, 102, 146, 159, 165, 180
Portugal, 227, 232, 236
Possession, long-term, 47–50, 169–70, 182

Privileges, royal and papal, 25–26, 127,
    142–43, 147, 150, 153, 159, 182, 200,
    239
Proofs, ix, 13, 58, 98, 111, 216–17
    destruction of, 109, 138, 241
    interdependence of different proofs, 13,
        120, 135, 140, 177–82, 242–43
    judicial ordeals, 10, 109–10, 119–40,
        166, 239–40
    oath-helpers, 81, 166
    witness testimony, 81, 106, 120–22,
        135, 138, 153–55, 159–60, 165–82,
        195–96, 201, 239, 242
    written proofs, 48, 120–22, 125, 135,
        138–66, 178–79, 237–39
Provence, 180, 229
Province of Narbonne, 16, 19–22
Public and private, 8–9, 212–15, 221–22

Quitclaims, 4, 188

Ramon (count of Pallars), 52
Ramon Berenguer I (count of Barcelona), 20
Ramon Borrell (count of Barcelona), 25,
    63, 100, 102, 187, 203–5
Recceswinth (king), 35, 170
Relics, 59, 73, 196
Reparatio scripturae, 155–58, 160–63, 174,
    177, 197, 228, 238
Reputation: of judges, 102
    of litigants and witnesses, 138, 166–68
Reynolds, Susan, 228
Ritual sanctions, 5, 56–80, 235–36
Roger (count of Carcassonne), 180
Romanité, 57–61, 68
Rosenwein, Barbara, 59

Sacrarias, 23
Saiones, 108–11, 123, 205, 224, 245
Saint Eulalia, 61
Saint-Genis, 146
Saint-Germain-des-Prés, 242
Saint-Hilaire, 108, 180, 221
Saint-Victoire de Marseille, 21, 198
Salic law, 41, 53–54, 62, 89, 234
Salla (bishop of Urgell), 71, 223
Sancho (king of Navarre), 235
Sant Benet de Bages, 3
Sant Cugat, 3, 25–26, 40–42, 62–63, 90–

91, 96–97, 100–101, 107, 109–10,
    122–24, 126–28, 131, 136, 138, 143–
    47, 152, 158–60, 173, 189–91, 195,
    201, 208, 216, 221, 231–32, 240
Sant Joan de les Abadesses, 143
Sant Llorenç del Munt, 3, 96
Sant Miquel de Cuixà, 1, 70–71, 79–80,
    143, 152–58, 174, 188, 220, 223, 241,
    247
Sant Pau del Camp, 96
Sant Pere de Besalú, 3, 143
Sant Pere de les Puelles, 90
Sant Pere de Roda, 112–13, 128–29, 133,
    143, 223
Santa Cecilia de Montserrat, 148, 152
Santa Maria de Lavaix, 52, 224
Santa Maria de Ripoll, 2, 84, 103, 220, 223
Scott, James, 202
Scripture, 13, 34, 54, 67, 78, 85–86, 90,
    99, 132, 166–67
Sendred (judge), 2, 5–9, 92, 96, 102, 111,
    150, 176, 205, 216, 219, 237
Serrateix, 8–9, 46, 146, 219–20
Servitude, 110, 123, 227
Settlement, of disputes, 12
    evidence related to, 185–86, 201, 243–44
    resistance to, 201–10, 174–75, 247
    varieties of, 186–92
    See also Compromise
Si quis clauses, 61–69, 193
Sicily, 231
Siete Partidas, 89

Theodosian Code, 36, 52, 57, 62, 68, 78,
    235
Theodulf of Orléans, 87–89, 94, 108, 215
Toledo, 231
Toubert, Pierre, 113
Toulouges, Council of, 65
Trial by combat, 127, 203
Truce of God. *See* Peace and Truce of God

Umayyad caliphate, 25
Usatges of Barcelona, 89, 133

Vendômois, the, 229
Vic, Council of, 129, 223
Vidal Mayor, 89
Violence, 7–8, 29, 211–28, 224–25

Visigothic Code, ix, 2, 5–6, 13, 15, 19, 29, 33–56, 59, 61–62, 67, 76, 108–9, 114, 127, 140, 142, 146, 161, 214–15
creation of, 35–36, 44–45, 54
divergent attitudes toward, 203–5
judges' use of, 94–99, 155, 167–68, 171–72, 175–76, 193–95, 205, 215–16, 219, 228, 230, 232, 241
judicial ordeals in, 129–34, 137
manuscripts including, 84–87, 92, 138, 169, 210
putative "survival" of, 36, 54, 76–78

White, James Boyd, 77–78
White, Stephen, 4, 59
Written law. *See* Law codes
Written records:
destruction of, 122–23, 138
survival of, 2–3
variability and bias of, 12, 185–86, 208
See also Proofs

Zimmerman, Michel, 214